Art
and the Committed Eye

Art
and the Committed
Eye

The Cultural
Functions
of Imagery

Richard Leppert

University of Minnesota

■ WestviewPress
A Division of HarperCollinsPublishers

FRONTISPIECE

Joseph Sacco (dates unknown)
Eye of a Young Woman (1844)
tempera on paperboard, in original hinged, standing case of leather with velvet lining, gilt detailing, and brass fillets, 3.2 × 3.8 cm.
Houston, The Menil Foundation, acc. no. X 3059. Photo: D. James Dee

Published in 1996 in the United States of America by Westview Press, Inc., 5500 Central Avenue, Boulder, Colorado 80301-2877, and in the United Kingdom by Westview Press, 12 Hid's Copse Road, Cumnor Hill, Oxford OX2 9JJ

Library of Congress Cataloging-in-Publication Data
Leppert, Richard D.
    Art and the committed eye : The cultural functions of imagery / Richard Leppert.
        p.   cm. — (Cultural studies)
    ISBN 0-8133-1539-5 — ISBN 0-8133-1540-9 (pbk.)
    1. Art and society—Europe.   2. Artists—Europe—Psychology.
3. Art and society—United States.   4. Artists—United States—
Psychology.   I. Title.   II. Series.
N72. S6L46   1996
701'.03—dc20   95-19092
                                                                                                              CIP

Printed and bound in the United States of America

The paper used in this publication meets the requirements of the American National Standard for Permanence of Paper for Printed Library Materials Z39.48-1984.

10   9   8   7   6   5   4   3   2   1

Contents

PART ONE   Sights/Sites for Seeing

PART TWO   Object

Illustrations

Color Plates

Acknowledgments

I am deeply grateful for the skilled, devoted, and tireless research assistance provided by Barbara Engh and Martha Mockus.

Several colleagues offered detailed critical readings of the text; I owe each of them a considerable debt of gratitude: Gary Thomas, Thomas Willette, Janet Wolff, and Rebecca Zurier.

Mez van Oppen helped me through some of the intricacies of seventeenth-century Dutch that exceeded my competence in that language.

I am indebted to the staffs of several research libraries: Witt Library, Courtauld Institute of Art, University of London; Interlibrary Loan Services and Special Collections, O. Meredith Wilson Library, University of Minnesota; and in particular Elaine Challacombe, Curator, Owen H. Wagensteen Historical Library of Biology and Medicine, University of Minnesota.

Numerous individuals, unfortunately too many to name, in the photograph departments and libraries of public art museums and private photo archives throughout the United States and Western Europe helped supply reproductions of artworks and necessary documentary information not available from other sources.

Gordon Massman, my editor at Westview Press, was invariably supportive—and, nearly as important, patient. Also at Westview and especially deserving of my thanks are Polly Christensen, Miriam Gilbert, David Jenemann, Jane Raese, and Michele Wynn.

I wish to acknowledge financial support received from the University of Minnesota Graduate School.

I acknowledge with gratitude other of my publishers who have granted permission to reprint excerpts from my previous writings: Cambridge University Press (*Music and Image: Domesticity, Ideology, and Socio-Cultural Formation in Eighteenth-Century England,* 1988), for Figures 4.3, 4.6, 4.7, 8.6, 8.7; and the University of California Press (*The Sight of Sound: Music, Representation, and the History of the Body,* 1993), for Figures 5.1, 5.2, 8.2, 8.3.

Richard Leppert
Minneapolis

Part One

Sights/Sites for Seeing

Representation need not be art, but it is none the less mysterious for that.

> —E. H. Gombrich
> *Art and Illusion*

Something [as] meaningful to us [as art] cannot be left just to sit there bathed in pure significance, and so we describe, analyse, compare, judge, classify; we erect theories about creativity, form, perception, social function; we characterize art as a language, a structure, a system, an act, a symbol, a pattern of feeling; we reach for scientific metaphors, spiritual ones, technological ones, political ones; and if all else fails we string dark sayings together and hope someone else will [elucidate] them for us. The surface bootlessness of talking about art seems matched by a depth necessity to talk about it endlessly.

> —Clifford Geertz
> "Art as a Cultural System"

Introduction

I<small>T IS LOST</small> on no one that a significant portion of our conscious and unconscious understandings of ourselves and our immediate world is framed by the imagery of advertising, both in the medium of print and on television. This imagery urges what sort of bodies to have and to desire—or to build (even the seeming natural "given" of our fleshly frames is terrain for future construction); it influences our sense of self, our belief systems, our individuality, and our status as social beings; it encourages what clothes to wear or car to drive, which political party to vote for, and so forth.

We understand several fundamental things about the advertising image. The information it provides is not unbiased or neutral (buy this instead of that, and you will be happier, better for it, more successful). It specifically exists to get us to do something we might otherwise not do. It promises future happiness, though by trying to make us dissatisfied with our past and, especially, with our present. And even when we recognize the fictions upon which advertising's pleas depend for their success, we commonly find ourselves being sucked in by the very possibility of the narrative. Thus the appeal to men made by jeans manufacturers of inordinate sexiness, coolness, group identity (lots of buddies), and athleticism; the appeal to women by pantyhose manufacturers of inordinate sexiness, beauty (long legs magnetically attracting an equally attractive man), being loved, and so forth. We understand—certainly once we've spent our money—that the promise remains just that. But despite our resistance and growing cynicism, we remain to one degree or another caught in the light of what we see—what we are *shown*.

Images show us *a* world but not *the* world itself. Images are not the things shown but are representations thereof: re-presentations. Indeed, what images represent may otherwise not exist in "reality" and may instead be confined to the realm of imagination, wish, desire, dream, or fantasy. And yet, of course, any image literally exists as an object within the world that it in one way or another engages. When we look at images, whether photographs, films, videos, or paintings, what we see is the product of human consciousness, itself part and parcel of culture and history. That is, images are not mined like ore; they are constructed for the purpose of performing some function within a given sociocultural matrix.

Outlining the Territory

This is a book about paintings produced during the broad expanse of time that marks historical modernity, from the early Renaissance to the beginning of the twentieth century. The images discussed are Western European and American, the earliest dated c. 1428 and the most recent, 1967, but most were painted between the early sixteenth century and the end of the nineteenth. This period encompasses the production of so-called representational art, the history of which ends near the beginning of the twentieth century, and the general move toward abstract imagery.

However broad the book's historical sweep, my purpose is not to map or otherwise survey chronologically the history of Western painting, or to introduce readers to the enormous variety of subjects represented during a five-hundred-year period, or to trace that visual history via an account of changing styles (the "moves" from Medieval to Renaissance to Mannerism to Baroque, etc.). Instead, my aim is to examine the complex relation between the "look" of paintings and the variety of social and cultural uses to which paintings have been put and to examine in turn how social and cultural forces have functioned to help determine the look of paintings.

In particular, I am keen to understand some of the ways that paintings function within the conflicting realms of power operative by definition throughout any social formation, especially those surrounding differences of class, gender, and race. Following the introductory chapters, I shall address art's relation to the material world—to objects—and to the ways that images mark our various ties to objects. The paintings discussed will be still lifes of things beautiful and, alternately, horrific, from flowers and fruit to human body parts, from the object world as coveted material luxuries to the object world as so much disgusting detritus—and all of it as a means of locating the self within (or outside) a viewing community. In the next section, I shall consider the representation of the human body as a sight—and sometimes as a spectacle—that is, as an object of display and intense interest upon which the viewer obsessively gazes. The represented bodies will be those of adults and children, males and females, of different social classes and races. Some bodies will be clothed, others nude. Some will be represented as pleasured, others as tormented. Throughout this encounter I shall question art's relation to the abstract realms of happiness, desire, fear, and anxiety, which are understood less as individual, private emotions and more as responses to social and cultural conditions.

Seeing and the Social Practice of Making Sense

An underlying and fundamental theme governing this project is that all meaning—thus including the meanings of paintings—results from social practices that are in a constant state of flux and are under challenge by people holding diverse, often conflicting interests. Art-making and its consumption (viewing) are social practices. But in order to consider how paintings have functioned—the "jobs" they have been assigned to perform, as it were—it is crucial to understand that visual representation "operates" with the specificity of the medium of painting—just as literature is specifically different from television, film, and music. Each of these media is richly expressive and communicative, and each is practiced according to its own set of principles. That is, the means by which visual art "says" something to us is in part unique to visual art, and that specificity must be investigated if we have any hope of sorting out how art "works" on us. Accordingly, another of my concerns is to address the question of how representations go about representing.

Sight is the principal means through which we learn to maneuver in time and space. Sight is a "device" for recognition, prediction, and confirmation: This person is mother and not a stranger. (Her identity is "seen" before her name is recognized and long before it can be spoken.) We also understand that seeing is not a simple matter of biology and physics, not a question of light waves' action on the retina. Seeing is very much about the mind and thought processes. The moment I invoke thought, the complexity of seeing increases geometrically, for I have introduced language into the equation—and not mere recognition, as with the basic identity bond between infants and parents prior to language acquisition.

Here again representation enters. The function of language is to represent in repeatable, abstract signs (morphemes) and sounds (phonemes) what comes to us by means of our various senses, sight being principal among them. (Without our senses language is impossible. To be sure, we can get along quite well without one or more of our senses, but not without all of them—which would end life itself.) Restricting ourselves to the sense of sight, what we make of it depends *in part* on thought, just as thought depends on language: again, representation. We cannot "escape" the web of representational devices—they are what allows us to make our way in the world.[1]

However, it is all too easy, and utterly false, to imply that paintings are simply nonverbal substitutes for what might otherwise be expressed or communicated in words—ironically, the vast body of writing *about* art confirms nothing more than that words often fail miserably to "account for" the communicative and expressive power of images. Paintings are products of human consciousness—thought and feeling—transformed through the physical act of painting into something visible, but *silent,* and usually devoid of words that might be read (relatively few paintings include texts that the viewer can read). Images are less visual translations of what might otherwise be *said* (in words) than they are visual transformations of a certain awareness of the world. Conscious (*and* unconscious) awareness of a given situation, to be sure, has ties in language, but language is only the most obvious, and not the only, means by which people attempt to make sense of their reality. Were that not so there would be little cause to explain the existence of either images or music. Further, it is important to point out that paintings are not simply assertions about the world; they are as much interrogatives, inquiries, and explorations. Images do not so much *tell* us anything, as make available—by making visible *in a certain way*—a realm of possibilities and probabilities, some of which are difficult to state in words.

Seeing to Know, Knowing to See

It makes no sense to think about a painting as though it were "a delivery van, conveying meaning to the customer."[2] Viewers do not wait for a painting's meanings to arrive prepackaged. Viewers are active participants in determining meaning. In order to "see" (that is, "to perceive"), I have to know something. At the most basic level this requires that I recognize what it is I am looking at, though mere recognition takes me but a short distance. Thus the ancient Roman scholar Pliny wrote: "The mind is the real instrument of sight and observation, the eyes act as a sort of vessel receiving and transmitting the visible portion of the consciousness."[3] It is easily understood that seeing requires certain "skills" that are in part historically and culturally specific.

What is "there" for me to see involves *me:* my own knowledge, beliefs, investments, interests, desires, and pleasures. Having acquired consciousness, I never approach an image as a tabula rasa—"the innocent eye is a myth"[4]—I come always already knowing, believing, wanting, and so forth, to whatever degree. Further, I know that the image's maker, like me, approaches the wood panel or canvas with knowledge, belief, investment, interest, and desire. Still further, artists historically most often worked directly *for* someone or something else—a patron, and later, an art market—wherefrom other, and not always parallel, knowledges, interests, and so on emanated.

Thus, "every image embodies a way of seeing."[5] Or better, each image embodies historically, socially, and culturally specific competing, and contradictory, ways of seeing. Precisely on that account, the "contents" of images are not simple substitutes for words, because they call upon so much more than words. Pictures call out not only to the mind but also to the body (consider the immediate physical impact of erotic images), to thought, and also to emotion, and so forth. The French novelist Emile Zola commented that artworks are "a corner of nature seen through a temperament."[6] Zola's remark acknowledges that artists do not operate as mere conduits moving information from point A to point B like electrical lines. Instead, artists *transform* their material. But the value of Zola's insight is limited by the fact that he tacitly reduces art to the isolated psychology of the individual artist, without acknowledging that artistic consciousness itself is formed within the boundaries of history, society, and culture. Further, it is perhaps ironic that what we label "individuality"—however we may imagine and treasure it—is endlessly duplicated in any given society. For example, the limits to individuality are evident in newspaper personals ads; despite efforts to make each message appear unique, the net result is often a striking, perhaps depressing, sameness.

Limits of Engagement

In writing about art, I seek to engage some paintings in a metaphoric dialogic process in which their "speaking out" to me, their function of giving visibility to something, elicits from me a response, an engagement. In the process, I hope that my readers will become engaged in that process as well. My intent is to make visible certain possibilities of meanings relative to certain images. Recognizing that art, as representation, is by nature inherently always "interested," and not objective, in what it makes available for me to see or to be shown, I respond in kind. That is, I recognize, and explicitly acknowledge, my own interests. Still, the reader must remember that these interests are not coterminous with the "everything" of art—but neither are they trivial.

It is critical to emphasize that all this will be partial, incomplete, impermanent, and for that matter, maybe wrong—but not disinterested. What I seek to do is in fact all that *can* be done. "Artworks are not like broadcasting devices perpetually sending out the same signal or set of signals: The construal of meaning is dynamically constructive for both user and maker; it is a ceaseless production galvanized by objects in historically and socially specific circumstances."[7] To talk about an image is not to decode it, and having once broken its code, to have done with it, the final meaning having been established and reduced to words. To talk about an image is, in the end, an attempt to relate oneself to it and to the sight it represents. The image is a place to see what we can see, a site of exploration, a place to travel, and like all sites worthy of a visit, worth returning to because there is always more to see. Art history is "a place to see seeing";[8] no more than any other site, it is assuredly not a place to see the end of seeing. As a signifying practice, it is a beginning without end, just as my own activity as an author of a book about images is an incomplete representation—about representations.[9]

To summarize: My particular interest in visual art lies in equal measure with the adjective, the "visual," and the noun it modifies, the "art." What is for me so essential about visual art is that it is first and foremost art (i.e., artifice) and, as it were, "incidentally" visual. The importance of vision to visual art is not in the physiological phenomenon of seeing (animals see; they do not make art) but in the perceiving, which of course is governed by the eyes in conjunction with the brain (conscious *and* unconscious thought) and indeed with the entire human organism (the body) in its perceived relation to external reality.[10] I am interested in how and why art functions as representation; in how and why people, objects, places, and events are *made* to appear in art; and in the means by which images attempt to call out to me.[11]

Basic Principles: Conventions, Social Interests, and Memory

The way any image "looks" is in part governed by the conventions of representation that operate at a given historical moment. Conventions, briefly put, are ways of doing things that have gained certain social sanction—for example, the social convention of eating with utensils, held a certain way, and not with the fingers; or the practice of using a napkin to wipe one's mouth as opposed to using one's sleeve (as was once conventional, hence socially acceptable). The conventional way of doing something involves predictability; as such, it can be comforting to the extent that we can expect the behavior or the style that results; alternately, of course, conventionality may eventually bore us or unduly confine our behavior.

If conventions, pictorial or otherwise, are simply the way people do things, they are neither innocent nor historically accidental, either in the common practice of daily life (for example, the conventions of table etiquette) or in art. Conventions are a means by which to make and keep social order; they function to regularize and regulate. Yet the effectiveness of conventions to some extent lies in the degree to which they manifest themselves as being "natural," thus seeming "universal" and not imposed or serving only certain social or cultural interests. And the greater the extent to which social practices have become naturalized, the more they are explicit responses to social pressure and specific definitions of culture. In other words, conventions are operative principles of order, just as order is the expression of power. In a social context, conventions are the rendered-unconscious expressions of ideology.

The conventions of painting—manifested in formal organization, the handling of color, light, space, and figural pose, and so on—sometimes have provided the opportunity to "naturalize" certain ways of seeing, as though what is represented is just the way things or people really *are* or ideally ought to be. For example, the conventions of European portraiture—by definition involving representations of the upper classes—required that the elite virtually never be shown to smile so as to expose their teeth (and usually not to smile at all), but it was quite the opposite for images of the poor, who commonly grin broadly. The history of this difference is deeply informed by class prejudices, notions of class-specific dignity, beauty, and, indeed, social and moral worth. The elite marked their identity not least by their physical reserve— their visual inaccessibility—a stance still very much adopted in the photographic portraiture of statesmen, business leaders, and others of stature. Thus in-the-flesh politicians grin a lot, but not when they are intent on projecting the conventional signs of statesmanship, upon which the social prestige of their position depends, namely, high seriousness and dignity. Conventions, put more radically, are fundamentally ways of telling highly selective truths. They are never objective, though always interested and partial. The effort to produce visibility likewise creates invisibility. That which is present marks also the absent.

Visual art reveals in the degree to which it simultaneously attempts to hide: Art "speaks" of one thing but remains silent on another. It draws attention to one issue not least by distracting us from, or otherwise ignoring, something else. Representation is necessarily and always highly selective; but I do not mean by this that paintings fail to tell the truth. That which is made visual is not intended only as the mirror of that which *is* but also as the indicator of that which *was* or *is to be.* That is, visual representation results from an act whose conscious or unconscious purpose is to engage a particular way of life, whether real or imagined. By definition the image re-presents the past (for time stops in art), but in one way or another art is *about* the future. It works either to stabilize or to change what is by marking what might be. Art engages an imagined future that is invariably social, involving others, including those who must be convinced, who must follow, or who must be made to follow.

Intention, Function, and History

This book is not an exploration of what artists meant to mean by their paintings. Recovering "original" intention is not my principal goal, not least because whatever the artist thought he or she meant, even if that could be known (and it usually cannot),[12] in no sense circumscribes what the image means, either to its original audience or to people living long afterward. My purpose is not to ignore the issue of intention, long a source of endless and often quite tiresome academic commentary, but to try to understand something about art that seems more crucial: namely, the functions of imagery within culture and society—in essence, what images were (and are) *made* to mean on the basis of how they were (and are) *used.* I cannot hope to sort this out with respect to each painting reproduced in this volume, but I will take the past-present use issue as central to the problems of looking and the production of meaning.

"A picture is a historical record of what its creator noticed and considered worth noticing within a given culture at a particular moment."[13] People study history in an attempt to understand the present; hence past and present are fundamentally joined—by a two-way street. As the past constructs us (we *are* to a certain extent what we *were*), we in turn reconstruct the past, perpetually rewriting it out of our own sets of concerns, understandings, investments, desires, and perceived needs. What we choose to "notice" about the past is dependent on our present, albeit invariably changing, sense of worth.[14] Thus not so long ago the histories of the not-powerful, the not-male, and the not-white were largely invisible, as though they had hardly existed. More recently people comprising these (in fact) majority communities have made themselves visible, commonly through enormous struggle. Citing the obvious examples of those who now *are,* but who all too recently seemed not to have been, is to acknowledge fundamental change in the production of history.

Like every object of human production, art exists in the past. Like the humans who make it, art ages from the moment of its making, perpetually receding from the viewer's own present. When I look at a painting, its historical moment is always already at odds with mine, to the extent that it represents a different time, place, and set of sociocultural circumstances of production and function. And though I *cannot* understand or otherwise make sense of it except within the contexts of my own concerns, this does not imply that an artwork's own first history is therefore absolutely out of my reach. Far from it.

Take, for example, the case of an ordinary flower. The seventeenth-century tulip in a Dutch still life resembles those in my garden, and on that account the oil-painted tulip is a tulip, as a rose is a rose. It is an object that produces a rush of visually induced pleasure. Now, as in the seventeenth century, the tulip is, simply, beautiful to behold. But in the seventeenth century the tulip *could* be much more, and that is the part I cannot know from ordinary experience. To gain access to something akin to the range of original meanings that are not part of my own cultural baggage I must make the effort to rediscover history. In so doing, I would quickly learn that the tulip's beauty-quotient came at the price of moral qualms, and even guilt, over the monies being spent in Holland to obtain real tulips—ironically, far more than might be spent on a painting of a tulip in many instances—and, for that matter, over the materialism implicit in the purchase of paintings themselves. Indeed, flower paintings belonged to a large category of pictures self-consciously intended to evoke thoughts about death and damnation, life and afterlife (of which more later), subjects that to us might seem to be far removed from the representation of "mere" flora—not much of that body of meanings attaches to the flowers growing in my garden.

Simply to recognize the impermanence of an image's function, and hence its meaning, is to come at least partly to terms with the history that produces the change. By so doing I incorporate a bit of the past into my consciousness, or my present, so to speak. I cannot look at an old Dutch still life with tulips without remembering what I have now learned. A gap is at least provisionally bridged, whatever the weight restrictions I must remember to place upon the bridge. That is, the insight I have produced will sustain only so much interpretative weight, though I can continue to buttress it to my heart's content and thereby structure an apparatus of historical memory that can support still more "weighty" understanding.

Bridging the gap between "then and now" is not just a matter of sorting out the contents of the past and bringing them forward in time. Allied to this challenge is the fact that when I see historical images today I do so with eyes fundamentally different from the ones originally doing the looking. This is not a question of biological difference; the effect of light waves on the retina is historically constant. Instead of physics and biology, the difference hinges on a culture of perception. I do not relate to images in ways identical to people in the past. For example, my world surrounds me with images; I cannot escape images. A few centuries ago, images—particularly painted ones—were likely to have seemed more unusual, hence more striking, not least because they were unitary objects, each existing in only one unique place. Paintings now compete for my attention with a plethora of other images—still, moving, colored, manipulable by the viewer, and so forth. Not least important, the aura that once attached to paintings because of their individual uniqueness is mediated by their being reproducible, as in this book. This says only that the meanings and experiences we can associate with art generally are not identical to those of the past. In short, looking is a historically specific activity.

Institutional Frames for Art

No small part of how we perceive paintings is determined by the various "frames" that surround them. To be sure, paintings hung on walls are nearly always set within a frame, whether simple or elaborate, which serves to demarcate the image and, not least important, which commonly marks a silent but evident claim to someone's idea (a museum curator, an art dealer, a collector) about the image's relative significance. More to the point, paintings are "institutionally framed," principally by the academy (via the discipline of art history), the museum, and the art market. Images exist within the context of a larger historical process in which all that is in the past is either being forgotten or, if remembered, is recollected in the light of current interests (never unitary, to be sure). This guarantees change in the functions of art. Decisions are made, as they must be, about *which* paintings should be "remembered" and *what* about them should be "recalled."

Images acquire "meaning" not only in relation to their internally specific "contents" and what people choose to say about those contents, but also in part according to where the artworks are exhibited, that is, their physical site. A typical eighteenth-century English family portrait, perhaps by Thomas Gainsborough, organizes its sitters, records their gestures, and valorizes their pretensions much the same as a portrait-studio color photograph that might (but does not) hang over my sofa. All this is both basic and familiar. But in spite of the painting's obvious resemblances to my world, much has changed, and not only as regards what is *in* the portrait. A family portrait originally served to define and memorialize for posterity the history and pedigree of the individuals represented. Hung in the long gallery of a great house, it formed part of a visual family genealogy. However, once removed from that setting and displayed in a museum, its function and meaning are transformed by its new location. In the museum, the people represented within the portrait diminish in importance in favor of the artist who painted it. Original evocations of family history, lineage, politics, and the power of social position are radically subdued, if not altogether erased, to the extent that the viewer first and foremost experiences the painting as an artwork in a repository (vault) of Art. In the museum setting, one of the painting's principal functions is to be part of art history because it has been *officially* deemed beautiful or otherwise significant as an artwork, without necessary regard to, say, the sitters themselves. (I am not necessarily criticizing this fact.)

That such a transformation in meaning occurs is in no small part supported by the physical space that the image occupies in the museum.[15] Not least important, the museum's architecture itself is a frame that "argues" for art as Art. The image is hung among other portraits in the same school (British, eighteenth-century), probably with some other Gainsboroughs, if the museum is a large one. It comes to the viewer's attention as part of a vast archive through which museum-goers walk. The painting at once becomes interchangeable with others of its kind, *and* it becomes autonomous to the extent that, as part of a vast genealogy of pictures, its own specific history and original function disappear.[16]

The physical conditions for looking in a museum are museum-specific and in no small way determine how viewers interact with paintings. A trip through the European and American paintings collections in the Metropolitan Museum of Art in New York City is a long journey indeed. Replicating the broad sweep of a textbook survey history of painting, the museum experience is not only physically challenging (if not exhausting) but to be done properly would require many repeat excursions. However, it costs money to enter, for many people a considerable sum (especially for non–New Yorkers with hotel and restaurant bills mounting), which encourages art "consumers" to get as much seeing for their buck as possible.

> At the Smithsonian . . . audiences are perceived as being either "streakers," who "roller-skate" through exhibitions, "strollers," who take more time to engage the exhibitions, and "readers," who spend even more time absorbing exhibitions and their texts. By grounding their exhibition strategies in audiences' time investments, curators and designers hope to "grab" and "hook" streakers and convert them into strollers, and lure strollers into becoming readers.[17]

The official rhetoric about art commonly promulgated by the art world demands that art be contemplated; the ubiquitous templelike architecture of many museums, including the newest, makes explicit the demand for reverence. Yet the actual experience of looking, given the conditions of large survey museums, encourages distracted looking, quick glances, and increased anxiety (How much more is there?) as visitors attempt (often futilely) to get through as much art as possible, either before the closing bell or their own physical collapse ends the visit. As we pass through the galleries, individual pictures compete for our attention like goods in a shop window. Museum staffs make judgments for us about what will be displayed and where. Those pictures that make the "cut" are hung in a hierarchy of judged significance and in a location that has the contextuality of school, period, and genre. Paintings hung in privileged museum sites and surrounded by guards (Leonardo da Vinci's Mona Lisa in the Louvre) usually attract notable attention. They convey different meanings than images receiving less obvious official attention.

It takes only a visit or two to an art museum to learn that a specific etiquette attaches itself to looking at art, involving the stated or unstated demand that we speak softly, in reverential tones, that we never touch—the oils on our skin are detrimental to such objects—and that we not say anything stupid about a painting within earshot of someone else who might after all be more expert. Beauty demands respect. All this necessarily has an impact on what we look at and how we will tend to see it; all of it is the product of decisions made for us by others—who are usually anonymous or at least unacknowledged. Museum visitors characteristically spend far more time in the first gallery they visit than in the last. The unspoken demands for concentrated viewing are difficult if not impossible to maintain; it is little wonder that museum-goers attempt to revive themselves just prior to leaving by shopping at the museum's department store, where can be had—and taken home for *relaxed* viewing—"authorized," or "official," museum reproductions of artworks (something like "real" fakes), as well as books, note cards, postcards, recordings, videos, apparel, jewelry, puzzles, art-related games, and even the odd cheap souvenir trinket to placate any irritable child in tow. In other words, museum shops provide a sanctuary for the sort of distracted looking (the kind we do in the malls) that the rest of the museum tacitly frowns upon.

Despite the critical edge to the foregoing remarks, I am not necessarily condemning what I am describing; instead, I am trying to account for some of the prevailing conditions that silently direct and in part govern looking. My own attempt in what follows is to involve in the discussion some of the history that is too often drained away from paintings under current conditions for seeing, whether in the academy or in the museum. Further, I hope to demonstrate that using social history to interrogate beauty (Art, writ uppercase) bears no grudge against beauty as such and also that beauty in the pretended absence of social history is sham. If, as Keats claimed, beauty is truth and truth, beauty, the truth embedded in beauty that must be ascertained and acknowledged is beauty's dialectical relation to human beings. Such beauty is understood not as a "universal" ideal, disembodied and abstract, but as it is embodied, in the form of actual people who struggle, suffer, and desire, seeking pleasure and happiness—people who are invariably social and political.

Privileged Seeing:
Painting and Power

To see an original painting the viewer must come to it, invoking the pilgrimage and the magic of the icon. In centuries past, to enter a gallery whose walls were covered with paintings from floor to ceiling (Figure I.1) was to enter a space of enormous privilege, not only because of the object's worth but also because the concentration of colored images in such a restricted space was extraordinarily unusual. The display recalled perhaps the stained glass of medieval cathedrals but was fundamentally different nonetheless, not least because the cathedral was an open space, the private gallery a closed one; admission as such granted status but also typically reminded the grantee that the owner's status was still greater than the visitor's.

Men of wealth and power collected paintings on virtually every subject imaginable (paintings need not be either of, or even about, the person buying them in order to reflect and perpetuate that individual's power). In Figure I.1, religious subjects dominate, taking up the top four rows of paintings on the back wall; the fifth, bottom row is given to portraits. Here and there are a few scenes drawn from myth, a genre scene or two (pictures of everyday common life, usually lower- or middle-class), and a landscape, as well as the odd piece of small sculpture. On the table at the left are some drawings and perhaps an inventory of the collection.

Paintings of picture galleries, like this one, were quite common in the seventeenth century, confirming the self-consciousness of the picture-collecting frenzy and helping at the same time to establish collecting's claim as a pedi-

Figure I.1
David Teniers the Younger (1610–1690), ARCHDUKE LEOPOLD-WILLIAM IN HIS PICTURE GALLERY, canvas, 123 × 161 cm. Vienna, Kunsthistorisches Museum, Gemälde-galerie, inv. no. 1611. Photo © IRPA-KIK-Brussels.

Figure I.2
David Teniers the
Younger (1610–1690),
STUDIO OF THE
PAINTER, canvas,
96 × 129 cm. Private
collection. Photo ©
IRPA-KIK-Brussels.

gree of status, wealth, and power. In virtually all of such representations the owner is included, though seldom by himself. He is accompanied by others who—like him—are caught in the spectacle, immersed in the business of art and viewing art, looking at the paintings that confirm the greatness of the host. It is not enough to have pictures as possessions; their final power comes from their being seen by others. The practice of painting picture collections was not characteristically a matter of fantasy. It was instead a matter of propagandizing *and* visually inventorying actual ownership. (Indeed, scholars have frequently been successful at linking the paintings within these paintings to the originals from which they were copied.) To the extent that the picture-gallery painting was itself hung in the gallery, it formed a kind of double proof, a redundant confirmation of the authenticities of privilege.

The connections between art and power and the various economies that support an art market can be described in relation to what occurs at modern art auctions, where, as Jean Baudrillard notes, money is exchanged not simply for art but for prestige. Baudrillard argues that money's meaning is transformed through its expenditure. In the art auction, the object itself gains value as a sign, directly linked to the fact that money—often a lot of it—is spent to effect the purchase. Expenditure constitutes not only a sacrifice but also a risked investment as part of a competition within a perceived community of wealthy, art-buying peers. Consumption, Baudrillard argues, "becomes the competitive field of the destruction of economic value for the sake of another type of value." That value is prestige, which he refers to as "sign exchange value."[18] Sign value is gained by exchanging a canvas for all that the money spent in buying it stands for and for all that was required to obtain the money in the first place. The painting becomes a visible *concentration* of that which stands behind money.

One final point needs to be made: The prestige accorded to owning art could also be visually claimed for making art (Figure I.2). In this regard David Teniers the Younger produced a scene markedly similar to the one formerly discussed, with one crucial difference. Pride of place is given to the painter himself, who is painted while painting, with an unfinished canvas in view, so that we can see his powers of representation at work. Lest we miss the crucial point, Teniers incorporates the dimension of time into his painting, as a device for marking his claim to power. He shows us his potential upper-class buyers *waiting for him.* Moreover, the picture collection he exhibits includes not only his own finished canvases (some of those resting on the floor are unquestionably by Teniers) but also many other pictures by other artists. Thus Teniers pictures himself as a collector, with all that entails vis-à-vis an argument for his own elevated economic and social standing. To *own* representations—and, in the second of these examples, to own as well the *ability* to rep-

Figure I.3
David Teniers the
Younger (1610–1690),
GUARD ROOM, canvas,
69.7 × 104.8 cm.
Baltimore, The Walters
Art Gallery, inv. no. 37.

resent—demonstrates to the viewer who the owner *is* by means of what he *has*. In each instance, identity is linked to having the sight of the other at one's command. In this respect, picture-gallery paintings bear more than accidental, if ironic, relation to representation of armories (Figure I.3). Like the latter, picture-gallery paintings remind spectators of the excessive means at the disposal of the owner to keep us in his sights.

Chapter 1

Representation and the Politics of Deception

T<small>HE SENSE OF SIGHT</small> is a fundamental means by which human beings attempt both to explain and to gain control of the reality in which they find themselves. Not surprisingly, the ability to represent that world mimetically, to "match" in two dimensions what exists in three, is conflated in some societies with magic or other special power.

Fooling

One sort of painting more than any other at once evokes and demonstrates that power: trompe l'oeil, meaning "to deceive the eye." This French term was pejoratively used for the first time in 1803 to describe a particular sort of imagery, whose earliest examples date back to the very beginning of Western history. The style is typified by an extraordinary naturalism that misleads the viewer, at least initially, to perceive that the image is the actual thing that it in fact merely represents.

Samuel van Hoogstraeten, a seventeenth-century Dutch theorist of painting, and not incidentally an accomplished trompe l'oeil artist, wrote that a perfect painting "is like a mirror of Nature, which makes things that are not actually there seem to be there, and deceives in a permitted pleasant and commendable manner."[1] Trompe l'oeil's ability *and purpose* to deceive the viewer, however pleasantly or commendably, bring into focus questions about the general nature of all representation, concerning which much philosopher's ink was already spilled many centuries ago.

What was bothersome to ancient philosophers about trompe l'oeil centered on the relation between representation and ethics, that is, the impact of images on human character lent imagery the power to shape a society and its culture. Put differently, from the dawn of Western civilization, representation was correctly understood to have an enormous potential to shape the polis; representation at its core was political. Thus, did representation help us to comprehend the nature of reality by stimulating thought, hence producing ideas, or did it deceive us with the replication of surfaces—mere appearances—by stimulating the senses, therefore producing a physical response devoid of cognition? Was its appeal to the noble mind or to the ignoble body? Was representation an avenue to insight or a highway to sham and a validation of fakery?[2]

These concerns notwithstanding, and as the ancients understood perfectly, we cannot live or "advance" as human beings without recourse to representation, notably including the visual. Further, sight—the transmitting sensory medium of and for visual representation—was commonly understood to be the crucial vehicle supplying "information" to the brain, together with hearing (taste, touch, and smell by comparison were ancillary). Sight and representation, in other words, operate in tandem to produce knowledge, and knowledge, as everyone knows, is a requisite of power. But a difficulty remains: Representation is dangerous; by its very nature it misleads to the extent that it never *is* what it represents; the essence of "real" reality remains outside our grasp, and all the while we may delude ourselves into thinking otherwise. Thus Plato's concern with representation derived in part from the perceived danger of believing that seeing is believing.

How to Fool

For a trompe l'oeil to effect a deception, which by definition is crucial to the image's success, no detail can be left unattended either "inside" or outside the picture. For example, the light source within the painting must match that falling on the picture itself; it cannot come from a different direction. The size of the images depicted must be identical to the things represented. There can be no evidence of the act of painting; brushwork has to be hidden. Colors and textures must match those of the real objects. Generally speaking, there should be no evidence of planning or formal organization of the objects, though in fact the composition must be carefully structured. On balance, intentionality seemingly surrenders to accident—until the visual deception is "discovered."[3] Shadows must be adroitly handled to give the objects a sense of depth—this despite the fact that the objects made most easily

convincing in trompe l'oeil are of course as flat as possible, thus closely approximating the painting's actual surface, which is literally without depth.
Most important, the space represented must seem contiguous with that in
front of the picture: Its space must also appear to be our space.

> It is something of an irony that flatness might trigger illusion, since it excludes
> precisely the device that was promoted to insure an effect of spatial depth [in
> paintings], namely fixed-point perspective. That requires a horizon at which
> parallels converge, but it is well known that the illusion works only from the
> fixed point that gives the device its name: If one moves about in front of the
> surface and uses both eyes, the mechanism of parallax will soon dispel that illu-
> sion. But flatness excludes the horizon, and with no depth there is little oppor-
> tunity for parallax to work, and illusion will survive the viewer's motion. The
> *trompe l'oeil* painter appreciates that parallax is the enemy to be defeated.[4]

Doubting Certainty

Sight offers certainty. Trompe l'oeil, however, says that it is *not* so,
that seeing is believing—in deception. One crucial means by which paintings attract our attention, getting us to look at them, is by making us aware
that they *are* paintings. Concerning that, as a viewer, I must reach two con-
clusions: first, that this is a painting, hence it exists to be looked at; second,
that this painting presumes my existence as a viewer. But with trompe l'oeil
it is as though I do not exist as an observer, as though I do not matter, which
in turn may raise doubt not only about the particular image that has deceived me but about all representation (which may be deceiving, but with a
subtlety that usually escapes me).

For all its wittiness trompe l'oeil engenders suspicion,[5] a matter well articulated by the Belgian surrealist René Magritte in a painting (about painting)
he called *La condition humaine* (Figure 1.1), which directly confronts Italian
art theorist Leon Battista Alberti's (1404–1472) famous likening of a painting to a window:

> Here the metaphor of painting as window is given material expression in an
> image of an easel picture standing in front of a window, where, like jigsaw
> pieces, both complete the view "to be seen," as it were, through the window.
> The question is begged, "What lies behind the painted canvas on the easel that
> stands in the window?" It is an aspect of the surrealist potential of the
> metaphor of painting as window, and, the title implies, of the human condi-
> tion, that we cannot know the answer to the question.[6]

Figure 1.1
René Magritte
(1898–1967), LA CON-
DITION HUMAINE
(1933), canvas,
100 × 81 cm.
Washington, D.C.,
National Gallery of Art,
acc. no. 1987.55.1, gift
of the Collectors
Committee. Photo ©
1995, Board of Trustees,
National Gallery of Art,
Washington, D.C.

To the extent that trompe l'oeil constitutes a kind of joke—we can hardly suppress a smile when viewing the Magritte—like all jokes it likewise articulates the very (unconscious) anxieties and doubts that representation otherwise supposedly functions in part to dispel. If trompe l'oeil hides what it is (a painting), it then seems not to address the viewer's gaze, as though it were a painting with no need of an observer. Norman Bryson articulates this well:

> Normally, painting controls the contents of the visual field by means of a sovereign gaze that subordinates everything in the scene to the human observer. But

in *trompe l'oeil* it is as if that gaze had been removed, or had never been present: what we see are objects on their own, not as they are when people are around, but as they *really* are, left to their own devices.[7]

Bryson's insight notwithstanding, the argument I am advancing can only be taken so far, since in the end the trompe l'oeil viewer *must* see the image for what it is (a painting) and by that means of course must recognize his own relative irrelevance. In other words, the viewer's gaze, in one sense irrelevant, is in another sense crucial. It is this is-but-is-not character from which trompe l'oeil simultaneously gathers its power and admits to its own limitations as a genre. In other words, the "subject matter" of any given trompe l'oeil is less what is actually represented and more the twin phenomena of representing and looking. The "content" or "narrative" in these literally nonnarrative paintings is their being seen, or perhaps more fitting, their being stared at as the viewer wonders, What is going on here? Thus the trompe l'oeil—oddly and ironically—marks the primacy, but uncertainty, of the gaze itself, in contradiction to Bryson's explanation cited here.

Furthermore, trompe l'oeil's deception must in the end be recognized, else the picture, in succeeding too well to deceive, fails as a painting. Were the representation taken for that which it actually (only) represents, it would effectively deny its own existence and hence deny as well not only the painter but also that the painting's owner possessed it. To the extent that all paintings function as property, and therefore function as sources of power and prestige, it is in the interest of neither the artist nor the owner for the possession not to be recognized. The ultimate value of fooling someone—more darkly, of making him or her a fool—is for the deception ultimately to become apparent. Such recognition confirms not only the authority of the owner-perpetrator (who knew the secret all along) but also immediately brings the owner prestige via demonstration of possession of the means to marshal the magical talents of the artist who painted the deception. Trompe l'oeil in other words, like all forms of visual representation, is inseparable from sociocultural mechanisms of power played out on the field of interhuman relations. Accordingly, the skills of the painter and the just-described benefits to the collector reinforce each other—at the expense of a nonartist nonowner. In this and other genres of painting the artist's identity was commonly confirmed by a signature, not merely as a sign of authentication but also as a form of self-advertising. Indeed, occasionally trompe l'oeil paintings take this a step further by including on some painted scrap of paper not only the painter's name but also his studio's address and precise directions— "Boilly peintre, rue faubourg St Denis no. 8, la deuxième porte en montant, à gauche, à Paris." One painting thereby becomes an advertisement for another, thereby serving as both consumer product and marketing technique.[8]

Representing the Desire to See

Trompe l'oeil painters in Europe and America from the seventeenth through the nineteenth centuries many times took the visual conceit of their practice a step beyond what I have so far described. One sort of trompe l'oeil—a kind of hybrid of the hybrid—accomplishes this task in a particularly curious and, indeed, problematic way via images that represent not the "front" of a picture, but, as it were, the "back" (Figure 1.2).[9] The or-

Figure 1.2
William M. Davis (1829–1920), A CANVAS BACK (c. 1870), canvas, 41.6 × 46.4 cm. Stony Brook, Long Island, N.Y. The Museums at Stony Brook, gift of Mrs. Beverly Davis, 1953.

dinary trompe l'oeil seeks to deceive its viewers into believing that what they see is, in fact, a painting and not what the painting represents. William Davis's little canvas, by contrast, announces itself *as* a painting, or rather, as the back side of a painting, a wood stretcher with wooden braces, or keys, at three of the corners. Two stamped and postmarked envelopes, one with a letter and a banknote protruding from its ripped-open side, are seemingly inserted between the canvas and the stretcher. If the deception succeeds, the viewer wants to turn the picture over in order to see what is hidden from sight, the "real" painting. In effect, the image produces a desire to see, to gain sight of, what it has no intention of satisfying.

With Davis's canvas, however, the tension that might otherwise develop from being "promised" a sight only to have it refused is drained off almost instantly. He paints a label at the top of the image that reads: "A Canvas Back/By Kro Matic," which simultaneously announces the deception and renders it comic—the title puns on the fact that American trompe l'oeil artists commonly painted still lifes of hunting trophies, waterfowl being especially favored (the canvasback was an especially prized species of duck). Obviously, the viewer does not need to be told, "This is the back of a canvas"; doing so in fact informs the viewer that it is *not* the back of a canvas, rather in the way that René Magritte painted a smoker's pipe and added a text clarifying that it was not what it was ("This is not a pipe"). The label, title, and artist's attribution together function as markers that we are in fact looking at the "right" side of the painting.

Cornelis Norbertus Gijsbrechts, probably the most accomplished trompe l'oeil painter in the history of Western art, engaged the connection between seeing and desire more starkly (Figure 1.3). His "reversed" canvas gives us nothing to look at but the image of a stretcher and a small numerical label ("36") that, far more than Davis's picture, promises something to look at on the "other side." The number 36 simultaneously informs us either that the image ("on the other side") can be bought or that it is already part of an inventoried collection. If the picture is turned over (Figure 1.4), the viewer confronts a three-dimensional "original"—but not a painting.[10] The representation confounds us; it simultaneously proclaims and denies its own being. It is a picture of "not a picture."

Painting Painting

Trompe l'oeil images do not tell stories; indeed they eschew them. They are not "about" things; they pretend to "be" things. They replicate not ideas but objects, though to be sure no object is without a network of ideas constructed around it. Nevertheless, once the viewer recognizes the deception, the image is no longer "about" either deception or the objects repre-

Figure 1.3
Cornelis Norbertus
Gijsbrechts (active
1659–1678), TROMPE-
L'OEIL: REVERSED
CANVAS (1670), canvas,
66.6 × 86.5 cm.
Copenhagen, Statens
Museum for Kunst, inv.
no. 1989.

sented. It is instead "about" *painting,* specifically the physical-technical act of making ("How was it done?"); at the moment of recognition, the painting's subject is the artist and the artist's craft.

Undoubtedly, the most self-conscious and direct efforts on the part of painters to make their craft itself the subject of looking are the surviving examples of trompe l'oeil painters' easels (Figure 1.5), this one by Antonio Forbera, also known as Fort-Bras.[11] In this instance the painting—what you see reproduced is a two-dimensional painting—exactly matches the size and shape of the objects represented, as is always the case in this genre, but with its outermost edges literally cut out, in cookie-cutter fashion, so as to conform to the three-dimensional model in every way except for the surrender of the third dimension. In order to be effective—to deceive—this "easel picture" cannot be hung on a wall, as with the conventional trompe l'oeil; it needs to be freestanding to occupy the same space as the object upon which it is modeled, otherwise no delusion could occur. But once this happens, the image's impact on us changes. It is physically intrusive. We have to walk around it, and arrange furniture with its three-dimensionality in mind. It makes a greater claim on our body, in that it shares the very space we otherwise command; by contrast, we cannot trip over a painting hanging on a wall.

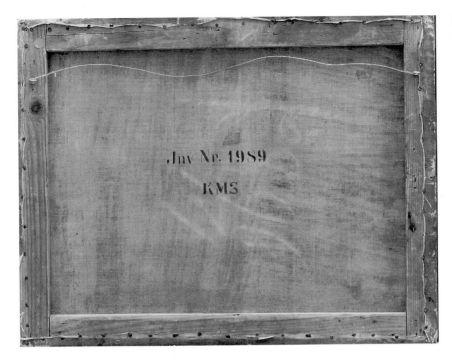

Figure 1.4
Cornelis Norbertus
Gijsbrechts (active
1659–1678), TROMPE-
L'OEIL: REVERSED CAN-
VAS (back side) (1670),
canvas, 66.6 × 86.5 cm.
Copenhagen, Statens
Museum for Kunst, inv.
no. 1989.

The easel's shape determines its subject and vice versa; this is not the case with paintings which, prior to the twentieth century, were conventionally rectangular, square, or, less commonly, round or oval. Alberti's metaphor—critical to the performance of linear perspective—that a painting was like a window onto the world, establishes that the painting (what we see) implicitly occupies a spatial cell beyond us, an outside to our inside. In effect, the painting maintains a distant relation to us. The effects of linear perspective that allow and indeed establish this relation keep representation at arm's length, spatially separate, and, to a degree, inaccessible.

The painter's easel by contrast is in the room with us; it is not seen through a window, either imagined or real. Its presence is therefore disconcerting to the extent that it seems simultaneously to be what it is and what it is not, in the instant we recognize the deception. This is critical, for what the easel trompe l'oeil claims—and demonstrates—is power, though not the power of its subject (as with the portrait, say, of a king), but that of the artist himself. And as if to erase doubt that the trompe l'oeil of a painter's easel is "about" the power of the artist, what is painted are the tools used for, and the results of, the artist's craft. The easel-picture trompe l'oeil is at once a demonstration of artistic ability and the product thereof, at once self-advertising and double proof.

Figure 1.5
Antonio Forbera (dates
unknown), PAINTER'S
EASEL (1686), canvas,
162 × 95 cm. Avignon,
Musée Calvet.

Forbera's painter's easel gives us the easel itself and, from bottom to top, a canvas back with the stretcher visible and a print inserted behind the center brace; his easel, the outwardly projecting but two-dimensional support upon which rests a painting in progress; his brushes; another print, carelessly hung from the "wrong" edge so that we see it sideways; and finally, a drawing serving as the basis for the painting in progress, attached to the easel by a large dartlike pin at the top. Everything we see in the reproduction is painted, including the easel's legs—canvas covers the actual wood of the legs, allowing the painter to paint exactly what is behind the canvas, the real legs.[12] Yet this is not all. The painting in progress is a copy of Nicolas Poussin's well-known *Realm of Flora*. This is crucial. The viewer is supposed to recognize not only a famous painting but also that the painting seen is in fact a copy, and *not a very good one*, based on the red-chalk drawing pinned to the easel. By remembering the original and recognizing a not-so-good copy, by seeing the drawing based on the original serving as the model for the painting in progress, the spectator sees a magical transformation in progress based on an *unseen* representation (Poussin's original), brought to a midpoint between the nothingness of drawing paper, the marked surface of the quite detailed sketch, and finally the representation of the representation(s). Beyond that, everything except the Poussin original is itself encapsulated in a new original—not a mere copy—the painter's easel itself. Thus representations are layered atop representations, and in the process the viewer is delighted and, with a little thought, confounded about what has happened in plain view. The painting confronts us in our own space, but what it aggressively claims by its spatial intrusiveness it denies in the uncertainty of what it purports to show. It comes forward, introducing itself to us, but when we reach out for it, it recedes into the actual spatial uncertainty that in part defines so much representational painting.

History preserves a reaction to this very image in an account by Charles de Brosses (1709–1777), a French magistrate, sophisticated connoisseur, historian, literary scholar, philologist, geographer, contributor of articles for the great French *Encyclopédie*, and even politician—neither a fool nor a man easily fooled. He saw Forbera's painting in 1739, more than one-half century after it was painted. Here is what he said:

> Upon entering, I saw an object which so took my fancy that it deserves considerable space in my narrative. At the end of the room there was an easel upon which had been set a painting, not quite finished, depicting the Empire of Flora, after the original by Poussin. The painter's palette and his brushes had been left next to the picture. . . . [He then precisely describes the rest of it.] I saw all of this at a distance first and then close by without noting anything out

of the ordinary; but upon attempting to pick up the drawing, I was astounded to find that all I have described was in fact one single painting, done entirely with oil colors. The plate mark of the metal plates on the paper of the two engravings; the difference in the textures of the papers; the threads of the turned-over canvas; the holes and the wood of the easel—all this was so wonderful that I could not help exclaiming. . . . The painting is unframed, not rectangular, but shaped so as to follow the outlines that would be those of the group of objects in reality; this device further deceives the eye.[13]

Indeed, de Brosses was so certain that the painted drawing was itself done in pencil, and not oil, that he moistened his handkerchief and tried erasing just a bit of it. At least on this one score, he thought that he had not been deluded; he was mistaken.

One thing more: This picture is thought to have been painted for a man with very deep pockets for buying art, King Louis XIV of France,[14] resented, admired, and envied by virtually every European sovereign of his time and long afterward, a man who spent vast sums of money commissioning the labors of painters to decorate his numerous residences. Forbera's painter's easel makes a claim on behalf of the artist himself to occupy the same space as that of his patron. The painter constitutes himself as a kind of present absence, who having finished his work, uncannily still remains there to finish it (the unfinished copy of Poussin's painting). His painter's easel is a bit like a computer-generated bill that refuses to go away, constantly reminding the owner of who the artist *is,* what he *did,* and—equally important—what he *does.* It is a promise to return made by a man who has no right to do so, though he may accomplish this feat nonetheless by creating the desire for his talents in his extraordinarily wealthy and powerful sometime patron.

Disclaimer

The viewer of a trompe l'oeil may attempt to make sense of its putative contents; indeed, that is to be expected as part of the conventional act of looking at anything. But the relations among objects that might in another sort of picture add up to a story, however loosely defined, in this instance commonly add up to very little, or at least very little to which one can point with certainty. How the painted "text" therefore reads remains up for grabs. More important, the effort to make sense of it, beyond the mere "facts" of appearance, and its impact as a deception or joke make the nature of interpretation itself problematic. The seemingly random character of trompe l'oeil paintings' contents undercuts the promise of clarity and certainty, thus also undermining the viewer's capacity to know.[15] In the same vein, however, it is necessary to acknowledge the limitations of the genre. Trompe l'oeil's lack of narrative ultimately condemns it to being "about" the same three things repeatedly—deception, representation, and artist—an insufficiency that permits the genre to lay claim to a radically narrow, though hardly trivial, set of insights. For better or worse, prior to the period of Modernism, the connection of paintings to texts was profound: "The greatness of Western art is a function of its narrative power, and that requires that pictorial space have something of the properties of theatrical space in which the great events—the annunciations, visitations, adorations, transfigurations, crucifixions, resurrections, and final judgments—can transpire."[16] Weighed against this tradition, trompe l'oeil is wanting. My interest in trompe l'oeil, quite specialized and specific, develops from the opportunities the genre allows for understanding some basic issues about the nature of representation *as such*, given that the "content" of what is represented is, by definition (and not merely by my whim), the issue of representation itself.

Deception and Erotic Desire

Raphaelle Peale's *Venus Rising from the Sea—A Deception* (long known as "After the Bath") (Figure 1.6) promises to be a painting of a female nude, one obviously turned frontally toward the viewer, judging both from her arm and right foot. Indeed, so presumably frank is the nude that a cloth or curtain shields precisely what the presumed viewer most wants to see, her sexual parts, her nudity. Yet what startles the viewer is not the woman, who is barely visible, but the curtain hiding her, strikingly real, a technical triumph in its own right, but one that maddeningly keeps out of view a much more desirable sight. All images

> involve the transformation of the present. The irreducible and untranslatable significance of images, then, is finally rooted in the intersection and inevitable contradiction between the world's always being present to us and its seldom being present to us as we desire it to be. *Desire for the absent constantly transforms the present* [emphasis added].[17]

The curtain feeds an appetite only so as not to satisfy it. It taunts, if only slightly, and not incidentally reminds the viewer—having "figured out" that the image is a deception—of the privileged gaze of the painter, who unlike us looked at the woman he does not allow us to see. (In fact, X rays show—no surprise—that Peale never painted any more of the body than what we see.)[18] Indeed, Peale paints the curtain to look more real, more tangible, than the woman, who appears to be what she "is"—not real, but painted. In other

Figure 1.6
Raphaelle Peale
(1774–1825), VENUS
RISING FROM THE SEA
—A DECEPTION (a.k.a.
AFTER THE BATH)
(c. 1822), canvas,
74.3 × 61.3 cm.
Kansas City, Mo., The
Nelson-Atkins Museum
of Art (Purchase: Nelson
Trust), no. 34–147.

words, the painting attempts to deceive us into seeing it as a nonpainting (the cloth covering) incorporating a real painting that is almost entirely kept out of our sight (obviously we could not otherwise be fooled, since the image is not life-size, which would be necessary were we to take the painted woman to be as real as the curtain).[19]

John Haberle's female-nude personification of Night (Figure 1.7, *Color Plate 1*), as it were, pulls back the curtain: We get to see—but what? The heavy velvet drape at the right is highly finished by the painter; he devoted

Figure 1.7
John Haberle
(1856–1933), NIGHT
(c. 1909), board,
200.7 × 132 cm.
New Britain, Conn.,
The New Britain
Museum of American
Art, gift of Mr. and Mrs.
Victor Demmer, inv. no.
1966.66. Photo: E.
Irving Blomstrann.

enormous care to make it appear to *be* what it merely represents. The nude by contrast is disappointing, a poor competitor for our attention. She is literally unfinished, merely a sketch, an *un*fulfilled "promise." Again, pleasure resides in the frustrated desire produced by *not* being able to see what we had hoped for, ironically, when we actually get to see it. Our attention drifts toward the drape that, as it were, "normally" hides the nude from view. Mere fabric becomes the subject of our marvel. What is left to imagine is this: If the painter can cause me to invest my pleasure in looking at velvet, what might he be capable of when he turns his attention to her "unfinished" body? With this, the trompe l'oeil moves us to a still more complex terrain, that of gender. The purported sight is for men, and it is controlled by a male artist. He alone determines if the viewer can see her at all, and what of her we "other men" shall see. This involves a game of one-upmanship, where the playfulness common to trompe l'oeil takes on an aggressive edge in the relation between producer (artist) and consumer (viewer).[20]

Deception and the Erotics of Money (Seeing for What It's Worth)

Now arrives the moment to modify my previous remarks to the effect that trompe l'oeil evokes only three narrow topics (deception, representation, and artist). Trompe l'oeil pictures do not stand outside history. Like all representation, they necessarily acknowledge the sociocultural terrain on which they rest and sometimes do so quite directly. Thus, to cite one historical instance, American late nineteenth-century trompe l'oeil paintings of money (Figure 1.8) invoke issues of social-class conflict, fascinatingly mapped onto questions pertaining directly to the nature and politics of visual representation.[21] Distinctly unheroic in dimension, this tiny image makes up for its lack of size by the predicate upon which it depends: someone's *seeming* to glue a twenty-dollar bill to a board in 1890, thereby removing from circulation what was for the majority of the population a considerable sum. The bill in question, in deteriorated condition, has previously passed through many hands—hands that until now had need of it. Thus the image pushes to the very edge of narration to mark the frank materialism of the American character first described by Alexis de Tocqueville (*Democracy in America,* 1835–1840) and later vigorously condemned by Thorstein Veblen (*The Theory of the Leisure Class,* 1899), who coined the famous phrase "conspicuous consumption" as regards the rapacious consumerist habits of the super-rich.

Figure 1.8
John Haberle
(1856–1933), TWENTY-
DOLLAR BILL (1890),
canvas, 19 × 24.1 cm.
Springfield, Mass.,
Museum of Fine Arts, gift
of Charles T. and Emilie
Shean, inv. no. 39.10.

Money per se was a topic of enormous concern in the post–Civil War decades, a period of high (and heavy) industrialization that produced the first so-named robber-baron multimillionaires and the historical moment that destroyed once and for all the myth of America as a classless society. As Edward J. Nygren puts it: "Money in the Gilded Age became a measure, perhaps *the* measure, of a man's moral as well as social worth. American materialism and worship of the dollar were subjects repeatedly discussed and often reviled in books, articles, novels, poems, songs, and caricatures by Europeans and Americans alike."[22] Paintings of money thus functioned as part of a vast network of discussion and debate about the economy and its power to define the very nature of American culture—increasingly centered around class divisions that had profound impact on principles of social justice.

We might argue that Haberle's painting functions as a particularly crass, if slightly indirect, sort of visual bragging about private wealth—but that "explanation" is by no means necessarily called for. Haberle's care to show a tattered bill, not one freshly printed, prepares the ground for a critique of a materialism whose logical end point is the private horde, the point at which money's social circulation ends not in its use but in the private determination to hold on to it for dear life. Late nineteenth-century paintings of money, paper money especially, were produced in large numbers. As with the image under discussion, many of them seem now to occupy—at best—a neutral position on the "question" of money. Other images are more obviously critical of the dominant economy. Thus painter Victor Dubreuil's *Money to Burn* (1898)[23] represents a close-up view of about one dozen barrels, neatly set in two rows, overflowing with greenbacks, a Midas horde in the presumed mansion of a millionaire, to judge from the patterned marble floor. The painting dates from the year of the Great Panic "when there was a shortage of currency and a need for money to stimulate the economy."[24] Dubreuil's *Safe Money* (Figure 1.9) takes up a complementary theme in a close-up of an opened safe, set on a marble floor of the identical pattern used in *Money to Burn*. The vault is filled to overflowing with large-denomination bills and gold and silver coins. Directly in the center of the image is an account sheet, a sort of visual audit, informing us that what we are looking at is a semiannual tally of dividends: $492,392,296.50. At the safe's top, the owner is specified as "N.S.E. & W.R.R.," a fictitious North, South, East, and West Railroad, symbolizing totalized monopoly capitalism and barely exaggerating the actual practice and financial success of the principal railroad magnates.

Antagonisms relative to rapidly expanding social-class differences are entirely obvious in the subject matter of such paintings, but these tensions also show, though they are less immediately obvious to late twentieth-century eyes, in the artist's choice to employ trompe l'oeil itself. Elite tastes were commonly offended by such powerfully illusionistic art, officially regarding it as mere trickery (hence not "really" art), intended for entertainment, not edification—it was middle-brow, middle-class (or worse, working-class) banality.

> To the elite, Harnett's crime [and that of his contemporaries like Haberle] was democratizing high culture—as well as debasing and displacing it—by diffusing it in unconventional exhibitions and by turning it into a spectacle. That threat had haunted the elite since the cultural revolution sparked by P. T. Barnum, who had created museumlike amusement centers in the antebellum period.[25]

The Greenback Party, which favored the continued use of paper money as legal tender (green bills were first issued during the Civil War), helped spark sustained national debates surrounding the relation between paper currency and the gold that stood behind it, as the standard that guaranteed the paper's worth. Here enter issues pertaining directly to representation and the nature of reality, both subjects of enormous interest during this period of American history.[26] A long tradition carried to America from Europe rendered the value of gold unproblematic. Its worth was taken to be obvious. Unlike pa-

Figure 1.9
Victor Dubreuil (dates unknown), SAFE MONEY (1898), canvas, 76.8 × 195.1 cm. Washington, D.C., The Corcoran Gallery of Art, museum purchase through a gift from the heirs of George E. Lemon, acc. no. 1980.65.

per currency, gold did not stand for a certain value, it simply *had* value. With paper money, the "real" (i.e., gold) was replaced by its mere representation, or stand-in. Whereas with gold, seeing (and feeling) was believing, with paper currency, belief depended more on an act of faith that what was represented (say, $20) really *was* worth $20. To complicate the matter further, throughout this period currency counterfeiting was endemic,[27] which exacerbated the uncertainties surrounding paper money's worth and brought into sharp focus the suspicious nature of an economy so apparently dependent on representation.

The "reality" and "real" worth of gold was replaced by gold's green representation. The mere *sign* of gold replaced gold's *reality,* a matter made still worse (and occasionally discussed to this day) when the nation abandoned the gold standard, that is, abandoned the promise that any greenback could be actually exchanged for that which it represented. Paintings of money joined the debate both by their subject and their very nature. Paintings of paper money, after all, were representations *of representations;* they themselves, in other words, referenced the troublesome relation between representation and fakery, or counterfeiting.[28] Indeed, artists like Haberle and his contemporaries William Michael Harnett and John Frederick Peto were investigated and even threatened by treasury authorities, a story repeated recently with the American-born painter J.S.G. Boggs.

Since the 1980s Boggs has specialized in drawing various international currencies with confounding precision, but with numerous readily visible tip-offs as to what he is doing; for example, his "bills" are drawn only on one side. He attempts to "exchange" his art-money for services rendered, for example, in restaurants when the bill is brought, always making clear, however, that what is being exchanged is not money but money's representation (that is, art). "The odd thing about art is that it recapitulates the confusion about paper money: Why, and how, is it worth *anything*?"[29] Boggs himself put the question more directly, alluding to the variety of responses he has received when attempting to carry out an exchange: "It's funny, though, how these transactions are themselves a lot like drug deals. . . . The same sorts of questions come up: Is it real? Is it a con? Is it good stuff? Is it worth it? Is it legal?"[30]

I will close with two vignettes about the "worth" of money—and art—rooted in the "worth" of representation. First, Pablo Picasso, ever smart about money, used to pay for his shopping with personal checks on the backs of which he would make doodles. The checks would, of course, carry his signature, the sign of double authenticity: The check is good *and* the doodle is a Picasso. The checks were seldom cashed—Picasso's signed doodle (not the check as such) served as the medium of exchange, as Picasso himself understood perfectly. In the second vignette, a Haberle painting representing a one-dollar bill and seventy cents in change sold in 1899 for $170; in 1987, the same painting auctioned at Sotheby's fetched $470,000,[31] in authoritative testimony both to art's historical relation to capital and to its status as a preeminent *sign* of modern worth,[32] by no means art's least significant social and cultural function.

Part Two

Object

Let us, from now on, be on our guard against the hallowed philosophers' myth of a "pure, will-less, painless, timeless knower"; let us beware of the tentacles of such contradictory notions as "pure reason," "absolute knowledge," "absolute intelligence." All these concepts presuppose an eye such as no living being can imagine, an eye required to have no direction, to abrogate its active and interpretative powers—precisely those powers that alone make of seeing, seeing something. All seeing is essentially perspective, and so is all knowing.

—Friedrich Nietzsche
The Genealogy of Morals

Chapter 2

Still(ed) Life, Beauty, and Regimes of Power

S$_{\text{TILL LIFE PAINTING}}$ is a neglected topic in the history of art, in part due to the low status it was granted in the hierarchy of art subjects by art theorists dating as far back as Pliny the Elder (23–79 A.D.) and Philostratus (170?–245 A.D.), who were responsible for some of the earliest substantial writings about Western art.[1] The designation "still life" first occurred only around the middle of the seventeenth century,[2] at which time the prestigious, royally endowed French Academy of Painting and Sculpture officially ranked the genre well behind paintings on historical subjects, that is, pictorial narratives about "important" persons real or imagined (secular, ecclesiastical, mythological, and legendary); and portraits (principally the representations of powerful people but without the narrative content of history paintings).[3]

> The theoretical issues that placed still-life painting at the low end of the scale of worthy subjects focused on the desire to demonstrate that painting belonged to the liberal arts. Primary to such arguments was that the role of the artist should be differentiated from that of the [mere] craftsman. The artist should deal with *abstract ideas that draw upon his imagination or intuition* [emphasis added].[4]

The "trouble," so to speak, with still life was its purported lack of narrative,[5] together with its privileging of mere objects. Still life eschewed text: history, scripture, epic myth, biography. It did not teach but only dazzled. It was about "goods," not people. Nonetheless, still life's attention to goods—possessions, things one could "have" and by having in part define oneself—guaranteed its popularity with and significance for an audience of principally rich buyers, whether old-moneyed members of the aristocracy or new-moneyed bourgeoisie,[6] who were sometimes willing to pay staggering prices for these images.[7] The lowly status assigned to still life by academic art theorists thus bore little relation to its status among those who bought such paintings. Further, sometimes art theory inadvertently sold art practice short by implying that art's importance did not arise from the skill and insight of the painter, without regard to the subject painted, but arose from the subject that was painted, with the inevitable bow to the purported interests of a real or imaginary elite—at least some of whom, not coincidentally, were also art patrons.[8]

Still life artists were characteristically, though not always, far lesser participants in the realms of power enjoyed by high-status painters of historical subjects, portraits, and the like. Most still life painters did not actually paint for particular patrons or on commission but worked for an anonymous market, painting pictures in advance of a more or less guaranteed sale. By contrast, Peter Paul Rubens (1577–1640), perhaps the most famous early-modern example of a high-status artist, was not only commissioned by various European heads of state to image (and imagine) their personal histories but also carried out numerous diplomatic missions on their behalf, acting as a sort northern European ambassador-at-large. Enormously talented, versatile, and politically astute, Rubens died as rich as he was famous.

Painting, Possessing, and Identity

Still life is *the* genre through which art and aesthetics most boldly encounter their entwined relation to privilege precisely because still life's typical object-centeredness seldom allows anyone to forget its relation to *buying* and *having*. Still life is commonly "about" money, and money is often its literal subject in the form of gold and silver coins and paper bills. Roland Barthes described seventeenth-century Dutch still-life painting as an "empire of merchandise"; speaking about Dutch paintings in general and their focus on the object world, he noted that they "require a gradual and complete reading; we must begin at one edge and finish at the other, *audit the painting like an accountant,* not forgetting this corner, that margin, that background, in which is inscribed yet another perfectly rendered object adding its unit to this patient weighing of property or of merchandise" [emphasis added].[9]

Still life is commonly about power, though of a raw and blunt kind, without the trapping and gilding of mythology's heroes, history's grand narratives, scripture's saints, or portraiture's men of noble stature or virtue. Still life is about what power gets you. It is the one genre that blatantly tells the unwitting story underwriting money: You are what you have, all the more visually inescapable given the "almost obsessive precision"[10] with which still life's objects, at least in their early history, were commonly painted. Thus, "the sense of awe elicited by a Dutch or Flemish still-life painting is not accidental. The artists who created these works wanted to convey the delicacy of a rose petal, the sheen of a silver urn, the rich textural surface of a lemon, and the shimmer of a satin drapery because they felt that the essence of a still-life painting is found in its illusion of reality."[11]

In its early manifestations the genre's epistemic "honesty"—sometimes regarded as vulgarity—is unsettling. And this story becomes all the more interesting if we factor in some account of still lifes that, in effect, cut across this grain—the grain of goods—to raise troubling questions, specifically visual questions, about the relation of goods and riches to power and privilege. My interest in this story will not be mapped as a kind of catalog of *what* is there in still lifes, but rather of *how* what is there is represented, arguably the more important issue. I will explore some of the ways that still lifes "work" on us—how their rhetoric or persuasive power operates—which very much involves the *evident* mastery of painting technique itself as part and parcel of such paintings' visual arsenal.

Still life raises significant questions about what people in a given place and time wanted to see and thus deemed worth seeing. In short, still life is a profound record of *interests,* yet it is never "objective" in its account and is all the more interesting and important for precisely that reason. Still life is a record of struggle over the "official" and changing account of reality, over the invariably frantic human effort to read out a particular version of what is "real," since whatever account of reality proves dominant defines people's ability to control their world. That this effort is necessarily political is obvious from the fact that the worldly terrain is one of scarce resources, unequal distributions, competing interests, and conflicting beliefs. We live out lives that are rooted in trouble and struggle, and painting has always provided versions of what these troubles and struggles are all about. My interest in painting in general, and for the moment with still life in particular, is that it is not merely a record of these phenomena but is likewise a significant "participant" in the debates, less a mirror of the past and present than an agent helping to shape a future.

Seeing Things to Want Them

Still life maps the intersections of economy and power atop an equally important series of categories at once intensely personal, specific, social, and cultural. These categories are desire, pleasure, and subjectivity. Still life ordinarily excludes people (or at least de-emphasizes them), but it is always ultimately about people and *not,* or not merely, about the objects actually represented. In other words, still life is about the relation of the object world to the human subject who is unseen but imagined. Still life specifically depends for its effects on an erotics—the desire and pleasure—of *looking,* triggered by the beholder's relation to the material world. Above all, still life is about the act of looking itself: "By default, what still life shows is the gaze. Since most of the objects in still life tend not to supply their own rationale for representation, what emerges when they are depicted is the act of representation as *bestowed,* unearned, as *conferred,* gratuitously, upon objects that exactly lack the power to summon representation."[12]

All painting requires looking, but still life evokes looking. Further, still life additionally often evokes smell, taste, hearing, and touch. Perhaps more than any other sort of painting, still life reminds us of our own embodiment, to the extent that it so specifically relates us as physical and sensory beings to the material world.

Still life privileges culture (things that are made) over nature (things that simply are)—and in this regard when it incorporates "nature" (as with food or hunting-trophy still lifes), it does so in ways that are often extraordinarily problematic, to the extent that nature is commonly sacrificed to culture. Indeed, the sacrifice regularly incorporates killing as such: Spilled blood is painted. This is paradoxical, if not ironic, to the extent that such paintings are intended to be decorative, which is to say that they invite us to take visual pleasure in death transliterated into something visually beautiful and presumably desirable.

Still life's imaging of the object world raises moral questions centered, at certain moments in Western history, around guilt about the very objects it otherwise invites us to take pleasure from. Once guilt is introduced, the still life returns to that from which art theory exempted it—to narrative, if of a particular sort, namely, theological and philosophical. Yet it does so in highly ambivalent, complicated, and indirect ways—sometimes, we might think, with enormous bad conscience. Certain genres of still life, that is, *intentionally* lead us on, inviting the pleasures of obsessive looking (scopophilia)—and then "ask" us to condemn the very thing we take pleasure in, thereby condemning ourselves for taking the pleasure in the first place but redeeming ourselves at the last minute (if all goes according to the supposed plan). An art that builds into its program a judgment about looking is a political art, one invested in long-standing debates about the connection of pleasure and desire to knowledge and power.[13]

Still life ranges widely between the extremes of visual scarcity and nearly shocking excess. It is high class and low class. It deals with the objects of the home and the objects of war. In essence still life is about every thing people can touch (and sometimes taste, smell, and hear) but which in representation we can only now see. Its rhetorical power in part is produced by the tension or frustration engendered in the move from the three-dimensional world of material reality to the two-dimensional world of representation. To "consume" visually the objects of the still life is to be invited to look—sometimes to the point of exhaustion or satiation—at the amount, the variety, the detail, the "essence," *but only to look.* "The pleasures [the still life] stimulates are not real, they are mere illusion. Try and grasp the luscious fruit or the tempting beaker and you will hit against a hard cold panel."[14] The tension produced by having only *not* to have is increased by the conventions of museum behavior, where the confirming touch on the painting itself is forbidden.

There is more to the story. The painting itself is a three-dimensional object: *It* could be possessed. And the possession of this singular object generates enormous pleasure, exactly to the degree that the painting concentrates into the visibility of its own material surface (color, texture, light, space) much more than merely the reminder of the objects represented. The painting, even when produced for a market, and thus of lesser cost than if individually commissioned, is inevitably an object defining excess, one that marks some degree of possible personal consumption above mere necessity. After all, paintings do not *do* anything; they cannot keep me warm or feed my belly. Their very uselessness as regards the basic requirements for living partially defines their importance. To have the painting to look at I not only have the pleasure of its company but also its visible-to-others confirmation of who I am. By having the painting I say to myself *and* others that I have exceeded the floor of mere sufficiency. I *have* more than enough. The painting bathes me in prestige.

Tulip Mania

Flowers might seem to be fairly innocuous, noncontroversial, and perhaps not very interesting subjects around which to organize a discussion about possession, power, politics, and desire in painting. The lack of an obvious match between flower paintings and these topics defines why I want to take up the topic: to establish a match where we might otherwise least expect to find one, thereby to assist an understanding of how thoroughly imagery operates as a sociocultural force. The tulip proves the single most striking example by which to develop this discussion. Its early history in Europe, following importation from Turkey in the sixteenth century, serves as an apt metaphor for the dynamisms of modernity itself as these were connected to profit motive, individual wealth, world trade, European colonialism, proto-capitalism, and not least, the new knowledges produced via science.

The tulip's early history is connected to the ambitious and enormously expensive botanical pleasure gardens owned by northern European aristocrats, bankers, and members of the intelligentsia.[15] Rare and exotic plants were transplanted from throughout the world, in effect from wherever European trade routes and colonization had made this possible.[16] Already by the early 1620s the tulip was the "unrivaled flower of fashion throughout northern France, the Netherlands and western parts of Germany."[17] The publication of tulip catalogs, alongside efforts to classify and rank tulip varieties, soon spurred its popularity well beyond an audience of the socially most privileged. Numerous plant breeders quickly and intensively experimented with bloom size, color, and petal shape, so that tulip varieties expanded exponentially.

The tulip trade quickly became big business. Whereas tulip trade early on involved professionals, by 1634 buying became common among people wholly without expertise, and what had begun as trade devolved into whole-sale speculation. Often no cash was traded; instead goods were pledged, running the gamut from farm animals to textiles, and including personal possessions like clothing, land, and house. Normally, these valuables had to be delivered or signed over immediately, often before the bulbs had been harvested. A futures market developed in which the seller had literally no bulbs to deliver—and the buyer had no money with which to make the purchase. At this juncture, new buyers and sellers entered the market, trading for the same nonexistent, on-paper-only bulbs. As the time drew nearer for the bulb harvest, the risk to the individual who in the end held the paper of sale—and hence was responsible to pay the grower—grew larger, but so did his chance for the greatest profit. Buying on speculation obviously produced immense profits for some and huge losses for others, the participants eventually involving all social classes, even the poor—very much like today's participants in the national lottery. The inevitable economic crash occurred in 1637.[18]

Tulip varieties were ranked in a hierarchy mirroring the social order itself. In the Netherlands, military leaders—public heroes (men only)—had tulips named after them. The flamed and irregularly striped varieties were the most admired, and these were grouped into three aristocratic "estates" according to dominant hue: the roses (red and pink on white background), the violets (lilac and purples on white ground), and *bizarden* (red or violet on yellow ground). "At the very head of this nobility were the 'imperial' rarities, the Semper Augustus (red flames on white) and the attempted clone, the Parem

Augustus."[19] One bulb of the Semper Augustus had sold for as much as 5,500 Dutch florins; for comparative purposes, in the mid-seventeenth century a skilled worker was paid a weekly wage of 2.8 florins.[20]

From Flower Speculation to Flower Fantasy

Many thousands of flower still lifes were produced in the Low Countries in the course of the late sixteenth and seventeenth centuries. They were principally sold to the wealthy bourgeoisie in the market towns of Antwerp, in the South, and Amsterdam, The Hague, Utrecht, Delft, and Middelburg in the North.[21] Among the most talented of all Northern European flower painters was one of the earliest, the Fleming Jan Brueghel the Elder (1568–1625).[22] In 1606 he was made court painter in Brussels and held the position until his death. Archduke Albert and Archduchess Isabella exempted him from taxes, duties, and export franchises; they also gave him free access to their private botanical gardens and menagerie of rare and exotic animals. He enjoyed not only success but considerable wealth—between 1604 and 1609 he bought no fewer than six houses. He was a close friend of the esteemed Peter Paul Rubens, with whom he sometimes collaborated on paintings.[23]

Brueghel's flower pictures (Figure 2.1, *Color Plate 2*)[24] were painted between about 1605 and 1621, during the years when the Dutch and Flemish taste for tulips and other exotic (or once-exotic) plants was on the increase, though full-blown tulip mania occurred after his death. During the years Brueghel painted flowers, the tulip was still a species enjoyed principally by the wealthy. He painted an enormous range of then-fashionable flowers, both indigenous and imported. His favorite was the rose, but he also favored tulips and the crown imperial, *Fritillaria imperialis,* imported from Asia Minor, the stunning flower he preferred for the apex of his pyramidal arrangements.[25] His large bouquets also included lilies, stocks, irises, orange blossoms, fritillaries, and cyclamen, among others. He liked painting fragile flowers like the cardamine, pimpernel, and forget-me-not. Indeed, the profusion and variety of blooms in Brueghel's flower still lifes can be astounding—in one painting up to as many as 130, each distinct.[26]

Brueghel took great trouble with his paintings, sometimes to the annoyance of patrons tired of waiting for delivery of their commissions. A master of technique, patiently painting with tiny and invisible brush strokes, he ren-

dered each flower only as it came into bloom, hence often requiring months
to complete a single picture.[27] Brueghel wrote of his first flower still life,
painted for Federico Cardinal Borromeo in 1606, that it would consist of
more than one hundred different flowers, all painted from life. The bouquet
was in no sense ordinary, for many of the flowers he included were at the time

so costly and rare that they were grown in gardens as single specimens.[28] Yet so many blooms are packed into the vase as to overwhelm its actual capacity to hold them.

Cardinal Borromeo, perfectly aware of the politics of visual aesthetics, wrote of his pleasure in possessing Brueghel's flower picture wherein "the variety of colors . . . [are] not fleeting . . . but [are] stable and very endurable," unlike those found in nature.[29] We may read this in at least two complementary ways. In the first instance, the brief life of natural blooms serves as a morally loaded metaphor for the vanity of all earthly things. In this respect the flower painting functions as an aesthetically charged memento mori. Indeed, in another flower still life, Brueghel incorporated the following inscription, here translated, at the picture's bottom: "Look upon this flower which appears so fair, and fades so swiftly in the strong light of the sun. Mark God's word: only it flourishes eternally. For the rest, the world is naught."[30]

In the second instance—and answering more to my interests—Brueghel's picture seemingly defies time (impermanence), nature, and geography. That is, the various natural blooming times of the flowers involved are compressed to a single instant, as though nature itself dares not keep the powerful viewer-owner waiting; and in oil paint they remain forever suspended in the moment of their unfaded perfection.[31] The various species originate on different continents; many were Eastern importations, that is, from the non-Christian, Muslim world, the centuries-old enemy of the Western church, here, as it were, surrendering its precious visual (and imagined olfactory) treasures to the private looking of a Catholic cardinal.[32]

To be sure there were still other ways to "read" flower pictures. Metaphoric associations were practically limitless. Such paintings were nominally and commonly constructed as allegories representing the human senses of sight and smell, about which more later. In a world still tied to the Christian Middle Ages, like most other things they were signs of the spiritual, a complete account of which would constitute a separate study. Thus the white lily, its color a sign of purity, might stand for the Virgin; the columbine, derived from the Latin *columba,* or dove, was associated with the Holy Spirit. The rose, whose beauty was thoroughly appreciated, was reminiscent of Paradise, though it also registered secular love. And so on.[33] Yet in any typical instance there is no *demand* for a metaphorical or religious reading and certainly little direct sign of such intentionality. To be sure, a stronger case for moral overtones is evident in those pictures where some of the flowers are already fading (an allusion to death) or in paintings that incorporate insects such as butterflies or dragonflies, symbols of redemption.[34] Yet the inclusion of insects also reflects an intense contemporaneous, and distinctly secular, interest in natural science.

Indeed, despite still life painting's low esteem in art theory, flower pictures enjoyed a link to contemporaneous—and highly prestigious—science, specifically botany. Antwerp, the city where Brueghel lived and painted, was the locus of the great Plantin publishing house, responsible for the production of important books on botany by Dodonaeus, Lobelius, and Clusius.[35] "It seems likely that some of the earliest efforts at rendering flowers came in response to the requests of flower lovers to see what new wonders botanists had developed."[36] A direct visual linkage to the classification practices of early botany is made by a painting of tulips produced about 1650 in which the artist dutifully numbered each variety's stem, keying the numbers to a sheet providing the identifications at the picture's bottom edge.[37]

What is striking about typical northern flower pictures is not only the abundance of blooms but the fact that no single flower is likely to be represented twice. An overall effect of rarity is preserved: "What is sought is not abundance but the Specimen." Norman Bryson connects this to the emergent move toward scientific classification, where redundancy would undercut or trivialize hierarchy. Thus, if more than one tulip is included, and this was commonly the case, different strains are represented. The relative lack of spatial depth in these early flower pictures may likewise be associated with the laying-out character of science, the "tabulation" effect being here dominant.[38]

Denaturalizing the Natural

There is a striking difference between flower still lifes by Rachel Ruysch[39] (Figure 2.2, *Color Plate 3*) and those by Brueghel. Most immediately obvious are the landscape settings into which she sets her "bouquets." Ruysch moves her flowers back to the outdoors, into a seemingly "natural" setting, one that would seem to deny the horticultural, as opposed to the natural or "wild," genesis of the blooms. Typically, the flowers in Dutch still lifes are the products of an intense horticulture; wild flowers are neither valorized nor paid much heed. Yet no sooner has Ruysch's image announced its naturalism to the eye than it denies it, and thrusts up for our consideration—and pleasure—precisely the opposite: its unnaturalness, its artificiality, its artifice, in a word, its Art. In other words, Ruysch's paintings render problematic the act of looking in a way that Brueghel's paintings ignore or cover up. On the one hand, the attention to detail that one quickly comes to expect from northern flower still lifes remains intact.[40] On the other hand, detail is used against itself, in a kind of defeat of the rational or quasi-scientific "proof" that we—and the original viewers—typically expect from detail: the *visible truth.*

For example, whereas the flowers are convincingly painted, their invisible "roots" defy reality, because they are apparently grounded in the trunk of a flowering elder tree. Nor do lilies and roses, and so on grow together in impossibly close proximity in nature. Indeed, these are "vase flowers" without their vase. Similarly, the reality of the natural setting, dependent on the illusion of spatial depth, is one of first glance, visually referenced only to have its reality denied upon closer examination.

Figure 2.2
Rachel Ruysch
(1664–1750), FLORAL
STILL LIFE (1686),
canvas, 114 × 87 cm.
Rochester, Memorial Art
Gallery of the University
of Rochester, acquired
with contributions made
in memory of Brenda
Rowntree by her
friends, and through the
Acquisition Fund of the
Women's Council and
The Marion Stratton
Gould Fund, inv. 82.9.

Landscape paintings produce their effects on the viewer in part according to the degree to which they effectively create the illusion of spatial depth and sweep. By this means, the enormity and enormous power of nature itself—or, conversely, the power of land ownership—is referenced. Ruysch reminds the viewer of the expectation of spatial depth and sweep—and then denies both. Her painting supplies only two spatial planes, front and back, the former having some depth, the latter—where depth might be virtually infinite—almost none.[41] In complementary fashion, Ruysch's handling of light exaggerates the naturalism of the horticulturally achieved blooms but at the expense of the "nature" into which they have been artificially situated. Subtly nuanced on the roses, lilies, iris, morning glory, morning bindweed, and opium poppies, light heightens the flowers' naturalism, but the fact that it illuminates only the blooms renders problematic the very naturalism it otherwise asserts. As regards color, it is as if all nature is drab apart from these blooms: Nothing else is permitted to detract from their display.

The image is a compendium of paradoxical binary oppositions: visually stark and yet celebratory; gorgeous and grotesque; real and unreal; "easy" and quite specifically *demanding*. It vastly exceeds its status as a commodity, precisely because of what it requires of the viewer, which is far more than a "natural" reaction to its attractiveness. Ruysch makes an issue of the power she claims as an artist by making visible the uncannily invisible, by making possible the impossible. Brueghel's equally astounding conceit gets there by technically denying the very artificiality of his enterprise. By contrast, Ruysch never allows viewers to forget that what we see is *her* seeing and *her* doing. For the sake of comparison, we might say that Brueghel's way of seeing denies itself in the naturalism of his representation, whereas Ruysch's way of seeing profoundly denaturalizes the naturalism to which she ironically nonetheless lays claim.

Ruysch maps a principal conflict at the forefront of early modernity. The new botanical science she learned from her scientist father evokes classification, registration, precision, and an explicitly eye-centered "objective" knowledge. Her odd-looking still lifes acknowledge the "objective" account of nature made possible by the new sciences, but via the filter of her own sensibilities, or subjective knowing. In essence, Ruysch attempts to see *through* science as though to understand and represent not only what science makes possible to see, hence know, but also what it masks in the process. Ruysch's horticultural still life, with its faked landscape, momentarily—hopelessly—sets back into the natural world the plants that have been removed forever from it. Her work follows by several decades the collapse of speculative tulip mania—and a parallel relative decline of interest in flower still lifes. Hers is a retrospective account of this history, deeply embedded in the Dutch national consciousness by the second half of the seventeenth century. In this painting, as in others she produced, tulips are avoided.

Ruysch's still life reproduced here incorporates fauna into the floral display: a tiny lizard, a snail, a snake, and a frog that spits fire, attracting attention to itself by the fire's bright dash of color. The fire-breathing frog is a mysterious creature of magic, a radically *non*scientific manifestation of superstition, an expression of the pre- or antirational. It marks an imaginary force that rational powers seem unable fully to suppress. As such it challenges the certainty and stability that early-modern advances in science seemed to promise. Quite apart from the emblematic or symbolic potential of the painting's several reptiles and amphibians, which are symbolically richly ambiguous, and morally contradictory, is the fact that these tiny painted creatures challenge the stasis, formal order, quiet, and peace evoked by the flowers, adding more than a hint of violence and change.[42] The precision with which the fauna is painted commands the eye to look—to look away, as it were, from the main attraction, the flowers—but to look at what? To look, at the least, to something like a narrative, a small drama, that sharply reintroduces time into the timelessness of the still life's stillness and putative claim to permanence.

Social Dynamics, Light, and Time

The social dimension of time as referenced in painting can be explored by moving forward roughly 200 years to one of Dutch artist Vincent van Gogh's well-known sunflowers paintings (Figure 2.3, *Color Plate 4*) produced near the end of his life at Arles, France, in 1888. This picture represents time in two complementary relations: first, as regards the time, and labor, necessary for van Gogh to paint it; second, time's relation to the subject painted, sunflowers.

In the flower still life by Brueghel the *work* of painting is made visible, ironically, by its *in*visibility; that is, Brueghel's technique involves the absolute hiding of the act of making brush strokes, combined with painstakingly precise drawing. Our recognition of his accomplishment comes indirectly. The beholder cannot "see how" the picture was painted and thus is led to wonder more at the apparent technical magic being worked. With van Gogh, the work of painting is not simply visible, it is obvious; we can easily trace the broad strokes of his brush, often heavily laden with paint, as when he painted the seed heads. In this respect, van Gogh's picture is striking for the entirely apparent haste of its execution. Many of the flower petals required only a single brush stroke; the most-faded petals consist of a series of parallel single-stroke orange and yellow lines.

To this day, how often do we hear, and are we troubled by, the comment that a particular art object betrays no apparent craft, as though a too-easy, or too-quickly-made appearance lessens its apparent worthiness? In a culture where time is money, sweat must show or at least be assumed, since the control of labor is perhaps one of the most obvious manifestations of power. What troubles us so much about "quick" art is not that we may think we are being had but that the art looks far too much like play. In the sixteenth century, Cardinal Borromeo *knew* that Brueghel had been kept busy. Van Gogh painted his sunflowers for himself—they were intended as decorations for his own room—and not for a market or a patron. Although he no doubt sweated mightily while painting in the Mediterranean summer, his perspiration takes on the effect of something like self-directed pleasure. In other words, the picture resists the interests and demands of others. It satisfies, if only momentarily—a self—though this says nothing about the painting's later history or function: One of van Gogh's other, very similar, sunflower paintings in 1987 fetched a record auction sale price of $38.9 million. It was purchased by a Japanese insurance company for investment purposes.[43]

The second manifestation of time in *Sunflowers* relates specifically to how the sunflowers are painted and, as a result, what they seem to represent—not simply blooms, but food. In turn, as food, the sunflowers reference life itself, just as food and life taken together reference light—the sine qua non for food, life, and not coincidentally, painting. (Van Gogh's sunflowers series are among the brightest paintings I know.) Introduced to Europe from North America in the sixteenth century and painted by Dutch artists of this period, by the late nineteenth century the sunflower was no longer an exotic species; indeed, it was utterly common. Whatever panache the sunflower may once have enjoyed on account of its non-native status had long since been forgotten. It was by now more an ordinary food crop than a flower—a plant of mundane utility, thus opposite to the inedible and uncommon blooms in the earlier still lifes, food only for the eyes.

In comparison with the flowers painted in the seventeenth century, usually if not always represented at the very height of bloom, van Gogh's sunflowers are already wilting and beginning to lose their petals and are thus represented at the moment when the flower heads begin their visible transformation into seed—into something less for the eye than the stomach, to be eaten directly by people or fed to animals that would in turn eventually be consumed. Arguably, the seed heads—not the blooms—receive van Gogh's principal labors. Of the fifteen sunflowers in this picture, perhaps only one smaller flower at the far right is actually in full bloom. In other words, van Gogh valorizes these plants at precisely the moment when under normal circumstances they would be pitched onto the compost heap, that is, when—in the florists' domain—they are no longer salable.

The still life flowers of the Dutch seventeenth century are fragile; their delicacy accounts for part of the awe they inspire. Van Gogh's sunflowers eschew fragility in favor of vitality. The veritable energy invested in their metamorphosis into seed heads is evident in their swelling shapes, which van Gogh in fact exaggerates. Their color is built up, dark and distinctly thick. Paint is heavily applied to create a spatial dimension that is sculptural, three-dimensional, even tactile. In other words, the seed heads have *literally* begun to swell, as though the two-dimensional surface of the painting were inadequate to contain their energy.

The magic of sunflowers lies in the way they seemingly take in sunlight, as if to reproduce it. Their shape mirrors the solar disk and its rays, as well as its intense colors. In van Gogh's *Sunflowers* it is as though everything *is* sunlight, manifesting life. Van Gogh himself referred to these paintings as "lamps or candelabra."[44] Whereas the "life" that seventeenth-century flower painters valorized was the spectacular moment of high blooming, for van Gogh the manifestation of life he preferred was that embedded in the sunrise and in the growth that sunlight promoted, the promise of a perpetually recurring spring. That promise pervades every part of the surface of his picture. The light banished in seventeenth-century flower paintings, except for that concentrated on the flowers themselves, as in Ruysch, in van Gogh is seemingly ubiquitous and by comparison almost overwhelming.

The blooming plants in Brueghel and Ruysch, undeniably gorgeous, are at once both more and less than living things; they appear to be surreal, fragile curiosities. Van Gogh's garish, fading sunflowers eschew awe in favor of bright promise: the simple and profound, utterly ordinary, cycle of life and death. To the extent that light is a technical device in the paintings by Brueghel and Ruysch, in van Gogh's work it is the picture's very essence, in a sense surpassing that of the sunflowers themselves. And in the work of all three painters, light is less an issue of mere technique than a deeply informative way of envisioning history.

Chapter 3

Death as Object

For several centuries beginning in the late Middle Ages, European painters and sculptors produced numerous images and tomb effigies that attempted to juxtapose the death of the body and the eternal life of the soul. Artists commonly focused on the *process* of the body's reduction to a skeleton, lavishing imaginative attention on its putrefaction. Death[1] was rendered both frightening and disgusting—the body literally made food for worms and vermin that slithered through or crawled from the body's cavities.

By the seventeenth century, death was no less a matter of concern, but it had some competition. Modern secularization, evident in the advance of European humanism, focused more on the here and now, and much less on the hereafter. The ubiquitous realization that life was short was tempered by the argument that, at least for people of means, living had its mighty and increasing pleasures. Death (still*ed* life) as a visual subject became at once abbreviated, abstracted, and rationalized, and rotting corpses disappeared from representation. Ironically, in the course of only a few decades the subject of death provided an excuse to deny death's reality in the very moment of representing it.

Vanitas

This chapter concerns a particular sort of still life painting known as "Vanitas" that took its title from the book of Ecclesiastes (1:2, "Vanity of vanities, saith the Preacher, vanity of vanities; all is vanity") and transformed textual allusions into emblems and attributes, based on work by Calvinist scholars from the University of Leiden—Holland was the principal, though by no means the sole, locus for production of these images. The still life objects represented were intended to encourage the observer to contemplate the frailty and brevity of life: human skulls, instruments for measuring time (clocks, watches, the hourglass), candles burning or extinguished but still smoking, soap bubbles that exist only for an instant, flowers at their height of bloom and about to fade, and ripe fruit about to rot. Luxury goods like rare shells, jewelry, silver plate, gold coins, purses, deeds, and so on alluded to the vanity of earthly treasures. Musical instruments and music books fell among a related group of attributes referencing life's tastes and pleasures, the so-called *vita voluptuaria,* intended to be viewed as activities that waste precious time better spent saving one's soul.[2] Similarly, books and scientific instruments alluded to the *vita contemplativa;* and the inclusion of weapons and in-signias of command, to the *vita pratica.* Finally, as a putative antidote to the condemnation of things transitory, Vanitas pictures often incorporated signs of the soul's eternal existence, such as a sprig of ripe wheat or ears of corn which, though dead, contain the seed of new life that will sprout after plant-ing, implying burial. (Few individual Vanitas paintings reference all of these categories.) Leaving nothing to doubt, mottoes were commonly incorporated as internal labels: *vanitas; vanitas, vanitatis; vanitas vanitatis et omnia vanitas; homo bulla* [Man is but a bubble]; *mors omnia vincit* [Death triumphs over everything], memento mori [Remember death]; and the like.

In light of this litany it is clear that by the seventeenth century the literary and visual textuality of death was extraordinarily well established, and indeed ordered. It had become, in a word, predictable, though the same could not quite be said of earlier death imagery, which, though conventionalized, main-tained a certain edge by always finding new ways to disgust and horrify. In earlier treatments of the subject there was less apparent order, due to the man-ner in which a body would decompose or be devoured by the creatures feed-ing on it. There were myriad *things* moving over the corpse that seemingly had intentions of their own.

By contrast, with the Vanitas still life all *movement* ceases, and in a retro-spective gesture, both life and death become subject to the sorting of data. Yet in this process, the end falls victim to the means, and data quickly becomes the imagery's real subject. Vanitas still life privileges *information.* To be sure, each object represented "officially" meant something beyond its literal self, having attached an elaborate set of textual conceits, each properly didactic and otherworldly. But all that textuality was nonetheless external to the im-age itself; it was invisible, apart from the aforementioned mottoes and some-times the painted representations of legal documents or titles pages of learned books. The challenge set before the viewer was to "see behind" or "see through" what was visible to the eye—gorgeous material goods, commonly luxurious—to the complex moral critique thereof as established by Calvinist intellectuals. As we shall see, this was no small feat. Unquestionably, the moral challenge was commonly not met[3]—but I am slightly ahead of the story.

Philippe de Champaigne's tiny Vanitas painting (Figure 3.1, *Color Plate 5*) relies on the barest essentials. Its setting is spatially shallow and confined, the three included objects nearly touching, so that the eyes can take in the entire scene with only the smallest of sideways shifts. The point of view is straight on: We meet death's "face" directly, whereas the angle controlling our view on the tulip and the hourglass is in both cases oblique. We look directly into the eye sockets of the skull and confront the blindness of death. The slab, necessary as a place upon which to set the three attributes, recalls the lid of a tomb, despite its small size.

All this notwithstanding, we have come a long way from the fattened worms and rodents devouring spilled bowels typical of medieval representations of human death. The skull is greatly aged and absolutely clean. The hourglass, although the symbolic attribute of passing time, is also eminently utilitarian, familiar, and homely; the same cannot be said of rotting corpses. The stunning variegated tulip, the type most prized, is pleasurable to look at, not least for the lack of other attractive objects competing for our attention.

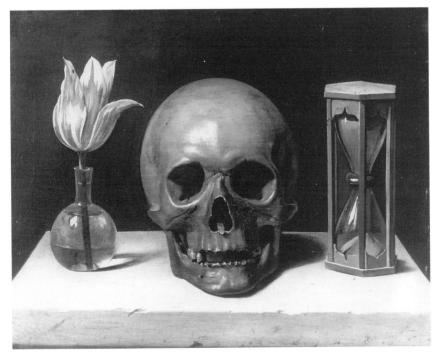

Figure 3.1
Philippe de Champaigne (1602–1674), vanitas, panel, 28.6 × 37.5 cm. Le Mans, Musée de Tessé, inv. no. 10.572. Photo © Musées du Mans.

Arguably, as we look at this image, the hourglass gets the least of our looking. The composition powerfully directs our eyes toward the central main event, the skull, yet the vibrant color of the tulip pulls our glance off center, an effect strengthened by the bright blotch of light reflected off the vase. There is a commanding simplicity to Philippe de Champaigne's painting, but its rhetoric is rife with an ambiguity characteristic of the entire genre. The pleasure brought by looking at the tulip's color seriously competes for the attention claimed by the skull, both because of the skull's compositional centrality and its obvious symbolic function, which in essence warns against pleasure. Looking means having to choose sides.

Death and Information

Spanish painter Antonio de Pereda's stark, small Vanitas painting (Figure 3.2) restricts the visual field to a startling close-up of three human skulls, two of which, including the principal one in the center foreground, border on the grotesque.[4] Indeed, were it not for the profiled skull at the left

Figure 3.2
Antonio de Pereda
(1611–1678), VANITAS
(1640s), canvas,
31 × 37 cm. Zaragoza,
Museo Provincial de
Bellas Artes.

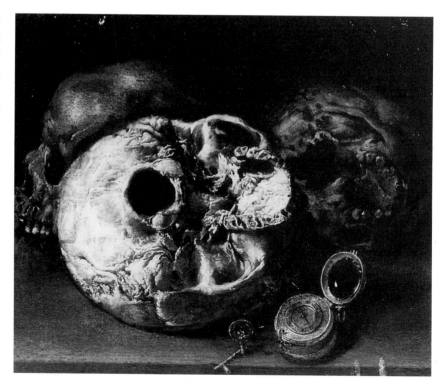

the principal skull might not immediately be identifiable. Once recognized for what it is, this skull in particular doubles its significance not only as a re-minder of death but also as a statement of the ugliness that lies beneath the thin layer of skin—a subject discoursed over endlessly for many generations prior to the seventeenth century in Christian Europe. Pereda provides visual access to the cranial void, the black hole that once cradled a brain. The skulls rest on a locking desk or tabletop, the key for which, compositionally placed at the frontmost picture plane and virtually at dead center, makes symbolic reference to crucial knowledge: The key to eternal life is to Remember death. A gold-and-silver watch provides mechanical confirmation of the natural fact of mortality.

The skulls' identities are lost. Whether peasant or patrician, we have no knowledge. That death "levels out" life's playing field restates the old Christian theme that in God's eyes we are all alike. Death, in other words, nullifies the categories of weak and strong, poor and rich (this is a common theme in the sculptural programs of medieval cathedrals and monastic churches relating to the Last Judgment). Still, the *replication* of skulls hints at the approach of secular modernity, hence the composition exceeds the tradi-tional Christian theological insight driving the Vanitas subject. To paint three skulls is to create a small archive, a little library of medical death *information,* and this effect is notably strengthened by Pereda's showing us the skulls from three different angles, as was common practice in contemporaneous scientific texts devoted to the study of human anatomy. In this way Pereda provides the viewer with visual data that clearly exceeds the requirements of orthodox re-ligious instruction. He directs the viewer's attention to new, distinctly secular knowledge that promises to unlock secrets about *this* life. Nonetheless, the significance of the anatomical information is strongly mediated by the fairly horrific "look" of the three skulls. The middle one especially garners our at-tention, principally because it is distinctly ugly, even repulsive—the pleasure of looking derived from Champaigne's colorful tulip in Pereda's picture is transformed into a morbidly fascinated gaze.

By contrast, repulsion is not the response elicited from a Vanitas still life by the Dutch painter Abraham van der Schoor (Figure 3.3). The artist incorpo-rates a variety of the standard visual-metaphorical allusions linking vanity to mortality: cracked pillar; hourglass, burned-down candle; roses (attributes of carnal love) that are out of water and thus soon to fade; books, documents, and seals, these last as attributes of vain learning and wealth. But the paint-ing's principal claim to visual interest is generated by a small pile of human bones—no less than six skulls, a jawbone, and what appear to be (left to right) a humerus, a femur, and a tibia. All the skeletal remains appear to be bleached

Figure 3.3
Abraham van der Schoor
(active from 1643),
VANITAS (c. 1660–1670),
canvas, 63.5 × 73 cm.
Amsterdam, Rijks-
museum, inv. no.
SK-A-1432.

or cleaned (unlike those in Pereda's painting), and this distinctly subdues any reaction of disgust or horror, evoking instead something closer to curiosity.

The pile of skulls seems almost arbitrarily scattered on the table, though van der Schoor takes care to spare us the most grotesque angles of view—the only one similar to Pereda's is set back and in shadow. Van der Schoor's presentation of skulls hints not only of anatomical information but also of art itself. The skulls' sheer numbers, their spatial volume, the play of light on their surfaces, the deep shadow of their recesses, the sheer draftsmanship, the subtle handling of color, and the complex formal composition together remind us of the painter's craft and the pleasures of looking—and distract us from the imperative of memento mori. In this instance, the repeated signs of "man at work" function to undercut the picture's putative subject: "men in death." The painting literally delineates mortality, maybe even morbidity; but subtextually it argues for vitality and the pleasures of making art.

The scene in Figure 3.4 by Jan van Oost the Elder is a study on whose table rest numerous objects, all symbolic: a sword (*vita pratica*); a violin, wine pitcher, glass, and pair of dice (*vita voluptuaria*); and books and manuscripts (*vita contemplativa*). On the parchment is written: *finis coronat opus* (death crowns work). In the background is a zodiacal sphere that is stopped at the point where the Lion replaces Cancer, thus marking the year's end. On the chair in the left foreground is an apple, the fatal fruit of man's fall, thus referencing the introduction of sin and death into the world, although next to it is a piece of bread, one of the signs of the Eucharist, therefrom the promise of life after death. A small manuscript enumerates the letters of the alphabet from A to Z, apparently an allusion to the Alpha and Omega, Christ as the beginning and end of all things.[5] An old man, Faustlike, sits contemplating a skull.

Unlike the compositional unity of the previous painting, this image bifurcates. At the right, the viewer is drawn to the sympathetically painted man, arranged so that we focus on his ancient face, downcast eyes, and wrinkled hands. Yet as affecting as his image may be, we are pulled away to the left, attracted by the clutter of objects on the table, so arranged that our eyes can find no repose among them. The composition is brilliant. Despite the individual detail each object offers, we are distracted by what lies in its proximity. Our eyes dart restlessly from one "trinket" to another. The only space where visual repose is offered is that occupied by the old man's face. Yet in looking

Figure 3.4
Jan van Oost the Elder (1601–1671),
MEDITATING PHILOSOPHER (VANITAS),
panel, 112 × 146 cm. Bruges, Comissies van Openbare Onderstand Museum, Burgelijke Godshuizen. Photo © IRPA-KIK-Brussels.

at him, we cannot avoid the temptation to look once again at the goods opposite. The painting's tension, the means by which it acts upon the viewer,
thus transliterates a moral choice into a physical one: We can *feel* it. What our
eyes can see, they can also sense in the urge to shift their glance.

Whereas the piles of stuff on the tables of these last two paintings might on
the surface seem to share the quality of excess, the effect of each is profoundly
different. Further, whereas van der Schoor's repetitive use of skulls may at first
glance strike us as the more honest Vanitas painting, I think that precisely the
opposite is true. In van Oost's painting, which gives us but a single skull, one
"safely" viewed only from the side and back, the pointlessness of life's mundane pursuits is made far more an issue than in the other picture, in which attributes like the hourglass seem by comparison almost boringly predictable—
if not preachified, then clichéd.

Eating One's Cake and Still Having It

Figure 3.5 shows a Flemish Vanitas concerned especially with
sonority; in its silence it emphasizes sound, mostly though not exclusively
musical. It marks sonority as a sign of life, but also marks its silencing as the
sign of death. No less important, it stresses repeatedly the age-old connection
of music to love, and even to sexuality—but of the coarsest sort. The connection of music to sensual pleasures is designated by a small pocket fiddle and
its bow, an instrument then exclusively associated with dancing, a practice
condemned by Calvinist preachers as an occasion for sensual improprieties.
There is also a bagpipe, another dance instrument, especially popular among
the lower social orders and the subject of a contemporary proverb: *Met een
goed gevulde buik wil het zingen beter lukken* (One sings better with a well-
filled belly); the instrument "sings" best only when its sack is well filled, an
earthy metaphor for male sexual performance, developing from the fact that
the bagpipe's chanter pipe and wind sack together correspond visually to the
male genitalia. The lute lying on its face likewise makes then-conventional
reference to carnal love; indeed, it was sometimes carried by prostitutes into
taverns as a sign of their identity.[6] Among the several high-caste instruments
is a harp, upon which is perched a macaw, a standard attribute of eloquence.

A host of the common signs of transience are incorporated, including flowers already starting to fade (Job 14:1–2, "Man that is born of a woman is of
few days, and full of trouble. He cometh forth like a flower, and is cut
down"). The figure of Death, wielding his scythe, intrudes from the right and

blows out the light in the lantern, a sign of life, located at the exact center of the composition and at the apex of the organizational pyramid of objects, just below which sits the ubiquitous skull. In the lower right, apples, associated with original sin, are put next to bunches of grapes, associated with resurrection by reference to Christ as the True Vine.[7] All the "proper" Vanitas components are present in abundance.

As sine qua non to any Vanitas, the conventional skull receives compositional prominence at the point of intersection of the X sketched from the painting's corners, but it sits in the background, small and indistinct. To be sure, its own relative obscurity in one sense helps to emphasize the fact that obscurity of meaning is a desideratum of the Vanitas still life, thus the image can produce its contemplative effect. This fact notwithstanding, the painting has a problem, of which the downplayed skull is a part. The picture provides pleasure—altogether too much pleasure—less in contemplating than in *looking,* via the myriad beautiful material objects, each of which not coincidentally references specifically sensual-corporeal activities.[8]

To help sort out the painting's apparent contradictory character, it is necessary to consider its function. Vanitas still lifes were principally painted for the market, not as commissions for a particular patron. Each Vanitas painting, as a source of a painter's livelihood, had to compete for attention among

Figure 3.5
Jacob Jordaens (1593–1678) and Peter Boel (1622–1674), VANITAS, canvas, 141 × 199 cm. Brussels, Musées Royaux des Beaux-Arts, cat. no. 237. Photo © IRPA-KIK-Brussels.

the others of its kind available for sale to a fairly large buying public—in point of fact this remained true even for painters who worked principally on commission, as was probably the case for the painters of this image. A picture like this one might compete very well for a spot on the walls of one's home against, say, the opposite choice of a severe representation of death and physical corruption, wherein visual pleasure and indeed decorative potential were necessarily quite compromised.

In this picture, the things of this world are rendered less with suspicion than with an admiration akin to fetish; each is afforded a nearly obsessive degree of the painters' attention (Peter Boel painted the objects, Jacob Jordaens the figures). Objects are displayed in a way that would never occur in real life, each gathered from its "natural" place and piled into a heap that registers dramatic abundance, however critically the excess might ideally be read. And there is one thing more: Vanitas paintings could themselves be very expensive; indeed, as with other paintings, they were in part bought for financial security and investment in *this* world. In other words, the very purchase of such pictures contradicts what their subject and putative function otherwise claimed: "Either one rejects the world or one does not. And decorating the house with framed pictures suggests one is not even going to try."9 Dutch buyer-viewers were unquestionably aware of this paradox, whose delicious irony acted as confirmation of human inadequacy to moral challenge. This being the case, the pleasure of looking is simultaneously a source of self-punishment. But if taking pleasure in looking constitutes a self-punishing self-condemnation, what true moral function does the experience hold? In sum, the cake remains after it has been eaten. Is material pleasure then the source of (real) spiritual suffering? I cannot answer the question; nor, I suspect, could the northern Europeans of the seventeenth century—which to no small degree was both the genre's aim and part of its success with what constituted an audience of connoisseurs.

Essentially, the extraordinarily imaginative allegorical didactics surrounding Vanitas paintings define particular objects as good or evil and, confoundedly, some might be either. The endless spinning out of associations of a given thing to its supposed referent and moral quotient included both the obvious (for example, skull = death) and the extremely obscure (dragonfly = resurrection). However one sorted it out, in the end everything came down to a profoundly simple—perhaps simplistic—set of binaries: good versus evil, mortal life versus eternal life. All the exercises of learning and imagination that one might ideally be expected to devote to the allegorical subtleties were in the end fairly pedantic and absolutely predictable, given the preordained conventional conclusion. All the mental gymnastics required to bridge the gap between the concrete and the abstract, the material and the spiritual, could never for long disguise this fact. This is not to "accuse" Vanitas paintings of bad conscience; the matter is more interesting and complicated than that. The image issues a challenge that exceeds the mere identification of allegorical relations in the degree to which, as Bryson aptly puts it, it "*enacts* Vanity"[10] rather than simply illustrates the theme. In the end we are left to admit that the Vanitas painting depends for its rhetorical impact on an unresolvable tension structured into such a picture's materially visible temptation: The Vanitas both *represents* and *is* itself what it condemns.

Vanity and Modernity

Georgia O'Keeffe's desert still life, *Jawbone and Fungus* (Figure 3.6),[11] painted in the American Southwest, bears relation to Dutch images in two fundamental ways: The donkey's jawbone, bleached and set prominently in the foremost picture plane, inscribes a death, and—as regards formal principles—the composition in its entirety is highly static and visibly, self-consciously ordered, rather like the painting by Philippe de Champaigne (Figure 3.1), though spatially O'Keeffe's is even more restricted in both depth and breadth. Thereafter, all is different. Most immediately notable, it is impossible to "make" the image textual, apart from mere naming in the absence of verbs: jawbone, death, fungus, heat. The relations of foreground (jawbone) to background (fungus) are formal, and nothing more; the compositional arrangements, in other words, eschew narrative.

O'Keeffe's painting disconnects the objects represented from their normal physical interrelations. The natural physical order, rigidly maintained among the objects represented in the earlier paintings, is here intentionally abandoned: The fungus, in reality a tiny thing, looms over the jawbone like a dark cloud filling the horizon. O'Keeffe's denaturalizing of physical relations thereby further detextualizes them. As a result, the "logic" of verbal expression proves inadequate to account for what is represented. Accordingly, the apparent "order" of the object world is O'Keeffe's own and cannot be confirmed in treatises on mammalian anatomy or desert botany. The two objects' compositional relation, in other words, defies their "reduction" to conventional language-based meaning, particularly to the extent that meaning in modernity supposedly operates as an analogue to facts. As objective data, both jawbone and fungus fail. But this failure in turn provides the painting with its distinctly spiritual charge—and as such, its protest. O'Keeffe's painting, that is, evokes an antimaterialism with less ambiguity, and perhaps with

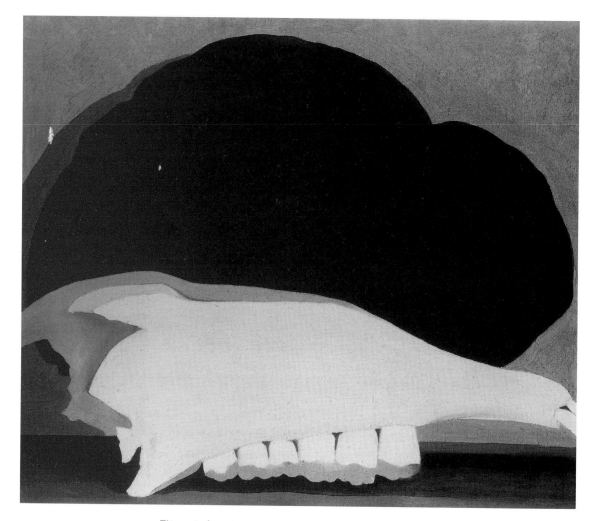

Figure 3.6
Georgia O'Keeffe (1887–1986), JAWBONE AND FUNGUS (1930), canvas,
43.2 × 50.8 cm. Rochester, Memorial Art Gallery of the University of Rochester,
The Marion Stratton Gould Fund, inv. no. 51.11.

better conscience, than is apparent in many Northern European Vanitas pictures that announce their topic rather like a badge of moral honor, simultaneously only inevitably to compromise on the claim.

Seventeenth-century still lifes in effect are visually public, to the extent that
they rely on both the common, shared optical visuality (the "real" look) of
things and, equally important, on *published* information. The images are part
of a common archive of knowledge relative to the material world. The objec-

tive information they contain can be verified. O'Keeffe will have none of that. Her image is visually private. Its connectives are uncertain, even arbitrary, based on the effect of shapes and the relations that can be imagined but not ascertained. O'Keeffe's still life, in other words, documents uncertainty and a distrust of "information"; at the same time, it evokes pleasure—and not a guilty pleasure—in the materiality of common things, for what could be more ordinary than a fungus or of lesser value than a donkey's jawbone?

Sociality and Death

Vincent van Gogh's *The Chair and the Pipe* (Figure 3.7) is one of a pair that forms a diptych; its painted mate is of the chair sat in by van Gogh's friend, the artist Paul Gauguin, when the two were together briefly at Arles in the last year of van Gogh's life. The pictures are painted so that when hung together the two chairs face each other, as if arranged for their putative occupants to converse. Van Gogh's chair, holding his pipe, is painted with nearly reverential care, to the extent that—for him at least—considerable attention to detail is evident, as in the many parallel lines of webbing in the rush seat.

Many Vanitas still lifes from seventeenth-century Holland, despite their presumed critique of worldly possessions, specifically valorize and even fetishize *things,* notably the degree to which they have been crafted, thereby showing the amount of human labor that luxury goods visibly concentrate in their material surfaces. The human beings "behind" the objects are invisible; both their individuality and identity are irrelevant. Indeed, no specific owner-user of the goods can be presumed; a tacitly dehumanizing anonymity, in other words, dominates the visual field (and, I suspect, contributes a melancholic tinge to one's viewing pleasure). With van Gogh what matters is hardly the cheap chair; instead it is the implied person who sits in it, directly acknowledged by the pipe and tobacco pouch. As an object the chair's significance derives entirely from its human occupant. The angle of view is such that we look down, as if approaching and intending to *use* it, thus to begin our smoking and our talk—Gauguin's chair, the companion to this one, has in its seat two books and a lighted candle, as though he himself is only momentarily absent. The two paintings together signify still more, not simply making reference to two distinct persons but to a social relation between them. The common materiality of the chairs, in other words, serves to help make possible one of the principal means by which people humanize themselves, namely, by bonding with others (the stormy friendship of van Gogh and Gauguin notwithstanding).

If O'Keeffe's desert still life and and van Gogh's chairs are intensely personal, Andy Warhol's *Big Electric Chair* (Figure 3.8) is simultaneously—and horrendously—both private and public, and it is a richly humanistic condemnation of a singularly dehumanizing phenomenon. It is private to the extent that the chair in operation is visible only to its victim and the execution witnesses; it is public as the virtually clichéd icon of state punishment and terror. Warhol seemingly plays off the irony that the chair in Western history is the sign of authority and power, as with ancient philosophers who spoke while seated, popes who address theological certainties *ex cathedra* (from the chair of Saint Peter), and Chair-men of the Board. With the electric chair there is literal power in the form of direct current that flows *through,* not *from,* the person seated, destroying him (more rarely, her). The spatial surround—not the magnificent medieval church or its secular analogue—has the character of a garage or a shop. The photojournalistic quality of the image—in fact a manipulation of a photograph—contributes to the effect. The image itself exudes a technical, mechanical, and operational dynamism, a force field at once electrical and threatening.[12] Although waiting for its human victim, the chair, and indeed the entire setting, is dehumanized and dehumanizing in the extreme, unlike van Gogh's, which exudes a nearly anthropomorphized warmth.

Figure 3.8
Andy Warhol (1930–1987), BIG ELECTRIC CHAIR (1967), acrylic and silk-screened enamel on canvas, 137.2 × 188 cm. Utica, N.Y., Munson-Williams-Procter Institute Museum of Art, inv. no. 86.56. Photo © 1995 Andy Warhol Foundation for the Visual Arts/ARS, New York.

Perhaps with Warhol we reach the logical end point to the Vanitas still life, to the extent that the big electric chair not only directly links the material object to human mortality but also is mortality's direct cause. Thereby, the stakes of the Vanitas are pushed beyond questions surrounding private morality toward ones that are public, social, and resolutely political. With Warhol we come upon still*ed* life—the chair as weapon, the instrument that silences human discourse absolutely.

Chapter 4

Death and the Pleasures of Meat

Perhaps what strikes us today, living in the age of endangered species, about many hunting-trophy still life paintings from the past is the alarming excess of the kill, more so to the extent that these pictures seldom reference eating, in order to legitimate the animals' deaths. Instead, the hunt is represented as arbitrary (literally unnecessary), in every respect a sport. The artist paints the game with precision and care, allowing us simultaneously to marvel at its beauty and at his skill in representation. For the spectator-owner, the image aestheticizes—makes beautiful—a fantasy of power and also transmits that fantasy into a semipublic visual and material claim to privilege.

The killing excess entailed in such images mirrors an episode from a recent novel by Carolyn Chute concerning poor people living in rural Maine. The local game warden comes to arrest Rubie Bean for poaching deer—in this instance less for food than as an expression of impotent rage against his own condition:

> For chrissakes, Bean, why can't you control yourself? . . . It ain't what's hangin' in your shed, Rubie. That isn't why I'm here. It's what's strewed all over the power line, drawing flies. . . . I can understand bein' a glutton for meat, Rubie, but what you left on the power line isn't meat . . . it's a friggin' holocaust. Haven't you got a sprig o' conscience? . . . Some people call it a waste of deer meat. Others would go to pieces to see those bleatin' motherless fawns. But when I came upon that puking scene, I says to myself, Cole, you've shot good dogs for less.[1]

The principal difference between Chute's narrative and that common to many early-modern hunting still lifes is that game killing in the former serves as a projection of power for a powerless man, but with the aesthetics gone: The scene is ugly and meant to be so. Killing animals without the presumption of then consuming them occurs in both instances, but in the novel, conscience is restored. The reader recoils at the episode described in *The Beans of Egypt, Maine;* the ideal and intended viewer for the early hunting still life by contrast is principally expected to revel in the pleasures of privileged identity bought by reference to the hunt.

The Social Utility of Representing Dead Animals

An understanding of the curious aesthetics of the hunting still life must ultimately be sought in an examination of its social utility. A case in point is Holland in the seventeenth century, one of the principal sites of production for gamepiece paintings. The territories of Holland, from its wetlands and dunes to its forests and fields, supported a rich array of fauna—ducks, swans, pheasants, grouse, rabbits, and deer. Migratory birds in large numbers passed through the territory. And virtually every species was fair game. Yet from the early years of the sixteenth century on, the sport was surprisingly regulated by seasonal dates, time of day, device (rifles, bows, snares, nets, and so on), strict bag limits, and—most notably—social class. Hunting was a privilege granted to the nobility and to a few others enjoying permission from the forest master. Members of the nobility were allowed to hunt hares and rabbits only between September 15 and February 2, with a bag limit of one and two, respectively; greyhounds, which could only be owned by people eligible to hunt, could be used only two days per week, and no more than five dogs were permitted in a hunt. The stag, or other deer, could only be taken on one day a year and then only by so-called bannered nobles, men enjoying such status as to be able to fight under their own banners in military campaigns. Other restrictions applied to game birds regarding how they might be hunted, the length of season, and which hunters were allowed to take them.

The Dutch gamepiece, despite its antecedents in the late sixteenth century, became popular only after 1650. Its emergence is tied to the success of the Dutch economy and to the rapid expansion of a wealthy, if not aristocratic, upper class. That is, the number of Dutch citizens holding title to nobility was far too small to absorb the large number of hunting still lifes produced, especially the elaborate trophy gamepieces. Accordingly, many more people bought these paintings than were actually allowed to take game—for even with the increased numbers of wealthy individuals, the license to hunt remained under tight wraps. Although the upper bourgeoisie's wealth might be nearly indistinguishable from the aristocracy's, only the latter possessed title, a crucial mark of distinction that remained restricted, even though the aristocracy held no special power in the state. The hunt, especially for the most desired animal species, served as a sign of difference and consequently was a sport of the highest social prestige. In essence, the gamepiece provided a means by which even the *non*hunting (or restricted hunting) bourgeois could mark his social position, in essence by claiming the visual results of the hunt, but only in the two-dimensional form of an image.[2]

Defeating One's Enemy

In the painting by the Amsterdam painter Jan Weenix (Figure 4.1), produced late in the story I am relating, the beholder is witness to a visual ecstasy linking the human-regulated deaths of animals to the triumph of men. Weenix is something of a special case; his paintings fed royal, not bourgeois, appetites; he received direct commissions for monumental hunting trophies from aristocrats from across Europe. The Dutch bourgeoisie, not allowed much hunting, typically bought ready-made gamepieces directly off the flourishing art market. The typical market-ready image was seldom a match for those by Weenix, a fact not lost on anyone buying gamepieces: Weenix's pictures are notably flamboyant and excessive; they raise death to the level of riveting spectacle. Accordingly, his paintings appropriately parallel the power of those who actually possessed the privilege to hunt. Indeed, their size alone made them unsuitable for anything but the walls of monumental buildings, which left out the Dutch burghers living in comparatively small canal houses, however richly furnished. Among Weenix's most important commissions, for Elector of the Palatinate Johann Wilhelm, were a dozen canvases in a series— "grand displays of booty and hunting scenes, often measuring up to 11 by 18 feet"![3] These paintings' scale confirms difference—and size always matters; it is a rhetorical device, if among the most overstated and obvious.

Most immediately striking about this enormous picture (roughly six by five feet) is the swan, among the most prized of all game birds, and especially preferred by Weenix, who painted it many times over. Indeed, the hunting regulations for swans were so restricted as to increase their value as highly prestigious trophies. Largest of all European waterfowl, the swan was noted for its

Figure 4.1
Jan Weenix (1642–1719),
DEAD SWAN (1716),
canvas, 173 × 154 cm.
Rotterdam, Museum
Boymans-van Beuningen,
inv. no. 1962.

beautiful plumage, and its regal, seemingly effortless, absolutely graceful, and
dignified movement on water. All of this mirrored the aristocracy's own most
idealized view of properly aristocratic physical grace—dutifully and obsessively taught and most spectacularly realized in social dancing, the treatises
and instructional manuals for which were legion throughout the period.[4]

The *dead* swan itself performs the metaphoric role of the vanquished enemy. This is no small matter in the proper functioning of the image.
According to age-old warrior codes dating back to the Middle Ages (as, for
example, in *The Song of Roland*), no personal prestige attaches to defeating
any enemy lesser than oneself. To gain fame and to increase one's authority by
killing, the opponent had to enjoy parallel stature. The trophy still life, in

other words, functioned as a kind of aesthetic transliteration of then-popular battle pictures, scenes that celebrated decisive military victories. The private sport of hunting down rare and markedly beautiful game mirrors that of publicly waged war. Painted representations of both types of event lay permanent visual claim to certifying the results because such works possess documentary, as well as aesthetic, value. Whether the person who commissioned the picture actually killed the swan is fundamentally irrelevant. In any event, the trophy bird Weenix used as his model was almost certainly the result of taxidermy—a studio prop—but its unusual "pose" makes it *appear* to be a fresh and specific kill *for this image,* which is no small commentary on the painter's technical skills. Its wings and neck alike, remarkably painted, appear limp, as though brought while still bleeding into the studio.[5]

Taken as part of a quasi-narrative, Weenix's swan is not killed to be eaten but killed in order to become a spectacle confirming the identity of the privileged putative hunter. Hunting trophies commonly indicate vanquishing by situating dead game in the most unnatural poses, like enemies fallen on a battlefield, but such a way as to appear heroic in death. Weenix accomplishes this effect but charges it further through the use of theatrical lighting focused on the white bird, set against the rest of the composition, which is relatively dark. Weenix's subtle modeling of the swan—his use of light and shadow—invites savoring the swan's "noble" form made pathetic in death. And to the same heroic end, the entire scene is formalized by the self-conscious classicism of the supplementary architectural detail of the column base and shaft at the right, a conventional class marker of the painting's owner (royal portraits commonly employ this motif). The column's perpendicularity operates as one side of a visual boundary. Its masculine phallicism contrasts sharply with the curvilinear form of the vanquished, hence feminized, swan. The death contest now finished, storm clouds seem about to give way to the sun, which, as every European aristocrat was aware, was the sign alike of Apollo, mythic civilizing force, and, more important, the emblem of Europe's greatest absolutist ruler, King Louis XIV (d. 1715) of France, *the* archetypal personification of sovereign masculine power.

It is sometimes suggested that even ostentatious and braggart paintings like Weenix's still retain traces of the Vanitas trope.[6] This I seriously doubt. Patrician paintings do not typically function as signs of defeat. It is not in the interests of those who rule to display gigantic paintings criticizing either their own vanity or acknowledging indirectly their own future mortality. Royalty do not buy paintings that might inspire doubt; paintings function for them as a means to help establish certainty. The very look of Weenix's picture is profoundly anticontemplative and celebratory; it has no devotional potential. His painting is not a plea for humility but rather is a cry of victory and a claim to future remembrance in history. The image is principally about the death of the Other and the resulting perpetual enshrinement of the self.

Weenix's monumental still life is an effective visual conceit that works to replicate a salient feature of the hunt itself: It catches *us* in sight. It acts on us through our vision, aiming its rhetoric partly at *our* identity. Few people seeing a swan had the legal right to take aim. By contrast, the image's original owner in essence displayed to all viewers what was, in effect, his hunting license—paintings of this size were public images by both intent and function—and simultaneously announced that he had his viewers directly in his sights as well. Although the swan receives the painting's principal emphasis, Weenix provides enhancing flourishes via the subsidiary "small deaths" lying beside it, in a kind of visual aside, a parenthetical "not only . . . but also," as if to emphasize that the license to kill was virtually unrestricted.

Ritual Hunting
as Political Spectacle

"Not Only . . . But Also" might name a gamepiece by the Fleming Jan Fyt (Figure 4.2) in which the principal victim is a stag. The stag's prestige as hunting booty exceeded even that of the swan, a fact reflected in tightly controlled hunting restrictions. Fyt's gamepiece, compared even to Weenix's painting, minces few words. As a manifestation of power and vanquishing it is heavy-handed, rhetorically beyond the pale. It valorizes slaughter and more. The disemboweled stag is displayed so that its sexual parts are prominent and highlighted, a visual thumbing of the nose at its defeat, masculinity made impotent. The pathos evoked by the stag is charged by the visual effect of its limp and dangling hind leg, the failed source of its awesome ability to outlast pursuers. Fyt presents the animal in a way that hints at no less than a ritual execution. By adding drapery to the outdoor setting, conventional reference is made both to an aristocratic owner-perpetrator (such drapery was common to aristocratic portraiture), and to a theatrical event, namely, the spectacle of contemporaneous and formally staged state executions, the final part of which was the public "humiliation" by mutilation of the criminal's body, an act that metaphorically restored full honor to the sovereign whose authority had been challenged by the crime committed.[7] (This subject will be taken up again in Chapter 6.)

A parallel sort of representation (Figure 4.3) directly references the hunting grounds as an execution site replete with a quasi-ritualized appearance of the "victor," who enters the scene of carnage like a sovereign making an entrance at court, utterly at ease, almost uninvolved, as if the animals were simply bowing down in his presence.[8] Here are displayed the assorted trophies of death—

Figure 4.2
Jan Fyt (1611–1661),
STILL LIFE OF GAME
(1651), canvas,
183 × 214 cm.
Stockholm, National-
museum, inv. no.
NM 433.

virtually every animal type having the misfortune to occupy his private woods, which by implication must be vast, given the assortment of species flushed from it.

In parallel fashion, Fyt does not limit his hunting trophy to the stag. He also presents full bag limits of numerous other bird and mammal species. Hardly a story celebrating the bounty of nature, the painting is quite simply one about the aesthetics and political metaphysics of killing, produced for an audience with some taste for it—Fyt has to his credit no fewer than 160 still lifes, most of which involve game.[9] Moreover, so far as the stag is concerned, Fyt most likely depended not on a studio prop but on a *fresh* kill—once the body cavity has been slit open for gutting, as here painted, spoilage comes quickly. To the extent that the representation at least appears to offer visual "proof" of a fresh and "real" kill, greater prestige rubs off onto the image's owner. Such an image not only claims hunting privilege, it also certifies it. Moreover, as was usual, Fyt provides no reference to eating. To acknowledge consumption would drain away the power derived from exhibiting the kill as sport, transforming it into mere necessity. In practice, however, there is no question that such a prized animal would in the end be consumed.

The relation of the gamepiece to raw power is nowhere traced more clearly than in Diego Velázquez's large canvas (Figure 4.4) representing Spain's King Philip IV, who commissioned the painting, engaged in a boar hunt (the king on his mount in the right foreground has lowered his pike to meet the boar's charge).[10] The painting represents the sovereign's power not via a hunting-trophy still life—the results of the hunt—but as a process that will culminate in a kill at the end of a lengthy hunting ritual held within a ritualized space, namely, the fenced areas in the center. In fact, the actual kill was left to huntsmen, once the king and his companions had exhausted the animal by repeatedly deflecting its charge by means of two-pronged blunted forks mounted on shafts.

Accordingly, the hunt per se is not the picture's subject. The crucial matter of finding the animals is insignificant, a matter left to underlings. Nor is the actual kill the true mark of the power possessed by the only possible victor, the king. What matters most is the king's ritualized demonstration of his power to suppress what can only be described as his putative enemy in an exercise that harkens back to medieval jousts involving knights on horseback wielding lances. The "hunt's" rhetorical impact is directly linked to its predictability and orderliness. The exercise, as ritual, has a preordained outcome; no benefit is to be gained from "giving the animal a chance." In the end the

Figure 4.4
Diego Velázquez (1599–1660), PHILIP IV HUNTING WILD BOAR, canvas,
182 × 302 cm. London, National Gallery, inv. no. 197. Reproduced by courtesy of
the Trustees, The National Gallery, London.

boar will die. But its death, necessary for closure, is otherwise quite irrelevant and hardly worth witnessing. Something of an anticlimax, it is handled by others.

As Velázquez makes evident, the event is entirely staged and tightly scripted. And yet the image is in no sense allegorical; its frank modernity is established by documentary accuracy and explicitness concerning what was an enormously expensive, actual event. Put differently, the "truth" of the hunt was so spectacular, so scandalously costly, that no allegorical dressing-up was necessary and would, in fact, have detracted from its dramatic reality, whose every detail affirms the resources under the king's control.[11] Not least striking about the painting is that the king's boar-jousting itself is merely a rather small detail of a pictorial surface containing numerous other human figures. Arguably, the painting's subject lies in what the crowd seems occupied with: *looking* at the central event. Velázquez, in other words, makes spectacle and ritual the true tropes of his principal concern. However, this choice in no sense diminishes the prestige attending the king. Far more important to his authority than the ultimate death of the exhausted boar (shown at the extreme left) is the fact that so many important people are present to watch his performance. They are present to watch him.

Hunting Game and Corralling Women

As a subject popular in the history of painting, the vanquishing of game is an indicator of male identity, yet one where gender *difference* is commonly made an issue with surprising self-consciousness, therefore sometimes unwittingly displaying not so much the perquisites of male power and masculinity itself as anxieties about the fragility of both of these. Oddly, reference to vanquished game often seemed to require reference to women—whose own vanquished state, to put it most darkly, was explicitly located in their domesticity.

What might be surprising is the degree to which dead animals were considered objects productive of pleasurable viewing. As I will suggest in what follows, that pleasure is driven less by any sort of "natural" response to the visual splendor of, say, animals' plumage or skins, and more by what their death allowed viewers to imagine about their own place in the "natural" order. Scenes of animal kills, from still lifes to family portraits(!), to which I now turn, are before anything else visual devices that link life to power via the driving force of the domination and death of the Other. These are images that aestheticize in the extreme and that demarcate beauty itself as a mapping and manifestation of identity as social power.

Sir Edwin Landseer started work on a large portrait of Queen Victoria, Prince Albert, and their daughter Victoria (Figure 4.5) in 1840, finishing it only in 1845, for which he was paid the considerable sum of £840. It was hung in the sitting room of the family quarters at Windsor Castle.[12] How can we explain the odd—indeed, seemingly gratuitous—incorporation of blood sport in this royal family portrait? One answer lies in the connection of the killing of animals to the maintenance of gender hierarchy in a situation that otherwise challenged the socially prevailing arrangement.

Prince Albert, as husband to the queen, sat in the shadow of his wife's power as head of state, a position profoundly out of sync with prevailing Victorian family hierarchy, and all the more troubling given the couple's position as first family and therefore "ideal exemplars" to the nation. Landseer negotiates this power reversal by asserting Albert's unchallenged authority as *family* patriarch, hence downplaying his severely limited national role as the

Figure 4.5
Sir Edwin Landseer (1802–1873), WINDSOR CASTLE IN MODERN TIMES: QUEEN
VICTORIA, PRINCE ALBERT, AND VICTORIA, PRINCESS ROYAL (1845), canvas,
110 × 140 cm. Windsor Castle, The Royal Collection, acc. no. 538721, © 1995,
Her Majesty Queen Elizabeth II.

mere prince consort. The painter accomplishes this in two ways. First, he
places Albert in a full-face frontal pose, with Victoria in profile, *and* he slightly
exaggerates Albert's size in relation to that of his wife. Physically she appears
both slight and delicate, and Albert seems physically imposing, especially due
to his long legs. Second, and more important, Landseer incorporates some
rhetorical insurance in the form of the favorite hunting dog (petted by its
master) and a hunting still life consisting of six dead game birds spilled out
onto the floor and furniture, one being held aloft by the girl toddler.

Shot birds bleed, hence they were not ordinarily displayed on expensive
carpets or fine upholstery. Yet their inclusion in this painting was obviously
thought necessary, presumably to help overdetermine a correct reading of the
image, however otherwise bizarre, or even tasteless, this incorporation into a
family portrait might seem. The birds establish the masculinity of the man
who has killed them, a man highly visible in the public sphere as partner in
the exemplary first family of the nation-state; yet it is a family in which the

power relation upon which Victorian marriages otherwise absolutely depended was reversed. There is no question as to Victoria's devotion to Albert, or her deference to him as her husband, all publicly and visually confirmed by her decades of dark-clothed mourning following his early death. There is equally no question that Victoria's queenship utterly compromised Albert in a society that had never been more obsessive about gender hierarchy. Albert's liking for the kill attempts to plead the case for patriarchal authority, the centrality of which is emphasized by the lesson brought home to his daughter, who examines the smallest of the dead game birds.

In English portraiture from the eighteenth century, the use of birds, especially caged birds kept as pets, was a clichéd device by which to refer to the wife in her domestic role. Arthur Devis's portrait of the Reverend Thomas D'Oyly and his wife Henrietta Maria (Figure 4.6) shows the husband handing his wife a letter he has read, to which he is apparently about to respond, as he holds a quill in one hand and writing supplies are on the table. The birdcage hangs directly above his spouse, its placement thereby marking its referent: caged bird = wife. Metaphorically it defines her dependent role as wife—cared for, attended to, and protected by her husband.

By contrast, it is no accident of representation that above Reverend D'Oyly is a landscape painting, that is, an open horizon, the world outside the closed and domestic interior. The painting hangs above the fireplace, archetypal metaphor for the home, which in English society it was the man's duty to protect.[13] The landscape picture contains more than scenery, however; it defines action, specifically a hunt (both a dog and a hunting horn are visible), the culturally loaded sign of an all-male activity among the English upper classes that, in the semiotics of actions, ritually asserted male dominance over property of all kinds *and* symbolic domination of the social order. The hunting vignette notwithstanding, Reverend D'Oyly's masculine identity needs his wife's subsidiary femininity, marked by the caged bird, in order for its full range of meanings to be evident. The caged bird complements his hunting scene.

Reference to the hunt is likewise evident, ironically, in a contemporaneous women's fashion plate for the month of November (Figure 4.7) illustrating a lady's fancy attire and at the same time defining her status in relation to that of her husband. In the background behind protective walls is the well-attended estate to which she belongs and from which she has ventured. By contrast, in the foreground she witnesses momentarily a world from which she has otherwise apparently been sheltered. To her right is a peasant cottage, mostly hidden by a wooden fence, meanly and obviously contrasted with the estate. To her left, a dramatic and striking image rivets her gaze. It is a scene

Figure 4.6
Arthur Devis
(1712–1787), REV.
THOMAS D'OYLY AND
HIS WIFE HENRIETTA
MARIA (c. 1743–1744),
canvas, 73.7 × 61 cm.
British private collection.

of death in two guises: first, that of a lifeless tree, in severe opposition to the evergreen topiaries (tended, flourishing, and regimented) behind the walls of the great house: and second, hunted birds hanging next to a gun, trophies of the husband's sport, ritual victims of his right to his property.

The woman's eyes, focused on the birds, marks her relationship to a well-established visual metaphor. In this dangerous exterior space she is protected by the voluminous cocoon of fur(!) and fabric totally encasing her body. Her latest fashions provide visual assurance of her preservation from violence, to

86

Figure 4.7
Robert Dighton (c.
1752–1814), FASHION
PLATE FOR THE
MONTH OF NOVEM-
BER, from a series,
The Twelve Months,
mezzotint, gouache and
watercolor, 38.4 × 26
cm. Minneapolis, The
Minneapolis Institute of
Arts, The Minnich
Collection, acc. no.
17,039.

be sure, but dialectically they also mirror the denial of her access to the non-domestic world. The fact that these matters are encoded onto a fashion plate reveal the extent to which the ideology of domesticity was naturalized in the culture. One might argue that such constructions in a genre as socially important as portraiture exaggerate reality by visually protesting too much. However, that assertion cannot be maintained in light of such ephemeral imagery as fashion plates, whose function bears only the most indirect relation to the self-conscious presentations of value in paintings but which nevertheless make the identical claim.

Meat and Life

Throughout the history of still life painting, even as far back as its beginnings in the ancient world, there is evident a nearly perpetual interest in food, whether represented before its consumption, during a meal, or as leftover scraps thrown from the table, as in some old Roman floor mosaics. The representation of food was an especially common theme in Low Countries painting at the dawn of modernity beginning in the late sixteenth century; indeed, the ubiquity of the subject defines something akin to a fixation. This should not strike us as particularly surprising. As elsewhere in Europe, people's lives and well-being depended directly or indirectly on an overwhelmingly agricultural economy. Despite numerous improvements in agricultural production, gastronomic abundance enjoyed no guarantee then any more than it does now. Lean years were regularly experienced, and the threat of famine always lay just behind the horizon.[14] Today our concerns tend not to be whether food exists in sufficient quantity but whether we have the means to put our hands on it. Both kinds of lack are devastating, but they are not identical, and each produces a different set of understandings and relations between human beings and their object world.

One of the earliest Northern European still life paintings with dead animals was *The Meat Stall* (Figure 4.8, *Color Plate 6*), by the sixteenth-century master Pieter Aertsen, active in both Antwerp in the southern Low Countries and Amsterdam in the northern.[15] In this very large picture, food dominates to a degree as in no painting before it. All the food is meat, all of it the consequence of slaughter. Meat is shown in the various stages of preparation prior to being consumable, from a whole carcass hanging in the background at the right to the various stuffed sausages occupying the central part of the image. Unlike what occurs in later food still lifes, Aertsen does not isolate food from other objects, privileging food for its look as such and separating it from the context of its production. Instead, Aertsen focuses our attention on how meat

Figure 4.8
Pieter Aertsen (1505/1509–1575), THE MEAT STALL (1551), panel, 124 × 169 cm.
Uppsala, Uppsala Universitet, inv. no. L-1.

and meat products become food. The contextual frame he provides not only
represents meat as food (food from the butcher, not the sportsman), but also
points to the fact that our lives are sustained by animals' slaughter. His is a
painting rife with the blood seldom included in decorative hunting-trophy
gamepieces.

   In particular, Aertsen provides an insistent reminder of life sacrificed to life
via the severed, partly flayed head of the ox (next to which are severed pig's
feet). Its grotesque, nearly horrific visage is dramatically foreshortened so that
it appears to project out from the front picture plane toward us, making it
unique in that respect to everything else represented. It is accompanied at the
upper center by the suspended severed head of a hog. The picture's dynamism is thereby compositionally linked directly to life itself: From the

dead come the living, from past to present, from deep space to a projection distinctly forward and, so it seems, out of the picture's "present" front into a spatial "future."

Aertsen's treatment of space is as compositionally extraordinary as it is culturally insightful; it is an engagement of the very nature of space as a parameter of human experience under conditions of change. That is, Aertsen links space to time—past, present, and future. The image essentially locates for the viewer three spatial domains, each treated differently. In deep recess is the imagined past designated by the New Testament story of the Flight into Egypt, a tiny detail just left of center. Here the link between life, death, and food is articulated by adding to the scriptural story of Mary, Joseph, and the infant Christ in flight from Herod's wrath: Mary, while sitting atop the donkey, leans down to give bread to a beggar boy. Food is thereby linked to charity and morality, and by being tied to the scriptural story, likewise gains a eucharistic tinge.

The chronological past in turn is linked to the present by a small For Sale sign attached to the shed at the top right: "Behind here there is now farmland for sale by the rod . . ."[16] The sign invites us to look back in space and time, behind what is in the front. It connects that spatial *hier achter* (behind here) to the dynamics of monetary exchange: farmland for sale. The past is encoded by a specific textual reference to change, namely, a notice that land ownership will pass from one family to that of another, indicated spatially by means of the representation of the land itself in deep recess. (I gloss over the background details at the right that exist in a temporal continuum with the main scene.)

The space occupying the picture's foreground is likewise highly rationalized via a linkage of space-time relations, involving an agricultural narrative. The food still life connects to a visual demonstration, at the right, of how meat is processed. By contrast, there is no such apparent logic to the Flight into Egypt. The scriptural event does not fit the scene, and we are supposed to be able to tell precisely that. The gap between a past that exists in faith is separated by a distinct spatial rupture from a present that is tacitly material and logical—literally, not metaphorically, visual, hence verifiable.[17]

The third spatial domain is one we cannot precisely see but are nonetheless invited to imagine, in the aforementioned shape of the ox's head. The point here is not simply that it is the one shape whose foreshortening seems to make a spectacle of itself, catching our eye by its singularity; rather, it is that the spectacular effect is accomplished with the aid of something else critical to the entire representation. The head is looking back at us; it looks beyond the frame. The ox's dead eye gives the foreshortening spatial, temporal, and *cultural* dynamism.[18]

In agricultural economies death and life operate cyclically, with the rhythm and promise of the seasons. Although life organized by the seasons incorporates change by definition, its fundamental character is eternal repetition. Modernity, in contrast, abandons the cyclical for the linear. In our own historical moment, time is experienced principally as a unidirectional vector. We perceive the past as forever lost. Aertsen's handling of space-time relations comes very close to breaking medieval perceptions of seasonal, cyclical time. To be sure, he represents time's linearity via the step-by-step process of butchering. Far more important, he represents the once-living animal itself as a linear entity designated by its division into its separate body parts and their individual functions. Thus, at the top center of the painting we see the parts of the boar *in order:* its head, esophagus and lung, heart, large chunk of fat, and intestine; this is altogether a neat summary of how a swine organism functions from the moment it first breathes and eats—head, heart, lungs, fat (the sign of comfort and plenty), intestines (the final logic of the alimentary process that began with the head)—until it achieves its status as food for us, becoming the animal in its butchered state.[19]

Aertsen connects life to life but also connects life to process and therefore to time as a developmental, not static, parameter of experience. Not coincidentally, he hangs these body parts in a linear row by means of a rod, foreshortened like the ox's head (just now, perhaps, we may notice this), the two foreshortenings precisely paralleling each other, hence visually relating the ox and the pig. The deaths of these two lives, the ox's and the pig's, do not allow us to visualize the future toward which their body parts point, and in one instance look. Instead they invite us *to see* that there is something about that future that is uncertain—emergent linearity replacing circularity in time-space relations—and perhaps troubling, given the means by which we are asked to look: grisly remains.[20]

Blood

Rembrandt van Rijn's *The Slaughtered Ox* (Figure 4.9), one of two paintings he produced on this subject, is a dark and brooding account of a subject fairly often painted in sixteenth- and seventeenth-century Northern Europe[21] and taken up several times again in the twentieth century. What confronts the eye in Rembrandt's image is the troublesome resemblance of the recently slaughtered animal to a victim of crucifixion: "In typological Patristic glosses, the killing of the calf was often compared to Christ's expiatory self-sacrifice."[22] The image thus traverses not only the nature-culture and

Figure 4.9
Rembrandt Harmensz.
van Rijn (1606–1669),
THE SLAUGHTERED OX
(late 1630s?), panel,
73.3 × 51.7 cm.
Glasgow, The Art
Gallery and Museum,
Kelvingrove, inv. no.
600.

life-death binaries but also the physical-spiritual. This not a painting so much about food, sustenance, or plenty, for all these might inscribe about human life and its perpetuation, as it is instead about an extraordinarily nondecorative vision of death in a tense relation to execution.

Rembrandt's painting is no visual celebration of earthly plenty. Arguably, it is instead an antifeast for the eyes and an opening to the soul—in the common understanding then that eyes provided access to spiritual interiority and spiritual truth. Still, the quite easy transposition from slaughtered ox to Christ crucified is inevitably interrupted by Rembrandt's reminder of the very ubiquity of the event he represents, the everyday ordinariness of animals' suffering to benefit human carnivores. Any easy communion between meat consumption and the Eucharist is broken, for the ox is not a willing victim but a dupe, slaughtered by the hand of its master. A bond is destroyed thereby, not forged. The paradox that death makes life possible is made unresolvable but no less pathetic on that account.

Rembrandt's striking picture is contemporaneous to myriad food and game pictures that mark little except the pleasures of consumption (and some the pleasures of killing), images "speaking" only to the delight of filling both belly *and* eyes with seeming endless bounty—a story that only increased in its excesses as Rembrandt's century wore on. Rembrandt's painting in comparison reveals a darker, infinitely more complicated awareness constructed from unquestionably intense personal and subjective sensibilities, thus it fundamentally differs from later fur-and-feathers manifestations of raw power, whether real or imagined (Figures 4.2, 4.3). The question of power, and even more of its attendant prestige, is deconstructed by Rembrandt. Choosing to paint the freshly butchered carcass, still virtually quivering, is not to evoke our pleasure in eating but to remind us of what it costs. Indeed, in this Glasgow version he positions our angle to the carcass and uses dramatic light-shade modeling in such a way that the ox's evisceration appears especially striking, as a hollowing out that seems to stress the mutilation aspects of butchering. (This effect is muted in his Louvre version, in which he employs more even lighting.) The effects I am describing are heightened in this painting by his inclusion of the animal's hide and head, in a pile at the lower right, and of the figure of a woman in the deeply shaded background mopping up the bloodied floor (unfortunately, the figure is so dark that it is virtually invisible in the reproduction).[23]

During the 1920s, Chaim Soutine, an impoverished Lithuanian Jewish émigré living in Paris, repeatedly painted beef carcasses (Figure 4.10, *Color Plate 7*), no fewer than twelve in a series, after having seen Rembrandt's Louvre version of *The Slaughtered Ox* (painted in 1655, some years after the

Figure 4.10
Chaim Soutine
(1893–1943), CARCASS
OF BEEF (1925), linen,
114.3 × 78.7 cm.
Minneapolis, The
Minneapolis Institute of
Arts, gift of Mr. and
Mrs. Donald Winston
and Anonymous, acc.
no. 57.12.

picture in Glasgow just discussed).[24] The version reproduced here, like Soutine's others, exhibits a kind of urgent violence. The carcass confronts us in a close-up, in-your-face manner, hung from spirals of rope and stretched open, freshly bleeding. The floor itself is bathed in red, and more reds are spattered against the wall. The background is painted with broad, almost slashing blue-black brush strokes. Painted as though by gestures out of control, it replicates the results of an attack on the canvas surface; the unforgiving hues of bruising are as apparently fresh as the animal's own slaughter. Images like this might well be associated with Kafkaesque interrogations, tortures, and executions: unexplained, as if unexplainable. The carcass appears to have been quickly gutted and skinned, as if by a man who has for too long not eaten, because the signs of skilled butchery are *not* evident; instead the carcass reveals something near to desperation, not business but urgent necessity. It is as far removed as possible from the prestige-power conjunction of earlier extravagant gamepieces.

Soutine's obsession with food (a subject he repeatedly painted) is psychologically and physiologically rooted in the documented poverty and hunger of his youth. Soutine's troubled relation to eating and to animal slaughter is driven by a memory that once-hungry people never overcome. Moreover, throughout his life he suffered from ulcers, so that his stomach was never far from his consciousness. Yet Soutine painted these pictures at a time when he had sufficient money, presumably, to be able to afford the purchase of an entire beef carcass to serve only as a prop—one that literally rotted in his studio, to the considerable complaint of his neighbors. It could not be eaten, due not only to its state of decomposition but also because Soutine's ulcerative condition did not permit him to include meat (or poultry or fish) in his diet. It is no surprise that he obsessively painted these foods during this period of his life.[25]

As if to intensify the obsession, Soutine purposefully fasted before painting these subjects. As a friend noted, "Well, he buys a piece of raw meat and fasts in front of it for two days before he starts to paint it. Look at that red: hasn't he put all his cannibal appetite into it?"[26] And while he fasts the meat rots, so that all of Soutine's senses are filled with it: empty, growling stomach; eyes; olfactory organs; and ears (hearing the nearby slaughterhouse animals crying out). He painted directly from the carcass, not from preparatory drawings. Unlike Rembrandt, who stood away from his subject, Soutine puts his face into it, seemingly standing close enough to touch it with his brush, as though the ox's own blood might be transferred to the canvas. In fact, Soutine brought a bucket of fresh blood from the slaughterhouse to dab over the carcass as it dried, so as to preserve the appearance of fresh butchering; he also hired someone to sit near it to brush away flies. Soutine's physical contact with this meat is profound and thorough, involving all his senses except the very one we would ordinarily take for granted: He does not taste it. For Soutine the ox's death is pointless except as a demonstration of violence and the potential of living things to suffer. His is not a painting likely to stimulate an appetite for consumption, as is the case with most food images produced in Western history.

I retell these well-known and gruesome details for more than their shock value. That Soutine repeated himself, with relatively little variation, in at least twelve paintings informs us of the painter's own subjective relation to his work growing out of traumatic personal experiences. But this singularity is not all that I am after: What also bears pointing out is Soutine's complex understanding—perhaps simultaneously conscious and visceral—of the relation between seeing and imaging. The act of imaging involves the interventions of as many senses as Soutine can muster. The act of seeing, in other words, is fully embodied, as well as being psychic and personally specific.

Meat, Terror, and Burial

Francis Bacon's *Head Surrounded by Sides of Beef* (Figure 4.11) was painted after photographic reproductions of Spanish artist Diego Velázquez's 1650 portrait of Pope Innocent X (Figure 4.12),[27] a subject to which Bacon returned obsessively. In this instance Bacon likewise borrows from the beef-carcass paintings by Rembrandt and Soutine. Like Soutine, Bacon acknowledged his lifelong attraction to slaughterhouses and meat; "he instinctively associated carcasses with the Crucifixion, which later, as a non-believer, he conceived as an act of inhuman cruelty."[28] Whatever the "inspiration" of Velázquez's portrait, though in fact not intentionally biographical as regards the pope's life and career, Bacon's rendition acknowledges power, dramatically evident in the "pope's" face, especially the penetrating eyes and (in the Velázquez) the hard-set jaw, but he also portrays powerlessness, equally evident in the passive, almost immobilized seated body. Bacon reworks his source. Velázquez's portrait of an accomplished church leader and adroit early-modern politician is transformed into the rendering of an insane monster intent on the kill—ruthless, foreboding, out of reach, and enraged. "Bacon's painterliness is a way of getting under the skin of things, of destroying their matter-of-fact surface appearance and revealing the flesh of feeling they are made of. . . . The unlocking of feeling in form, as Bacon calls it, does violence to the image."[29]

Figure 4.11
Francis Bacon
(1909–1992), HEAD
SURROUNDED BY SIDES
OF BEEF (1954), canvas,
129.9 × 122 cm.
Chicago, The Art
Institute, Harriott A.
Fox Fund, inv. no.
1956.1201. Photo ©
1994, The Art Institute
of Chicago. All rights
reserved.

Figure 4.12
Diego Velázquez
(1599–1660), POPE
INNOCENT X (1650),
canvas, 140 × 120 cm.
Rome, Principe Doria-
Pamphili, Galleria
Doria-Pamphili, inv.
no. 118.

Representation itself comes undone before our eyes. The picture's impact hinges on its unstable formal composite of spatial-geometric "logic" (the lightly outlined box that creates the effect of both volume and order) and the implosion of that logic as regards what is housed within the box, two sides of bloody beef, one pierced by a black arrow, and a portrait head principally defined by the black hole of its gaping mouth, apparently engaged in a half-scream but in any event registering incomprehension and ironic loss of control. The boxlike internal frame also acts as the imprisoning "order" of a psychic cage, no less effective than one of iron. The figure is in solitary confinement. Everything social is erased. As in so many representations of food throughout the visual history of modernity, this image is not about eating and thus about life but is about killing—and the destruction of the self—as the defining force of human power over everything, most especially over human life itself.[30]

Bacon once confided that he hoped one day "to make the best painting of the human cry."[31] "If we scream, it is always as victims of intangible and invisible forces that obscure specific events, and which are not limited by pain and feeling. This is what Bacon means when he speaks of 'painting the scream rather than the horror.'"[32] He repeatedly painted the gaping mouth shown here (some are still more obviously screaming), at once horrific and exuding impotence. What might at first seem a scream of rage is also one of pain. The man's mouth, like the rest of his distorted figure, necessarily resonates with art history itself, to the extent that the viewer recognizes the picture's relation to portraiture in general, more so if the viewer recognizes the source in Velázquez's famous image. Bacon violates the portrait convention of screening out human emotion in favor of a kind of universal mask that hides as much as it reveals about the sitter, in part to idealize and flatter. Bacon's screaming pope is antiportraiture attempting to expose the deeply hidden, repressed, and suppressed interior that bursts forth explosively and uncontrollably through the mouth. "For of all the bodily parts, the mouth alone has the potential for spontaneously converting from a matter-of-fact local feature to a general area where the feeling of the whole body can be expressed."[33]

Time is frozen in all paintings, but the passage of time can be referenced by direct or indirect allusion to an external narrative (myth, story, historical occurrence, and so forth), by which means we can locate what came before and what will occur after the moment represented. Portraits, however, conventionally represent sitters in a state of temporal suspension—doing nothing, reacting to nothing, *just being*, which itself implies a kind of magical "nowness," as if unique to the lives of (would-be) important persons. Bacon's image undoes all that in the specificity of a particularly violent emotional moment registered exclusively on the sitter's face, the most expressive region of the body, the expression being completely at odds with what appears to be an otherwise relaxed, seated body. The difficulty for the viewer is caused by not knowing *why* the physical rupture has occurred, though the bloody beef carcass provides a surreal clue. The viewer is not provided a narrative to explain the given moment or to define a later outcome—and thereby be let off the hook. The logical progression of time (what has happened, and what will happen), and time's logical relation to space (here, the "cage") is uncertain, up for grabs, surreal, and obviously unsettling. It is also quintessentially modern.

To the extent that we can project a narrative, it is one involving the diametrical opposite to what we expect of portraiture: not life, but death. Thus even portraits literally painted after someone's death are not efforts to bury the individual in question but are attempts to resurrect him (usually him) into permanent memory. Bacon's figure, by contrast, is one who leaves us with a memory we would under "normal" circumstances prefer to forget, not least because it is a face that is so rarely—and understandably—to be found in the history of painting, whose social functions usually precluded making visible the profound, politicized darkness that Bacon insisted on representing. Bacon references this darkness via violent death—the beef carcass is pierced with an arrow—blood, and a screaming man. But more, that man references art itself via Velázquez's famous antecedent. Art history is thereby implicated.[34]

Part Three

Body

Sight opens all space to desire, but desire is not satisfied with seeing.

—Jean Starobinski
The Living Eye

*The painting is not a pure vision that must then be transcribed into
the materiality of space; nor is it a naked gesture whose silent and
eternally empty meanings must be freed from subsequent interpretations.
It is shot through—and independently of scientific knowledge and
philosophical themes—with the positivity of a knowledge.*

—Michel Foucault
*The Archaeology of Knowledge and the
Discourse on Language*

Chapter 5

Sensing

IN THE EARLY SEVENTEENTH CENTURY, at a defining moment of early modernity, there developed an intense humanistic and scientific interest in the human senses (sight, hearing, smell, touch, and taste). The visual arts, literature, and philosophy, as well as the new sciences of anatomy, biology, and medicine delved into the subject. In humanistic and philosophical inquiry, the senses were studied as keys to human identity, principally as vehicles of our embodied "apparatus" for knowing. In painting, the theme of the Five Senses received particularly dramatic treatment.

The Sensing Body

The subject first established its pedigree, as we might expect, as a mirror reflecting, hence putatively reinforcing, long-established religious belief: the Old World theory of knowledge according to which the here and now makes ultimate sense only in terms of the hereafter. The way to knowledge was described as a series of pathways marked by the senses—but the senses' role, as it were, was to confirm principles of religious orthodoxy.[1]

An alphabet of images related to the Scriptures was established: Sight, symbolized by the eagle, was linked with the theme of the healing of the blind man by Jesus; the mirror, with the theme of the expulsion of Adam and Eve from Paradise; Hearing with the preaching of John the Baptist; Taste with the miracle of the bread for the five thousand; Smell with Mary Magdalen's anointing of Christ's feet, and Touch with the miracle of Christ walking on the waters.[2]

Yet in the most striking of all the Five Senses paintings (Figures 5.1, 5.2), those produced by the Fleming Jan Brueghel the Elder, whom we met earlier as a painter of flowers, something else comes to the fore. With Brueghel the radical abstraction of the senses as theological metaphors is abandoned. What "his" senses sense is this-worldly, made strikingly concrete and supercharged with a visually gorgeous materialism. Accordingly, the senses' more traditional role as pathways to theological knowing is shifted toward the secular. Not least important, these paintings likewise silently argue for the earthly pleasures available to be consumed by seeing, hearing, smelling, touching, and tasting. Brueghel's Five Senses paintings, in other words, hail the *body* (not the soul).

As viewers, Brueghel's *Hearing* (Figure 5.1) calls us to our own bodies by providing us a level of pleasure that vastly exceeds mere knowing. Brueghel gets us to look by giving us so much to look at. That we *want* to look in the first place is partly the result of the cultural value placed on worldly goods, products of human manufacture that in virtually every instance are luxury items, and none a basic life necessity. To take in the myriad material contents of the painting we must look wholeheartedly. The act of visual consumption becomes a feast, not a snack; it requires time and even focused attention sim-

Figure 5.1

Jan Brueghel the Elder (1568–1625), HEARING (c. 1617/1618), panel, 65 × 107 cm. Madrid, Museo del Prado, inv. no. 1395.

ply to make basic identification, to name the objects (though principally musical instruments, there are also devices of the hunt, expensive timepieces—at the time, collectors' curiosities—paintings within the painting, interior decoration, exotic animals, background landscape, and so on).

One of the pleasures we are invited to experience is derived from the naked woman at the picture's center. Her bare flesh attracts our eyes partly by its whiteness in contrast to the richly colored materials surrounding her, including the carpet that frames her body, thereby setting it off as a "special sight." The fact that she is naked, of course, changes everything, for it marks the pleasure to be had as specifically erotic, that is, *sensual* (of the senses)—and also at odds with lived experience. That is, her body is made available as a sight in ways that profoundly exceed what is available for us to see in ordinary daily life. The painting's visual pleasures, in other words, are extraordinary, hence supplying all the more reason for us to look. Brueghel's painting *illustrates* a human sense (hearing and, since it is a painting, seeing as well). It also activates our own sensing bodies to the extent that it makes us *want* to look. In a culture where, already in Brueghel's own lifetime, seeing is believing, paintings of the human senses—no matter which sense is represented—mark the hold that looking as such enjoys in modernity. Put differently, Brueghel's *Hearing* is hearing for the eyes, to the extent that the eyes can confirm hearing's function, even when there is literally nothing to hear.

Pleasure as Serious Business

Since paintings are silent, what matters in this representation is not aural phenomena per se, but the social importance and function of certain kinds of sound and audition. Brueghel's painting illustrates not simply things that make sounds,[3] but those which make socially *prestigious,* and principally *private* sounds. That is, the musical instruments illustrated are solely those of high-caste music: The hunting devices recall an activity restricted to the nobility, and timepieces were expensive collector's items during this period. Accordingly, human hearing is represented less as a natural phenomenon than as one of social privilege. Hearing, in short, is politicized—and its politics are made to appear beautiful.

The pleasures immanent in Brueghel's picture are to no small extent produced by the degree to which the accumulated objects make no functional sense, except as a kind of archive of related things. As an inventory, Brueghel's sound-making collections please by their function*less* excess. Their visual logic, so to speak, lies in their apparent lack of logic, the degree to which the inventory seems impossible, a mere fantasy. Yet fantasy is brought back to reality—and to the chronologically present moment—by the inclusion of a specific landmark visible through the central archway at the back, namely, the

Château de Mariemont, the favorite, though not the only, residence of the region's rulers, Albert and Isabella, Brueghel's patrons. This single indicator of specific terrestrial geography specifies a marriage between embodied pleasure and concrete power, a sort of reality check that determines the nature, source, and boundaries of the senses being stroked. It specifies that our looking is not free but is firmly anchored in debt to those through whose eyes, in effect, the image is previewed. This presumed previewing has nothing to do with abstract theological symbolism or secular allegory and has everything to do with ownership: tactile possession. What is here for us to look at (but not to touch or to have) is *theirs*.

Norbert Schneider wisely points out that Five Senses paintings of this sort work not so much to satisfy cravings as to produce them. The seventeenth century marked the emergence of new wealth and the accompanying demand for things to buy. The great port at Antwerp—where Brueghel spent his life—later in the seventeenth century could accommodate 2,000 ships at one time, bringing trade goods to northern Europe from the far corners of the already fast-shrinking globe. "The stimuli provided by the new range of luxury goods triggered off a compulsive urge in the viewer to enhance his own sensual pleasure and to keep increasing his long-term needs."[4] More to the point of my concerns, these desires are both *classified* and *structured* in paintings like Brueghel's: Our consuming pleasures, in other words, are organized *for* us— exactly as with advertising.

Brueghel's series, five paintings in all, isolates each sense, thereby paralleling the practices of contemporaneous anatomy lessons carried out on cadavers that took up one discrete body part after another for examination. This parallel is neither accidental nor trivial. At the same historical moment that Brueghel's paintings both visualize and valorize sense-derived physical pleasure, the viewer's own sensing body itself is in effect objectified, taken apart, and appealed to in a kind of aestheticized *science* of pleasure. This science is structured as an inventory of the objects that reference and stimulate each sense, each in turn—wonderful sounds to hear, exotic flowers to smell, bountiful feasts to taste, and so on. Science meets and allies with consumption and the desires that drive consumption. As Roland Barthes reminds us, "Ownership depends on a certain dividing up of things: to appropriate is to fragment the world, to divide it into finite objects subject to man in proportion to their very discontinuity: for we cannot separate without finally naming and classifying, and at that moment, property is born."[5]

Thus a direct relation is established between the epistemology underwriting these pictures and that which governs contemporaneous scientific classificatory schemes more generally. That is, these images are doubly modern, de-

spite their otherwise old-fashioned allegorical structures. They mark the pleasure of excess consumption, linking it directly to power, and they situate
physical, embodied pleasure in a quasi-medical discourse about the *mechanics*
of pleasure. Pleasure becomes something not simply to be enjoyed but something to be isolated into its component parts, then studied. Moreover, these
representations evoke modernity's troubling conflation of work and play (or
perhaps the erasure of play):[6] The pleasure in the seeing comes from the effort
expended to make sense of the classification schemes underwriting the painting's material contents.

Keeping Her Body in Sensory Range

Brueghel's illustration of the sense of smell (Figure 5.2),[7] from the
same series, presents a paradisiac garden with a nude personification (probably) of Flora, at ease in her nakedness, comfortable in her total safety, and unaware of our stare. Hers is a private, walled world of silence and sweet scent
where nothing foreign intrudes—except our eyes. In the painting, scents, to
which as mere viewers we are denied access, abound to such a degree that
their excess—always in such paintings, excess—is harvested. At the left in the
background there is a vignette of Flemish perfume-manufacture, reflecting
the desire to push beyond the scent-limits set by nature. Perfume becomes an
indicator not only of culture but of identity and difference. Smell, in short, is

Figure 5.2
Jan Brueghel the Elder
(1568–1625), SMELL
(c. 1617/1618), panel,
65 × 109 cm. Madrid,
Museo del Prado, inv.
no. 1396.

a dimension of the political. Perfume was a means by which the European aristocracy engaged smell as a vehicle for social self-definition. By dabbing themselves with expensive manufactured unnatural scents, they established social difference by appeal to olfactory sensation. In an age when bathing was thought unhealthy, hence an age when, to our noses, most people would otherwise have smelled bad, perfume helped mark caste boundaries.[8]

The smells in Brueghel's garden were not in any sense complementary to those of the countryside, for in several regions of Flanders the rich pungency of ploughed earth and cut hay were replaced by the stench of death produced by the Eighty Years' War, so recent that historical memory was certain to have been still sharp. In the painting, only the skunk at Flora's feet marks antithesis to the sweetness that pervades, yet the animal is completely domesticated, a pet whose musk is presumably never sprayed. However apparently unreal, the scene is neither wholly fictional nor imaginative. Indeed, it is a confirmation of Brueghel's access to the physical spaces of the most totalized privilege. As I have already mentioned in an earlier chapter, his position as court painter provided access to the sovereigns' botanical and zoological gardens to study plants and animals.[9] In parallel fashion, the painting's possessor—its ideal viewer—had privileged visual access to the sight of Flora's nudity and by analogy had access in fantasy to her sensual odor, given the valorization of desirable smells around which the painting is organized.

Five Senses paintings, unified by a philosophy of the hoard, are nonetheless underwritten by an anxiety about loss, driven partly by the fact that "having" in the two dimensions of a painting is not analogous to having in three dimensions the actual objects represented. Imagery stimulates desire precisely by frustrating it, except for those individuals who have both the paintings *and* what the paintings represent. But for other viewers, those who have only the sight of what is represented, such paintings mark the enormous gap separating the realm of having from the realm of having merely a look. For the painting's viewer-owner, looking confirms—and makes more beautiful—what is owned, thereby helping define both the owner's private and social self. The image functions as a kind of psychic and visual insurance policy against all future claims to the contrary. But trouble still looms on the horizon. Establishing a claim by getting us to look is limited by the fact that we will eventually look away—and once out of sight the representation moves toward the border of out of mind. The very knowledge of that fact led patrons and artists alike to want to hold us in the thrall of the painting's look as long as possible, not least to help us better to commit it to the memory bank of our perpetual desires, which not coincidentally is the same function as attention-grabbing in ever more over-the-top advertising.

By freezing time, painting suspends action and reaction; it both permits and encourages us to imagine a permanence that does not exist. The objects Brueghel represents are "there" only for the eye, as a stimulation passing through the retina and nothing more, that is, apart from the literal value of the picture itself, no small matter to be sure. In that regard, what is seen in an image makes a promise it cannot fulfill. The "seeing" in painting frustratingly leads no further; we cannot pick up one of the musical instruments and make it sound; we cannot smell a single bloom. We can only *imagine*. What seems in representation so concrete, so available, so "real," pulls back from us, always out of reach, to the very senses that otherwise confirm it. When we move too close to a painting, what made perfect "sense" from a short distance suddenly blurs into the colored fog of the image's own material surface—just so much paint on wood or canvas. The eye that establishes what painting "is," likewise confirms that it is not what it claims to be.

Sensing Difference

Later in the century and in the same region, another sort of Five Senses representation rose to popularity, indeed eclipsing the elegant examples produced first by Jan Brueghel the Elder, and later by his son Jan the Younger. David Teniers the Younger, an enormously popular, prolific, and financially successful artist, time and again returned to this topos, either in single-sense paintings or in ones that accommodated each of the senses in a single image, as is the case with the two examples reproduced here (Figures 5.3, 5.4). Obviously, everything has changed. Like Brueghel, Teniers appealed to his well-to-do patrons (but not likely confined simply to the aristocracy) by marking their class privilege, although by means entirely different from those employed by his predecessor.

Brueghel pictured luxury, producing visual fantasies of quasi-imaginary Midaslike sanctuaries. By contrast Teniers pictured nothing worth having (or being). Teniers did not paint goods. He painted bodies, specifically those of the lower social orders, Flemish peasants, in scenes of vulgarity, drunkenness, and—critically important—contentment with their simple pleasures and surroundings. At once nonthreatening and visually entertaining, Teniers's Five Senses pictures are grist for comedy bordering on derision. The rude pleasure of the peasants' sensing provides pleasured looking for their social betters. For Teniers the peasantry *have* nothing but their embodied senses, distinguished by crudeness bordering on the subhuman. The issue turns on bodies portrayed to function seemingly without minds. The visual claim is made that

Figure 5.3
Attributed to David
Teniers the Younger
(1610–1690), THE FIVE
SENSES (PEASANTS
MAKING MUSIC AT AN
INN) (c. 1635?), panel,
26.9 × 35.1 cm.
London, National
Gallery, inv. no. 154.
Reproduced by courtesy
of the Trustees, The
National Gallery,
London.

Figure 5.4
David Teniers the
Younger (1610–1690),
THE FIVE SENSES
(1634), panel,
36.5 × 54.5 cm.
Karlsruhe, Staatliche
Kunsthalle, inv. no.
1902.

peasants *feel* (sense) but do not think. And that in part not only claims to define the peasants' principal character but also serves as the moral determinant for the prevailing social order. To extend the metaphor back to Brueghel, if the nobility smells sweet, the peasantry stinks.

In Teniers people replace objects, but the people are fundamentally objectified. The body returns—clothed. Material goods are reduced to a minimum so that what we as viewers stare at are other people, lesser than ourselves. Critically important, the implicit ownership of the senses evoked is the reverse of what occurs in Brueghel. In Brueghel the appeal is made to the viewer's senses. The only bodies present, unless we count tiny figures in the background, are those of naked women who function as fantasies. While looking at these images, it is our senses that are supposed to be stimulated. In Teniers's paintings what is provided of the material object world is the bare minimum necessary to establish the setting and to mark clearly which senses are evoked. In place of objects, the pictures are "all bodies," though funny bodies doing silly things.

If Brueghel provides the viewer with a five-course sensual banquet, where first we get our fill of, say, hearing, then smell, and so on, with Teniers the viewer is provided with a combination appetizer and nothing more—all of it in the form of a joke. Teniers's images are akin to today's cartoons; the punch line is put right in front of us, as in the ridiculous form of a squat peasant— they are always squat with Teniers, *lumpen* types close to the ground—holding a lute. This was an instrument that in real life a peasant would never have held, since it was principally an instrument of artistic music. (Nor is he playing it, a matter requiring some skill and considerable practice, but merely trying unsuccessfully to get it in tune, and this very much part of the joke.) At the extreme left, at the open window, sits an emblematic owl, a bird long associated with wisdom, looking in with its penetrating sight and accordingly no doubt enjoying the joke as much as the rest of us.

In the second of these pictures (Figure 5.4), also set in a tavern, a man smokes (Smell) and drinks (Taste); another plays a pocket fiddle (Hearing); a man vulgarly sitting spread-legged, with his pants coming open, looks out at us while singing (Sight); and a man with his back to us relieves himself (Touch)—with another owl looking down on the scene. (The gesture of holding in his hand his organ of sexual pleasure is a degraded version of the sensual erotics evident in Brueghel.) Finally, a man in the middle at once passes judgment on the entire scene and alludes to smell by holding his nose. Thereby even the participants acknowledge the scene's pervasive raunchiness. In sum Teniers's paintings reframe the question of human sensing into one principally about the differentials of class and privilege,[10] as filtered through bodies. Here, once again, enter pleasure and erotics.

In the first (Figure 5.3), Teniers sets up a putative duet between lovers—the lutenist and the old woman holding the song sheet. As though the physical ugliness and age of the couple were insufficient to guarantee the joke, Teniers places between them a music part-book but with its title-page inscription wrongly facing us, on which Teniers has written the word "BASO" (for the base part) serving as a judgmental pun (base, coarse). What in aristocratic tradition would be defined as the manifestation of a chivalric exchange is here rendered vaguely disgusting. Seeing these paintings, the original and ideal viewer could delineate his own refined sensing, at the expense of a social inferior and via the biting edge of sarcasm and cynical derision.

Teniers's exegesis into class relations is as heavy-handed as it is entirely obvious. Subtlety was not his long suit. What is far more interesting about these paintings, indeed about all paintings from this period concerned with the human senses, is their invocation of the body as a visible ground upon which to imagine and map human identity in its specific relation to social and cultural practices and institutions. In the remaining chapters, this will be the subject, principally defined by the differences of class, gender, and race.

Chapter 6

Body Examination: Scalpel and Brush

Throughout much of Western history the public execution of criminals by torture occupied an important niche in the regulation of social order. Staged in part for their educative value to the population at large, physical punishments of this sort were neither arbitrary nor carelessly performed. Instead, they were carried out in measured fashion specifically calculated according to the effects on the individual punished and as a specific and logical response to a particular crime. Torture executions for the most serious of offenses (for example, assassination and treason, among a very large number of other crimes) provided the opportunity to reassert by demonstration the reordering of society disrupted by antisocial acts. As highly rationalized rituals, torture executions symbolically restored to the sovereign the authority that had in essence been challenged by the miscreant.[1]

The Body Punished

The prisoner's punished body was the star feature in a regularly performed piece of urban theater, there being one plot with the same ending, though with numerous variations. Torture executions were commonly performed on an elevated platform that functioned as a stage by providing an unimpeded view from throughout the city square. People of "quality" enjoyed reserved seating in areas roped off and insulated from the standing rabble. The drama's conclusion was not reached with the death of the criminal but with a kind of epilogue revolving around a final insult to the victim's remains through mutilation, and in particular, through dismemberment.

Crucial to the social success of punishment was its visibility as a spectacle, governed by a process, and commonly advertised in advance in order to attract the greatest crowd. Such notices regularly informed the populace of the specific and varied means by which torture executions would be carried out: "This morning Pietro, son of Gio. Battista of Borgo Panigale is to be executed: tongs, the bar, quartering." Pulling flesh from the body with red hot tongs, a favorite device used for centuries, made its impact on witnesses via the senses of sight, hearing (screams), and smell (seared flesh). Convention required that the prisoner's body be punished sequentially, as though following a strict logic as part of an obvious plan or protocol. Arbitrariness had no place: "This morning Andrea Malagù is to be sledge-hammered, his throat cut, and then he will be quartered." Punishment was rationalized by its connection to the specific crime committed, that is, the most directly offending body parts were first attacked, after which the entire organism was destroyed. Thus in Venice a forger first had his hands cut off, after which his eyes were put out.[2]

Visual art's relation to spectacular bodily punishment is contradictory. Principally serving the interests of official institutions—state and church especially—art conventionally functioned to extend and perpetuate institutional and personal power. We might therefore expect that painting, the most prestigious vehicle for representation, would be called upon by the state to record punishments. Yet this is not usually the case. In fact, Western images of physical punishments often seek viewers' sympathies for victims, though the determination of guilt—who really is the victim—is inevitably open to extreme manipulation. Among the most moving are the series of etchings by Francisco de Goya called the *Disasters of War,* offering an immensely sympathetic view of human sufferings and a searing criticism of myriad cruelties; and his horrific painting of the mass execution carried out by the French army of occupation against a randomly selected group of Spaniards near Madrid, the date of which serves as the picture's title, *The Third of May, 1808* (1814).

The history of Western painting is tied closely to the church, for which painting served as a principal educative force for an illiterate populace. Painting in this guise focused attention on the lives of the saints and on martyrs in particular, often punished as resistors to secular authority—despite the church's own direct involvement in such contemporary punishments as the torture executions associated with the Inquisition. The church thus established a large visual archive recording executions carried out by secular authority against the innocent. This fact considerably limited the usefulness of painting to later secular authority as a device for promulgating its own position vis-à-vis the punishment of criminals.

The prime source for painting's repertory of victims ultimately depends on the visual history of the sacred victim, Christ crucified. It is his punished body from which all other unjustly punished bodies derive, if not directly, then culturally. As though to impart the greatest rhetorical impact from the scriptural lesson of Christ's sacrifice, painters commonly emphasized precisely those aspects of his Passion that would resonate most effectively and directly with ordinary experience. Thus painter Pieter Brueghel the Elder set the scene of the Crucifixion in his own sixteenth-century Flanders, replete with its hated foreign army of occupation playing the role of Christ's executioners in the costumes of his day. But more to the point of my concerns are those images referencing Christ's tortured body per se. Two noted examples will suffice.

Annibale Carracci's *The Dead Christ* (Figure 6.1) represents the body after its removal from the cross, immediately before burial. It is a tour de force of compositional foreshortening, a striking bit of visual rhetoric that draws our attention to the image and not incidentally to the young painter's considerable technical skills. We survey a mutilation. The angle of view gives us access to the multiple penetrations of Christ's body and the principal means by

Figure 6.1
Annibale Carracci
(1560–1609), THE
DEAD CHRIST (c. 1582),
canvas, 70.7 × 88.8 cm.
Stuttgart, Staatsgalerie,
inv. no. 2785.

which his body was wounded: the crown of thorns and, especially, the stilet-tolike nails, their irregularly flattened heads visually reverberating with the force of the invisible hammer strikes used to drive them home. In the lower left foreground, paralleling the line of Christ's foreshortened leg, are the pincers used to remove the nails—the removal having caused the nails to bend. Yet scripture makes no reference to this tool. The pincers in effect are modern; they resonate with the here and now. That is, the pincers are fundamentally contemporary not to Christ but to the viewer, to the extent that they mirror but do not literally replicate the conventional function of the flesh-ripping tongs long popular with executioners.[3] Christ's body is made an object of pity, not derision; his tortured form, in other words, forms an "argument" against his executioners.

Painters ordinarily direct their attention toward the human face, the specific indicator of individuality and the principal terrain for identity. But in Carracci's painting the face is deemphasized by darkening it in background shadow while relatively highlighting the torso and feet and by angling the head away from the powerful parallel lines of the legs that, in turn, lead to a visual climax in Christ's pierced hand and side. Christ's body gains its identity, in other words, from its wounds and the blood dripping from them—and not from his visage. Thus Carracci emphasizes the violation of the sacred body as a ground upon which to map the supreme outrage of human injustice against which all other, historically subsequent, bodily punishments can be made to resonate.

Hans Holbein's painting of the dead Christ (Figure 6.2), equally striking, approaches the victimized Christ differently, but his victimization and humiliation are principal subjects nonetheless. Here Christ is already—and unceremoniously—entombed, the body lacking even the honorific shroud. Painted to the size of a male adult, the corpse is shockingly squeezed into a sepulchre that begrudges any waste of space. The very form of the image, longitudinal to a degree that even today still surprises, violates pictorial convention and thereby produces the rhetorical effect of grabbing our attention. The emaciated corpse, unlike Carracci's Christ, is antiheroic. Christ's hand is grotesquely misshapen in stiffened reaction to the the iron nail; and its greenish cast, the shade even more evident on the ghastly profiled face, indicates the onset of decomposition. In fact, tradition has it that Holbein used as his model the body of a drowning victim taken out of the Rhine. Christ the king is posed as no portrait of an earthly king could ever permit: mouth agape, visually acknowledging the physical loss of control, the absence of agency guaranteed by death. Our angle of sight permits our eyes to penetrate this king's body, to look into his mouth and nostrils; Holbein is very careful to empha-

Figure 6.2
Hans Holbein the Younger (1497–1543), THE BODY OF CHRIST IN THE TOMB
(1521/1522), distemper on limewood panel, 30.5 × 200 cm. Basel, Öffentliche
Kunstsammlung, acc. no. 318. Photo: Martin Bühler.

size this accessibility and, compositionally, even to invite it. Our stare confirms the nearly total degree of his humiliation—and not incidentally implicates us in shared guilt at the same time as our sympathy is invoked.

Holbein's visual account of physical death is so convincing that it challenges the possibility of Christ's Resurrection, as Julia Kristeva has suggested.[4] This is no small matter. In theological terms, resurrection is the guarantee of final justice and at once the sign and means of reestablishing order (as in divine law and order). Doubt notwithstanding, the scene represented is part of a very well known scriptural narrative that "guarantees" Christ's Resurrection, thereby closing the gulf separating appearance (Christ's death) from "reality" (ultimate resurrection). By forcing acknowledgment of the absolute nature of physical death, in effect by shoving the look of death in our face, Holbein allows us to confront the nature of faith as a leap, not a step. Holbein challenges the believer to recognize that proof and faith are contradictory. The proof he apparently offers confirms death's finality; it is the visual equivalent of the signed and certified coroner's report. In sum, Holbein's *The Body of Christ in the Tomb* maps the uncertain relation of seeing to believing directly on a body. Christ's body, that is, serves as a locus for determining the limits of sensory perception and hence also the limits of representation. It questions what can be known and how what might be known can be shown. The reality we see in the decomposing Christ is, after all, not intended to be taken as real. Holbein wants us to see that our senses lead us astray—that representation fails (and, ironically, by failing, it succeeds, to the extent that the failure invites believers to the safe harbor of faith). But however the viewer reacts to Holbein's painting, it is crucial to recognize that the terrain upon which the issue is mapped is the body, in representation the repository not only of subjectivity and identity but also of history. The body in representation—any body, not only Christ's body—is the ultimate visible sign of the attempt to know.

Anatomy, Knowledge, and Defilement

According to the sixth-century textual account detailing the martyrdom occurring in the year 303 of Saint Erasmus (Figure 6.3), the tools of torture included "red-hot tongs, boiling oil, nails and spikes driven under the fingernails." Dieric Bouts's altarpiece, painted c. 1428, locates his execution in the technique known as *evisceratio,* then widespread in Europe—but having nothing to do with the Erasmus story—involving the cutting open of the stomach in order to pull slowly from the victim his intestines, winding them round a windlass while the victim remained alive.[5] Despite the particularly gruesome nature of this form of execution, the characters in Bouts's picture are most noteworthy for their reserve. The greatest physical reaction to the event is registered on the face of the man at right working the windlass. Saint Erasmus himself, his body entirely relaxed, appears absolutely stoic. The scene seems quiet, as though no utterance or scream will pierce the air. The wound in Saint Erasmus's belly is neat; there is no blood. In the absence of what we would expect to be shown, Bouts draws our attention to the mechanics of the execution machinery and its chronological working on the body. The windlass framing the saint's body draws attention to itself; we pause to sort out how the simple mechanism works.

The drawing out of the guts visually acts as a drawing out of the representation, unfreezing the painting's stasis. The long vertical line leading from the cut leads the viewer's eyes to the discrete turnings on the shaft, lapping and overlapping. The machine itself, the painting's central object, is accurately drawn and, more to the point, is familiar, an object whose contemporaneous public function sharply contrasts with Bouts's imaginary and stylized landscape. Bouts's modernity locates itself in the degree to which he sets up the event as a kind of *demonstratio,* a lesson in how evisceration is done. Accordingly, Bouts's picture serves not only as a statement about a great martyr and the banality of cruelty but also as a foretaste of a knowledge crisis that would later ensue when society confronted the new science of the body—anatomy, dependent upon the systematic mutilation of the body through dissection. The particular parts of the story I want to develop are the connections among anatomical science, state-sanctioned executions, and the history of painting, on the one hand, and emerging contradictions in the cultural meaning of the human body, on the other.

The place to begin is the literal end itself: execution as mandated by judicial authority, a decision of the state on behalf of the society it purports to represent. That executions are affairs of power in its rawest manifestation is obvious. More crucial to consider is their connection to knowledge, notably

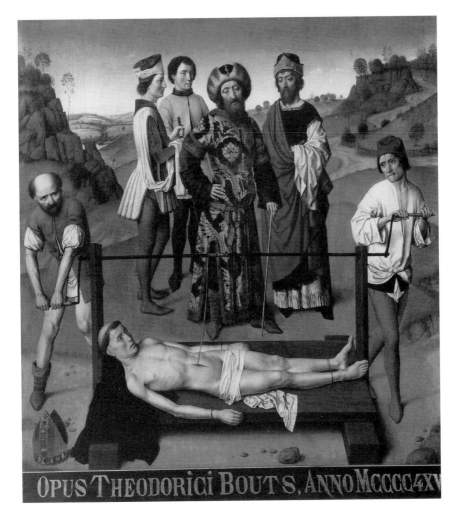

Figure 6.3
Dieric Bouts (died 1475), THE MARTYRDOM OF ST. ERASMUS (c. 1428), central panel of a triptych, 82 × 80 cm. Louvain, Belgium, Collegiate Church of St. Peter. Photo © IRPA-KIK-Brussels.

modern science, and this turns out to be as direct as it might at first glance seem curious. Thus in Germany and the Low Countries, between the sixteenth and eighteenth centuries, executioners—hangmen, beheaders, men responsible for quartering the body—"also practiced medicine and carried out autopsies."[6] Indeed, throughout most of Europe the principal source of cadavers for anatomical dissection was execution, a fact well embedded in popular consciousness and regarded with dread.[7] The final humiliation against the body of the accused was that it be turned over to the anatomist, against which surviving family members and friends frequently fought. Postmortem dissection plagued the mind of many criminals who commonly bargained with judicial authorities to avoid it. In fact, anatomists' dissections literally and officially were made to serve as deterrents to crime. The penetration of the deceased body, now reduced to the probing interests of a stranger wielding knives, was widely viewed and feared as the final act of dehumanization, indeed, of demonization of the executed.

Artists occasionally produced horrifying images of dissections as the wages of sin and crime (Figure 6.4), none more effectively than William Hogarth, who "rewards" the dead criminal's cruelty by returning the favor in kind. A screw is drilled into the executed man's skull and a rope attached, so as properly to accommodate the anatomist's convenience—and likewise recalling that hanging was the favored device for public executions in eighteenth-century England. Indeed, the rope by which the man was strangled remains around his neck, a fictional liberty on Hogarth's part that makes more visually emphatic the connection of punishment to dissection. The identical connection is reinforced by Hogarth's conflating the overseer-surgeon, seated on an elaborate raised chair, with a judge passing sentence.

Hogarth gratuitously spills the victim's entrails to the floor, at the end of which the viewer's eyes are led to the victim's heart now in the jaws of a skinny, obviously hungry dog. The "punishment" enacted by the anatomists is driven home by the fact that three men cut into the cadaver: one at the feet; a second pushing his hand into the body cavity while holding an enormous knife in his other hand; and a third at the head literally gouging out an eye. Hogarth translates dissection into the realm of a second murder. And all of this is presented as spectacle, a bizarre combination of classroom exercise and quasi-public entertainment. Not one to leave things to chance, Hogarth included his typical verbal gloss to the scene:

Behold the Villain's dire disgrace! *Those Eyeballs, from their Sockets wrung*
 Not Death itself can end.   *That glow'd with lawless Lust!*
He finds no peaceful Burial-Place;
 His breathless Cor[p]se, no friend. *His Heart, espos'd to prying Eyes,*
           To Pity has no claim:
Torn from the Root, that wicked Tongue, *But, dreadful! from his Bones shall rise,*
 Which daily swore and curst! *His Monument to Shame.*[8]

Hogarth in fact was only reporting, with hyperbole, on common, even longstanding, practice. In the seventeenth century in Holland and elsewhere

THE REWARD OF CRUELTY.

Behold the Villain's dire disgrace!
Not Death itself can end.
He finds no peaceful Burial Place,
His breathless Corse, no friend.

Torn from the Root, that wicked Tongue,
Which daily swore and curst!
Those Eyeballs, from their Sockets wrung,
That glow'd with lawless Lust!

His Heart expos'd to prying Eyes,
To Pity has no Claim:
But, dreadful! from his Bones shall rise,
His Monument of Shame.

Designed by W. Hogarth.

Published according to Act of Parliament Feb 1 1751.

Figure 6.4
William Hogarth
(1697–1764), THE RE-
WARD OF CRUELTY
(from *The Four Stages of
Cruelty*, Plate IV, 1751),
engraving, 40.3 × 32.4
cm. Brooklyn, The
Brooklyn Museum,
bequest of Samuel E.
Haslett, inv. no.
22.1874.

throughout Europe, annual public anatomies were held "with clock-like regularity[;] they marked the height of the winter season." Carefully staged over
several days (usually not more than five, given problems with decomposition), as instructional spectacles they were intended to be both entertaining
and profitable. Entrance for the general public was by purchased tickets—
and these were expensive if the corpse was female (audiences were male).[9]

Science mixed freely with prurience and not incidentally simultaneously complemented the scopophilia informing the painting of female nudes. Audiences were situated in tiered scaffoldings, amphitheater-style, inside pre-existing buildings, often chapels! These events even had a specifically tactile element in that human organs might be passed from hand to hand among the spectators—though under threat of fine if theft was attempted.

In mid-eighteenth-century England punishment by hanging could be assigned to roughly 160 crimes. In 1752 Parliament raised the stakes for murderers by either hanging their bodies in chains or assigning them for dissection. The function of the latter was as much for public warning as for the advancement of science, as is made clear by a 1759 speech given in London by a surgeon-anatomist, immediately prior to the actual dissection of a murderer's body.

> And it being well known, in how great horror dissection was held by almost all mankind, more especially the lower class, as the most harden'd villains, tho' they braved death, still shuddered at the thoughts of being made an Otomy (as they called it) they very wisely ordained, that every such malefactor, (not hung in chains) should be delivered to the surgeons for dissection. . . . I would wish [those here merely out of curiosity] to consider the crime which has occasioned their present assembling in this place: that crime, which death is not looked on as an atonement for, but that every one hereafter guilty of it, may expect to be exposed on that table. . . . Let therefore the Anatomical Table in the Surgeons Theatre, be a preacher to all this audience.

The speaker, having remarked on the ignominy of public hanging, warns of the executed body's final and public humiliation over which he now presides: "afterwards to be prepared and exhibited again, a publick spectacle, as the present subject now appears." All that on a Thursday. The dissection ended on the following Saturday, concluding with a sermon that reprised the first: "I think few who now look upon that miserable mangled object before us, can ever forget it. It is for this purpose our doors are opened to the publick, that all may see the exemplary punishment of a murderer, and that it may be impressed on their minds, and be a warning to others to avoid his fate."[10]

Vesalius and Skeletal Remains

The greatest of the early anatomists, regarded as the founder of the modern science, was Andreas Vesalius (1514–1564).[11] His gigantic treatise, *De humani corporis fabrica,* was published in 1543, with a second edition in 1555.

Richly illustrated and printed in folio, the volume includes 824 pages of text, plus an extensive, unpaginated index. Most of the images are of particular body parts, but a small number, seventeen in all, involve the full human form shown from different angles, either as a skeleton or an *écorché* (anatomical model with skin flayed away to expose musculature). These are the largest illustrations in the book, each taking up a full page. And unlike the illustrations of human body parts that are shown in isolation, each full body figure is set into a narrative frame that seemingly either accounts for the figures' deaths or alludes to philosophical issues surrounding death. Not least important, a number of these illustrations connect the new science of anatomy to the execution of prisoners. Vesalius concentrates these images between pages 203 and 248 of his book, but he introduces the series with a half-page illustration of the tools of the anatomist's trade (Figure 6.5), a fearsome collection that distinctly, if inadvertently, recalls contemporaneous tools of torture illustrated in numerous representations of saintly martyrdoms that the general populace could see displayed on the walls of churches (Figure 6.6).

In effect, Vesalius begins at the end (Figures 6.7, 6.8). Employing full-page images for the first time in the book, he illustrates these "bodies" as skeletons, the final remains after the anatomist finishes his dissection. And his skeletons—put back together for their first and final "showing"—literally confront their own deaths. Thus the first holds a grave digger's spade while looking toward heaven and opening his mouth as if crying out in anguish (an effect undercut by the very relaxed pose of the arm resting on the spade handle); the second contemplates a skull while resting the left arm on the lid of a classical sarcophagus, replete with appropriate Latin inscription: *Vivitur ingenio, cætera mortis erunt* (Genius lives on, all else is mortal). The upper half of the image resonates directly with the memento mori Vanitas paintings that would become popular in northern Europe one-half century later. The lower half, by contrast, replicates the cross-legged pose then (and long afterward) characteristic in portraits of elegant gentlemen who by this means marked their self-assurance and social position (Figure 6.9). To be sure, the messages are mixed and mark a confusion resulting in part from the as-yet uncertain relationship between anatomists and artist-illustrators in their employ.[12] It is certain that artists brought to the task their own sets of practices and expectations, notably including those growing from the conventions of narrative: Pictures told stories—and that was the rub.

The *story* of any image marks a location in history, society, and culture; it is the means by which the human figure is made *to relate* and without which the human being not only makes no sense but cannot fully be human. The problem facing the anatomical illustrator is how to think about, hence represent, the human being without any story and, simply, as information.

Figure 6.5
Andreas Vesalius (1514–1564),
INSTRUMENTS OF ANATOMY (from *De
humani corporis fabrica,* 2d ed., rev.,
1555, p. 200), woodblock engraving,
39.3 × 26 cm. Minneapolis, Owen H.
Wangensteen Historical Library of
Biology and Medicine, University of
Minnesota.

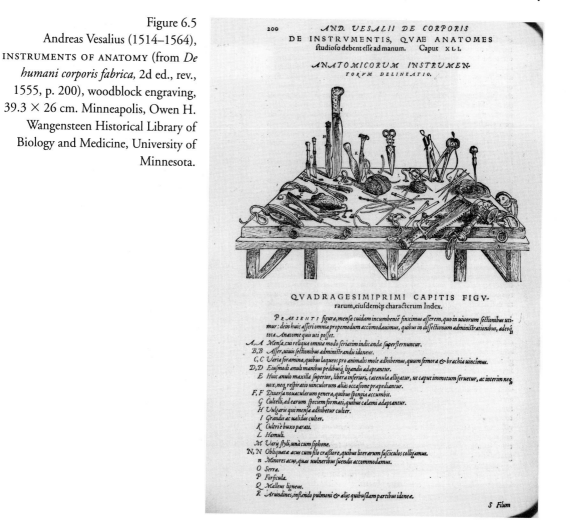

Anatomy is about the *data* of the body, which in essence can be gotten at by penetrating the skin and seeking out the body's depths, the human interiority that seems to lie beyond the reach of culture and history.

Anatomical illustration marks the fly in the ointment of Renaissance humanism and the dark background to the surface sheen of modernity. The secularism of early modernity increasingly acknowledged the terrestrial here and now; as a result, ancient philosophies claiming the nobility of the human regained some currency, fighting back against the Christian theology of human degradation. But the victory was problematic. The eye that once focused on heaven and the soul now focused more on the earth and the body, about

Figure 6.6
Stefan Lochner
(died 1451),
MARTYRDOM OF ST.
BARTHOLOMEW
(c. 1430), canvas.
Frankfurt am main,
Städelsches
Kunstinstitut, inv. no.
826. Photo: Ursula
Edelmann.

which there remained much to know. That knowledge depended on the scalpel and the saw—thus the knowledge of life depended upon death. The full-page illustrations that appear for the first time in Vesalius were plagiarized repeatedly for two full centuries and more—they are replicated with small variation in the illustration volumes (published 1762–1777) accompanying Denis Diderot's great French *Encyclopédie*. For a very long time these images, and a number of others like them, served to remind readers that the anatomized body was also the body punished. This can be stated more boldly: Artist-illustrators, in maintaining the skeleton in a cultural setting, often made direct reference to execution. Thereby, they visually reinforced anatomical science's link to politics, state power, cruelty, and fear.

Vesalius's illustration of an *écorché* (Figure 6.10) is literally of a man hanged, as though the anatomist's task was so urgent that the cadaver was worked upon while still on the gibbet. In fact, anatomists did suspend the

Figure 6.7
Andreas Vesalius (1514–1564),
SKELETAL FIGURE WITH GRAVE DIG-
GER'S SPADE (from *De humani corporis
fabrica,* 2d ed., rev., 1555, p. 203),
woodblock engraving, 39.3 × 26 cm.
Minneapolis, Owen H. Wangensteen
Historical Library of Biology and
Medicine, University of Minnesota.

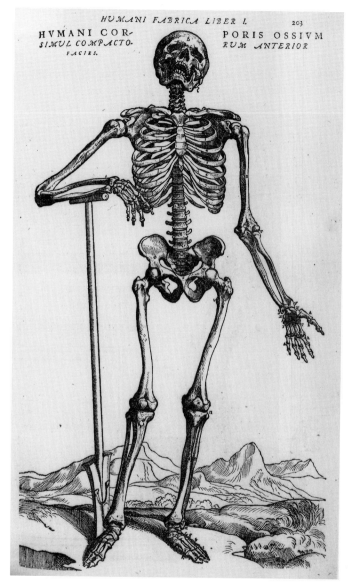

body so as better to display, among other things, "the caval, esophageal and
aortic openings" (the cadaver's diaphragm is pinned to the wall at the upper
right).[13] But the adding of scenery moves the lesson from the examining theater to the execution yard. Nonetheless, already with Vesalius there is an alternative gesture that seemingly attempts to cleanse some illustrations of their
unsavory associations with criminality and punishment (Figure 6.11). In this

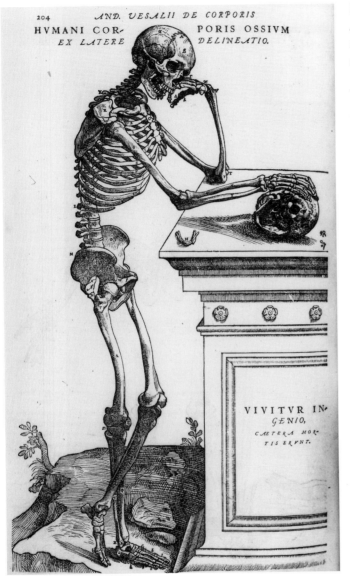

Figure 6.8
Andreas Vesalius (1514–1564),
SKELETAL FIGURE CONTEMPLATING A
SKULL (from *De humani corporis fabrica,* 2d ed., rev., 1555, p. 204), woodblock engraving, 39.3 × 26 cm.
Minneapolis, Owen H. Wangensteen
Historical Library of Biology and
Medicine, University of Minnesota.

instance, the *écorché* still breathes—this quickly became the common type—and, indeed, lives a "normal" life. Shown in back view, he becomes like us, a viewer; standing on a hill, he surveys an Italianate landscape with a village and gestures as elegantly as the most cultivated of gentlemen, while sporting the body of a young Apollo: beautiful man, beautiful body.[14] As viewers we are invited into the image: "Look at this," the *écorché* seems to say, "what a splen-

Figure 6.9
Nicholas Hilliard (1537–1619), A YOUNG
MAN AMONG ROSES (c. 1588), parchment,
14.3 × 7 cm. London, Victoria and Albert
Museum. Photo courtesy of the Board of
Trustees of the Victoria and Albert Museum.

did vista." Stripped of his skin, he remains ignorant that our eyes feast instead
on his exposed body, a nude made still more naked by the anatomist's
striptease. However, art does more in this instance than hide what needs to be
hidden; it also compels us to look, and it does so, oddly it might seem, by being rather old-fashioned about its illustrating. By setting the *écorché* "back
into" a narrative, a conventional mode of representation, the artist hails the
viewer not only to look but to contemplate and admire, to the extent that the
image still resonates with the pictorial aura that viewers would associate with
art and not with "mere" scientific drawing. In other words, one cultural role

usefully played by artists on behalf of anatomists was to transfer some of the prestige long associated with art onto the upstart and still suspicious practice of a new science.

Painter-Anatomists

During the Italian Renaissance, with the rise of humanism and the parallel development of secular painting, artists' interest in the body increased dramatically. Surprisingly quickly, the body's outer surfaces were regarded as insufficiently revealing of the physical essences of physical form and human identity. The source for surface appearance was sought more deeply in the body's interiority. Painting met anatomy and dissection. Artists sought information from cadavers. They penetrated the body with their eyes, and also—like anatomists—they got their hands bloody. Visually and tactilely they probed the innards of real bodies, all that lay between the skin and the skeleton. Leonardo da Vinci and Michelangelo were among the earliest and best.[15] Leonardo drew 228 anatomical plates. Like Michelangelo, he "procured cadavers, attended public dissections, and even performed them himself on freshly deceased bodies at the hospitals of Santa Maria Nuova and Santo Spirito in Rome."[16]

> Artists thirsting for immortality may have wanted to see death at close quarters, to touch it with their eyes. And so they made it their model, one as privileged as the live model. . . . When the live model did not suffice, the corpse was called in. . . . Dead or alive, the body was a rich mine of information. And so artists stalked it throughout its transformations into its last and least recesses.[17]

Tableaux: Living Death

The distance separating art from science was by no means great, nor for that matter was the distance separating artist from scientist. "Anatomists could turn, as we know they actually did, to works of art to study muscles and sinews. The adjustment from one to the other was comparatively easy: all that had to be provided to turn a martyrdom into an anatomy was a change in emotional climate."[18] An indication of how the divide between art and science was sometimes bridged involves the case of the long-lived Fredrik Ruysch (1638–1731), father to still life painter Rachel Ruysch, discussed in Chapter 2. Ruysch took his doctorate in medicine at the University of Leiden and later worked in Amsterdam, where for a time he held the post of city ob-

Figure 6.10
Andreas Vesalius (1514–1564),
ÉCORCHÉ AS HANGED MAN (from *De
humani corporis fabrica,* 2d ed., rev.,
1555, p. 230), woodblock engraving,
39.3 × 26 cm. Minneapolis, Owen H.
Wangensteen Historical Library of
Biology and Medicine, University of
Minnesota.

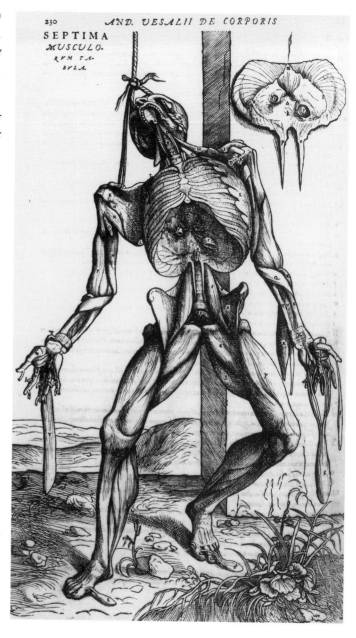

stetrician, taught anatomy, worked as a forensic expert on behalf of the court
of justice, and studied and lectured on botany.[19] Closer to the point, for a period of sixty years he prepared injected specimens, using a variety of preserving fluids (whose recipes he closely guarded) and highly adept embalming

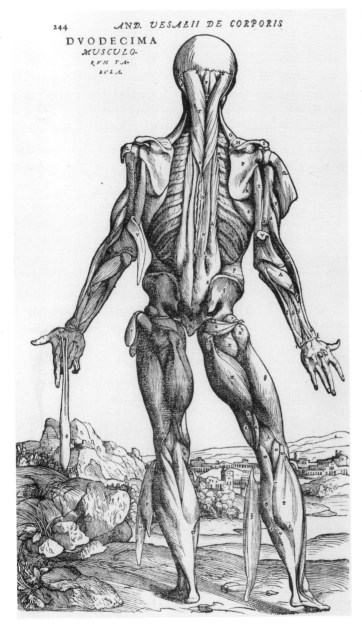

Figure 6.11
Andreas Vesalius (1514–1564),
ÉCORCHÉ SURVEYING AN ITALIANATE
LANDSCAPE (from *De humani corporis
fabrica*, 2d ed., rev., 1555, p. 244),
woodblock engraving, 39.3 × 26 cm.
Minneapolis, Owen H. Wangensteen
Historical Library of Biology and
Medicine, University of Minnesota.

methods. And these specimens he put on display in a vast "cabinet"—really a
protomuseum—available for public viewing, where *display*, or spectacle, in
fact, was a driving force, as we may surmise from a 1743 account by Robert
James.

His museum, or repository of curiosities, contain'd such a rich and magnificent variety, that one would have rather taken it for the collection of a King than the property of a private man. But not satisfied with the store and variety it afforded, he would beautify the scene, and join an additional lustre to the curious prospect. He mingled groves of plants, and designs of shell-work with skeletons, and dismember'd limbs; and, that nothing might be wanting, he animated, if I may so speak, the whole with apposite inscriptions, taken from the best Latin poets. This museum was the admiration of foreigners: generals of armies, embassadors, electors, and even princes and kings, were fond to visit it.[20]

Rachel Ruysch practiced her developing craft by painting background displays for her father's specimens, and she also prepared lace costumes for preserved infants, or body parts of infants, kept either in fluids or as part of open-air displays—various specimens survive to this day in their original fluid-filled jars in collections in Leiden and St. Petersburg.[21] The whole collection took up five rooms of Ruysch's Amsterdam house. He sold the collection, roughly 2,000 specimens in all, to Peter the Great in 1717—and for a huge sum, 30,000 Dutch guilders. The czar, so the story goes, was sufficiently moved by the results of Ruysch's skills as an embalmer—which practice took place in his house—that he kissed the face of an embalmed child, reacting to the corpse as though it were still alive.[22]

Bits of Ruysch's anatomical curiosities, nothing if not ingeniously imaginative, were illustrated in his major treatises (Figures 6.12, 6.13). Science *and* death are made decorative, literally spectacular. The body—better, body parts—is transformed into sculptural art. Ruysch delivers more than anatomical information; he is concerned as well to mingle science with aesthetics, and not least, with morals. Thus (Figure 6.12), Ruysch sets three tiny fetal skeletons, together with a stuffed bird, into a landscape whose raw materials were mined from cadavers. The rocks are kidney, bladder, and gallstones; and the foliage is partly from human vascular "trees," which Ruysch was especially adept at preserving.

Ruysch presented these displays as tableaux, replete with "dialogue," in the form of labels or inscriptions, as referred to in the passage just quoted by Robert James. These inscriptions are cited in those volumes of Ruysch's collected works that provide a sort of catalog to the huge collection, only a small portion of which is illustrated by engravings such as these. Indeed, the display tableaux receive principal attention in the books. They are placed at the head of major sectional divisions and are printed four times larger than the engravings illustrating the scientific specimens that actually form the bulk of the collection.

The introductory display engravings reproduced here are actually large foldouts that the reader has to open up in order to see. Accordingly, the prints re-

veal their startling contents only gradually. Once fully open, each invites con-
templation. This is partly because once the engraving is unfolded, the book
cannot be turned to another page, nor can its subsequent pages be casually
flipped through, until the print is refolded. Further, the thinness of the paper
requires that the volume be set on a table rather than be handheld, otherwise
the engraving will tear. Setting the image on a table raises the stakes of looking; it becomes work. And yet these images tell the anatomy student very little
about anatomy that would not better be learned by specimen displays of the
more conventional kind. The display prints, and the three-dimensional originals to which they refer, are not about anatomy as such but about the artist-
anatomist himself, overlaid with a profoundly well-established if entirely predictable gloss that can be summed up in the familiar phrase, memento mori.

The portions of Ruysch's collection introduced by these two displays focused on the anatomy of fetuses and infants. Thus, regarding the first (Figure
6.12), the text catalogs more than one hundred specimens of body parts,
many preserved in fluids and kept in bottles. Sexual parts receive noteworthy
attention ("No. V. Pueri Penis cum annexo scroto, naturali colore præditus";
other examples are cited further on), along with abnormalities, for which, like
many others of his time, Ruysch had considerable taste, of which more momentarily ("No. IX. Phiala, in qua portio Cerebri hydrocephali, 8 circiter an-
nos nati").[23]

In the first display piece (Figure 6.12), a tiny skeleton at the top adopts a
stage pose and appears to deliver a brief soliloquy provided in the form of an
inscription cited in the text: "Why should I long for the things of this world?
Death spares no man, not even the defenceless infant."[24] Two other fetal
skeletons act out in pantomime conventional gestures of death itself (at the
left, wielding a scythe) and mourning (at the right, wiping away tears with a
cloth—formed from a piece of preserved stomach lining). In the second example (Figure 6.13), the effect of mourning is evoked by musical sonority
involving the largest skeletal figure, a fetus of four and one-half months
placed in a kneeling position, playing a "violin" formed out of a thigh bone
"through sharp humours rotted out," the bow formed from a dried artery,
and the figure adopting a stance conventionally marked as melancholic—
"its head turned heavenward." There are five fetal skeletons in total, ranging
in age up to roughly twenty weeks, with the one at the top being the oldest.
This exhibit, like the other, stands on a walnut base. Its core is a large rock
that is invisible because of all that is glued to it. Most of what catches the
viewer's eyes are the many stones mined from cadavers, each given a letter label and described in the accompanying text, in regard to size, surface texture,
and a bit about the donor ("taken from a drowning victim"; "from an old
woman who lived in an almshouse"). Some parts are from animals, such as a

Figure 6.12
Fredrik Ruysch
(1638–1731), and C. H.
Huijberts (engraver),
DECORATIVE-ANATOM-
ICAL DISPLAY: THREE
INFANT SKELETONS
(*Thesaurus anatomicus
primus. Het eerste
anatomisch cabinet,*
1739, plate 1), engrav-
ing, 41.4 × 38 cm.
Minneapolis, Owen H.
Wangensteen Historical
Library of Biology and
Medicine, University of
Minnesota.

calf's spleen; the skeleton at the far right holds in one hand a fluid-filled
sheep's intestine and in its other hand, a sort of spear fashioned from "the
hardened vas deferens of an adult man."[25] The supine skeleton resting on the
display base clutches in one hand a mayfly (in Latin, *ephemeris*), to which an
accompanying inscription comments on the brevity of life. A tiny skeleton
to the immediate right of the fiddle player holds in one hand a thin piece of
artery and in the other, a stick fashioned from part of a woman's bladder. At
the extreme left, and standing on its own small pedestal, is an odd object that
looks very much like a vase, in fact the air-inflated *tunica albuginea* that en-
cases the testes, with blood vessels visible, filled with red embalming fluid.

The background is completed by an elaborate, red-fluid-filled arterial and venous forest.

The textual commentaries are of a kind: "What are we, anyway? What remains of us after our death? Oh, see, it is only bone. . . . Oh, fate. Oh, bitter fate! . . . When my life was given to me in the first hour, at that same moment my death was forecast. . . . Oh, how horrible is the condition of men in this life."[26] In still another display (not illustrated here) Ruysch reestablished visually the connectives among anatomy, medicine, and morals via "an infant's leg kick[ing] the cranium of a prostitute, which shows syphilitic changes."[27]

Figure 6.13
Fredrik Ruysch (1638–1731), and C. H. Huijberts (engraver), DECORATIVE-ANATOMICAL DISPLAY: FIVE INFANT SKELETONS (*Thesaurus anatomicus tertius. Het derde anatomisch cabinet,* 1744, plate 1), engraving, 42.1 × 35.5 cm. Minneapolis, Owen H. Wangensteen Historical Library of Biology and Medicine, University of Minnesota.

Ruysch's apparent morbidity parallels his by no means unique fascination with anatomical grotesqueries, in short, with monstrousness, in the form of physical deformity (Figure 6.14). In essence, at the first light of Western modernity, the anatomy of the real replaces the anatomy of the imaginary in medieval art. The demonology of the fabulous and of the dream becomes not only tactile but sought after. Human physiological aberration, part of an undeniable and perceptible reality, needed accounting for, not least of all because it interrupted the logical order of a world supposedly in balance. Aberration gave truth to nightmare; science in turn was needed to return nightmare to the fog of myth, to the unreal. The difficulty of the task is evident in Ruysch's illustration: The representation takes over from the text, and no amount of narrative can quite satisfy the viewer's own physiological thrill at the sight of it—especially when the severed hand is part of a museological display, precisely the sort of object that makes worthwhile the trip to Ruysch's house (the surviving analogues of this in the late twentieth century are "freaks of nature" shows in carnivals). The monstrous is always explicitly visual; it begs to be represented by an image rather than by words that, at best, take so much time to complete the "picture." The true effect of the monstrous is in the immediacy of the shock it produces.[28] In its most affecting forms, the monstrous is presented less to be contemplated than to be literally startling.

Figure 6.14 Fredrik Ruysch (1638–1731) and C. H. Huijberts (engraver), HUMAN HAND DEFORMED BY GROWTHS (*Epistola anatomica, problematica, quarta & decima,* 1732, plate 17), engraving, 23.9 × 34.8 cm. Minneapolis, Owen H. Wangensteen Historical Library of Biology and Medicine, University of Minnesota.

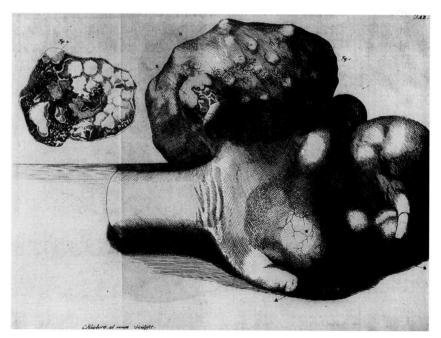

The monstrous tugs against all human claims to human perfection and perfectibility; it restates the ancient religious wisdom regarding the filth and corruption of the flesh. The ennobling principal of human rationality, the bulwark of new science, seemingly demonstrated human godliness. Yet the knowledge that rationality produced brought to light what could not be sufficiently explained—or whose effects could not properly be contained. Two questions remained up for grabs: What *was* the body? What did it *mean*?

Secular heroic and historical paintings (the stuff of myth and legends, kings and courtiers) and also religious pictures (Christ and the saints) embodied greatness in the perfection of idealized bodies, a practice transferred easily into secular portraiture. However, artist-illustrators of anatomy in effect removed the makeup of idealization, and what was left open to view was not simply that the emperor had no clothes. What was made shockingly visible was the body as a universalized *mechanism* about which notions of individuality and identity were, simply, irrelevant. The impact of this realization could never be forgotten; the sight of it changed everything. Art, among other forms of human discourse, was assigned the task of rehumanizing the body and, no less important, particularizing it against the claims of universal sameness. It should come as no surprise that portraiture rose to particular importance at the same moment as anatomical illustration. Art's task, to put it succinctly, was to confront the body after its radical scientific separation from beauty, whether because of its occasional monstrousness or its having been cut apart on the dissection table.[29] The task of anatomy, in contrast, was to cut through the cultural baggage of visual representation—art—to get at what lay behind and supposedly beyond culture. Science claimed essence, culture was left with appearance; the first would come to be increasingly judged true, the latter false—but useful. In reality, which is no surprise, the entire matter was a good deal more complex and paradoxical.

Art into Data

Dutch anatomist Bernhard Siegfried Albinus (1697–1770)— Ruysch's most famous student—and his illustrator Jan Wandelaer moved to secure the transition from art (the body in culture) into science (the body in nature) (Figures 6.15, 6.16). The engravings are paired and bound directly opposite each other on the open elephant folio pages. The image on the right-hand page (Figure 6.15), by established convention, replicates a narrative about death. It shows a skeleton-man gesturing elegantly, standing with his back to the viewer while looking at an elaborate tomb set in a landscape.

Figure 6.15
Bernhard Siegfried
Albinus (1697–1770)
and Jan Wandelaer
(1690–1759, engraver),
SKELETAL FIGURE
STANDING NEAR A
SARCOPHAGUS (from
*Tabulae sceleti et muscu-
lorum corporis humani,*
1747, plate 2, right), en-
graving, 55.5 × 38 cm.
Minneapolis, Owen H.
Wangensteen Historical
Library of Biology and
Medicine, University of
Minnesota.

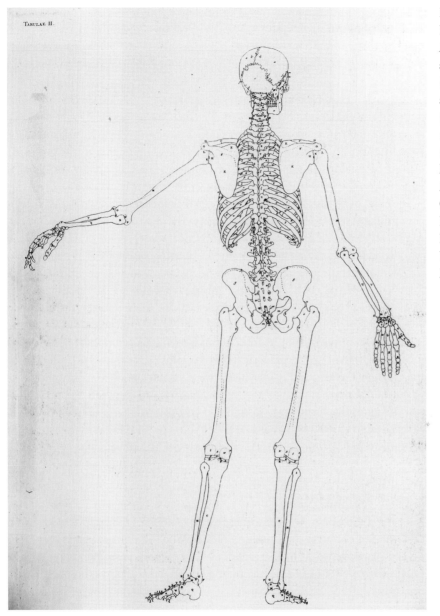

TABULAE II.

Figure 6.16
Bernhard Siegfried
Albinus (1697–1770)
and Jan Wandelaer
(1690–1759, engraver),
SKELETAL FIGURE
(from *Tabulae sceleti et musculorum corporis humani*, 1747, plate 2,
left), engraving, 53.5 ×
38 cm. Minneapolis,
Owen H. Wangensteen
Historical Library of
Biology and Medicine,
University of
Minnesota.

Albinus recorded his explicit concern for perfecting the *beauty* of illustrated figures like this one; he literally saw them as art. The result was accomplished by using as his model an ingeniously preserved skeleton with the connective ligaments still attached, the whole suspended and movable via a system of ropes and pulleys attached to rings embedded in the ceiling.[30] Albinus and his artist-collaborator compared each position of the skeleton to that of a living male model whom he hired to pose naked nearby.

Opposite this image is, in effect, a skeleton of the skeleton, an engraved outline of the same figure (Figure 6.16). Here the narrative implied by a cemetery-landscape setting is expunged in favor of pure information—naming, or the identification of the bones. Whereas in the first image the skeleton maintains the name "man," in the second he loses his identity in favor of the identification of his separate parts. Only the delicate tracing of the gesturing outline of his former self recalls his manhood. The context for his being is gone; he is now merely a catalog, an object of reference.

In many earlier anatomical illustrations that incorporated narrative scenes, the intrusion of "science" was apparent by the inclusion of alphabet letters, Arabic numerals, or other symbols as reference points for an explanatory text. Albinus avoided that by the left-right formatting I have just described. His narrative illustrations contain no such intrusions, and as such, they fall back further into the realm of art. Thus, Albinus's format visually marks the beginning of the end for the age-old connection of art to science. It indicates a growing antipathy—but not as yet a divorce—of the qualitative from the quantitative, of spirit from reason. And not least important, his format delineates this difference on a grid that will eventually be more obvious than is here the case, one on which the "hardness" we now associate with science and the "softness" of the humanities also mark the division between the masculine and the feminine,[31] the mind and the body. The terrain on which these binaries are mapped and confronted on this staging ground for early modernity is the body itself—often, but by no means always, still male.[32]

Fashion and Odor

Dutchman Govard Bidloo's (1649–1713) anatomy treatise is an odd, though elaborate, production. In large folio format, the text is illustrated by 105 plates designed by Gérard de Lairesse, whose prominence as an artist vastly exceeds that of Bidloo's as an anatomist. Yet for all the book's production values, it falls far short of the best anatomical observation of its time yet was too costly a text for the beginner.[33] It is nonetheless a fascinating book due to the impact of its illustrations. Bidloo and Lairesse, in essence, take the dissected body on an alternate route to modernity. Without abandoning the appeal of the body as information, they return it to the domain of spectacle. Put differently, the body-as-anatomized-information is reacculturated. And in the process art *as such* plays a crucial role.

Let us start at the book's beginning. Bidloo's first plate (Figure 6.17) is not anatomy but art: a very "loose interpretation of the original," the *Apollo Belvedere,* at the time among the most famous sculptural survivals from the ancient world and the quintessential cultural example of Renaissance humanism's fascination with the male "body beautiful." Various parts or divisions of the body are marked with letters. Thus the reader begins with what contemporaries regarded as among the most perfect of imagined male bodies—paired, incidentally, with a female counterpart, an antique Venus, on the following plate. Thereafter, Bidloo-Lairesse's illustrated bodies literally deteriorate. In plate 30 (Figure 6.18), for instance, are the partly exposed back muscles of an adult whose residual humanity is encapsulated in the sensitive representation of the fully intact hands, carefully shaded and expressive. The figure is draped so as to appear made nude, and the drapery is distinctly feminine. "She" is located into a narrative hinting of violence and punishment via a rope around the neck holding her up to view and by the thin strings tying her wrists together, which Lairesse carefully models to show how they dig into the flesh. And there is more. The print is colored: The rope and string are brown, the drapery green, and the musculature red. Color, in other words, hints that a story accompanies the image, hence intrudes on science. Colored rope, string, and drapery in a book on anatomy is entirely irrelevant to science. Indeed, it produces a dissonance that smacks of sensationalism associated with execution-mutilations.

In plate 52 (Figure 6.19) the process I am describing is vigorously pursued. In this instance, the drapery at the illustration's bottom is more specific than in the other image. Here it takes on the look of a woman's dress, for it is both patterned and colored; in a word, it resonates *fashion* in brownish-green, pink, and red. And one thing more. Lairesse includes something otherwise utterly extraneous to the putative issue at hand—the rendering of the human body as information for the advancement of science—a common housefly. He colors it brown (it sits on the top edge of the drapery left of center, with the insect's head pointing to the open body cavity). Thereby, the association of the image with that of a beautiful woman (or her portrait) is not so much undercut as mocked: She is now a stinking corpse, soon to be food for maggots, though no visual hint of decay is provided, which would be antithetical to the purported use of the book. Not one of the anatomical images I have previously discussed contains the slightest hint of the olfactory. In this instance, by contrast, smell is not only referenced but morbidly gloried in. The viewer's engagement with looking at the anatomized body is transformed into a confrontation with soon-to-be-rancid meat. The presence of the hand-colored fly, a deep brown present nowhere else in the print, organizes a cultural

Figure 6.17
Govard Bidloo
(1649–1713) and
Gérard de Lairesse
(1641–1711, engraver),
APOLLO AS ANATOMI-
CAL FIGURE (from
*Anatomia humani cor-
poris*, 1685, plate 1),
colored engraving, 44 ×
27.5 cm. Minneapolis,
Owen H. Wangensteen
Historical Library of
Biology and Medicine,
University of
Minnesota.

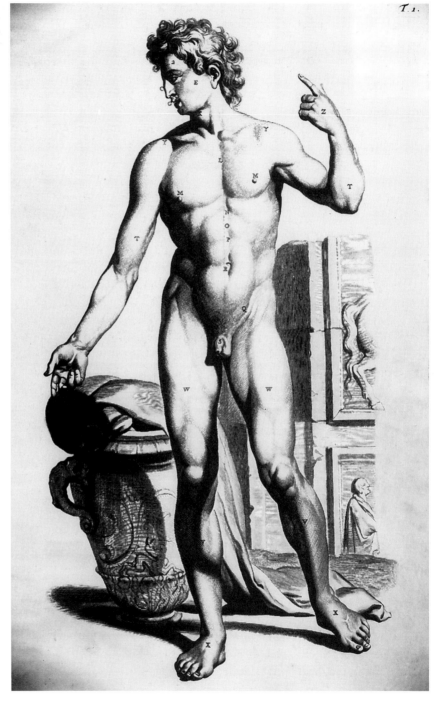

Color Plate 1
John Haberle
(1856–1933), NIGHT
(c. 1909), board,
200.7 × 132 cm. New
Britain, Conn., The
New Britain Museum of
American Art, gift of
Mr. and Mrs. Victor
Demmer, inv. no.
1966.66. Photo:
E. Irving Blomstrann.

Color Plate 2
Jan Brueghel the Elder
(1568–1625), VASE OF
FLOWERS (c. 1609–1616),
panel, 101 × 76 cm.
Antwerp, Koninklijk
Museum voor Schone
Kunsten, inv. no. 643.
Photo © IRPA-KIK-
Brussels.

Color Plate 3
Rachel Ruysch
(1664–1750), FLORAL
STILL LIFE (1686), canvas,
114 × 87 cm. Rochester,
Memorial Art Gallery of
the University of
Rochester, acquired with
contributions made in
memory of Brenda Rown-
tree by her friends and
through the Acquisition
Fund of the Women's
Council and The Marion
Stratton Gould Fund, inv.
no. 82.9.

Color Plate 4 *(opposite)*
Vincent van Gogh (1853–1890),
SUNFLOWERS (1888), canvas,
92.1 × 73 cm. London, National
Gallery, inv. no 3863. Repro-
duced by courtesy of the Trustees,
The National Gallery, London.

Color Plate 5 *(above)*
Philippe de Champaigne
(1602–1674), VANITAS, panel,
28.6 × 37.5 cm. Le Mans, Musée
de Tessé, inv. no. 10.572.
Photo © Musée du Mans.

Color Plate 6 *(above)*
Pieter Aertsen (1505/1509–1575),
THE MEAT STALL (1551),
panel, 124 × 169 cm. Uppsala,
Uppsala Universitet, inv. no. L.1.

Color Plate 7 *(opposite)*
Chaim Soutine (1893–1943),
CARCASS OF BEEF (1925), linen,
114.3 × 78.7 cm. Minneapolis,
The Minneapolis Institute of
Arts, gift of Mr. and Mrs. Donald
Winston and anonymous donor,
acc. no. 57.12.

Color Plate 8
Jacques Gautier d'Agoty
(1711–1785), BACK
MUSCLES (from *Myologie
complètte en couleur et
grandeur naturelle,* 1746,
plate 14), multiple-plate
(color) mezzotint, 60.4 ×
45.8 cm. Minneapolis,
Owen H. Wangensteen
Historical Library of
Biology and Medicine,
University of Minnesota.

Color Plate 9 *(opposite)*
Philippe de Champaigne (1602–1674), PORTRAIT OF
CARDINAL RICHELIEU (c. 1637), canvas, 259.7 × 177.8 cm.
London, National Gallery, inv. no. 1449. Reproduced by
courtesy of the Trustees, The National Gallery, London.

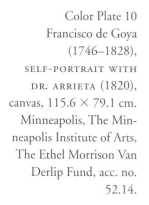

Color Plate 10
Francisco de Goya
(1746–1828),
SELF-PORTRAIT WITH
DR. ARRIETA (1820),
canvas, 115.6 × 79.1 cm.
Minneapolis, The Min-
neapolis Institute of Arts,
The Ethel Morrison Van
Derlip Fund, acc. no.
52.14.

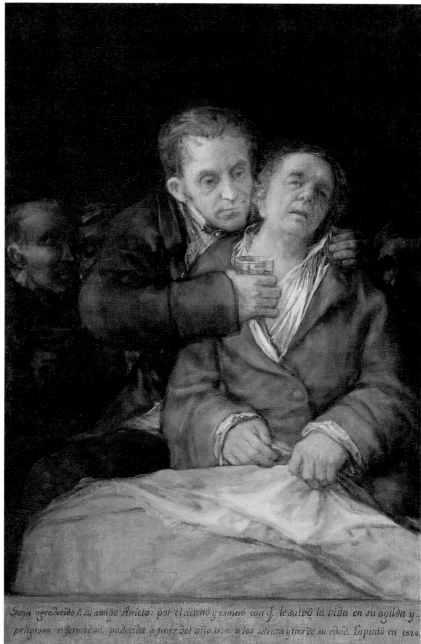

Color Plate 11
Giuseppe Arcimboldo
(1527–1593), RUDOLF II
AS VERTUMNUS (c. 1591),
panel, 68 × 56 cm. Skok-
loster, Sweden, Skokloster
Castle.

Color Plate 12
George Stubbs
(1724–1806), THE
REAPERS (1785), panel,
90 × 137 cm. London,
Tate Gallery, inv. no.
TO2257.

Color Plate 13 *(opposite)*
Jean-Léon Gérôme (1824–1904),
THE CARPET MERCHANT
(c. 1887), canvas, 83.5 × 64.8 cm.
Minneapolis, The Minneapolis
Institute of Arts, The William
Hood Dunwoody Fund,
acc. no. 70.40.

Color Plate 14 *(below)*
Théodore Chassériau (1819–1856),
STUDY OF A NUDE BLACK MAN
(1838), canvas, 54.8 × 73.3 cm.
Montauban, Musée Ingres, inv. no.
867-180. Photo © Musée Ingres.

Color Plate 15 *(opposite)*
Bronzino (Agnolo di Cosimo)
(1503–1572), AN ALLEGORY WITH
VENUS AND CUPID (c. 1540s),
panel, 146.1 × 116.2 cm.
London, National Gallery, inv.
no. 651. Reproduced by courtesy
of the Trustees, The National
Gallery, London.

Color Plate 16 *(below)*
Jean-Auguste-Dominique Ingres
(1780–1867), ODALISQUE WITH
A SLAVE (1839–1840), canvas
mounted on panel, 76.5 × 104
cm. Cambridge, Mass., courtesy
of the Fogg Art Museum, Harvard University Art Museums,
bequest of Grenville L. Winthrop,
acc. no. 1943.251.

Color Plate 17 Jean-Léon-Gérôme (1824–1904), THE SLAVE MARKET (c. 1867), canvas, 84.3 × 63 cm. Williamstown, Mass., Sterling and Francine Clark Art Institute, inv. no. 53.

paradox in the form of a question that to this day finds no satisfactory solution in living reality: Are we subjects or objects?

Erotics of Dissection

Jacques Gautier d'Agoty was an early maker and publisher of colored copper prints of anatomical images. Poorly regarded by historians of anatomical illustration (he himself dabbled in dissection), his work follows an uncertain path between art and science, knowledge and prurience. His work was of little use to the advancement of science, not least because his elaborate, large-scale images, sold in bound sets, never provide visual replication of a complete dissection. Only certain parts of the process are shown. The cutting and probing goes a certain distance, but never surrenders the spectacle of dissection for the scientific knowledge that might be gained from minute, systematic examination. Gautier d'Agoty attempts less to deliver science than visual (and quite morbid) pleasure (Figures 6.20, 6.21, 6.22). Thus the final gigantic prints that close his *Myologie complète en couleur et grandeur naturelle* . . . (Paris, 1745), plates 17 and 18, are of the twinned male-female sexual organs of a hermaphrodite, presented as the climactic visual experience of this volume, whetting the appetite with one print and offering a repeat experience with the next. This contributes an extraordinary and confessional organization to this pictorially ambitious publishing venture.[34]

A man's head and neck in profile (Figure 6.20) is partly flayed to expose musculature. Yet the principal features remain intact—eyebrows, lips, eyes— and they are expressive. The body is half cadaver, half sculptural bust (anatomies did not separate the upper torso and head in the manner represented here). It is anatomically informative but only at a very basic level. At least as apparently important as the anatomical data is the affecting look of the man himself. As his work was of little interest to scientists, Gautier d'Agoty provided wealthy amateurs with private and leisured viewing on sexualized interiorities that no living body could provide in conventional experience: What exudes from print after print is an erotic charge driven by a putatively bloody narrative of which the viewer can make little sense. I stress narrative precisely because his models wear expressions; arguably, their expressivity is as significant as the anatomy they illustrate. Expression is something every person strives to read as a crucial task of life experience; hence, we cannot look at these images without trying to fathom the faces. The expressiveness of figures' features can only make sense, however, in relation to the entirely apparent activity to which they are subject: here, not dissection, but vivisection. Gautier d'Agoty renders anatomy as blood sport.

Figure 6.18
Govard Bidloo
(1649–1713) and
Gérard de Lairesse
(1641–1711, engraver),
WOMAN'S BACK MUS-
CLES (from *Anatomia
humani corporis*, 1685,
plate 30), colored engrav-
ing, 47.9 × 29.8 cm.
Minneapolis, Owen H.
Wangensteen Historical
Library of Biology and
Medicine, University of
Minnesota.

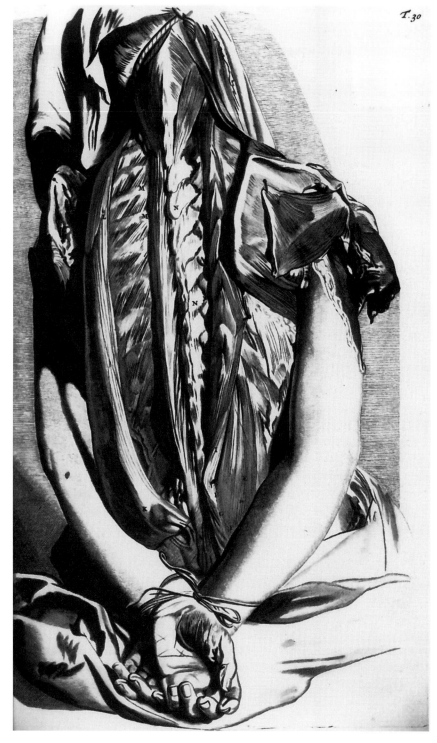

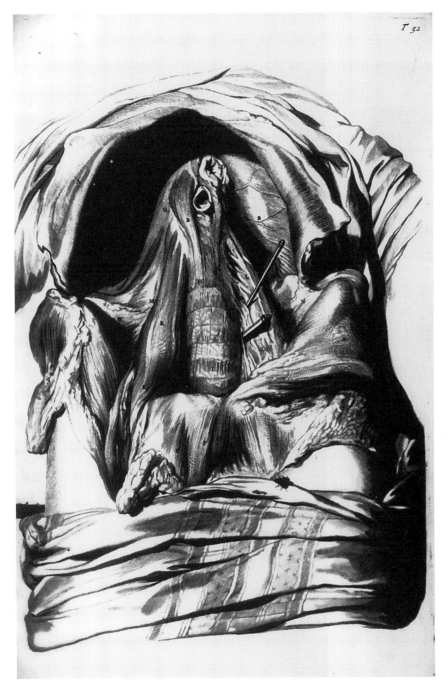

T 52

Figure 6.19
Govard Bidloo
(1649–1713) and
Gérard de Lairesse
(1641–1711, engraver),
WOMAN'S ABDOMINAL
MUSCLES (from
*Anatomia humani cor-
poris*, 1685, plate 52),
colored engraving,
47.3 × 32.1 cm.
Minneapolis, Owen H.
Wangensteen Historical
Library of Biology and
Medicine, University of
Minnesota.

Figure 6.20
Jacques Gautier d'Agoty
(1711–1785), FLAYED
HEAD (from *Myologie
complètte en couleur et
grandeur naturelle*, 1745,
plate 1), multiple-plate
(color) mezzotint,
41.3 × 32.4 cm.
Minneapolis, Owen H.
Wangensteen Historical
Library of Biology and
Medicine, University of
Minnesota.

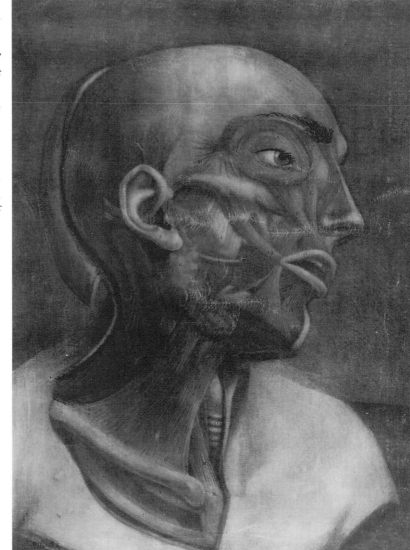

The erotic quotient in Gautier d'Agoty's imagery sometimes directly references sexual attraction. Thus two heads (Figure 6.21), of a man and perhaps of a woman[35] nearly touch, the lips of one to the cheek of the other. They *relate* as a couple. Her eyes are closed; she gestures the kiss. His eyes are open and bright, as though marking his consciousness of her presence. Drapery hides their presumably severed necks and functions simultaneously as clothes or bedding. No actual dissection would place heads in such an arrangement; science is *not* referenced. But her cranium nonetheless is cut open to reveal the brain, and his face is half-removed, though accomplished in such a way as to preserve its expressive character. The semblance of anatomical information, profoundly elementary, plays second fiddle to the thrall of sensationalism for which Gautier d'Agoty strives.

And finally Gautier d'Agoty's tour de force (Figure 6.22, *Color Plate 8*), less a female cadaver than a mutilated nude. Gautier d'Agoty dryly remarks at the beginning of his textual description of this plate that "on y a laisse la Tête pour agrément" (loosely translated, "We left her head intact for your viewing pleasure"). Indeed. She lies not on her stomach, as would be necessary for the dissection of the back muscles, but sits up and peers slightly over her shoulder, as if looking at us looking at her, smiling slightly, altogether not unlike the myriad coy nudes in contemporaneous paintings. Indeed, the intertextual relation between this image and the painted nude is increased by the effect of Gautier d'Agoty's varnishing his prints to give them something of the luster of oil paintings—the prints veritably glisten with a sheen that deepens their colors and contributes to our pleasure in looking. The mutilated woman is alert,

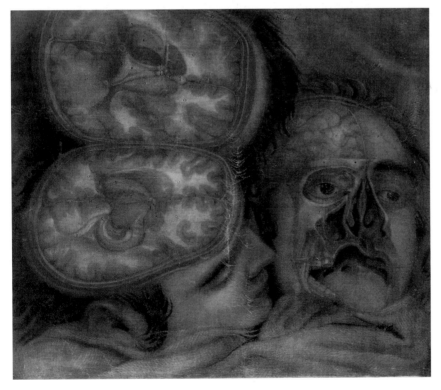

Figure 6.21 Jacques Gautier d'Agoty (1711–1785), TWO DISSECTED HEADS (from *Anatomie de la tête*, 1748, plate 5), multiple-plate (color) mezzotint, 32.7 × 39.5 cm. Minneapolis, Owen H. Wangensteen Historical Library of Biology and Medicine, University of Minnesota.

Figure 6.22
Jacques Gautier d'Agoty
(1711–1785), BACK
MUSCLES (from
Myologie complette en
couleur et grandeur
naturelle, 1745, plate 14),
multiple-plate (color) mez-
zotint, 60.4 × 45.8 cm.
Minneapolis, Owen H.
Wangensteen Historical
Library of Biology and
Medicine, University of
Minnesota.

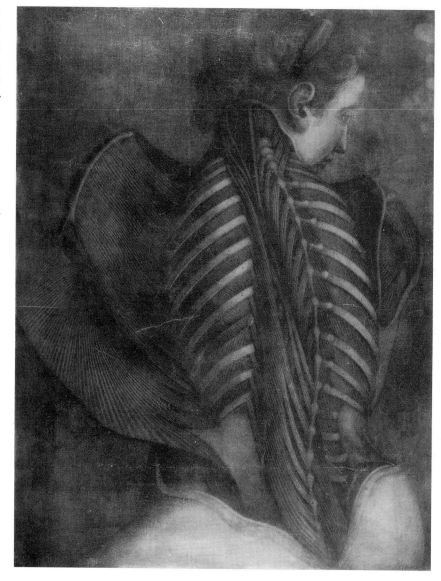

and seemingly made up to receive us, hair carefully coiffed, eyes bright, and
ears pink. She is, in short, *alive* and expressive. She is also predominantly the
color of blood. (Gautier d'Agoty's use of color printing favored red.) The
"wings" formed by her folded-out back flesh and muscles—the Surrealists
named her the "anatomical angel"[36]—seem to vibrate with blood flow,
though not a drop of it is shed by the procedure.

Body as Detritus

With the paintings by Théodore Géricault of human body parts (Figures 6.23, 6.24, 6.25), seen by few people during the artist's own lifetime, we have arrived at an end point in the history of the body.[37] Géricault got his body parts from Parisian hospitals, notably including Bicêtre, whose basement contained the cells to which condemned men and women were sent immediately prior to their executions. After the sentence was carried out, the decapitated bodies were returned to Bicêtre for dissection. Géricault kept the remains in his studio,[38] like Bacon and Soutine in our own century, until decomposition's assault on the visual and olfactory senses became unbearable.

The paintings are as paradoxical as they are visually riveting. In the first instance, once the initial shock of their appearance wears off, we become aware of their painterliness. The component body parts—two heads in one, two legs and an arm in the others—are clearly *arranged* into compositions that are aesthetically evocative despite the subject matter. The paintings are finished

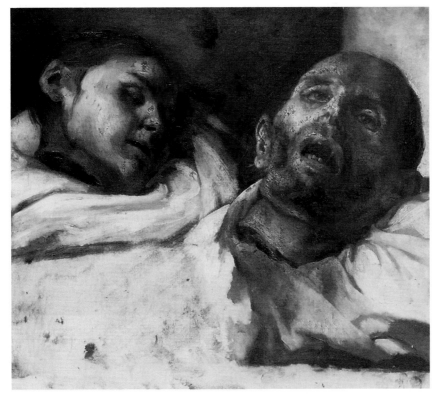

Figure 6.23
Théodore Géricault
(1791–1824),
GUILLOTINED HEADS
OF A MAN AND WOMAN
(1818), canvas, 50 × 61
cm. Stockholm,
Nationalmuseum, inv.
no. NM 2113.

Figure 6.24
Théodore Géricault (1791–1824), TWO SEVERED LEGS AND AN ARM (1818–1819),
canvas, 52 × 64 cm. Montpellier, Musée Fabre, inv. no. 876.3.38. Photo: Frédéric
Jaulmes.

projects, not quick studies. The play of light on the surfaces of skin, set
against a dark and nonspecific background, provides a modeling of the body
parts that gives them a lifelike essence, especially in the case of the limbs, since
it is difficult to otherwise ignore the death-stare of the male head. Uncannily,
the severed remains are made specifically to relate to each other, as one person
might to another, as if in muted defiance of the dehumanization of both execution and dissection. These images may engage contemporaneous debate
over capital punishment in general and the purported humaneness or, conversely, the horrific cruelty, of the guillotine in particular.[39] Thus the relation
of the two heads is that of woman to man, husband to wife, as though in their
connubial bed, covered by bedsheets (the model for the male head was that of
a guillotine victim, whereas the model for the female head was in fact alive,
although Géricault also paints her head as if severed). She turns toward him,
as if in sleep (compare Figure 6.21). Yet their relation is cemented not by love

but by death, made horrific not so much by his gaping mouth and blank stare as by the small strip of bloody neck and the hideously stained sheets. The care with which the painter delineates severed necks, together with the slightly propped up presentation of the heads atop drapery, increases the painting's surreal impact.

Severed necks and bloodstains mark the aesthetics of the horror—that which makes us *want* to look, even to take pleasure in looking. The blood of passion, lovers, and the red rose is here leaked onto white, the color of virginity and the sign of perfect and selfless love. The self-consciousness of Géricault's gesture is evident to us the moment we recall that the blood he painted did not come from direct observation, the result of death by beheading. The head in his possession would have arrived drained of blood; he enlivened it for rhetorical purpose. In other words, Géricault does not, as we might at first suppose, provide us with the body as information, as death data, so to speak. He is assuredly not an anatomist. Ironically, perhaps, given the source of his visual information, he rehumanizes the grotesque remains once the executioner and anatomists are done with them, taking them from the

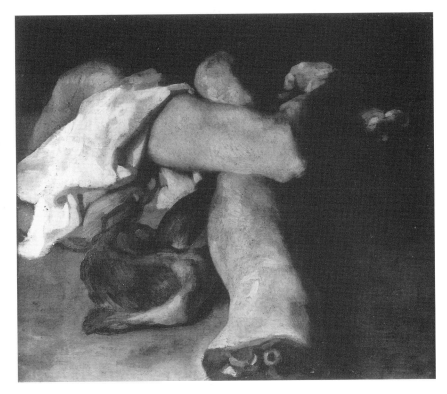

Figure 6.25
Théodore Géricault
(1791–1824), TWO
SEVERED LEGS AND
AN ARM (1818), canvas,
37.5 × 46 cm. Rouen,
Musée des Beaux-Arts,
inv. no. 972.1

garbage heap. Yet he makes no effort to reassemble the bodies, and no purpose could be served by such a perverse act in any case. He decomposes the
body parts and *thereby* makes them human once again.

This is the effect of the severed-limbs paintings (Figure 6.24 especially),
both of which mark the trace of the human by the paradoxical sensuality inherent to the limbs' shared relation.[40] It matters little whether we ascertain
the body parts to be from one person or two (man and woman); the only narrative that would logically account for their apparent relation is a story of
lovers who through their sexual encounter experience life in its most pleasurable, self-affirming, and explicitly social engagement. As if to anchor this
quasi-narrative, Géricault makes a decision to include in both paintings of
severed limbs a bit of cloth, again bloodied, that he drapes around the arm, "a
woman's camisole strap sensuously slipping down her bare shoulder."[41] A moment's reflection tells us that no dissected body entered his studio with rem-
nants of clothing intact; it has been added in order to *mean* something. The
artist focuses his attention, and ours, particularly on the hand and crooked
arm that seem virtually to caress the leg around which it is entwined. The
hand gesture is especially delicate, as though caressing. The bodies in effect
entwine as those of lovers in collapse. The criminal's dissected body thus displays not its guilt but the trace of dignity that the society responsible for passing sentence summarily denied it.

Accordingly, with enormous subtlety, Géricault engages not simply life in
death, but the politics of death, wherein the "sociality" of power in the rawest
form of social discipline destroys what it otherwise claims to save. Géricault
takes to his studio the soon-to-be-stinking detritus of the human body, the
vile body of his society's rejects, usually its poor and downtrodden, and he visualizes what the verdict of the executioner effectively sought to extinguish:
He paints life *and humanity* into the mangled remains. This is literally the
case with the limbs, which still possess the color and texture of flesh nour-
ished by flowing blood, though not so with the male head. Géricault suspends the viewer's visceral revulsion and disgust by transfusing the body
parts, placing them in a state between life and death. By this means, he makes
visual a rhetoric of protest constructed on social contradiction and representational impossibility: an aesthetics of outrage; beauty that means something.

Chapter 7

Portrait: Dramatizing the Body

JOHN EVANS wrote at the end of the eighteenth century in "On the Utility of Paintings":

> A Portrait is the best mean devised by the ingenuity of art, to substantiate the fleeting form—to perpetuate the momentary existence. It is thine, O Painting! to preserve the form, which lies mouldering in the tomb. . . . Portrait-painting subserves. It teaches beneficial lessons. It calls to mind the example of great men, when they are fled beyond the reach of observation.[1]

Portraying in All Seriousness

By definition, portraits are "about" specific people whose identities, and not mere identifications, they serve to establish and perpetuate. Identity, however, commonly understood in terms of personal character, is profoundly abstract, even quasi-spiritual. It is not located in the physical body as such. Challenged to make identity visible—in essence, objectively concrete—portraits must "employ" the physical body as the proving ground of the soul, since the body is the only available terrain onto which the nonphysical can be visualized.

Whether painted or sculpted, portraits have existed since the ancient world, but their production reached particularly staggering numbers only with the advent of the fifteenth-century Renaissance. Principally a genre put to use by people of means and social position, portraits allowed preservation of the look of one's ancestors and immediate family. Serving more than mere commemorative function, they helped concretize family genealogy as an indicator of class status and general worthiness. Indeed, portraits were less a matter of sentiment than common and principal tools of propaganda, most easily recognized in official state portraits of sovereigns. A long gallery filled with the painted evidence of several generations of one's family members operated as proof of long-standing familial importance, due to the prestige—and cost—of oil painting itself. Portraiture was an extraordinarily important business, on which large sums of money were spent—and, for some artists, literal fortunes were amassed.² Always more than monuments to personal vanity, portraits served as primary tools for managing culture. They often did so forcefully, particularly when the political stakes were high.

Confronting the Likeness

Portraits usually confront viewers, to the extent that such images are always ready to be seen: They stand prepared to be looked at. "Essentially *advertent* in form, they show their sitters as turning a persona, decked out and waiting, toward the one who will come and view."³ Philippe de Champaigne repeatedly painted the portrait of Armand Jean du Plessis de Richelieu (1585–1642) (Figure 7.1, *Color Plate 9*, and Figure 7.2), French aristocrat (of lesser nobility, but later given the title of duke), cardinal of the Roman Catholic Church, and longtime chief minister to King Louis XIII. Richelieu was a man of immense power and political ambition. Indeed, during the eighteen years of his service as the king's minister, Richelieu's personal biography was "the history of France and to a large degree that of Europe. His work was directed toward a twofold aim: to make the royal power—his power—absolute and supreme at home, and to crush the rival European power of the Hapsburgs."⁴ Richelieu behaved ruthlessly, mercilessly, toward his political enemies. His appetite for vengeance was well appreciated.

The king himself quailed before that stern, august presence. [Richelieu's] pale, drawn face was set with his iron will. His frame was sickly and wasted with disease, yet when clad in his red cardinal's robes, his stately carriage and confident bearing gave him the air of a prince. His courage was mingled with a mean sort of cunning, and his ambition loved the outward trappings of power as well as its reality; yet he never swerved from his policy in order to win approbation, and the king knew that his one motive in public affairs was the welfare of the realm—that his religion, in short, was "reason of state."⁵

Figure 7.1
Philippe de Champaigne
(1602–1674),
PORTRAIT OF
CARDINAL RICHELIEU
(c. 1637), canvas,
259.7 × 177.8 cm.
London, National
Gallery, inv. no. 1449.
Reproduced by courtesy
of the Trustees, The
National Gallery,
London.

Figure 7.2
Philippe de Champaigne
(1602–1674), TRIPLE
PORTRAIT OF CARDI-
NAL RICHELIEU (1642),
canvas, 58.4 × 72.4 cm.
London, National
Gallery, inv. no. 798.
Reproduced by courtesy
of the Trustees, The
National Gallery,
London.

Richelieu received enormous financial reward for his efforts. His income when he arrived at court in 1617 amounted to 25,000 livres; in his later years it exceeded 3 million. He lived like a prince among princes in his so-named Palais Cardinal in Paris (now the Palais Royal), one of three that he maintained for his use.[6]

In both of the Champaigne portraits reproduced here, the cardinal prominently wears around his neck the Order of the Holy Ghost, established by King Henry III in 1578,[7] an honor whose badge unambiguously marks the link between the church and the French state. Both portraits are specifically "official"—not for the obvious reason that Richelieu would have posed for them but because they conform to a type of facial representation to which he gave specific approval in 1640. Not only did he order that all future portraits be done according to this model, but he also ordered that his earlier images (thus including Figure 7.1) be retouched.[8]

In the full-length portrait, the face occupies only a small fraction of the total composition. It is nearly overwhelmed by the drapery that dominates the composition, most notably the traditional ceremonial red robe denoting Richelieu's elevated church rank. The function of this costume is its aggressive excessiveness. It is so voluminous that its totality cannot be contained within the canvas; the train tails off out of the frame at the lower right. It is not worn for comfort (quite the opposite) but for show, and its showiness is played to the hilt. Champaigne exaggerates the play of light and shadow on the gown, darkening the recesses of its folds to give the whole a sense of almost over-whelming volume and reflecting light off the highlighted surfaces to create a paradoxical hardness, a mark of unapproachability. The drapery at the figure's back, two curtains, one gold and the other royal purple, bring the conven-tional trappings of power and sovereignty into Richelieu's private domain, the working center of his power. His elaborate chair, an entirely conventional symbol of authority, helps anchor this meaning. At the left, there is a view onto a garden. The identification of the space, whether his château at Rueil or the Palais Cardinal, remains uncertain, but what is more important is the sense of place that Richelieu commands: an architecture of authority as con-stituted by the classical pier and arch and a garden of delight in which nature is organized for his private use.

Richelieu's right hand holds his cardinal-bishop's hat. Champaigne draws attention to the hat in two complementary ways. First, he paints it as the brightest object—by far—in the painting, a fire-engine red that makes the cardinal's red drapery seem somewhat dull in comparison. Second, he shows Richelieu holding it far away from his body in a gesture that seems unnatural, hence the more noteworthy. To a degree, the hat's color and the reaching-arm gesture together distract the viewer's gaze from Richelieu himself, the strong line of his outstretched arm leading the eye toward the hat and away from the cardinal's face. Still, the two are connected, that is, the arm establishes a dif-ference but also a linkage. The red hat, standing apart from Richelieu himself, marks the sovereign and independent authority of the church. Thus church and Richelieu are *not* one and the same. Richelieu's apparent reaching for the hat indicates this difference, for a purpose far more important than the value of false humility. It situates the church outside the control of the king and the state, as an untouchable force. It situates Richelieu as the intermediary, as the person who negotiates the crucial relation between church and state. Without church sanction, the king's authority is directly threatened, literally the case at this historical moment, as both Richelieu and Louis XIII knew all too well.

Richelieu's own relation to the hat is crucial, and Champaigne brilliantly captures it. Two clues are noteworthy: the gesture of reaching, and the rela-tion of that gesture to Richelieu's face. It is at this stage that we can begin to understand the centrality of facial representation and grasp why the cardinal seems to have ordered up one official face to show the world repeatedly. The arm gesture suggests the outer limits of reaching, one that if extended further would incorporate discomfort, the suggestion of which would undercut the picture's greater purpose. Yet the reach in particular is crucial in two ways. First, holding the hat at a distance indicates a separation, a distinction, and a threat: "*This* (hat) is the church. *I* am not the church. Note well the difference." The church stands outside its human representative, in which role Richelieu serves. Second, the arm gesture, by its nearly extreme extension, dramatically emphasizes the hat-head relation. The hat is not, in fact, held forever at bay; it "normally" sits on Richelieu's head: "My arm is the link. The hat (church) is mine. You must deal with me. But even after I am gone, the church remains."

The church is symbolized by the hat, but once Richelieu places the hat on his head, as he "promises" to do in the gesture subsequent to the one represented, the abstract power invested in the symbol is made concrete and operational. We must note that Richelieu, however actually immobilized by his costume, appears entirely at ease and relaxed. His hands in particular exude a confidence because of the familiar manner with which they grip both drapery and hat. He "wears" these signs of authority with total familiarity, as though his power is fully entrenched and entirely unthreatened. Accordingly, we are not invited to assume that he will long hold out his arm. On the contrary, we see him for a brief moment when the separation between his person and the church is acknowledged, for the ironic purpose of immediately thereafter inviting us to see the functionality of his enormous power. In France he *is* the church. Yet the portrait carefully encodes Richelieu's own cunning, his awareness that the position he enjoys depends not only on the difference between his person and the church but also on the simultaneous collapsing of that difference in actual daily operation. The paradox is simultaneously a brilliant confirmation of his extreme capability at political maneuvering and a tacit warning, inevitably a threat. One thing more: Richelieu *stands,* a singular mark of his position, to the extent that it notably violates pictorial convention, a fact that would not for a moment be lost on contemporaneous viewers. Church figures were conventionally painted while seated (compare Figure 4.12)—it was *kings* who stood for their portraits.[9]

Putting Face to Threat

And now, the face: The two representations are very alike. But the *Triple Portrait* (Figure 7.2) produces a different effect because of the twin flanking profiles, now oddly resonating with the conventions of police mug shots, and the lack of any background to establish a context or narrative. The *Triple Portrait* was not intended for public display but was created as the model for a sculpture (an inscription on the painting's back indicates that it was intended for Roman sculptor Francesco Mocchi). Showing the head from three angles provides the necessary information for a three-dimensional representation. Champaigne put great effort into getting the face "right"; after all, the *Triple Portrait* was needed to supply a far-off sculptor with all the information pertinent for the proper "look" the cardinal would demand.

In paintings, Richelieu wanted full face, not profile; profiles, after all, severely limit the depth of possible visual characterization to the most basic elements, thus the attraction of profile for use in caricatures. Over the right-side profile an inscription (not reproduced here) indicates that this one is the better of the two. What might this mean? It is very curious, since the sculptor would have no choice but to "supply" both profiles for a sculpture in the round. It cannot be that Champaigne flubbed the left profile, rendering it somehow inaccurate. In that instance he would simply repaint, to make improvements before sending it out. Something more is at stake, central to all portraiture, that goes well beyond accuracy—or rather, that renders accuracy a subsidiary expectation.

The human face is never static—an ironic fact, given the degree of stasis and sameness evident in the various Richelieu portraits. In life as in portraits, we read people first and foremost via their facial features, specifically on the basis of how the living being behind the face consciously or unconsciously molds the face, giving it meaning. In a portrait, however, a "single face" must account for all the complexities of the person represented; it must encapsulate a meaning or set of meanings that define the portrait's very purpose. Portraits are never painted simply to document that "I am" but rather to document that "I mean." Thus for an inscription to be added to the right profile in the *Triple Portrait* indicates two things. It is an acknowledgment, first, that the profile as such presents a problem for official and intended meaning (the front view is preferred); second, that the right profile is the better of the two as a complement to the front view.

The front view in both images is not difficult to fathom: Extreme reserve, seriousness, intelligence, and watchfulness are apparent. The eyes reflect at us uncannily, as if to acknowledge that they see us seeing; the lips are closed and appear slightly tensed, as if signaling judgment. By contrast, the difficulty with either profile is the limitation placed on Richelieu's own act of seeing. That is, everything about the frontal face relates to the eyes and their capacity for taking in information, all of which will be used to Richelieu's own advantage. With the profiles, the commanding power of the eyes is almost entirely undercut. But what the right profile adopts as compensation is a degree of apparent hardness that is less evident in the left profile. This is largely accomplished by the slightly sharper delineation of the right profile's outline and by a greater degree of modeling of the features, emphasizing contours, depth of the wrinkles, and so on. Clearly the two sides of his face were not different in this respect. Champaigne in effect experiments for the sculptor, taking into account the possible play of light in three-dimensional modeling, trying to sort out potential effects. Finally, to our eyes, these distinctions seem minute, perhaps even unconvincing. Yet the extreme degree of subtlety evident in the claim made by the inscription—that the right profile is the better—helps establish for us the enormous challenge facing portrait artists; the slightest change in modeling may adversely alter the identity projected by the sitter. Arguably, the noted distinction between the two profiles is a lesson in what to do and what not to do.

Champaigne's two images certify the painter's own prowess in getting the meaning right, in giving visible form to the self-interest of the sitter. The two pictures also mark the contemporaneous perception of art's function in the day-to-day reality of state politics as highly sophisticated mechanisms of propaganda. The history of portraiture provides ample evidence that the much-lamented cult of personality is no recent invention but is instead a central element in the establishment of certain types of identity as the gold standard for human prowess.

Money and the Look of Modernity

Jan Gossaert's *Portrait of a Merchant* (Figure 7.3) is at pains to anchor the young man's identity in the objects surrounding him and thereby also to explain, justify, and finally valorize his "look." The look is the principal defining characteristic of the sitter's individuality, though it is nonetheless governed by established conventions for representing merchants and bankers. The face is not difficult to read:[10] Before anything else, it conveys wariness, distrust, separation, and privatization.[11] The head is turned slightly away from a perpendicular angle to the viewer, allowing Gossaert to shift the eyes to the straight-on view. This marks the viewer as an interloper, an unexpected intruder into a distinctly private space wherein balance sheets, inventory, and business orders are kept. The viewer enters, as it were, moving up to the desk, whose invisible yet distinct boundary establishes a concrete barrier to going any farther.

Gossaert's painting promises information but actually withholds it. To construct the sitter's identity, the artist surrounds him with paper, not as a sign of literacy, though that is implicit, but as a symbol of an economy of numbers—yet they are numbers that can only be imagined, not actually seen.

Figure 7.3
Jan Gossaert
(called Mabuse)
(c. 1478–1532),
PORTRAIT OF A
MERCHANT (c. 1530),
panel, 63.6 × 47.5 cm.
Washington, National
Gallery of Art, acc. no.
1967.4.1, Ailsa Mellon
Bruce Fund. Photo ©
1995, Board of Trustees,
National Gallery of Art,
Washington, D.C.

The business records that define the man's identity and social position are kept entirely from sight but within his easy reach. It is the very fact that information is his alone that matters. Thus the two stacks of papers hanging on the wall are explained by two labels: "Alrehande Missiven," and "Alrehande Minuten" (miscellaneous letters, and miscellaneous drafts of letters that have been sent). These labels correspond roughly to the In and Out baskets of the modern workstation; they signify the dynamics of commerce. They are the data of record keeping, the "carbons" of the bureaucracy of profit on which his identity as a merchant depends. The man *is* what he *does*. The painter's care to keep every object and every detail in sharp focus helps inform the viewer of just how much private information is within the man's reach (but not within ours)—and which if necessary he can ponder still more carefully with the magnifying glass next to him. The physical space he occupies is designed for writing, in a culture where the paper trail of emerging economic bureaucracies first took firm hold, the great northern trading centers. The man is writing, copying from a handwritten bound volume—a distinctly private ledger of sorts and not a printed, hence public, text. In fact, the painting overdetermines the act of writing by including no fewer than five pens. The conventional inclusion of a pair of scales and some gold coins is virtually superfluous here as the badge of the merchant or banker.

The image is profoundly modern to the extent that it visualizes a world order in which the concentric social circles of mutual dependence defining medieval feudalism are giving way to aggressive individualism—what will eventually be named economic and social Darwinism, the competitive "survival of the fittest." Gossaert provides the sitter with an identity defined by extreme self-control; he is a man of all business. The physical reserve characteristic of nearly all portraits comes across in this instance as highly self-conscious and specifically determined. The man's face exudes hardness as an enviable quality. In the end, everything resonates with the face, sharply lighted from the upper left and entirely framed by a dark band insuring no competition for rhetorical significance. This notwithstanding, the objects that in turn frame the dark band provide the necessary gloss to the face, without which he would remain a cipher. The objects work to translate him into the vulgate of a rapidly changing present: The light on his face is distinctly cool (crucial to producing the effect of unapproachability), whereas that on the painting's many objects is quite warm by comparison, the familiar warm light characteristic of early Flemish art in the Jan van Eyck tradition.[12] Light in this instance manifests profound social and political change. Light warms to objects and cools to the person. As a result, the viewer's ability to identify with the representation is redirected along a modern, if not necessarily admirable, pathway. The merchant's identity is valorized by his appearing *less* human (more a hard, cold, and calculating *object*). Objects themselves are made to appear warmer, hence more invested with the quality of being "alive"; this is especially obvious with the man's expensive and highly elaborated costume. It is made desirable for what it is. The man is desirable for what he has. The value of identity is visually transferred from the person to what he possesses.

Whereas the elaborate gown worn by Richelieu (Figure 7.1) functions principally as a symbol, that worn by the merchant functions as fashion.

Portraying the Self

Francisco de Goya's *Self-Portrait with Dr. Arrieta* (Figure 7.4, *Color Plate 10*), painted nearly two centuries after the Richelieu portraits and nearly three centuries after that of the young merchant just discussed, is profoundly different in both look and meaning from these others. It provides us with an opportunity to sort out the crucial role that function or purpose plays in what the viewer sees. Self-portraits by their very nature look inward. That is, whereas all portraits strive to mark identity and not mere likeness, official portraits like Richelieu's (Figure 7.1) also attempt to take in the viewer during the viewer's act of looking. The viewer, in other words, paradoxically becomes an object of surveillance. But in self-portraiture the viewer stands at a greater metaphorical distance from the image, to the extent that the painter's task is distinctly personal, sometimes to a degree that the viewer might seem almost, but never quite, irrelevant. Self-portraiture does not respond to the concerns of a patron but to those of the self. The self-portrait's immediate audience involves the painter as his own subject—as viewer of the self "being made." The gap ordinarily separating producer from consumer is collapsed.

Goya's painting is a hybrid, since it is at once a portrait of someone else and a self-portrait. It was given as a gift to his physician, Dr. Eugenio Garcia Arrieta, whom Goya credited with saving his life after a brief but serious (and unknown) illness—it was the last of his self-portraits. The painting carries an inscription in Spanish at the bottom, a textual label that identifies the sitters and helps forestall the forgetting that characterizes the fate of most portraits' sitters—ironically, the very thing that portraits are intended to prevent. Equally important, the inscription supplies an interpretation for the painting. Its text translates: "Goya gives thanks to his friend Arrieta for the expert care with which he saved his life from an acute and dangerous illness which he suffered at the close of the year 1819 when he was 73 years old. He painted it in 1820."[13] The inscription is highly specific: It names the actors, establishes date and age, gives thanks, and certifies the date of its execution. However, it accomplishes all this in a highly impersonal, matter-of-fact way that parallels a catalog entry. Only the handwriting personalizes the statement.

Viewers commonly confront labels in museums next to paintings. At the least they provide basic identification, but more and more frequently they elaborate on the image. Either way, they remain extraneous to the image it-

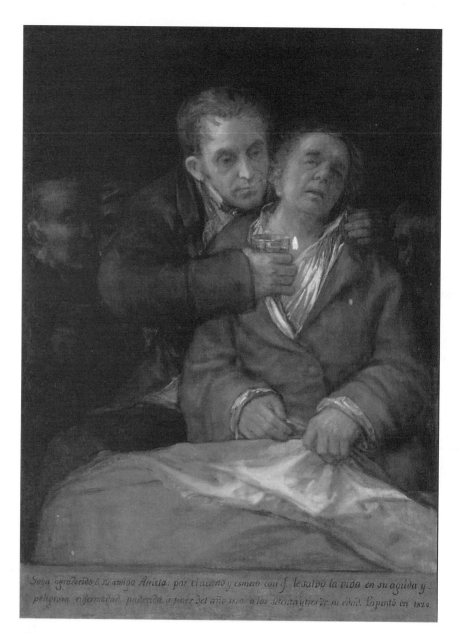

Figure 7.4
Francisco de Goya (1746–1828), SELF-PORTRAIT WITH DR. ARRIETA (1820),
canvas, 115.6 × 79.1 cm. Minneapolis, The Minneapolis Institute of Arts, The
Ethel Morrison Van Derlip Fund, acc. no. 52.14.

self. But the intrusion of language directly *onto* the visual field of a painting is a different matter, since this virtually demands the viewer's attention. Writing on the painting's own surface requires the viewer's eyes to shift back and forth between two competing forms of representation, one visual and the other linguistic. What a painting may gain from the presence of words as anchors for intended meaning may all too easily be lost by the distraction of having something to read. Text, in other words, comes to painting with a bill attached. Goya mitigates this difficulty by very evidently "personalizing" the writing. It is in his own aged hand; and it is made to appear as if it were almost a fragment from a letter—note how the inscription resembles a piece of manuscript separate from the painting. Fred C. Licht suggests, convincingly, that the inscription resonates with then-popular ex-voto religious paintings that represent a person in a catastrophic situation together with a statement that characterizes the event and acknowledges the divine intervention that saved the day.[14]

Relatively little of the painting's surface demands notice; ironically, in due course this becomes quite noticeable. In comparison to the standing portrait of Richelieu, where detail, or surface clarity, is crucial to the characterization of the cardinal's power, Goya's painting blurs every detail but two. All of the artist's attention is focused on two heads and two pairs of hands; that is all— and everything: an extraordinary achievement of portrait and self-portrait characterization. Bedding, clothing, and the mysterious background characters[15] are there to a degree sufficient only to clarify their presence and hence to help establish a narrative supporting the painted inscription.

Concerning the hands: In essence the most important of the hands is compositionally situated at the painting's very center; Arrieta's hand grasps a glass filled with medicine for Goya to drink. Exuding strength, it is distinctly masculine, a bit large and obviously strong, and attached to a large arm. Its mate is very different, about which Goya makes a powerful visual point. Only partly visible, this other hand virtually caresses the infirm artist. It touches Goya's shoulder with an extreme delicacy of the sort usually reserved for lovers. Thus the strength and resolve of the hand holding medicine for the body is matched and complemented by the hand whose gesture provides medicine for the soul. Arrieta's hands in turn are set in a binary relation to Goya's. The artist's own hands, very carefully painted, are large but robbed of strength, accomplished by showing them grasping weakly at the bedclothes with the first joints of the fingers.

Portraits characteristically deemphasize the representation of strong emotions or reactions. Usually excluded, for example, are facial signs of "surprise, disgust, sadness, anger, fear, and happiness" in favor of some unnameable foundation of true character, as opposed to fleeting response. What we are left with is what Richard Brilliant names "masks of convention," that both reveal and hide—in art and sometimes in our outward behaviors—"self-imposed disguises allowing the wearer to impersonate someone, even himself, in a favourable guise."[16] Arrieta's fully frontal face is almost entirely illuminated by the light that enters from the left. The face is uncomplicated. It exudes one emotion, caring, an effect increased by his virtual embrace of Goya, but it is also a professional care, less that of a friend, in other words, and more that of a healer (Goya on other occasions had produced scathing images of physicians as quacks). This is a subtle compliment: Arrieta cares for the sick, who *in this instance* is Goya, but Goya himself is not a special case. I think that this accounts for the slight reserve in Arrieta's features.

The artist's own features are sharply different and deeply complex, partly due to all that is involved in the representation of the self no matter what the circumstances. However, an image replicating one's own confrontation with death meets the issue of identity with particular poignancy. Further, the self-portrait in old age demands the representation of self-evaluation when there is little opportunity to go back; the matter of "last remarks" hangs heavy. (Rembrandt's self-portraits in old age are among the most profound of this sort.) Yet in Goya's last self-portrait something a bit different seems to occur. The painting does not actually penetrate deeply into the insights that old age can offer, though it probably lets us know that these insights are buried within Goya's being. Instead it emphasizes exhaustion, an ebbing of strength when breath itself is a struggle. The face, in short, manifests not only suffering but the inward turning that suffering near death often brings, when what is revealed is that which cannot be spoken. In part Goya accomplishes this by the way he paints the two men's eyes. Arrieta's are open, almost too widely perhaps, and his eyebrows and the bags under his eyes are rounded so that the full effect is riveting. These are eyes that see with the advantage of full physical vitality. Goya's eyes are mostly closed and his head is leaning back and toward the right, so that we see that he can see little; darkness closes in. The two men's emotions are complementary, not least because the depth of revealed feeling is so rarely represented in art.

In the end, however, the painting remains a painting: Goya, having recovered his health, paints a picture of himself on the brink of death and for the benefit of his physician. But through the act of painting Goya reclaims his own agency, his strength and vitality, as a man and as an artist. He reclaims his own identity— utterly dependent upon his life as a painter—by painting. When our looking occurs we do not in the end marvel at Arrieta's countenance or his gift to Goya. We marvel at Goya himself, both at the Goya in the painting and the Goya standing outside it, laying claim to the work in which he locates the very identity that self-portraits are charged to provide. Walter Benjamin points out that "the portrait becomes after a few generations no more than a testimony to the art of the person who painted it."[17] With self-portraits this is the situation from the start.

Transformations

A basic requirement for a portrait is that its sitter be recognizable to its original and intended audience. Most portraits produced between the sixteenth and early twentieth centuries attempted to accomplish recognizability by mimesis, that is, by matching or approximating fundamental aspects of the specific "look" of the persons portrayed. Yet as obvious as this might seem, the parameters within which painters worked to accomplish such recognition were very wide and, in fact, were seldom a matter of mere "copying" in paint. Indeed, the conventional boundaries of portrait representation were sometimes pushed against very forcefully, and occasionally exceeded, well before the abstract and expressionistic portraits of the early twentieth century. A case in point is the work of Giuseppe Arcimboldo (1527–1593) (Figure 7.5, *Color Plate 11,* and Figure 7.7), who served for many years as painter to the Hapsburg Court in Vienna and Prague during the reigns of Ferdinand I, Maximilian II, and finally, Rudolf II.[18] Arcimboldo's paintings provide the opportunity to demonstrate in particularly dramatic fashion that portraiture's principal function has far less to do with marking *who* someone is than *what* that person is—or at least would claim to be.

If we compare Arcimboldo's painting (Figure 7.5) to Hans von Aachen's portrait of Rudolf II (Figure 7.6), it is reasonably clear that the sitter was the same person in both instances, though his identity would in fact be very difficult to establish on grounds of mimetic relation alone. In the painting's original setting, however, no problem over identification would occur. The "right" people (at court) would know exactly who Arcimboldo had in mind; the sitter's identification would have been a given. The first task of establishing identification accomplished, the portrait's real work—composing identity—may begin: first by denotation, then by connotation. However, with the work of Arcimboldo, denotation—conventionally the elementary part of portraiture—is made an issue. In *Rudolf II as Vertumnus* the sitter is demarcated indirectly, by assembling into the form of a likeness a group of objects that have already acquired a set of functions and meanings entirely separate from Rudolf himself.[19] Arcimboldo's constructed head is a horticultural and agricultural concoction that may resemble Rudolf but hardly looks like him—to the extent that we can never *not* see the individual objects of which he is composed. Like all portraits, but demonstrated in an especially dramatic manner, this portrait is not "about" Rudolf's identification but about his

Figure 7.5
Giuseppe Arcimboldo
(1527–1593), RUDOLF
II AS VERTUMNUS (c.
1591), panel, 68 × 56
cm. Skokloster, Sweden,
Skokloster Castle.

identity—marked as a public and political issue. Precisely by radically denaturalizing the portrait process, Arcimboldo's picture reminds us that representation is the visual enactment of a *strategy*.

Von Aachen's portrait, painted about a decade after Arcimboldo's, produces no surprise. In its own time it might have neatly fitted a gallery's walls along with dozens of others more or less like it, a large memory album wherein no one in particular among the privileged and powerful sitters particularly stood out. By contrast, Arcimboldo's image, harder to fix as regards identity once taken from its intended setting, does not fit. Then as now, it steps forth, demanding attention. In museums we commonly tend not to spend much time focusing on portraits, especially if a number of them are hung together—as was commonly also the case when portraits were hung in palaces. They tend to blend together, a little like faces in an old high-school yearbook. But most viewers coming upon an Arcimboldo for the first time are caught in its commanding appearance, the purposeful result of its unconventional rhetoric. *Rudolf II as Vertumnus,* by Arcimboldo, gathers us before it and has its say—makes its speech. Portraits by their very nature are propaganda; they function, and justify the expenditures to produce them, as ex-

Figure 7.6
Hans von Aachen
(c. 1552–1615),
PORTRAIT OF RUDOLF
II (c. 1603–1604), canvas, 60 × 48 cm.
Vienna, Kunsthistorisches Museum, inv.
no. 6438.

Figure 7.7
Giuseppe Arcimboldo
(1527–1593), THE
LIBRARIAN (early
1570s), canvas, 97 × 71
cm. Skokloster, Sweden,
Skokloster Castle.

pensive and highly specialized advertising for the sitter (the sometimes notable exceptions are artists' self-portraits). In this instance, Rudolf II got his money's worth.

Such images were produced for more or less captive audiences, people with access to the court. Part of the image's success lay in the sitter believing what the painter said of him (flattery is usually irresistible), but the rhetoric was necessarily more generally directed. The "statement" needed to be convincing, or to be imagined to be convincing, to others. Arcimboldo's achievement to no small degree lies in two closely related elements: his technical ability to paint and his intellectual acumen in conjuring up, probably with assistance, an extraordinarily imaginative allegory by means of which the composite head of Rudolf II *is* what he has accomplished and not merely a reflection thereof.

Arcimboldo had earlier painted two series of four composite heads, one devoted to the seasons and the other to the elements (Earth, Air, Fire, Water). Although highly imaginative metaphors for physical creation and time, these images are not likely portraits of specific individuals. *Rudolf II as Vertumnus* in essence compresses the "nature head" type with the royal portrait. Rudolf II portrayed as Vertumnus becomes protector of the garden and the orchard, the deity of the changing seasons.[20] The result is distinctly political. Rudolf II is conflated with the essence of the elements and the seasons, with the dynamism and vitality of Nature. Thereby, the head of state in effect becomes (a) head of everything, a microcosmic manifestation and encapsulation of the macrocosm itself. "Fruits and flowers from all seasons flourish in harmony in Rudolf's face, suggesting not only the peace, prosperity, and harmony of his clement beneficent reign, but that the eternal spring of the new Golden Age is to come with his rule, as this image portends."[21] Time's threat, as the ultimate guarantor of death, is suspended in favor of a bountiful and timeless simultaneity, the end of history, as it were, the closest thing to heaven on earth.[22]

We might raise a considerable objection to this quite preposterous bit of puffery. We might point out that the painting is, well, funny. Indeed, but humor has its purpose. Admittedly, the smile that comes to our face as we stare at this garden-concoction of a man is in part related to its being funny-looking. But our smile, or our laugh, is a recognition of the ingenuity very much in evidence. Wit, so to speak, marks itself everywhere on the panel. And in the Renaissance, a period of highly self-conscious premodern statecraft (Machiavelli's time), wit functioned as a mark of intelligence, wisdom, and insight. Baldassare Castiglione, for example, makes this clear in his famous treatise on the ideals of courtly behavior, *Il Cortegiano* (1528, *The Courtier*). Wit was that faculty that sought out resemblances and connections between things, the more obscure the better to demonstrate one's powers of thought and language. Arcimboldo's paintings are manifestations of his own wit, to be sure, but they serve to claim wit for his patron as well. To paint the emperor, with his knowledge and approval, as a composite of vegetables and flowers assumes and demonstrates both the sovereign's own appetite for wit and the security of his political position. No ruler uncertain of his hold on power would permit, let alone commission, a painting that might evoke laughter. Arcimboldo's wit is part and parcel of Rudolf's imaginary Ministry of (Self-) Defense and Information. A man who "spoke" well on behalf of the sovereign was invited to tell Rudolf's story.

Arcimboldo's bust of a librarian (Figure 7.7) shifts gears to emphasize the comic.[23] The image's wit is derived from Arcimboldo's making the man appear as a composite of the objects defining his occupation: The librarian literally is what he does, though no serious allegory develops from this conceit. Comedy is emphasized by Arcimboldo's giving the man rather too much the face of a monkey, perhaps bringing to mind the academic pedant. The man's book-torso simultaneously looks like a pile of books being carried into the room by a befuddled functionary, brought home by Arcimboldo's draping a curtain over the man's shoulder as though he were unable to push it aside since his hands were full. Still, the painting's comedy serves a greater function than purposeless laughter. It pays an explicit compliment to the emperor, who is indirectly referenced at the librarian's expense. Arcimboldo painted for a select courtly audience, no one among whom would have forgotten for a moment who owned the tomes from which the librarian is fashioned—and presumed ownership is a far weightier matter than the knowledge the books might contain. Arcimboldo offers not a clue—no titles appear on the spines.

Consider this painting's impact on the viewer. It manipulates us psychically, like all images, but physically as well. And by this means, in spite of the mirthful response the image elicits, the painting demonstrates the power of representation *and* the power of those who control representation. As we confront *The Librarian,* our bodies move, and not only our eyes. The act of looking is always one of deciphering: What is it I see? Viewed close up Arcimboldo's painting seems like the agglomeration of closely related things. It is when we step back—and this is a metaphorical as well as physical necessity when viewing the actual painting—that we can perceive the "unity" for which the composite strives, a "human" form. "In short, Arcimboldo's painting is *mobile:* it dictates to the 'reader,' by its very project, the obligation to come closer or to step back, assuring him that by this movement he will lose no meaning and that he will always remain in a vital relation with the image."[24] But the meanings change as we move near or step back. What we see is unstable. In the end, Arcimboldo's "portrait" denotes ambiguity and paradox, while claiming status as a spectacular manifestation of and invitation to the scopic realm—ironically a realm in which certainty (seeing is believing) gives way to doubt, where what is revealed remains hidden. What remains constant and certain is the performance of painting itself.

Chapter 8

Others' Bodies:
Class and Race

THE RHETORICAL TRADITIONS of Western painting have long traded in the coin of social class and racial difference as a principal means of marking human value. Thus there is a radical distinction between portraits, whether of individuals or small groups, and scenes from everyday life, especially those involving the lower social orders, representing not individuals, but types—simply "people" defined en masse. As the English in the eighteenth century charmingly put it, those defined by bloodline and pocketbook were "The Quality"; everyone except this tiny minority was, in essence, The Non-Quality. Pictorial practice handled the distinction by means of comparisons that were characteristically encoded onto the physical bodies of those represented.

Body Type and the Representation of Social Harmony

Sir William Beechey's portrait of two upper-class children giving alms to a beggar boy (Figure 8.1) is archetypal, if heavy-handed, in its delineation of class difference. Beechey's painting was unquestionably commissioned by the children's father, Sir Francis Ford, with whom the artist would have discussed the picture's size (portrait cost was significantly determined by size), the setting, and the putative narrative situation. The presence of the beggar boy, in other words, came with the approval of the man paying the bill. A specific and "legible" rhetoric must be assumed. That is, the painting has a textual intentionality that necessarily goes something like this: "My chil-

dren are sensitive and good, attuned to what they have and what others less fortunate have not; I've taught them to give alms freely and willingly." Behind this perfectly obvious narrative, however, lie other stories informed less by intentions than by cultural practices, social attitudes, and the means of representing both. For the principal and intended narrative to be evident, in other words, other submerged narratives must operate, otherwise the image cannot make sense to its intended audience. At least three "submerged" and interlocking narratives occur that involve bodies in opposition; space conceived as

political; and time understood as a specifically social, and not merely chronological, dimension.

Beechey represents extremes of costume difference. The beggar boy is shoe-
less; his clothing is in tatters and does not fit his growing body. His walking
stick and mongrel pet are the clichéd signs of his homelessness and wander-
ing rootlessness. His dog is posed so as to appear walking, and its momentary
looking back serves as a visible sign that a journey (to nowhere) has been
halted, for alms. The child intrudes into the physical space of the Ford estate.
(The landowning English beheld the geographically unstationary underclass
with special alarm as a potential threat to the social order organized around
property.) Although the boy is a creature of the outdoors, *this* outdoors is not
his own.

The Ford children, similarly posed as in then-popular husband-and-wife
portraits set on estate grounds, stop the beggar's forward advance. The bodies
of the girl and the beggar incline toward each other, outlining a kind of compositional circle whose center is given to the dramatic, all-governing gesture
of a single coin changing hands. Compositionally, the painting radiates outward from the visible driving principle of money and its possession, the fetish
of one's greater worth, and the guarantee of individuality. We know who the
Ford children are; the identity of the boy who modeled as the beggar, if ever
known to Sir Francis Ford and his family, is entirely irrelevant.

The two boys' bodies are arranged differently. The poor child is significantly taller, the better to bend him more dramatically from his knock-knees
and from the waist. He is made to appear both weak and, equally important,
submissive. His hair unkempt, one hand stuck inside his shirt as if for
warmth, he engenders his misery and the misery of his station, all of which is
opposed by the other boy. Young Ford, smartly, even dashingly dressed,
stands posed like a Gainsborough gentleman, at ease and entirely comfortable
in his own surroundings. The larger boy poses no threat to him or to his self-
confidence. His sister, like a properly deferential female of her social class and
time, keeps such a distance from the young male intruder that she has to lean
forward to extend the coin. The faces are very different, as we would expect,
but most interesting for my purposes are the eyes and where they look. The
Ford children look directly at the beggar boy, whereas his eyes are not allowed
to confront theirs. His face marks shame.

The time required for the encounter is an instant and no more. The painter
signals this fact redundantly. No real social encounter between the two classes
of children can be so much as hinted. Thus the dog, its tail between its legs in
both fear and deference, barely halts its advance. The sky is threatening,
hence the Ford children must quickly retreat to the house. The girl's pose is

very unstable; her weight is shifted forward onto one foot and must immediately be rebalanced. Finally, the gestures of reaching and taking, involving the coin, serve less to establish a link between the boy and girl than to mark precisely the opposite. The proximity of their hands will last no longer than the time required for the coin to drop. And Beechey is careful to show that their fingers will never touch.

The beggar presents a pictorial challenge to the extent that his presence draws attention away from the Fords. But the risk was obviously deemed worth taking. The presence of the Other—the Not Us—provides a visual measure by which distinctions of social and cultural merit may be drawn. To be greater, in other words, the lesser *must* be acknowledged. The danger to the greater that is posed by the lesser's presence may be circumscribed by limiting the latter's agency, a task Beechey attempted via the usual, rather fanciful, beggar's costume and theatrical pose (a beggar from Central Casting) and with greater subtlety and skill via his handling of the rhetorics of spatial relations and time.

The Animalistic Other

Social class differences, mapped onto bodies, were often incorporated in seventeenth-century allegorical paintings whose narratives were complex, hence requiring contemplative response and, in fact, special knowledge. One example will suffice, a portrait commemorating a marriage (Figure 8.2) produced in 1633 by the Dutch artist Jan Miense Molenaer.[1] In this instance, the allegory concerns the demand for marital fidelity and employs music as the principal device by which to mark this virtue. Specifically, the self-restraint and measure required for a musical ensemble to perform harmoniously substitutes visually for the order, self-regulation, temperance, and fidelity required in marriage. This is stressed most notably by the woman sitting in the middle holding a part book, at once singing and marking time with her right hand, a gesture that serves to keep together an ensemble that includes a lutenist and cellist. Reinforcing this theme, a male figure, standing directly behind that woman, in a spectacular, indeed, preposterous gesture borrowed from a contemporaneous print representing the virtue Temperance, pours water from a jug into a wineglass at his side. The importance of this detail is evident not only from the singularity of the man's action but also from the prime compositional location of the pitcher at the upper center of the picture.

The painting's thesis concerning marital temperance is both defined and clarified by its being set against a subsidiary antithesis—intemperance. An-

Figure 8.2
Jan Miense Molenaer (c. 1610–1668), A MUSICAL PARTY (ALLEGORY OF
FIDELITY IN MARRIAGE) (1633), canvas, 99.1 × 140.9 cm. Richmond, Virgina
Museum of Fine Arts, inv. no. 2542, The Adolphe D. and Wilkins C. Williams
Collection.

tithesis is shown in two vignettes: one in the background at the extreme left,
where two men in small scale stab each other with knives, hence representing
anger (*ira*); and one in the foreground at lower left, where a chained monkey
ridiculously embraces a cat, representing enslavement to the senses and to
pleasure—in a word, lust, the cat being a common symbol of libidinous temperament. The cat and monkey are offset by the dog (*fides,* or fidelity), standing guard by the newlyweds. P.J.J. van Thiel comments that the picture is a
"mirror of virtue" for the husband and wife alike, what he terms a "key to an
harmonious married life."[2]

I wish to pursue two additional points closer to my own concerns. First,
moderation or temperance is articulated as a class issue. Moderation is a possibility for and the obligation of the upper classes. It is the peasants who are

violent and who behave with anarchical excess; hence, they are threats to themselves and to the social order whose calm they disturb. The painting's sights engender sounds in opposition: namely, the sounds of art music versus the sounds of brutality, for fights are punctuated by animal-like grunts and groans and often by cries of pain. The painting invites, perhaps even compels, its viewers to *envision* and to *hear* the difference between chaos and order, the antisocial and the social, the lower class and the upper class. Sonority therefore serves a social parameter whose representation provides a means of delineating class difference—ironically so, considering that painting is a medium of actual silence.

In the main part of the image, where the musical performance takes place, sonority is accorded privilege, even though we cannot actually hear any sound. This is so because of the visually commanding presence of the instruments, the lute and violoncello. They are striking objects in a painting in which every object included has been carefully chosen; and they occupy considerable, and compositionally prestigious, pictorial space. By contrast, the fighting peasants, whose sounds in reality would doubtless greatly overpower and upset the musical tranquility of the main scene, command attention only by the visual incongruity; even as a small detail, their inclusion is striking—and purposely worrisome. They possess what the well-to-do burghers had to surrender in exchange for their status and their art: physicality, though vested in squat, somewhat *lumpen* bodies, entirely unlike the svelte and elegant figures of their class superiors. The peasants' movements are spontaneous and unpredictable, whereas those of their betters are planned and constrained. Indeed, the spatial logic enshrined in the paved terrace on which the central characters stand helps emphasize the opposite of spontaneity.

The vignettes of watering down the wine, of the monkey and cat, and of the dog are fundamentally emblematic.[3] Their function in this image is clear. They are presented to the viewer as allegorical because something about each of them simultaneously registers a visual slippage from lived experience and appears to participate in a narrative. In reality, watering wine in the manner represented would produce a mess; monkeys and cats do not embrace; dogs, of course, do stand guard, like Molenaer's, but his painted dog, with its exaggerated stiffness, takes on symbolic character.

I think there are two reasons for incorporating music, the importance of which is sufficiently great to require Molenaer to locate the newlyweds well off the center at the painting's right side. First, music's association with love and sexuality was entirely enshrined in the culture and had been for many centuries. Marriage was the approved locus for sexuality and for the sexual availability of the woman. Music as an expression of desire, and as a well-practiced device for the production of desire, was fully theorized and valorized. Ribald song texts, not to mention the literary feast of Dutch proverbs, preserve such references in abundance, just as numerous published Calvinist diatribes condemned them and the practices they described.[4]

The second reason, I think, has to do with class difference. The practice of art music in the Dutch seventeenth century was increasingly emerging as an important component of class distinction in a world rapidly changing from a feudal order to a mercantilist, precapitalist order. Medieval economic stasis was being replaced by economic dynamism, by the building of new fortunes. However, the cultural implications of these changes were being invented as the socioeconomic changes occurred, following the successful separation from the rigidly feudal political hegemony of conservative Spain during the religious wars of the late sixteenth and early seventeenth century.[5] Dutch culture was middle-class in the ways that historically later determined what that term meant in the West generally. Dutch culture created for itself the challenge of class self-definition. It is not surprising that the habits it adopted included conspicuous consumption, in which it effectively aped the acquisitional habits of the European aristocracy, even though the price paid was enormous guilt.[6]

Music was a prime component of the new habits—visually, in the form of expensive musical instruments; sonorically, in the music that was played. The music was increasingly sophisticated and complex, inevitably composed and notated, and collected in printed form. Expensive musical instruments made with precious or rare materials (exotic woods, ivory, silver, and so on) were clear signs of excess wealth. Because they did not "do" anything except produce sound, they were perfect signs of social position, the very ethereality of what they "produced"—sound—assuring the correct reading. Indeed, sermons condemning music during the seventeenth and eighteenth centuries in Holland and elsewhere commonly stress this point. To make music well takes much time, yet music made well is nothing—simply air.[7]

The musical sonorities that can be assumed in Molenaer's painting stand in silent opposition to the noise[8] judged characteristic to the music making of peasants. By noise I do not mean that peasant musicians played poorly or that their instruments were incapable of producing pleasing sounds. Indeed, quite the opposite was undoubtedly true, though extremely few instruments of this sort have survived on which to base a judgment. The issue is not circumscribed by the skills of players or instrument makers. It develops instead from the ideological necessity to differentiate the sounds of classes according to principles that delineate *sociocultural* superiority, the sounds of one class over those of the other, as established by the particular group enjoying power. The

Figure 8.3
David Teniers the Younger (1610–1690), A VILLAGE WEDDING (1648), canvas,
76.5 × 114. cm. Vienna, Kunsthistorisches Museum, Gemäldegalerie, inv. no.
1160. Photo © IRPA-KIK-Brussels.

sounds of the lower classes are associated with anarchy, registered *visually* as
vulgar physicality, drunkenness—and as leering sexuality (Figure 8.3). For example, David Teniers the Younger, Molenaer's Flemish contemporary,[9] specialized in arch representations of peasants in paintings obviously produced
for the upper, especially urban, social strata (compare Figures 5.3, 5.4). By
contrast, the sounds of the upper classes are associated with the high degree
of order, registered visually as extreme physical self-control, as in the case of
Molenaer's painting, one among many similar representations.

Teniers's painting, like Molenaer's, concerns a new marriage, though
treated with extreme irony and condescension. Being a peasant affair, it provides Teniers with the opportunity for caricature. The visual argument, and
the sonoric one on which it depends, reverses the situation constructed by

Molenaer. Teniers places the newlyweds beside a bagpiper and, like Molenaer, he moves them to the edge of the image. The bagpipe is the location of sexual energy,[10] since its chanter pipe and wind sack together replicate the male genitalia, a likeness noted in contemporaneous proverbs, as I have previously described (see Figure 3.5).[11] Further, the bagpipe is decorated with the head of Pan, whose lechery and fertility go hand in hand. The husband's coarse arousal is captured in his face; the bovine stupidity and incomprehension registered by his bride's profile is made more ludicrous by the conventional bride's crown she wears.

The visual differentiations between Molenaer's and Teniers's images could hardly be more extreme, and the same holds for sonoric distinctions. The sounds of Molenaer's ensemble are soothing, easy on the ear. Those of Teniers's bagpipe are raucous, especially with the instrument blaring virtually into the ears of the whispering lovers, who under the circumstances could not have heard each other. But that does not matter. For in this image marriage is not temperate. It merely follows the guidance of biological rhythm, whereby the peasantry is objectified as little more than animals whose responsibility it is the noblesse oblige of the upper classes to control and their right to belittle. And it is the *noise* of peasants' music that provides their degraded identity and subjectivity, as much as the non-noise of Teniers's and Molenaer's patrons that by contrast marks the distinction of their class. The political difficulty here, of course, is that only one side is empowered to represent these judgments in historical memory by preserving the image of the social order of sound long after the sounds themselves have dissipated.

The elegant body of the seventeenth-century bourgeois lays claim to the visibility of its status in large part by means of its repose. If the body shows movement, as with Molenaer's young husband (Figure 8.2), gracefulness is its defining characteristic. And as always the face is mostly a mask, giving us very limited access to the privacy of its owner's subjectivity. The interiority of the privileged sitter is visually remarked, but only by that which is specifically exterior to this interiority: gait, body shape, and clothing. The face that would conventionally provide visible access to the sitter's "soul" remains expressively inexpressive. In comparison, Teniers's peasant newlyweds seem principally incapable of subjectivity; their interiority, such as it is, is available for the looking—and the laughing. Their personhood, or what remains of it, is cause for a viewer's smile, if not smirk, and little more. As Roland Barthes puts it, writing about the Dutch painter Adriaen van Ostade in a way that mirrors what happens in Teniers:

> Van Ostade's peasants have abortive, shapeless faces; as if they were unfinished creatures, rough drafts of men, arrested at an earlier stage of human develop-

ment. . . . As the ape is separated from man, here the peasant is separated from the burgher precisely insofar as he is deprived of the ultimate characteristics of humanity, those of the *person*.

Barthes goes on to compare the blobbish bodies of peasants with those of the burgher: "Turn now to the young patrician . . . frozen into the proposition of an idle god. He is an ultra-person, endowed with the extreme signs of humanity. Just as the peasant face falls short of creation, the patrician face achieves the ultimate degree of identity."[12]

Molenaer's sitters are finished artistically, much worked over by the laboring painter. Thus the bride's costume is complexly layered and painted in different colors, with a lively play of light and shadow across its many surfaces and drapery folds. Her dress includes a distinctly patterned outer garment and a finely worked lace collar. Much the same follows for all the figures *except* for the fighting peasants off to the left—even the household servants are ornamentally liveried. Neither Molenaer nor Teniers expended much energy on the peasants (apart from the three peasant faces at the extreme left in the Teniers). Especially in Molenaer, they are quickly painted, using a minimum of brush strokes. The relative lack of painter's effort demanded for their representation is visible and plays a rhetorical role in establishing the differential worth of the two social classes.

Difference and Protest

Occasionally in the regime of class representation a painter handled things differently (Figure 8.4). The short-lived Dutchman Adriaen Brouwer (1605/1606–1638) is such an artist. Brouwer painted lowlife with an insider's knowledge. A frequenter of taverns who set his scenes in the space he knew so well, Brouwer was found dead at age thirty-two outside a drinking den. He lived a generally miserable and consistently marginalized existence. He witnessed wrecked lives, hard living, raucous, if drunken, pleasure, lust, and rage. He painted all that and a good deal more. But unlike Teniers he painted none of it for the putative amusement of a presumed audience of picture buyers, inevitably his economic superiors. Brouwer eschewed the easy "charm" that always threatens to overwhelm Teniers's representation of peasants—when he is not overtly deriding them.

Brouwer sees differently, as is clearly indicated by the literal and metaphoric darkness of his never-decorative work. He painted with a broad stroke that suggests haste, at least in the late pictures, though that is not a sign of carelessness. Representing only what was necessary, Brouwer's paintings contain few objects, and none that are valuable. The inventory effect characteris-

Figure 8.4
Adriaen Brouwer
(1605/1606–1638),
BITTER MEDICINE
(1635), canvas[?]
47 × 35.5 cm.
Frankfurt am Main,
Städelsches Kunst-
institut, inv. no. 1076.

tic of so much northern art (compare Figures 5.1, 5.2) is absent. Thus, as re-gards the picture in question, our eyes take in the man at a glance, everything reduced to the minimum. We are provided with little context to explain the man's strong emotional outburst. The vial he holds is the only clue, apart from the look of the man himself. There is no indication of the space he in-habits. We see only a close-up that crops most of his body, tight and unre-lenting in its focus on the man's contorted face. He is young, perhaps attractive. But he is above all—what? Enraged? Drunk? Rowdy? Merely swallowing a bitter draft? It is impossible to say. But expressive he is—and visually "loud." (He likely illustrates the old bromide that good medicine always tastes bad.)[13] There is nothing much to sort out about his clothes. His hands are like those of other men, notably those of his class betters. Neither stumpy nor coarse but almost delicate and refined, they signal the sitter's underlying dignity because of the evident care that Brouwer devotes to them, as if to suggest, "This man has worth."

Whereas Teniers often painted large canvases (for the aristocratic Flemish market), Brouwer's are nearly always very small. *Bitter Medicine* is his only picture whose sitter is painted close to life-size scale. The late pictures are often sketchily painted, as here, dimly lighted, and executed in dark colors with low contrast—this one is entirely in brown apart from some purple in the cap and green tints in the jacket.[14] Despite their small size and dim colors, Brouwer's paintings are consistently arresting, in no small part because he grants his sitters the humanity that is so conventionally and conveniently erased by most of his contemporaries. The contorted features—highly unusual in paintings—of the man in *Bitter Medicine,* possibly sketched in a tavern and later painted in the studio, as was Brouwer's usual practice, make us curious about him and his *non*contorted look. The refined hands, his obvious youth and apparent character focus the viewer as effectively as if we were within earshot of his outburst. Brouwer stops us in our tracks by representing what was conventionally unrepresentable: the body of the impoverished whose identity is encoded not in imagined typecast simplicities but in the chaos of protest, if rendered as a cry in isolation. Brouwer's subjects are nearly always men, commonly young men, but without women, hence without love. And very often his men are alone with their loneliness, drunk or doped, but making no pretense in representation for any claims to fictive happiness for the benefit of those who enjoyed greater claim to material pleasure.

In most of Western painting, common men's bodies, as repositories of often raw sensing, define the totality of their being. Their bodies are treated as surface entities deprived of depth; viewers could easily see what little there was to be seen. By contrast, the bodies of the social elite signified principally as vessels less of sensing than of "soul." Their bodies possessed surface *and* depth. Soul, the interiority that produces identity, was made evident but inaccessible. It was public to the extent that its presence was marked but private in that its complexities should not be exposed to the gaze of the other. Brouwer seems to insist that the bifurcation I am describing, constructed on economic, social, and cultural foundations, is in the end just that: a construction. His all-too-common men, in their brutalized state, inevitably and invariably lay claim to their hurt, to their ability to know pain. Yet the pain they know is not physical (Brouwer's peasants never starve) but psychic, that is, lying in the domain of the soul—the very soul that most painting denies them.

Controlling Smiles

Looking back to all the images of people thus far considered in this book, we encounter an extremely limited range of facial expression, especially regarding people's mouths. Smiles are rare; and grins that expose the teeth are virtually absent. For many centuries, toothy smiles were appropriate, with rare exceptions, solely as part of the representational vocabulary for the lower classes (notable exceptions include some of the Dutch burghers painted by Frans Hals in the seventeenth century). Western painting on the whole has looked askance at smiling people, reading the gesture as a sign of social irresponsibility and lack of self-control. The smile represents pleasure, and pleasure, or fun, was seldom regarded as an important pictorial topos. Art had larger fish to fry. The smile, which conflated too easily with mirth, worked against the serious business assigned to painting. The smile had nothing to do with issues of social power, and it betrayed too much of the interior life (life as lived for itself) of otherwise responsible sitters whose identity was well anchored in the value placed on extreme physical reserve. In short, the smile said the wrong thing about important people. Above all, it marked a common touch, when common touch carried no special merit. In large part, smiles served as signs of irresponsibility reserved for children, more precisely, the children of the poor. They set off the child from the adult and the lower social order from its responsible, hierarchically superior other.

The children allegorically represented by Molenaer (Figure 8.5) wear costumes, not clothes. They play assigned roles as metaphorical musicians in a dubious ensemble whose apparent sonorities produce not music but noise. The allegory plays off a long-standing Western cultural tradition wherein music stood for order, and noise or nonmusic, for chaos.[15] Molenaer's youths sing and play fiddle (but not well; the boy does not know how to grip the fingerboard), hammer with spoons on a military helmet, and perform on a folk instrument, the rommelpot. (The rommelpot was played principally by children as a toy, and by beggars as a device for attracting attention to themselves in pursuit of alms. It consisted of a crockery pot partly filled with water over the top of which was stretched a pig's bladder, through which a small stick was inserted. The instrument's sound, dull and rumbling, was made by rotating the stick or pulling it up and down.)[16]

The painting exudes irresponsibility, however charming the children may appear to the modern viewer. The boy affecting an adult burgher's outfit, re-

Figure 8.5
Jan Miense Molenaer (c. 1610–1668), CHILDREN MAKING MUSIC (1629),
canvas, 68.3 × 84.5 cm. London, National Gallery, inv. no. 5416. Reproduced by
courtesy of the Trustees, The National Gallery, London.

plete with fancy collar, is entirely careless; he is a good burgher gone bad. He
plays the role of the worldly drunk. His leggings fall down; his shirt is undone; his sleeve patched at the elbow. He is a fake. His adult-size pants are
baggy on him; his shoes do not match and one is much too large and the other
too small. In complementary fashion, little girls were not raised in Dutch culture to become soldiers, but rather, domestics; hence the young girl reverses
what is required of her gender. But she is only playing, after all. The little fel-
low at the right, with the rommelpot, apparently "aspires" to be a beggar:

Molenaer gives him no socks, removes his shoes, and paints his bare legs so that they appear filthy. In other words, the painting in comic fashion transmits a standard Calvinist moral constructed on the reversal of proper behavior and mapped on age reversal; here, children play the roles of dissolute or disreputable adults. The children's smiles convey the mark of disruption.[17] For morality to reassert itself, child's play must cease—and the grins be banished.

Farmers' Daughters

The concern to articulate class difference by sharply delineated distinctions among body types even applies to the bodies of children. Nonetheless, Molenaer's children's bodies, independent of the props and tasks used to define them, are no different from those of children of the upper social orders. Indeed, their basic body types are visually attractive. This situation changed. With the rise of the middle classes and the greater social mobility gradually afforded the lower social orders occurring in parts of eighteenth-century Europe, in England especially, a new visual vocabulary of bodies emerged. The distinctions in body types long employed by painters to delineate class difference were radically increased by caricaturists who did not so much create a wholly new vocabulary as extend by hyperbole the one already in place. In short, the lower social orders were made visually ridiculous and often ugly. Physical grossness gained ground as the preferred sign of lower-class rank—especially for those whose recently improved economic positions allowed them access to some of the traditional trappings of their social betters. In England, for example, few things irritated the upper classes more than the discovery of people lower on the social ladder aping the habits of those higher up. The preferred medium, hardly surprising, was cheap, quickly produced prints, whose means of production allowed wide dissemination and hence a large audience to hear the cry of outrage against social mobility.

It is to one such example that I now turn (Figure 8.6). In eighteenth-century England upper-class girls were expected to learn the so-called ornamental accomplishments, including music, dancing, needlework, and the like. These were judged to be unmistakable signs of one's social station. The acquirement of these accomplishments by girls and women from the lower-middle orders that gradually occurred as the century wore on was strenuously objected to, especially by upper-class men who regarded the instability of social boundaries as particularly threatening. Thus, Arthur Young, writing in the *Annals of Agriculture* (1792), noted his considerable annoyance at finding a pianoforte in a farmer's parlor: "I always wish [it] was burnt."[18] Allatson Burgh in 1814 sarcastically noted that "the Daughters of Mechanics, even in humble stations, would fancy themselves extremely ill-treated, were they de-

Figure 8.6
James Gillray (1757–1815), FARMER GILES & HIS WIFE SHEWING OFF THEIR
DAUGHTER BETTY TO THEIR NEIGHBOURS, ON HER RETURN FROM SCHOOL
(1809), engraving, 32.5 × 47.5. cm. New Haven, Yale Center for British Art, Paul
Mellon Collection, no. L296.3 folio B.

barred the Indulgence of a piano-forte."[19] A distinctly ill-spirited, anonymous
statement published in the *Gentleman's Magazine* (1801) reflected clearly the
underlying class consciousness affecting these attitudes: "Instead of dishing
butter, feeding poultry, or curing bacon, the avocations of these young ladies
at home are, studying dress, attitudes, novels, French and musick, whilst the
fine ladies their mothers sit lounging in parlours adorned with the fiddle fad-
dle fancy work of their daughters."[20] However impotent these sarcasms, each
exhibits strong reaction to a changing social order, and blame for the loss of
tradition (the good old days) is specifically, ridiculously, and ironically laid at
the feet of girls and their doting parents. It is the rising-yet-inferior class and
the unempowered gender that are at fault.

The farmer's daughter seeking the accomplishments appropriate only to her social betters was meanly satirized by the always trenchant James Gillray in a print from 1809. The older generation of women gossip cattily behind a fan, having already examined the needlework signed "B[etty] Giles" atop the table. Farmer Giles and his wife feel satisfaction and give encouragement as daughter Betty, upon her return from boarding school, demonstrates her talents on the square piano in a performance of the "Bluebells of Scotland," hardly high art but apparently all she can handle—and clearly more than her younger sister is able to sing.

Betty's needlework is no better. A framed sampler on the back wall, signed by the young girl at age sixteen, includes an alphabet in upper and lower case, numbers from one to twelve, a proverb ("Evil communications Corrupt good Manners"), and a pair of birds flanking entwined hearts, an incomparable and incongruous mix. Betty's drawing is a good deal worse; her rendition of the family estate, titled "Cheese-Farm" (!), on the wall above the piano, shows elementary problems with perspective: In the foreground a woman milks a cow, beside which stands a gigantic rooster; a two-story-tall horse looms above the cottage roof in the background.[21]

Looking beyond these details to the bodies of the sitters, particularly striking is their *lumpen* quality: short, squat, fat, and with piggishly stupid faces. Betty at the piano wears an almost diaphanous gown, a fashionable coiffure, and a pearl necklace. But she wears none of it well. And in this she resonates intertextually with a large number of contemporaneous images—portraits, especially—of "respectable" girls of superior class, who have the "right" bodies to adorn with such fashion (Figure 8.7).

In sharp contrast to Betty Giles, everything about the Binney sisters contributes to an iconography of prestige centered on the unrelieved femininity, delicate and hyperrefined, pervading the composition. The painting's very roundness replicates the emphasis on the young women's breasts, whose shapes are barely disguised. The sisters are softness personified: Their skin is unquestionably beautiful and flawless, but they seem to have no skeleton beneath this perfect surface. The arm of the girl at the left appears utterly limp, as delicate as Betty Giles's is beefy.[22] It is important to note, however, that John Smart's portrait is not on that account a feminist image but a fetishization of the "eternal feminine." The Binneys are principally decorative. Drained of movement, they are "empowered" to be utterly immobile. Miss Binney's hand on the piano seems barely to have the energy to depress keys. Bovine Betty, silly as she is made to seem, is nonetheless acknowledged as a force to be considered, whereas the Binney sisters can be dismissed as very pretty and absolutely unthreatening.

The Working Body
and Social Order

The history of human labor in the West, until the early twentieth century, was principally concentrated in agriculture. Throughout Europe, though varying considerably from country to country, peasants constituted the majority of the population. I want to examine one important subject, the harvest scene, by which means artists referenced the peasant laboring classes from the sixteenth century to the end of the nineteenth. I will be particularly attentive to the representation of bodies.

French court painter Simon Vouet's large canvas representing *Ceres and Harvesting Cupids* (Figure 8.8), painted c. 1634, was probably intended to decorate the house of the French surintendant des finances, Claude de Bullion, who worked for Cardinal Richelieu (Figures 7.1, 7.2). The picture's subject and handling perfectly represents the interests and self-interest of M. de Bullion, who was responsible for the crown treasury and thus answerable to the ruthless Richelieu and King Louis XIII, in whose name Richelieu served. The French state was largely supported by taxes from the country's rich agricultural lands, and these lands were worked by a vast army of peasants.

Vouet's painting transliterates the awesome responsibility of agricultural production, inevitably and invariably an uncertain, unpredictable business,

Figure 8.8
Simon Vouet (1590-1649), CERES AND HARVESTING CUPIDS (c. 1634), canvas, 147.6 × 188.7 cm. London, National Gallery, inv. no. 6292. Reproduced by courtesy of the Trustees, The National Gallery, London.

into a mythology of plenty watched over by a mythic deity, Ceres, goddess of agriculture, hence fertility. As Earth Mother, since the Middle Ages Ceres was conflated with Holy Mother Church.[23] She was All: food for the body and for the soul; in short, Ceres stood for Life. In state-political terms, she was the mythic guarantor of the sovereign's power, since state power is money driven, a fact never lost on the perennially pinched Bourbon line.

Vouet's painting aestheticizes the process of collecting taxes. Ceres's chubby minions, watched over, gather the wheat and tie it in bundles, like cash packages duly to be counted in the central bank. The desire encoded in the pleasures of cash is transliterated into Ceres's nude body; not least of all, her ample breasts serve the dual purpose of a sexual sight and an overdetermined site for food production. Vouet, however, is not content to relocate French agriculture entirely in some horticultural Arcadia of the distant past. Instead he anchors the image as well in "real" space, whence the money comes, and in the present. He accomplishes this feat by the incorporation of two French peasants, dressed in modern garb and working with scythes to cut the standing grain. Vouet connects the French peasant to the process of food production, hence to production of wealth, hence to tax collection. Ceres and her cupids were useful for show. But the peasants are included because they must be: No minister of finance had any illusions as to the centrality of the labor force that did the work.

Yet within the field of vision, Vouet devotes far greater attention to the four putti than to the "real" workers in the field. Indeed, so far as Vouet's own labor is concerned, the sheaves of wheat in the lower foreground required at least as much effort to paint as the peasants. Thus, what counts is not the peasants but the effort that they expend. The fact that they are human—the only humans in the image, men upon whom everything depends—is irrelevant. Vouet paints them in profile or from the back, stooped to their job, *faceless*. The peasant at the right—low to the ground, squat, heavy, and strong—is shown from an angle impossible to imagine for a man of any social stature; he is essentially reduced to his buttocks.

Turning the pictorial clock back, something different—but not entirely different—occurs in Pieter Brueghel's magnificent *The Harvesters* (Figure 8.9), painted nearly seventy years earlier. Brueghel sets his scene with a high degree of local specificity in Flanders, unlike Vouet's rather generic landscape. Brueghel's painting is replete with all the local color he so consistently preferred: villages with churches, castles in the distance, and myriad details of peasant life and labor. Deities and mythologies are banished in favor of the patently local and the present-day—though in the representation of peasant life and agriculture, a sense of cyclical timelessness is nearly always pervasive. Indeed, to the extent that agriculture and its labors resonate with cyclical eternity, the viewer is assured of the predictable continuation of the political process and social structure upon which quasi-feudal economies depended. To no small degree this explains the enormous visual appetite among the European aristocracy, dating back to medieval manuscript illuminations, for representations of the twelve months and the four seasons.[24] Picturing the future in the present, these images provided a convenient promise of continuation that their viewers very much wanted to believe in, all the more so as the seemingly timeless feudal world was coming apart in the excitement of mercantilism, new manufacture, and world trade associated with maritime northern Europe.

Figure 8.9
Pieter Brueghel the Elder (c. 1525–1569), THE HARVESTERS (JULY-AUGUST) (1565), panel, 118 × 160.7 cm. New York, The Metropolitan Museum of Art, Rogers Fund, 1919, inv. no. 19.164.

Western painting often, but by no means always, represents peasants as few and isolated, both from their class superiors and—more important—from each other. Agriculture was enormously labor-intensive, yet few paintings acknowledge the gathering of workers. Workers were feared, and no fear was stronger than of workers massed. This fact renders Brueghel's painting unusual. The picture marks the noontime meal, when tired and hungry peasants gather under the shade of a tree to eat, drink, and sprawl for a brief snooze. Brueghel acknowledges community, via the binding force of shared labor and the shared meal.[25] The subjects are totally engaged in their activities, unaware and uninterested in being pictured. Conversely, the putative constraints of their small world cuts them off from all that lies beyond the lands they work but which we can see from our privileged perch, whose point of view gives us a long-shot cinematic panorama.[26] A few peasants "inadvertently" face us, and Brueghel particularizes their faces. The centrally positioned and compositionally largest peasant, sleeping soundly, is treated comically; laid out as though dead beneath the tree, his mouth is agape. A young man carrying water pitchers and walking through a gap cut in the wheat field shows exhaustion from his long walk and climb. Other figures, stooping to their work, are handled more cursorily, like the men in Vouet's painting.

To acknowledge Brueghel's representation of a laboring community defines in his work an important distinction among the large numbers of related images. But we must be careful not to make too much of it. To whatever degree Brueghel supplies agency to his peasants, he is equally attentive to establishing the severe limitations to their power. Brueghel painted pictures for the rich (including a cardinal, a city councilman, a geographer, and a merchant), and to be successful he had to respond to their ideological investments, without regard to whether he shared their view. One of a series of six paintings (five still survive) dedicated to the twelve months, *The Harvesters,* was painted for an Antwerp banker-financier, Niclaes Jongelinck, and was intended for display in his villa at Ter Becken.[27]

Thus in *The Harvesters* two coexisting worlds are envisaged, by means of which social difference serves as a defining characteristic of the social fabric. What bodies *do* is definitive. In the far distance (in tiny detail, just a few flecks of paint, but sufficiently important to be included nonetheless), some people recreate—bathe in a pond, or engage in lawn bowling—while in the foreground, others exhaust themselves. The difference in activities is no small matter: The season is harvest, that crucial moment when the winter's food supply and the fundamental source for the region's wealth is gathered. During harvest, time is a critical dimension, because with its passage comes weather change and the threat of crop ruin posed by the onset of fall rains. Yet at this juncture, some continue to play. And the difference between play and work acknowledges an unbridgeable and definitive social gap. Brueghel concentrates on the peasant laborers, but he provides his audience with other signs of a stable social frame within which the laborers function. The peasants work for others whose situation is entirely secure—if not in reality, then in their visual fantasies. *The Harvesters* is "tinged with the nostalgia of a mid-sixteenth-century city-dweller for the bucolic existence of the fading feudal age; this attitude was fashionable in Antwerp, the rapidly expanding mercantile center where the artist found his friends and patrons."[28]

Brueghel's *The Harvesters* is *about* heat. Its surface is dominated by the "hot" yellows and golds of the wheat; the sky is the grayish pink of noon, the sun at zenith. The four surviving panels that form other parts of the series each display different atmospheric effects, thereby exacerbating the impression of nature's dominance—and of simple peasants held in nature's thrall. This fact alone would have provided Brueghel's intellectually cultivated banker-financier patron with what he had to have in order for the series of panels to be *decorative,* that is, politically correct. Along similar lines, and entirely characteristic of his work in general, Brueghel prefers to see his peasants from above, from a bird's-eye view, as though surveilling them. The harvesters of this summer scene are on a hillside, sufficiently high to provide a view to the distant sea. Brueghel himself is still higher.[29] Brueghel does not stand among the peasants, but remains at a safe distance, observant but uninvolved. The spatial distance echoes cultural distance.

Orderly Bodies

Three-quarters of a century after Brueghel, David Teniers the Younger painted a four-seasons series, each season delineated by the actions of a principal adult male. *Summer* (Figure 8.10) employs the usual wheat harvest. But in this instance, in comparison with Brueghel's work, the decontextualization of peasant labor into a sort of basic schematic is pronounced. The lad holding up the sheaf of wheat is rather like a cutout figure plunked down on a stage. Teniers devotes some attention to all three figures, though most of it settles on the man in the foreground. The two figures at the back are a foretaste of so-called staffage figures typical to later landscape paintings (roughly the equivalent of movie extras) and what John Barrell describes as "tokens of a calm, endless, and anonymous industry, which confirm the order of society . . . [and] objects of colour, confirming the order of the landscape."[30]

Figure 8.10
David Teniers the
Younger (1610–1690),
SUMMER (c. 1644),
copper, 21.9 × 16 cm.
London, National
Gallery, inv. no. 858.
Reproduced by courtesy
of the Trustees, The
National Gallery,
London.

Teniers's three peasant workers constitute a kind of labor-logic, a three-part progression of activities that moves from right to left and from background to foreground. One man cuts the grain, a second stacks it in bundles, and a third holds a bundle up for view, the finished product. In the end, the bundle is the man's equal, perhaps his superior. The peasant holds the grain shock as the sole object of attention, as he looks backward over his shoulder, hence deflecting any importance that might otherwise accrue to him. As if this were not sufficient, Teniers plays with relative scale. The standing wheat field at the back reaches a height just above the waist of the man wielding the scythe. But the shock of wheat held by the young peasant in the foreground is well over his head, despite the fact that he is represented as a boy in his late teens. In representations of the seasons, nature dominates men, but the men it dominates are nearly always those of low station.

Nearly one and one-half centuries after Teniers's little painting, the English artist George Stubbs produced his *Reapers* (Figure 8.11, *Color Plate 12*), a large picture showing a group of six men and women gathering the wheat harvest while watched by a mounted overseer.[31] On the verge of modernity, on the cusp of the Industrial Revolution, Stubbs produced one of the last major nostalgic evocations of a pastoral agriculture, yet one unable to contain, suppress, or hide the actual history across whose grain the image attempts to navigate. As with Brueghel in 1565, Stubbs in 1785 bathes his painting in the golden hues that seem to reflect against the sky, giving even the heavens a yellow tint. The bare earth beneath the laborers' feet is golden; the men's pants and the women's dresses show the same color, though in different gradations. The trees' green leaves are given a pronounced yellow cast, apparently reflecting the sun now low in the sky. From this point, similarities to Brueghel disappear. In Brueghel surveillance is veiled, made implicit by the bird's-eye view, but off-camera, so to speak. In Stubbs, surveillance is part of the now-naturalized order of things. The painted overseer takes over the role that Brueghel gives to the viewer, allowing the viewer to relax. We come onto the scene at eye level. The overseer literally stands between us and the "them" of the labor force and stands above them. Enjoying a private all-seeing bird's-eye view, he literally over-sees.

Space is ingeniously organized to encode an immediate clarification of its relation to time, specifically to the developmental or dynamic aspect of space-time relations. The overseer has ridden his horse in from the right, past that part of the field already cut, past grain that has been stacked. He has now caught up to the workers near the end of their workday: The low sun reflects on the trees. Stubbs's delineation of the space-time relation is a map for and a certification of a stable social and economic order. But unlike earlier representations of the summer harvest season, Stubbs focuses principal attention on the work itself—and *not* on the worker. The issue is less to decorously celebrate harvest, however nostalgically, as in Brueghel, than to represent and explicitly valorize discipline. In the process, each laborer is privatized into his or her own task. Agricultural labor is transformed into a prophecy of the factory assembly line, whose monotonous tasks, relative to the massive English textile

Figure 8.11
George Stubbs
(1724–1806), REAPERS
(1785), panel, 90 × 137
cm. London, Tate
Gallery, inv. no.
TO2257.

industry, were reflected in labor riots and smashing of looms by one-time farm laborers whose lives had been reshaped by the disciplines of machine and clock. Each worker performs a single task, in a precise line that begins with scything the wheat and ends with stacking it in bundles for transport to the threshing barn.

Each body reacts uniquely to the singular physical task assigned, each a sign of efficiency, regularity, dependability, and productivity. It is as though a twentieth-century Taylorist efficiency expert has trained them. The workers are transformed into extensions of the tasks they perform. They are *that* to which their tools are attached. Spontaneity is entirely drained from the scene in favor of an overdetermined rationalization of labor. Stubbs makes this rationalization distinctly aesthetic, though also frank and unapologetic. And yet, despite the assurance of productivity via the stacked bundles that frame both sides of the image, none of the workers precisely works. The signs of labor upon their bodies are entirely absent. Their clothes are unmussed; indeed, the women are dressed more like ladies. No one seems to sweat or get dirty. On balance, the painting walks an uncertain line between demonstrating how harvesting is done and rendering agriculture aesthetic. In other words, Stubbs makes his appeal to the landed class by attempting to mix business with (visual) pleasure. It would require several additional decades of European history before artists like Jean-François Millet,[32] and later, van Gogh,[33] would reformulate agricultural imagery into something that could at least begin to pass for a critique of what inspired Stubbs.

Color, Racial Difference, and Embodied Fantasy

The terrain of racial difference, invariably evoked by the physical body of the Other, for centuries has received enormous attention in Western visual art. In a representational medium so dependent upon color for producing its rhetorical effects, the differentials of human color have served well as a measure for representing certain claims on the "scale" of human worth. On this scale, it will come as no surprise, white is the standard against which all other colors of the human are measured and, for the most part, found lacking. It is on the specific issue of color that I want to concentrate in the remarks that follow: the color in paintings of the colors of people. This will hardly exhaust the topic of painting's relation to race, but it will permit exploration of what I would term first effects, the differences that are encoded into painting, and pertaining to race, that are not only most immediately available for the seeing but also fundamental to all other differences within the visual code.[34]

Color is the driving principal of *The Carpet Merchant* (Figure 8.12, *Color Plate 13*), by Jean-Léon Gérôme, the most important nineteenth-century French painter of orientalist subjects.[35] With attention given to the smallest detail, Gérôme represents the courtyard of the rug market in Cairo that he had visited in 1868. Filtered golden light gives the architecture a warm glow and enlivens the varied and rich hues of both carpets and costumes. The merchants are each garbed in different colors—gold, blue, red, green, blue-black, and so on—virtually neon in intensity. With one exception, their faces are seen in profile, if at all, hence they possess no separate identities. They are typecast as exotics. In essence reduced to their skin color and costume, they are human analogues to the equally exotic—and decorative—carpets piled up on the floor or hung for viewing. With Gérôme, as with countless others among the dozens of orientalist painters of the nineteenth century, color *is* the Other. It defines difference, fuels desire, and feeds an appetite for goods—carpets—*and* for bodies, as with his (in)famous nudes, about which more

Figure 8.12
Jean-Léon Gérôme
(1824–1904), THE
CARPET MERCHANT
(c. 1887), canvas,
83.5 × 64.8 cm.
Minneapolis, The
Minneapolis Institute of
Arts, The William Hood
Dunwoody Fund, acc.
no. 70.40.

later. It also marks a hierarchy of cultures and does so by explicit reference to and employment of a long history of Western pictorial tradition.

Western theorists of art, principally but not exclusively those attached to the French Academy of Painting and Sculpture in the late seventeenth century, defined painting in terms of two basic principles: line (drawing), and color. Long-winded debates ensued concerning which of the two principles contributed to the production of great art, an art that was—no surprise, here—expressly put to the service of the French state, whose propaganda interests artists had long served directly. That is, what might appear to be an issue of rather obscure interest, a seemingly narrow debate about aesthetics, was in fact anchored in perceptions about art's social role, narrowly understood to be sure. The argument about whether to favor line or color was never settled. However, one aspect of the old debate enjoyed a particularly long life, lasting well into the nineteenth century and directly affecting the imagery of the racial Other. It centered on gender.

Briefly, line (drawing) was commonly characterized as a vehicle of the mind, appealing to reason and rationality. In effect, it was masculine, hard, and—culturally speaking—"responsible." By contrast, color was judged to be a vehicle of the emotions, hence it was antireason. It was the pictorial vehicle for affect. It was feminine, soft, and "irresponsible." If the former appealed to the mind, the latter appealed to the hierarchically lower body. Gérôme's *The Carpet Merchant* explicitly feminizes his conception of the Orient, the Orient itself being a literal figment of the Western imagination, as Edward Said has so convincingly shown.[36] The color that shimmers throughout the painting both defines and limits the culture as one, simply, for the seeing—and the buying (Gérôme and his party of friends "bought rugs with great enthusiasm, ordering their purchases to be crated and sent ahead of them to France").[37] The Oriental Other is *available* as a viewing pleasure. Fundamentally *like* the carpets, what is visually interesting is the gorgeous—and to nineteenth-century Western eyes—nearly riotously colorful drapery that marks "them" as Not Us. *The Carpet Merchant* employs the body of the Other as little more than a mannikin upon which to hang electrically colored drapery. The shimmering quality of Gérôme's drapery, however, was commonly transferred to the *skin* of nonwhites, one of the most powerfully evocative surfaces ever to attract oil paint and to elicit the transfixed gaze.

Measured Difference:
A Matter of Black and White

The representation of racial difference in Western painting has historically depended on visualizing submissiveness, without which a gendering via effeminization cannot occur. The power begrudgingly allotted to the black Other (it is principally *blackness* that defines Western color-fixation) is ironically acknowledged by the lengths to which efforts were made to deny it in Western painting. One of the most striking examples of this effort is a gigantic painting, *Queen Victoria Presenting a Bible in the Audience Chamber at Windsor Castle* (Figure 8.13). Here a white woman—already in the nineteenth century the imagined object of black sexual desire—*and* the queen of the world's largest colonial empire—symbolically puts Western religion into the hands of a bent-kneed submissive black. Christianity is transformed into a visual metaphor of masculine (!) control over a feminized paganism, re-

Figure 8.13
Thomas Jones Barker (1815–1882), QUEEN VICTORIA PRESENTING A BIBLE
IN THE AUDIENCE CHAMBER AT WINDSOR CASTLE (c. 1861), canvas,
167.6 × 213.8 cm. London, National Portrait Gallery, inv. no. 4969. Reproduced
by courtesy of The National Portrait Gallery, London.

garded as irrational, invariably primitive, and dangerously sensual. Queen Victoria subdues the black man via the prophylactic of scripture that will in turn control his sexuality.

Carl Linnaeus (1707–1778), the great Swedish botanist, classified human beings into four groups: European, African, Asian, and American; and he designated for each what he regarded as their "natural" physical and character traits, the two being closely bound. The African had "black skin, black, curly hair, an apelike nose, and swollen lips; was phlegmatic, crafty, and careless; ruled by authority." Europeans, Linnaeus's gold standard against which all others were measured as lesser, had "white skin, blonde hair, blue eyes, was sanguine, very intelligent, a discoverer [read: conqueror, colonizer], and ruled by religious custom."[38] Thomas Jones Barker, the painter of the Queen Victoria painting, follows Linnaeus closely, though with several crucial adjustments. In order to make visible the full degree of credit claimed for Victoria's triumph, it is necessary to acknowledge in paint the strength of the Other now subdued. Thus the unnamed, hence anonymous, surrogate for the black world is invested with a powerful sexual energy. His physical animalism is strengthened by the leopard skin in which he is wrapped; his own tribal leadership by the jewelry and colorful dress, as well as by the usual (phallic) sword. Racial difference is concentrated in skin color. Barker makes a great rhetorical point in the sharp contrast between Queen Victoria's right arm and his left. The blackness of his skin is made a visual issue especially by the bright reflection off its surface, very unlike the absorptive hues provided to Victoria.

Barker paints the man as both young and physically beautiful. His face especially is explicitly refined (indeed, altered), both feminized and made sexual: full lips, high cheekbones, arched eyebrows, earring, and so forth. One only need contrast his features with those of Prince Albert at the left, standing in protective proximity to his wife, to sense the difference. As scholars like Sander Gilman and Leonard Bell, among others, have noted, European artists commonly adjusted and transformed the facial features of racial Others, "Europeanizing" and effeminizing those who were to be deemed "good others."[39] As Bell points out, this African chief is physically ennobled for having accepted colonialism via the religious metaphor of Christianity, itself an aestheticization that serves as a moral justification of imperialism (Christ to the natives, and Good overcoming Evil, with the convenient white-black color binary in tow).[40] Such an image, in its own time, resonated intertextually with endless numbers of pictures of the unsaved, uncivilized, resistant Africans, who "were characterized by ugliness and suggestions of brutality and lecherousness." By contrast, Barker's African is "docile

Figure 8.14
Théodore Chassériau (1819–1856), STUDY OF A NUDE BLACK MAN (1838), can-
vas, 54.8 × 73.3 cm. Montauban, Musée Ingres, inv. no. 867-180. Photo © Musée
Ingres.

and passive—the ideal native."[41] Moreover, he seems to be nobody in particular (in other words, the anonymous, all-purpose black from Central
Casting)—no such event such as Barker depicted is known to have taken
place. The painting does not record an event; instead, it stages a metaphor of
cultural difference, cultural hierarchy, and the beneficent progression of the
West over its far-flung domains.[42]

Exoticism, as Harriet Guest has demonstrated, "inscribes its object with an
acultural illegibility, isolated from any coherence of origin."[43] A study of a
nude black male (Figure 8.14, *Color Plate 14*), painted in 1838 by the French

artist Théodore Chassériau, radically erases context except for that of color, whose choice—by using a black model—makes color per se an issue, hence invests the man's physical body with a textuality of difference. The image is acultural only insofar as the black man is concerned: We know nothing of him or his circumstances. (Chassériau sets the model against a shimmering blue background, as if he were floating among the clouds.) But we know that he is Other, and it is his otherness that acculturates him to us. In essence he inhabits "our" (i.e., white) pictorial space, namely, Western European painting and its representational traditions. He interlopes, but he is pictorially useful. What matters is his blackness, precisely because that color, when "attached" to human skin, makes reference to an enormous number of cultural codes and social practices.

This painting was commissioned by another artist, the great Jean-Auguste-Dominique Ingres, then living in Rome. He wrote to a friend in Paris to say that he needed a painting of "a simple figure of a Negro in this attitude," demonstrating the appropriate pose with a quick sketch. The task was given to Chassériau. Ingres's explicit instructions on how he wanted the figure painted made reference to wanting "the most correct rendering of the forms *and his color*" (emphasis added). The model was someone special that Ingres had in mind, "Joseph the Negro," a man of obvious physical beauty judging from Chassériau's picture, presuming it was Joseph who posed. Chassériau was given no hint concerning the purpose of the study. Without this information to guide him, he rendered the man in the preordained pose and in the process provided him with an unusual degree of visual power precisely by making him appear both beautiful and heroic. His body possesses idealized proportions, youth, and strength. Moreover, it is neither submissive nor vanquished. He is in essence the black analogue to the classical *white* male that made its way into Western art via antique statuary depicting gods. But so far as this study picture is concerned the man is something more than an analogue; he exceeds the putative model or white referent. He "has" or "is" all that *they* are, *and* he "has" color besides. Color under these circumstances immediately transforms itself into the paradoxical matrix of fear and desire that "blackness" registers in white consciousness. There is of course a visual rupture caused by the two hand studies set alongside the full figure; these unambiguously "name" the image as a study piece not intended for public viewing. Here is the final irony. The secret Ingres kept from Chassériau was that the study was for a figure representing Satan, to be shown chased by the Lord from a mountaintop—a project Ingres never completed[44]—the remasculinized, heroic black male as Evil Incarnate fleeing the wrath of the white God.

The Evil Other

"Physiognomics was body criticism. As corporeal connoisseurship, it diagnosed unseen spiritual qualities by scrutinizing visible traits."[45] This pseudoscience, all the rage in the nineteenth century after a long incubation that began with Aristotle,[46] sought to classify and organize the human species always with the white European male as presumed Adam. It was a "science" of the visible, measurable body, organized around the differences of gender, class, and race. Physiognomics' credibility was insured by the millions of words spilled on the subject. Saying repeatedly that "this was so," physiognomics was functionally *made* true and was taken for granted in the West for decades. It was from the start sexist, classist, and racist. More to my interests, it was not only widely practiced as social science, it was as well an art project about bodies.[47]

The founding father was the Swiss Johann Caspar Lavater (1741–1801), whose first works on the subject appeared in 1775 and by 1810 had appeared in fifty-five editions, with twenty in English translation.[48] Lavater studied and measured the face in order to understand the supposed inborn, *natural* character traits—assigned in the most essentialist ways—of every diverse group of people then known to inhabit the planet. Lavater and his myriad followers sought archetypes, and they found them in abundance. They measured human heads with an obsessiveness that is difficult to overestimate, filling countless pages of large volumes with engravings of noses, lips, eyes, foreheads, and so on, each duly typed, labeled, and associated with internal character, and each having a distinct moral component—some lips, for example, showing "the greatest affinity to genius," and others appropriate to a "degenerate race."[49]

Among the more prominent nineteenth-century physiognomists was Samuel R. Wells, whose *New Physiognomy, or, Signs of Character* covers nearly nine hundred pages in small type, replete with numerous engraved faces of the good and evil, the famous and infamous, serving as archetypes of whatever character trait, race, or ethnic group was under discussion. Following common practice, Wells divides the face into minute but quantifiable and specific regions for manifesting character, 157 in all (for example: "123. Envy," "136. Patriotism").[50] He provides separate chapters with titles like "The Human Chin, What It Indicates," and "The Jaws and the Teeth."

Typical of physiognomic characterizations, individual body parts provide a road map for hierarchical cultural difference. Thus of the nose, Wells says,

> alone in each [person, it] tells the story of its wearer's rank and condition. The one is elegant, refined, and beautiful; the other gross, rude, and ugly. The one is

fully and symmetrically developed, the other is developed only in the direction of deformity.

It is the same with nations as with individuals. The more cultivated and advanced the race, the finer the nose.

Next to this paragraph there appears in profile the engraved head of a female "Ethiopian," whose nose Wells compares to that of what he calls "the snouts of the lower animals."[51]

For Wells, as for other physiognomists, the nose of noses is Greek, by which is meant nose measurements taken not from "real live" modern-day Greeks, who by Western standards were considered fairly primitive, but from ancient Greek *statuary*. Wells's discussion, entitled in bold "The Greek Nose—Refinement," describes what he names the "classic nose," which "takes its name . . . from the wonderful art-loving Greeks." Famous sculpture is cited. Once again, the body *in art* becomes the body by which to measure the body in flesh. Typical for Wells, he follows up with a list of famous Greek noses worn by famous poets and, especially, *painters* (Raphael, Claude Lorrain, Rubens, Murillo, Titian)—none of whom were Greek.[52] Elsewhere we are given "The English Nose" and "The Irish Nose"; finally "Miscellaneous National Noses," beginning with those from Eastern Europe and ending in Melanesia, lumped together as ones of not much importance. There follows a section, duly illustrated, of "Noted Noses"—including those belonging to Tasso, Chaucer, and others.

Of eyes, Wells claims that poets praise blue ones "more perhaps than any other kind."[53] Of necks, murderers are "observed" (always scientific, always objectively *seen*) "to almost always have big [ones], which corresponds with the gross, animal, and destructive tendencies of their minds."[54] The Caucasian skull "is distinguished by the symmetry and beauty of its parts." Wells's enthusiasm now fully charged, he reports on the "beautiful proportions of a well-formed Caucasian skull, with its magnificent intellectual and moral developments"—this from an engraved skull, seen frontally, without the lower jaw. He then makes direct comparison with what stands for the radical opposite, the skulls of "savage and barbarian tribes."[55] As ridiculous, and comical, as this now seems, it was taken seriously in its own time and regarded as genuinely "scientific" (that is, as true). Not coincidentally, physiognomics served the convenient purposes of the Third Reich in the supposed delineation of the Master Race and the literal failure of the Jew, among others, to "measure up." The measurements of physiognomics, in other words, eventually helped provide "scientific" basis for justifying genocide.

In a section called "The Englishman," Wells notes that "the English cranium is large"; soon thereafter he explains this as "the secret of the domination of the English race in the four quarters of the globe. Brain is power; and the more you have of it the better, provided it be in the right place and you have a physical system to sustain it (as the Englishman has) correspondingly developed."[56]

At the end appears "The Ethiopian Race," and the concluding, deeply racist paragraph establishes the bottom rung of Wells's human ladder:

> We may say of the typical negro, that from temperament he is slow and indo-lent, but persistent and capable of great endurance [crucial to the success of slav-ery, recently abolished]; and from cerebral development sensuous, passionate, affectionate, benevolent, docile, imitative, devotional, superstitious, excitable, impulsive, vain, improvident, cunning, polite, and unprincipled. [These are qualities during the period principally associated with either women or domes-tic pets.] He lives in the real rather than the ideal, and enjoys the present with-out thinking much of either the past or the future. He is a child in mental de-velopment, has the virtues and faults of a child, and like the child is capable of being controlled, disciplined, educated, and developed.[57]

The trace of Wells's remarks remains in evidence in the typecasting that commonly occurs in today's racist jokes and put-downs. More to the point, Wells's views are entirely typical of a profoundly influential discourse about the body of the Other, existing principally *in representation,* essentialized and debased, that allowed the colonialist and capitalist Western bourgeoisie to es-tablish a "natural" (but in fact constructed), hence moral, explanation for their social, cultural, and economic hegemony. For example, Irish-American painter Thomas Hovenden's *Ain't That Ripe?* (Figure 8.15), like numerous other images of African Americans, weaves a visual discourse from the long-standing cultural claim that the nonwhite races are simpler, more primitive, and indeed fundamentally childlike in comparison with Caucasians. Ho-venden's painting is dominated by three colors: the boy's black, light-reflective skin, framing his very white teeth that in turn attract the viewer's gaze to his broad smile, the white shirt that sets off his skin color so dramatically, and an almost luridly red watermelon. It requires no special insight to sort out the power of the racist cliché that merges African Americans and watermelons and fuses the black male in the permanent state of man-child. The operative words, each connected to the others, serve to weave a familiar discourse: black = primitive = child = simple = nature = happy = nonthreatening ("good" Negroes in Western paintings seem always to be grinning).

We must keep in mind that images like Hovenden's were painted for mid-dle-class whites not blacks. They were designed specifically to appeal to the people who were economically superior, people who viewed themselves as culturally superior as well. The painting provides no hint of paradox, prob-

Figure 8.15
Thomas Hovenden
(1840–1895), Ain't
that ripe? (c. 1865),
canvas, 55.7 × 40.5 cm.
Brooklyn, The Brooklyn
Museum, gift of the ex-
ecutors of the estate of
Colonel Michael
Friedsam, inv. no.
32.825.

lem, or criticism. Indeed, it celebrates a system that operates to keep the racist linkages intact, without regard, incidentally, to whatever might have been Hovenden's own conscious thoughts or motives, to which we have no direct access. *Ain't That Ripe?* phrases the simplest question in nonstandard English, informing the viewer that the rhetorical phrase is actually not a question at all but a statement that the African American, recently freed from legal slavery, remains nonetheless no more *by nature* than what the physiognomists claimed:

> Prosperous collectors created a demand for depictions that fulfilled their own ideas of blacks as grotesque buffoons, servile menials, comic entertainers, or threatening subhumans; these depictions were, for the most part, willingly supplied by American artists. The vicious cycle of supply and demand sustained images that denied the inherent humanity of black people by reinforcing their limited role in American society. More fundamentally, these images expressed an inability to comprehend a people whose appearances and behavior were judged to be different from their own, and thus inferior.[58]

The power of otherness is derived not in least part by the manufactured cultural fear of incorporation. Separateness established in myriad ways by government policy and enforced by law is represented in painting by the antithesis of black to white. These colors are not often mixed, and when they are, as, say, in the representation of brown-skinned people, other parameters of representation than color conventionally are brought to bear in order to inform the viewer that brown skin is, after all, simply another shade of the detested but riveting and awesome black.

Chapter 9

The Female Nude: Surfaces of Desire

I̲ₙ PAINTING, NUDE OR NAKED: What to call it? What are the stakes of the difference? A generation ago Sir Kenneth Clark, in his monumental study of nudity and nakedness in art, established the principles defining a difference. Nakedness, he said, describes a state of being without clothes; nudity, by contrast, is a category of artistic representation. The former, he argues, "implies some sort of embarrassment" most people feel from being deprived of clothes, but the latter "carries, in educated usage, no uncomfortable overtone. The vague image it projects into the mind is not of a huddled and defenseless body, but of a balanced, prosperous, and confident body: the body re-formed."[1] Nudity for Clark operates as a manifestation of aesthetics, as representation and at a remove from mundane reality. The claim to aesthetics provides Clark with the source of his book's subtitle: "A Study in Ideal Form." Clark developed his project along formalist lines, investigating the representation of the naked human body in art as a type of painted or sculpted composition—which to be sure it is—governed by the regularities and symmetries of geometry.

Within the confines of a broadly defined Western tradition, Clark universalized the body as an unproblematic entity, divorced from history other than the history of art and art-making. In particular, he ignored any specific investigation of the function of the nude (the "why" question) or of the act of spectatorship (the "who's looking" question). As a result, his book (immensely insightful regarding formalist art history) oddly separates the nude from discourses about power and, a little ironically, from the politics of gender difference. Further, it identifies but quickly backs away from eroticism's role as a driving force to portray the nude in art from time immemorial. "It is necessary to labor the obvious," Clark says, "and say that no nude, however abstract, should fail to arouse in the spectator some vestige of erotic feeling, even though it be only the faintest shadow—and if it does not do so, it is bad art and false morals."[2] The pleasure of looking at beautiful naked bodies in art, for Clark, is principally contemplative, not physical, a view predicated upon preserving "in educated usage" a sharp division between mind and body.

The first substantial, if brief, critique of Clark's book was mounted by the art critic John Berger in 1972.[3] He argues that the nude in art responds to, and in turn reinforces, the principal power differential that partly defines the social and cultural functions of gender hierarchy. He reasons that man's "presence" in the world articulates a "power which he exercises on others," whereas a woman's presence articulates "what can and cannot be done to her" (while effectively critiquing Clark, Berger perpetuated a male discourse concerning women's supposed lack of agency). As far as art is concerned, he relates gender difference to the separate acts of looking and of being looked at: A man's look is directed outward toward others, a woman's inward toward herself. One surveys and surveils; the other is surveyed and surveils herself. Berger sums up:

> *Men act* and *women appear.* Men look at women. Women watch themselves being looked at. This determines not only most relations between men and women but also the relation of women to themselves. The surveyor of woman in herself is male: the surveyed female. Thus she turns herself into an object—and most particularly an object of vision: a sight.[4]

Berger argues that the painted nude is, essentially, the painted nude female. Historically, however, this is the case only since the nineteenth century, before which there is a reasonably close balance between the sexes in representations of the nude. Berger further notes that the female's nakedness is not expressive of her own feelings but is a sign of "her submission to the [art] owner's feelings or demands." To be naked, Berger suggests, is to "be oneself"; but to be nude is to be seen by others "and yet not recognized for oneself. . . . Nakedness reveals itself. Nudity is placed on display."[5] Finally, Berger reiterates the character of power difference by noting that female nudity in art conventionally, though by no means always, includes men who are clothed or no men at all, leaving but one man implicit, the spectator-owner of the image who stands, clothed, outside the frame. In sum, whereas Clark defines the nude in terms of beauty, Berger defines it in terms of politics.

Berger's thesis about the painted nude and spectatorship has its counterpart in film studies, in a famous essay by Laura Mulvey, written in 1973 (a year after *Ways of Seeing* appeared) and published in 1975.[6] Employing the term scopophilia (pleasure in looking), she suggested that the conditions of watching movies, together with the narrative conventions of film, promote "the illusion of voyeuristic separation." Viewing a movie manifests itself as a private act in a darkened theater (looking in on a private world, like a Peeping Tom), with attention focused on the human form itself, upon which the spectator may project his own desires. The pleasure, and the anxiety, of film, she argues, derives from the gap that separates image from self-image, a divide that can be bridged at least temporarily by fantasy. (This is the same gap exploited by advertising.)[7] The woman in film (her body and the character it reveals) receives Mulvey's principal attention, and her understanding of the woman's visual function is summarized by the following: "Traditionally, the woman displayed has functioned on two levels: as erotic object for the characters within the screen story, and as erotic object for the spectator within the auditorium, with a shifting tension between the looks on either side of the screen."[8]

For Mulvey and Berger, and implicitly for Clark, woman *is* image, and man is the bearer of the *look* on that image. The former is passive, hence it lacks agency; the other is active, hence it possesses agency.[9]

Who's Got the Look?

Is it sufficient to suggest, like Berger, that there exist only a relative few "exceptional" female nudes painted by male artists that fall outside the parameters thus far described? What happens when women themselves look at painted female nudes—or when women artists paint male (or female) nudes? Can women in effect "look back"?[10] The terms of debate have largely been defined by the academic discipline of art history, which for most of its existence has been practiced almost entirely by men who rarely saw a need to raise issues of the sort articulated by Berger, who is a critic, not an academic, or Mulvey, who is an academic, but not an art historian.

The seemingly obvious connection of the art nude to sociocultural questions about sexual difference was made an issue only with the advent of feminist art history in the early 1970s. The issue surfaced much as the result of the increased presence of women in the discipline who, through their own experience as women in the society at large and through experiences within the academy—historically not a site of empathy toward women—began to constitute a new discourse.[11] Some of the most interesting new work of this sort has addressed the contradictions inherent in the male gaze.

Marcia Pointon, for example, alludes to the deep-seated anxiety embedded in the male look concerning female sexuality, calling upon an Freudian psychoanalytic account of the male fear of castration, first experienced in childhood, generated by the appearance of physiological sexual difference—the female's "lack" of a penis. In other words, her account of the male gaze tacitly acknowledges not only strength but weakness. A difficulty with this formulation, however, is the degree to which it preserves the phallus as the locus of imagining the visible, or as Luce Irigaray puts it, "The male sex becomes *the* sex because it is very visible, the erection is spectacular" in a culture that privileges sight over other senses[12]—though as I will suggest in the next chapter, the male phallus *in art* borders culturally on being unrepresentable.

Nonetheless, Pointon demonstrates through her own practice as an art historian—a professional "looker" at art—that she can "see through" the visual technologies that operate to objectify women, thereby helping to undercut or overcome the effect. Her own gaze possesses the power to name patriarchy and to demonstrate how its rhetoric operates in representation.[13] This still acknowledges that the female nude is a category of painting mostly by and for men, of which "woman as spectator is offered the dubious satisfaction of identification with the heterosexual masculine gaze, voyeuristic, penetrating and powerful . . . negating women's own experience and identity."[14]

Pointon's most important insight is to regard the female nude as a form of rhetoric in which the subject is not fully contained or controlled either by the (male) artist, or the "author," or by the (male) spectator, or the "reader." In essence, the female nude *exceeds* her characterization by men, and this excess is not simply the result of external analysis by feminist spectators but in fact is inherent in the object itself. Put perhaps too simply, the female nude, even (perhaps especially) in its most objectified and objectionable form—usually what we call pornographic—constitutes an acknowledgment by men of the ability of women to satisfy a desire that men cannot satisfy themselves. Moreover, the female nude represents an *imaginary* female body to which the male spectator has access only psychically, not physically. In representation, she remains explicitly out of reach, except in fantasy. In other words, the desire to look, and to "possess" by looking, in the end only demonstrates that looking is *not* the same as "having." Assuming for a moment that all representations of female nudes are sexist (a blatant falsehood), we would still be required to specify that men's domination of women develops simultaneously from both strength *and* weakness. The *need* to dominate is the surest sociocultural indicator of the latter—and is no comfort to those being dominated, to be sure, but neither is it to those exercising that form of coercive power.

The desire of men to look at women, *and vice versa,* whether clothed or naked, is after all deeply informed by sexual necessity, an activity fully sanctioned by society when involving lovers. Herein, of course, lies the problem: There is no single road map for looking at the body of another. The look may define desires driven by love or hate, desires mutual and reciprocal or selfish and self-serving. Accordingly, the rhetoric of a given image is defined by more than itself, by more than what it is made to *look like*. It is driven by the function to which it is put. In the generation of my youth, boys' experiences with *National Geographic,* for example, were probably not always in line with the "official" discourses surrounding that magazine's exploration of the world and its myriad cultures. Yet however we account for the sexual desire produced by a woman's pictured body, whatever intentions her body may be designated to serve, the very act of picturing her, and not something else, marks the power her body possesses over her male counterpart, as Pointon has shown.[15] What this adds up to, in the end, is that the female nude occupies a space that is inevitably open to contestation, hence that space is profoundly ambiguous. And for all the insightful talk about the male and his controlling gaze, whereby women are objectified, I would argue that the female nude also defines fundamental limits to the agency of the gaze and its ability to objectify. The dominating power of the male gaze rests on the same fragile foundation as male identity itself, and although this can neither explain away the actual psychical and physical battering many women experience at the hands of men, it can perhaps provide a less essentialist account of the complexities surrounding the problem. The trouble with much current theorization about the male gaze is that it is itself essentialist, a vast simplification alike of both female *and male* identity and subjectivity, as I hope to show.[16]

Needing to See

The nude body in art is always "about" the removal of clothes; nudity does not constitute Westerners' natural state. To make available the sight of nudity in art is to respond to sociocultural needs not otherwise met in lived experience.[17] The question to ask is: What is this need, and how is it met in representation? The fact is that the need is not singular, nor is the means by which representational response (the making and the seeing) occurs. Whatever the representation, viewers project back onto and into the image their own sets of interests, desires, investments, phobias, and the like. We see differently from each other because our lives are never identical. Nor is any individual an unchanging cipher through which impressions flow without modification: Sexists and bigots are not born, but made; people who strive to liberate themselves and others are not genetically programmed for this activity—and, of course, people change.

Seeing helps make us what we are, whether we choose to confirm, to deny, or to mediate the "reality" we construct. Yet neither the misogynic nor the feminist image leads us toward any necessary or specific response. Either may strengthen or weaken our beliefs, whether they are regressive or progressive. This does not mean that no moral consequence attaches to either, only that no moral consequence is guaranteed from looking at one image as opposed to another. Each response is located within personal and general history, embedded in experience and belief, never the same in two individuals, and established within the complicated dynamics of culture, which is always a changing process and never static.

Originating in Sin

The glorification of the naked male body in ancient pagan art is matched by the denigration of the female body in much of Christian art. Eve's *sin*—not Eve herself—is the source for the female nude in Western painting. Her eating of the apple from the forbidden Tree of Knowledge, the meal shared with Adam that "universalized" the sin, produces the necessity of clothing to hide the shame that both, having sinned, suddenly experience. Their sense of shame is not the product of sensitivity to nakedness as such. Instead, shame develops from an awareness that nakedness is constituted by uncovered genitals made vulnerable by being visible to others. Having sinned, Adam and Eve do not wrap their entire bodies; they merely sew together fig leaves to wear—just that much and no more (Genesis 3:7). Since the late Middle Ages, nudity and sin are linked, and the *visual* account of the sinning body is marked by the appearance of sexual organs.

In the clothed culture of the West, the removal of drapery references Eve's sin, even when female nudity is represented in purely secular subjects. Indeed, the arousal upon which the functional success of the painted nude depends is connected to Eve's shame. The pleasure of the painted nude is driven in part by the act of looking *in judgment* on evil personified. Eve's importance to the history of art is not because she was "first mother" to Adam as "first father." Her real significance is her sin and its catastrophic consequence, the Fall of Man (the word is gender-specific). Scripture and art alike acknowledge Eve's power to influence Adam, *hence* to cause general misery. It is not surprising, therefore, that Eve in pictures is almost always positioned upright—phallic—visually very much Adam's equal; they usually form a matched pair. But in Western painting those later women who, posed nude like Eve, were "heirs" to her sin, are usually preferred supine. In essence, they are toppled from their phallic position, no longer able to share the uprightness granted to men. (In most painting, supine males are fallen heroes, wounded and dying: Their stance references activity, vitality, and potency, even while showing all of these in a state of collapse.) In art, female nudes are overwhelmingly longitudinal, anchored to the horizon, to nature, to earth—and to bed. The bed serves as the sign of eternal submissiveness for a woman's having led Adam astray. As such, the bed in art often represents less the site of mutual pleasure and love than a place for the punishment of females, the locus of sanctioned revenge. Only, as I will soon show, it is actually not quite that simple.

Hans Baldung's *Eve, the Serpent, and Adam as Death* (Figure 9.1) is an extraordinary visual text in the history of the female nude. In particular, it situates Eve as both a biblical figure and a modern sinner. Her body is provided with the consummate beauty of youth and (blond, Germanic) perfection, and it is displayed without shame. By crossing her legs, she displays a degree of modesty despite her nakedness. But her most distinct trait is a frank sexuality typified by a lack of self-consciousness about her nakedness. To be sure, before their fall from grace, both Eve and Adam's "innocence" is scripturally marked by an apparent lack of awareness of nakedness as such. Baldung plays off this fact by painting a trace of her pubic hair—the vast majority of Western paintings of female nudes eliminate all traces thereof. Yet this is a body sign of adult sexuality that, in the history of representation, simultaneously defines her innocence *and* her guilt. Eve's historical modernity is marked especially in her face, which is at specific odds with the rest of her body. Her expression hints of sophistication, allurement, and seductive power. It is the look of a coquette, dangerously like that of a whore—the "sideways glance" that would establish itself so firmly in Western iconography as one mark of female sexual evil and power of entrapment. Eve's modernity is further evident in the slightly smug mouth and, of course, by her hiding behind her back the apple that she will produce for Adam once she has worn down his resistance.

Like Eve, Adam marks the uneasy relation of prehistorical timelessness to the historical time of Baldung's modernity. He reaches up to pluck the apple that will be his poison but in fact has not yet tasted the fruit, the act of consumption that will guarantee his physical death. This notwithstanding, his body is fast decomposing before our eyes. Before Adam can sire his future children, his flesh rots: His own agency disappears, and that agency—so Baldung makes visually clear—was phallic. (The serpent biting Adam's wrist is profoundly phallic, emphasized by its engorgement.) In effect, because of the advanced decay of facial flesh that exposes his teeth, Adam appears to leer at Eve. His blank stare not only implies sexuality but also sexual violence. The relaxed hand he lays on Eve's fleshy arm does not grasp but seems virtually to caress; by contrast, his shoulder muscles are tensed as though he were attacking. This mixed message of body language suggests that he will eat the apple, then rape her—but she, in the meantime, will have seduced him. The male force is transmitted from first father to father of Death (Adam's rotting body),

Figure 9.1
Hans Baldung
(c. 1484–1545), EVE,
THE SERPENT, AND
ADAM AS DEATH
(c. 1510/1515), panel,
64 × 32.5 cm. Ottawa,
National Gallery of
Canada, no. 17011.

and Death equates with violence, with Eve's just desserts. Moreover, sexuality itself is mapped onto a grid of mortal combat.

Baldung's painting is organized around the sight of Eve's body. The background is black; the tree and Adam's body are both mostly brown. Eve is the picture's light. Her body's surface relates to the rest of the painting in such a way that she holds no single focal point: Her whole body *is* what is to be scanned and not merely her breasts or genital region, as would later become the rather clichéd norm of compositional focus—Baldung devotes more care to her feet and toenails than to her genital region. Baldung acknowledges Eve's power as a whole woman, not merely as a sexual part. Her agency is her *being,* and that being is sexual.

Indeed, Baldung fashions "an erotic art that itself arouses the desires that reflect a viewer's kinship with Adam. And Baldung punishes those desires through the viewer's experience of revulsion in encountering himself in the habit of the corpse."[18] Our eyes are not held entirely in the thrall of Eve's nudity. The painting's focal point, following a line traced by Eve's right leg, is occupied by Adam as Death's ugly hand laid atop Eve's arm, and Eve's hand fingering the snake. This connective link to the price of sin's pleasures is compositionally powerful and marks a transference of action and reaction. Eve grips the tail of the phallic snake or, better yet, seems to stroke it lightly with her fingers in a gesture of marked sexuality. It is toward this activity that she directs her glance, compelling ours as well to follow her eyes. She knows exactly what she is doing.[19] The metaphoric excitement of this foreplay accords with the symbolic excitement marked by the reptile's engorgement and, not least important, by the bite it delivers to Adam as Death's arm. Baldung is careful not to show the jaws tensed: This is virtually a perverse love bite,[20] a physical, and human, response in sexual play, yet one that feeds only on itself, to the extent that the serpent, Satan, *is* death. Sin—defined as sexual—procreates destruction.

It is necessary to keep in mind that Baldung's remarkable painting operates via a pervasive eroticism that invites our libidinal investment; this makes us complicit children of the first parents and acknowledges that we bear the stain of their guilt. As other scholars have noted, Baldung is the first painter to have linked the Fall to an erotic act.[21] As Joseph Koerner so aptly puts it, describing another Eve by the same artist:

> Baldung demonstrates that human representation cannot pretend to be the purveyor of an unspoiled, prelapsarian innocence of vision. This "message" is instantiated in the way that we, as beholders, interpret his images. To say, for example, that Eve's gesture . . . is a deliberate, seductive, and erotic concealment of

sexuality, or to interpret her as possessing a "knowing" look, is to betray our knowledge of sexuality and deception and therefore to admit our own fallenness.[22]

By the late nineteenth century the moral implication of this insight will be reduced to a *pleasurable tinge* of guilt embedded in a rhetoric of titillation and to the outrage (moral and otherwise) with which Western middle-class men framed female sexuality, as the means of defining their own (see Figures 9.7, 9.8). But in the meantime, Baldung's painting helps us understand the stakes of looking. In essence, the history of the nude in art finds in Baldung's Eve its driving force. In the Beginning, it seems, *Eve* possessed the look, a look so powerful that men thereafter have been made to pay the price—and to seek revenge. Put differently, Baldung's Eve controls everything. She is what the viewer desires to see, and within the painting, her act of looking controls a world-changing event. The history of Eve provides visual representation with the moral excuse and the social function at once to keep women in sight while rendering them metaphorically blind.

Cold Comforts

Bronzino's *An Allegory with Venus and Cupid* (Figure 9.2, *Color Plate 15*), painted only a few decades after Baldung's picture, is a product of Italian mannerist sensibilities par excellence that anticipates the wholly sexualized secular nudes that principally define the subject in modern consciousness. The rhetorical power of Bronzino's painting, when set against the tradition of painted nudes as a whole, derives from its overtly frank acknowledgment of the erotic pleasure of scopophilia, with none of the tiresome overlay of moral justification, a shadowed reference to bad conscience, that so heavily marks the female nude in the nineteenth century.

Bronzino's Venus is surrounded by other figures who factor into a complex (and now very uncertain) allegory dominated by the male figure of Time, who spreads a neon-blue cloak as an enfolding frame or mantle around the central figures. The other figures may be Folly, at the right, Pleasure behind and to Folly's left, and Jealousy, behind Cupid. I will focus my remarks on the nudity and interaction of the two central foreground characters.

Cupid, provided with a highly sexualized adolescent body but the face of a child, moves to kiss Venus while sexually exciting her by fondling her breasts, whose nipples are erect. Venus, no stranger to the ways of love, takes pleasure in Cupid's attention *and* disarms him. She has reached down to his quiver and has taken from it the sharply pointed, emphatically phallic arrow that she

Figure 9.2
Bronzino (Agnolo di
Cosimo) (1503–1572),
AN ALLEGORY WITH
VENUS AND CUPID
(c. 1540s), panel,
146.1 × 116.2 cm.
London, National
Gallery, inv. no. 651.
Reproduced by courtesy
of the Trustees, The
National Gallery,
London.

now holds delicately and *provocatively* in her hand. His body is tensed to his
sexual "work"; her body, no less contorted but nonetheless extraordinarily relaxed, shows every sign thereby of controlling the situation of their mutual
excitement.

Bronzino paints Venus as physically powerful, and she is literally posed so
as to maintain complete control over her own dramatically elongated body.
She dominates the much smaller boy. Cupid's body, however, as much a spec-

tacle as Venus's, is also made sexually accessible to a degree that hers is not. In an extraordinarily homoerotic pose, Cupid's phallic sexuality is diminished—metaphorically, it is visually taken from him by Venus. He is emphatically feminized. In essence, Venus's sexual parts are transferred to Cupid, whom she overpowers. His backside is made as attractive a sight of pleasure's site as Venus's breasts (or better, her nipples). Venus's genital region "promises" virtually nothing; Cupid's buttocks "promise" much. His pose, in other words, renders him physically available for the sexual penetration that in most Western painting is conventionally "due" Venus and women generally. Further, X rays of the canvas indicate "a series of curves in the region of Cupid's buttocks," suggesting that Bronzino lingered over their function in the painting's visual rhetoric. The buttocks he ultimately painted appear to be the most radical, sexually provoking of these compositional "experiments."[23]

However, the painting's kinky and incestuous[24] omnisexuality (Cupid is Venus's son) is not quite all it might at first seem, especially when seen in color. Bronzino's Venus and Cupid violate a host of sexual taboos: incest, homoeroticism, prostitution via Venus's wantonness, and gender reversal via Venus's sexual domination of Cupid. But the sexualized bodies we gaze upon seem oddly distant and inaccessible. The light illuminating both figures is nearly fluorescent, giving a distinctly cold cast to their skin, and the painting's overall highly reflective surface only increases the impact of this lighting effect. As a result, their bodies appear, if not exactly corpselike, not quite alive.

The patriarchal figure of Time "controls" the allegorical text by framing the various figures within his cosmic-blue cloak. And to complicate matters further, the mantle matches the blue drapery then conventional to imagery of the Virgin-Mother of God. Hence, Bronzino subtly hints at a paradoxical conflation of sacred love and its most secular analogue. Time, in everything, is the essence. Time is wasted, *and* time wastes. The intense pleasures of sex, pleasures most desired and most sought, are profoundly time bound. Relative to other experiences, the time of sex is as short as its realization is often uncertain. People most strongly realize time *in* their own bodies (development, aging, and the rest). In short, time is a principal dimension of life within which the body "makes sense" and within which it senses. Time, in other words, is an external and abstract manifestation of the experience of life lived through the body. Embodied life is made possible by sexuality. Our sense of the sexual body is largely determined by desire, just as our sense of time is in part determined, and made an issue of, by our awareness that it is a finite dimension eternally working against our abilities to realize our desires (Time flies).

Erotic desire, driven by the viewer's response to the sights offered by Bronzino's painting, remains paradoxical. Bronzino visualizes for us the violation of taboos, evoking desires of the most culturally dangerous sort. But while holding us in the momentary thrall of sexual possibility, he seems to hint at two sobering facts. First, the pleasures of looking are just that. What we see is not only not real, or realized, but impossible. The highly sexualized bodies of both Venus and Cupid are the result of visual fantasies; their contortions are physiologically impossible. Both are posed unnaturally, as distorted figments of desire. Cupid's invisible neck, for example, is impossibly long, stretched unduly so as to allow his lips to reach Venus's. Her pose defies gravity; her torso should topple, as it does not appear to be propped up by Cupid's counterforce. The pleasures that both presumably enjoy, as do we as viewers, are masochistic to the extent that the poses would be uncomfortable, if not painful, to maintain for long. In other words, Bronzino deftly informs us that the delicious omnisexuality he is offering produces a desire that cannot be satisfied except in the imagination; it has no fleshly parallel. Its reality is abstract: The nude bodies of woman and boy ultimately keep their distance in the bluish-white cold of a technicolor dream.

To be sure, the image is controlled by an elaborate conceit, one I have barely glossed over, though I would suggest that keeping the academic at arm's length is not the least indication of Bronzino's success at evoking paradox. Whatever the impact of his nudes, we cannot "get away from" all else that goes on in the image. The other figures stand nearby as though to protest, "There is more to this." The painting insists on our recognizing its textual complexity and by that means, of course, acknowledges the educated audience for which it was intended. In any event, the undeniability of the allegory, whatever it may turn out to be, confirms Bronzino's deference to his patron, usually thought to be Cosimo de' Medici (1519–1574), the first grand duke of Tuscany and a moral puritan, which by itself might suggest the paradoxical nature of the picture, that it is more than high-grade pornography. Cosimo is supposed to have sent this painting as a gift to King Francis I (1494–1547) of France,[25] providing him with (1) a striking sexual fantasy, (2) an allegory about life but with quasi-moral overtones—nothing explicit—appropriate as a gift from one Catholic sovereign to another, and (3) an elaborate riddle that the French king by presumption had the ability to solve, an implicit and diplomatically valuable compliment to his intelligence (the task might in fact have been beyond him, but that is not the point).[26]

Turning the Tables

François Boucher's *Pan and Syrinx* (Figure 9.3), painted more than two centuries after Bronzino's *Venus and Cupid,* is an altogether less compli-

Figure 9.3
François Boucher (1703–1770), PAN AND SYRINX (1759), canvas, 32.4 × 41.9
cm. London, National Gallery, inv. no. 1090. Reproduced by courtesy of the
Trustees, The National Gallery, London.

cated image as far as its "story" goes. Boucher does not concern himself with
allegory, and concerning any textual source, or excuse, he simply calls on an
entirely unsurprising, virtually stock subject (if it can be called even that) demanding a female nude—and includes two, for good measure. The old story
of the Arcadian nymph Syrinx, whom the randy Pan pursues, is transformed
into a ménage à trois. According to Ovid's[27] account, Pan chases Syrinx to the
banks of a river that impedes her escape from what is, after all, an intended
rape. Syrinx successfully pleads for deliverance and, just as Pan grabs for her,
she is transformed into a bunch of reeds. Hearing the sounds made by wind

blowing across the open ends of the plants' hollow stems, Pan fashions from them/her the first panpipes. Music is thereby accounted for as the twin result of violence against a woman and *as* woman in another, disembodied form. To avoid a sexual assault, she becomes music, though at the expense of her body.

The Pan and Syrinx myth thus has a serious side. It tells a male story, yet it acknowledges paradox and contradiction as it addresses gender, desire, violence, and loss. And not least important, it posits music as a consolation for failure: Pan's being outwitted by a woman, but also a woman's sacrifice of her selfhood to avoid a presumably worse alternative. When Ovid arrives at the point of having to describe Pan's proposal to Syrinx, he interrupts the narrative and only quotes Syrinx's firm "No," leaving us to imagine the vile things Pan suggested. Pan's sexual desire, mapped in this instance as an unadulterated biological drive (a convenient justification for his sexual aggression), is in the end redirected into work. For the moment, Pan becomes a woodworker-artisan, fashioning a musical instrument that will bear his name and mark his identity. He makes good use of his pipes: They provide him with the means not for rape but for future seductions. He will use the instrument's sweet sounds to charm the ladies, to make them desire him—with considerable success, judging from his later sexual exploits with the orgiastically inclined bacchantes. The complication to this sexual Horatio Alger story arises from the fact that Pan's success depends upon a woman, transformed. By himself he is not up to the task. Still, the price paid by a woman to make the man a man—his sexual performance—is supreme: She ceases to be.

Western mythology slowly transformed Pan from handsome youth to half-man half-goat, as in Boucher's painting. Driven by his lower region, he has only partway "evolved," being provided in art with the torso of a heroic, if a bit beefy, god and the lower, furry torso of the quadruped. His head is human, but usually has a goat's horns and ears, though not in Boucher's picture. The point is that, although he may be something of a bad joke, for example, when stood against the elegant and wise Apollo, Pan is nonetheless all too recognizable as "us." In textual allegories of the Renaissance, Pan's lust defines him, but that characteristic is, for the male sex, an ambiguous character trait. It exemplifies coarseness, on the negative side, but dominant aggression, on the positive. As an imagined inhabitant of Arcadia, as a pastoral shepherd, Pan marks a time of male "innocence"—when the world was presumably less complex, when a boy could just be a boy, with the girls there to help him, wittingly or not, play the role well.[28]

A massive Arcadian revival (a fascination with the ahistorical never-never land of shepherds and shepherdesses) was played out at the courts of Western Europe from the Renaissance to, roughly, the French Revolution.[29] In part, the revival represented a reactionary response to a complicated series of new questions about the nature of human identity, defined by evolving conceptions of individuality and competitive individualism. At the precise moment when Western humanism undertook the effort to redefine a gender-specific mankind, in other words, a powerful wave of nostalgic melancholia swept the consciousness of the educated, aristocratic elite. Their fantasy of an Arcadian paradise was grounded in a growing awareness of fundamental sociocultural change that would, within the course of roughly three hundred years, topple the aristocracy in favor of the bourgeoisie. Not surprisingly, the Arcadian revival reached its most intense state of performance at the French court immediately before the Revolution in 1789. Thus when the uprising had literally reached the front gates of Versailles, Queen Marie Antoinette had to be summoned back to the main palace from her toy-village "backyard" hamlet, where she and her courtly friends enjoyed dressing up as (well-heeled) peasants. (Much of the hamlet, a proto-Euro-Disney Fantasyland, survives to this day and can be visited.)

By the late eighteenth century, the threat of the distinctly non-Arcadian new bourgeoisie—businessmen, in modern parlance, newly monied—caused a crisis in the old aristocracy, with its old money, agriculturally based. The overriding issue was economic but was quickly translated into a story involving class and gender identity, an important feature of which centered on masculinity. If the European aristocracy wasted its substance in sexual degeneracy (Panlike)—or so the bourgeoisie eventually told the tale—then the bourgeoisie's moralistic-political response was a move toward containing the temptation. Indeed, it was ironic that the degeneracy attributed to the aristocracy was located as much in the sexual bodies of their women as in the sociopolitical privilege and power wielded by the male nobility who actually ran things.[30] Either way, not much space was left for women in what was principally a war between competing groups of men. Women were part of the war materiel for both sides, not the least result being the rampant misogyny evident in the late eighteenth century and throughout the nineteenth, and the phenomenal level of male hysteria concerning female sexuality, though this puts me ahead of the story.

Boucher's *Pan and Syrinx* was designed for the courtly gaze at Versailles. In that its subject involves a female nude, it is significant that the picture acknowledges a *female* rather than a male spectator, though it otherwise offers up the usual image of Arcadia. Boucher is an adapter who pays lip service to widely known textual sources but makes significant changes to suit the historical moment and presumed function of his commissions. In particular, Boucher's work, and his female nudes especially, resonate intertextually with the enormous Baroque propaganda pieces that decorated the walls and ceilings throughout the palace of Versailles—older, gigantic images, often profoundly and aggressively masculine, and invariably, heroic (Louis XIV on horseback metaphorically crushing his enemies, and the like). Masculinity in Boucher is reduced from performance on the battlefield to performance in the putative bedroom, masculinity's most vulnerable site. Masculinity in *Pan and Syrinx* comes up less as wanting than as vaguely irrelevant.

Boucher's Syrinx is *not* the victim of naked male sexual aggression, as Ovid's story recounts. Boucher's Syrinx does not flee for her virginity or her life. Instead she *relaxes*. Boucher gives his audience an early version of a beach party picture, where boys pursue and girls egg them on. Pan seems to rush onto the scene, his fur trailing behind him, as though still the mythically sanctioned aggressor. The nymphs, meanwhile, privately disrobed in the deep woods at the river bank, their pink skin entirely unused to exposure, simultaneously engage him *and* each other. Aside from one nymph's surprised look and upraised arm with opened hand—the standard theatrical-rhetorical gesture for fending off attack—both women are virtually languid. In other words, Boucher places the viewer at a critical moment, ripe with ambiguity and possibility: rape or seduction, with the question of who is seducing whom left open.

Boucher plays off a theme of lesbianism, to the extent that the nude women, positioned to provide a back and front view, one complete female anatomy, seem to move apart from an embrace, as though their bodies, just prior to the moment represented, had enmeshed (the hand of one lies atop the other's shoulder, and their lower torsos are composed like two puzzle pieces destined for perfect interlock). Meanwhile, a little Cupid illuminates Pan's way and holds a daggerlike arrow that defines an anticipated action—that will not occur. Pan is set to resituate this all-girl love scene back into "natural" order. He will come between the women, in essence penetrating their ovular pink enclosure, a fact broadly hinted at by the line of separation Boucher delineates between them, as sign of Pan's sexual interpolation. What is interesting here is that Boucher provides no hint of Pan's failure. As the myth insists, Pan grasps with his powerful arm but comes up with only an armful of "reeds" (yet not the kind from which to make panpipes). Nonetheless, the woman remains a woman, not merely untransformed but doubled. Pan has gotten the making of his music, *and* he has gotten *them,* too. Pan is a real winner.

Taken just this far, most of what John Berger and Laura Mulvey have maintained about the objectifying male gaze rings true. But there is more to be said. Boucher lavished considerable labor on the picture, especially regarding the commanding presence claimed for the women's bodies, seen in the care he takes to model their every fleshly fold. He explores their bodies' surfaces with enormous attentiveness, subtly shading and modulating every square centimeter of the canvas that their bodies occupy. Boucher cannot take his brush from them, and he adeptly works to insure that neither can we divert our glance. What might this say, beyond the legitimate claim of male objectification and self-interest in the representation of women?

It seems to me that Boucher frankly plays to the well-documented rampant libidinal pleasures of the court of Louis XV—long exploited by the artist's chief patroness, Madame de Pompadour (1721–1764). Madame de Pompadour became the king's mistress in 1745 when she was twenty-four. In 1750 their sexual relationship ended, though they maintained a close friendship until her death nearly fifteen years later. Boucher began to work for Madame de Pompadour in the same year that her sexual partnership with the king ended.[31] This painting (from 1759) acknowledges her interests, at the same moment that it putatively exists to please and help entertain the king via pictures of young, pretty, and naked women—his appetite for their three-dimensional analogues being well known and endlessly demonstrated.

Boucher explicitly acknowledges women's own sexual desires, via his lightly veiled reference to lesbianism (which, to return to the myth, may *not* be set straight by Pan). His nymphs, in other words, can succeed at their own pleasures, ones in which the male presence seems clumsy and almost comical. Pan intrudes on the nymphs, and he intrudes on the pleasure of our looking, in essence interrupting or preventing a more pleasurable voyeurism. Boucher's Pan has a notably stupid, uncomprehending face; he just "doesn't get it." He may push ahead, at the urging of Cupid, who seems to promise success, arrow properly poised. But Pan himself is profoundly confused. The nymphs on the other hand are not. Accordingly, it is equally possible that the wide-open eyes of one of the nymphs allude not only to surprise or shock at the intrusion but also mark sexual excitement that has nothing whatever to do with Pan. Ultimately, however, the issue in question is not female homosexuality; that would be a ludicrous claim. The issue is female sexuality, a sexuality that men cannot ultimately understand, control, or—like a problem—"solve" to their satisfaction. It literally remains out of grasp.

Grasping is the gesture that defines both the myth and the picture. (The current cliché, in male business parlance, of "grabbing the ring" is of related cultural genealogy.) Pan goes for the girls but ends up with an arm full of blooming plants—not reeds—whose flower heads bear a distinct resemblance to the fleur-de-lis (the iris), the symbol of the French state and the king, in essence the emblem of the sovereign's identity and authority. Pan takes (pitiful) hold of power as a poor substitute for what escapes him. Desire is deferred; Pan gets a shot at its realization, and he misses. In Boucher's version of the story, the bittersweet aftermath allows us to imagine Pan going off to make a raft of panpipes, and the phallic impact of this instrument was lost on no one, either in the ancient world or in Boucher's own day: a replication of phalluses, which in the end add up only expelling a bit of hot air. The nymphs meanwhile go back to their embrace, complete, and judging from their appearance quite happy.

Boucher makes it patently clear, by means of a few subtle decisions, how easily the cultural discourse can be changed. To paint a nude woman for the delectation of a man guarantees nothing, least of all woman's objectification as such. To represent a woman's delicate touch on the shoulder of another woman, delineating a trace of their arrested self-absorption, remakes the meaning of the women's nudity. The sight of them posed accordingly takes back what it promises at first glance. Their bodies remain their own and, in this instance at least, at the specific expense of a man.[32] (It is worth noting that Boucher painted this picture at a time when Madame de Pompadour was at the height of her influence over Louis XV, "an influence which she exercised for twenty years with tact, intelligence and charm"—long after their brief sexual relationship ended.)[33]

Figments of an Imagination

The nude woman in Jean-Auguste-Dominique Ingres's early nineteenth-century *Valpinçon Bather* (Figure 9.4) displays her back and a small bit of backside. Her nakedness dominates the canvas, yet it yields surprisingly little as a sight for voyeuristic pleasure, despite promising more. The tiny waterspout at the lower left explains her nakedness as resulting from her preparation for a bath, and that fact marks the viewer as an unseen intruder in a distinctly private space. The woman's red-and-white turban (borrowed from paintings by Raphael) stands out against the plain background and provides her with an exotic air that complements an association with the white-sheeted (virginal) bed, the picture's only furniture. The picture's basic elements are these: young woman, vaguely exotic, sitting naked on a white-sheeted bed. The connotations are as unambiguously sexual; they also are made to appear less than "natural." Ingres thus puts distance between the viewer and what the viewer looks at by defining the view as imaginary. What is "there" is not really there except as a fiction. The painting's event promotes itself as unabashedly *staged.* Indeed, theatricality is hinted broadly by the curtain at the extreme left, which, by being dropped, makes the tableau visible to the audience.

For a nude study, Ingres's painting is noteworthy for its extreme reserve, evoked not least by a pervading sense of *silence.* The only sound to be imagined comes from the small stream of water flowing from the bath spout. Moreover, the picture space is mostly given to sound-absorbing drapery: bed-

Figure 9.4
Jean-Auguste-
Dominique Ingres
(1780–1867),
VALPINÇON BATHER
(1808), canvas,
146 × 97.5 cm. Paris,
Musée du Louvre, inv.
no. RF 259. © Photo
R.M.N.

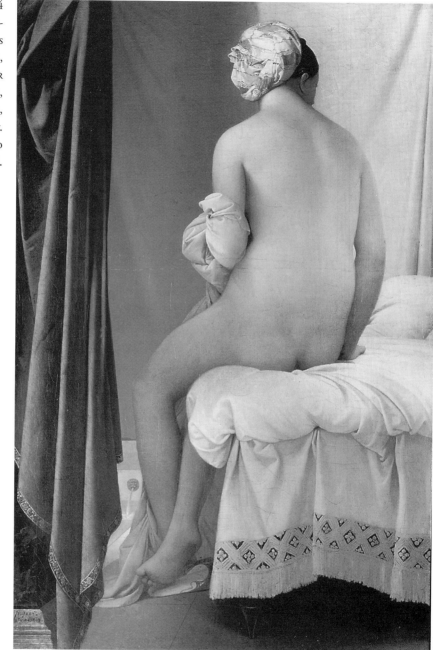

ding, a white sheet suspended at the back, and the greenish drape at the left. What our looking produces, at least with a little concentration, is an awareness of the act of *listening*—not looking.[34] (The nude herself has nothing to look at but a piece of unadorned cloth.) She cocks her ear. She listens, yet with absolute relaxation, as though still fairly certain of her privacy. The evocation of hearing and the painting's pervasive silence affect the viewer's stance in two ways. First, viewing becomes more a self-consciously intrusive act; second, the viewer's invasiveness remains virtually irrelevant. We seemingly cannot psychologically project ourselves into the space she occupies, precisely because the pervasive silence has a spatial impact: It distances us.

Ingres's picture organizes the female nude around a paradoxical association of two human sensing organs. The first, hearing, is located inside the picture frame, in a distinctly feminine space (overwhelmingly *soft*—including her own body that seems almost without skeleton—white, pure, moist). The second, seeing, is external to the image and referenced only indirectly as an abstraction—the fact that any image exists to be looked at. Hearing, by contrast, is represented and appears concrete. Hearing is visibly embodied, and it is what she *does*. Culturally speaking, hearing is usually regarded as enveloping and incorporating, and as such, is viewed more as a mark of the feminine. Hearing defines proximity and connectedness but also wariness (listening for trouble). The bather listens *for* something, and given the apparent attentiveness of her visible ear, the suggestion is that she listens for an unseen other. Sight, in this case, establishes not proximity and connectedness, but distance and separation.

Ingres's allusion to hearing and sight, his separating one from the other, establishes the limits of the masculine gaze at precisely the point at which its purported powers should claim victory—the visual taking-in (metaphorical possessing) of the vulnerable female body. Ingres acknowledges that male voyeurism is a self-defeating principle for the establishment of masculine supremacy (I am not arguing that he was a feminist). In essence, the power of the male gaze depends on its being *noticed* by the person subject to the gaze. Male identity, in other words, hangs in the balance of being acknowledged. She *must* somehow display her awareness of, and reaction to, male spectatorship, or the power supposedly embedded into the act of his looking is principally undercut. In essence, for the male spectator to rise above the level of Peeping Tom (a form of self-defeating self-infantilization) she has to catch him at it, particularly when the scene involves private space. In the end what Ingres leaves us with is uncertainty. He in no sense disregards scopophilia; instead he clarifies the uncertainty of its effects. The *Valpinçon Bather,* ironically named this by art history after one of the painting's owner's, reflects by its title an unwitting displacement of possession, as though owning the *canvas* substitutes for owning control of the spectacle.

Near his life's end, at age eighty-two, Ingres returned to this same nude via the exotic orientalism of *The Turkish Bath* (Figure 9.5), but in this instance as a Peeping Tom intent on getting himself quite a sight. Indeed, the picture's shape takes on the aspect of a peephole, or perhaps a camera lens—the original shape of the painting was rectilinear; it was later repainted by Ingres. It is not a coincidence that one of the first major initiatives for the documentary possibilities of photography came from Europeans' toting their cameras to the Middle East, as early as 1839. The link of the early history of photography to orientalism is firmly established,[35] together with its employment for mass production of erotic and pornographic images, contrived harem scenes

Figure 9.5
Jean-Auguste-
Dominique Ingres
(1780–1867), THE
TURKISH BATH (1862),
canvas, mounted on
panel, diameter 108 cm.
Paris, Musée du Louvre,
inv. no. RF 1934. ©
Photo R.M.N.

prominent among them. Ingres never traveled to the Near East. Indeed, his source for this image was textual, not visual, in the form of a letter written long before, in 1717, by Lady Mary Wortley Montagu, whose husband was British ambassador to Constantinople. She described a women's bath with two hundred in attendance. Ingres copied the passage into his own notebooks as early as 1819, obviously interested in the visual possibilities.[36]

The borrowed bather occupies the center left foreground, still with her back to us but with her breast visible; she wears a close approximation of her original turban. Now a musician plays the oud, and again she listens with her head cocked. No longer a solitary figure, as a nude she is replicated by Ingres with seeming abandon, as though he could not stop—and many of the other nudes are also taken from his earlier paintings.[37] Some are quasi-classical, like the face of the woman in full profile just right of center; others, like the frontally nude woman at the far right, are her excessive opposite, all physical and expressive reserve thrown aside. A few are lithe, like the woman at the center left, but most of the twenty-seven women are heavy; and all of them, without exception, have enormous breasts. Indeed, the painting might aptly be named "Turkish Breasts," so fixated is Ingres on this physiological feature. The desire to fondle them is prominently displaced from his own fantasy onto that of a young woman at the right who very firmly grasps her companion's breast, to the point of distorting its shape. Indeed, the grasping hand, its thumb slightly enlarged, attracting attention to itself, is not only obvious, but coarse.

Ingres not only signed his painting, on the table edge at the very bottom of the picture, he also inscribed his age, as if to suggest that his capacity as an artist to paint women at an advanced age was a sign of undiminished virility. And yet the claim falls somewhat flat, mostly because he protests too much: too much promise of erotic adventure in swollen bodies, too many women squeezed in, though with Ingres's characteristic compositional flair, as through a compulsive attempt to assert his capacities by multiplication and technical bravado. For all this, the painting is oddly desensualized; it remains as much a compositional study (a formal problem to be solved) as an erotic fantasy. The gap between the eroticism that his subject demands and the cool rationalization of a complex compositional challenge provides still one more indication of the elusiveness of the female body to masculine control. Even the bodies of young women fantasized by an old man remain beyond reach: They are for the most part impossible oedipal conflations of maternal nurture and sexual allure—as it were, breasts for nursing *and* fondling.

But as Marilyn Brown has written, it is insufficient to consider this image solely in light of Ingres's psyche. It is, after all, an image for an audience, one

Figure 9.6
Jean-Auguste–Dominique Ingres (1780–1867), ODALISQUE WITH A SLAVE
(1839–1840), canvas mounted on panel, 76.5 × 104 cm. Cambridge, Mass.,
courtesy of the Fogg Art Museum, Harvard University Art Museums, bequest of
Grenville L. Winthrop, acc. no. 1943.251.

Ingres knew well how to please. It can come as little surprise that Ingres's
painting has rather little to do with the Turkish bath, Turkish culture, or history. Instead, the painting contains a fictive accumulation of Western fantasies that attempt to fix the Middle East as the epicenter of orientalism, conflated with forbidden sexual possibilities and primitivism.[38] Nonetheless,
finding "what you want" in the vast archive of Western painting's female
nudes is by no means an uncomplicated task. This enormous library of images, duly cataloged in the myriad texts of art history, resists the gaze. Ingres's
Odalisque with a Slave[39] (Figure 9.6, *Color Plate 16*), commissioned by his

friend M. Marcotte d'Argenteuil, whose portrait he had previously painted, is a case in point. It employs a visual rhetoric quite different from either of the previously discussed paintings. This time Ingres resorts to color and abundant detail to establish a cultural and visual ground against which to set his inordinately white-pink, and *distinctly* (northern, blond) European, nude model. Her own color is striking, in comparison with what surrounds her (a black eunuch, a brown slave playing the *tar;* red curtain and column, green-and-red tiled floor, red-and-blue tiles on the back wall, with much of this being richly patterned) and when set against the other nudes in the Ingres paintings just discussed.

Ingres adapted this nude's supine pose from numerous European paintings of the reclining Venus dating back to the Renaissance, though with one distinct alteration. He rearranged her body into a quasi-contortionist pose, at once both unnatural and uncomfortable to maintain, but nonetheless particularly frank about the function of her state of undress. That is, Ingres unabashedly arranged her *as a sight* defined compositionally by a pronounced geometric triangulation of navel and nipples and by a soft anatomy, virtually deskeletalized. In effect, Ingres disciplined her soft flesh for his and our viewing, shaping her into complex curvilinear outline *and* twisting her into something of a corkscrew. She is like silly putty in his hands. And yet despite Ingres's attempt to subject her to his and our gaze by placing her in a pose that responds to the command, "I want to look at you," she comports herself as a figment of the male imagination and not as the representation of a real woman—though ironically of course she was: that is, he employed a model. The issue does not hinge on the faulty ethnography of Ingres's fabricated seraglio or on his supplying a Nordic Brunhild instead of an odalisque. Rather, I think, it hinges on the limited ability to represent a fantasy without making it apparent that what is represented *is* merely a fantasy. Indeed, Ingres's overload of gorgeous, colorful details comes off as profoundly staged. For example, the balustrade and columns, both quite distinctive visual features of the picture, seem flat, undercutting the viewer's sense of space, the reality-confirming third dimension. (Norman Bryson aptly refers to these details as cutouts.)[40]

When Ingres deals with the nude, paradox asserts itself and entirely unmasks the elements of theatrical realism as mere props belonging to the theater of the absurd. In the end what is available is something to be seen and something to be wished, but *not* something to be had. Access to the secret interior of the seraglio provides the male European voyeur no greater access to the European woman of his dreams. Not able to claim her, he can only acknowledge her ability to traverse his imagination. Ingres's nude, for all her seeming vulnerability in the voyeuristic eye, remains distant precisely to the extent that her very form and compositional arrangement delineate her literal impossibility. She is not objectified in and by the male gaze; instead she invites the recognition that sometimes a look is just a look. And the purported all-encompassing power of the look sometimes deceives.

Colonizing the Body

Jean-Léon Gérôme's *The Slave Market* (Figure 9.7, *Color Plate 17*) is the product of one of the most successful French painters of the nineteenth century, a man who enjoyed fame—and an immense fortune—but whose reputation quickly faded after his death. He sold his work to European nobility and wealthy businessmen in both Europe and America. A contemporary of the Impressionists, he denigrated their work, though he was a friend of Edgar Degas. Gérôme moved in a very different circle as the foremost orientalist painter in the world. Two-thirds of his roughly 550 paintings were devoted to orientalist subjects. He traveled widely in the Middle East between 1856 and 1880, going to Palestine, Syria, Sinai, and North Africa, but he especially favored Egypt and the cities of Cairo and Constantinople.[41] On these excursions he made numerous sketches and obtained many photographs; these served as stock images—some were used repeatedly—for paintings produced later in France, sometimes long afterward. He also purchased numerous items to serve later as studio props: "clothing, shoes, armor, helmets, swords, daggers, rifles, pistols, yards of materials, tables, stools, saddles, boots, tiles, pots, hookahs, and other artifacts. At his death the inventory of his studio included an immense store of oriental costumes and properties."[42]

The nude in *The Slave Market* is not exhibited supine, like so many female nudes positioned that way to demonstrate their sexual powers of attraction; instead, she is standing—in order to be examined. Her owner, just behind, has stripped off her white drapery, which he holds. Its pure white color unsubtly marks her presumed virginity. Her would-be buyer is luxuriantly overdressed, his costume conventionally then perceived in the West as a sign of oriental decadence—and even effeminacy! His face is mostly hidden, but a bit of it shows, along with one hand: He is very dark, the Certified Other, his color in sharp contrast to the nearly white (European) skin of the young woman he violates. His examination involves her teeth, a humiliation in the West associated with commerce in horses. Gérôme, a supposed stickler for nearly photographic accuracy of detail, actually *enlarges* the hand, notably elongating the outstretched fingers that penetrate her mouth—the better to make a point of this lurid detail.

Figure 9.7
Jean-Léon Gérôme
(1824–1904), THE
SLAVE MARKET
(c. 1867), canvas,
84.3 × 63 cm.
Williamstown, Mass.,
Sterling and Francine
Clark Art Institute, inv.
no. 53.

That the penetration is sexual requires little imagination. The man's gesture is profoundly phallic and assertive, and her response, head languidly flopped to one side, utterly passive and *receptive,* hints of pleasure and offers no sign of revulsion. Indeed, Gérôme paints her to stand *relaxed,* weight shifted to one leg, the other leg bent at the knee. Her pubic area is shaved (this was the custom), to Western eyes not only making her more available to the gaze but also more fully obliterating her agency.

Gérôme's own involvement as the painter is both present and absent—present to the extent that any buyer or spectator would know, or be made to know, that the work is his, but absent to the extent that he denies his own labor. Gérôme painted in tiny, exacting brush strokes that are invisible on the finished surface. In this way, his paintings vie with contemporary photographs for clarity of detail. Gérôme's paintings distance themselves from photographs because of their dramatically deep colors, a principal means by which he successfully competed with the new black-and-white technology. Moreover, the close attention to detail—such as the architecture in the background of *The Slave Market*—seemingly rendered with photographic "accuracy," provided Gérôme with a way of meeting photography on its home turf. His paintings could claim—and indeed came to depend upon—similar degrees of "objectivity," hence "scientific" accuracy and truth.[43]

Gérôme could thus provide his Western spectators with a painting of a slave market under the guise of "this is just how it is over *there,*" at once laying the necessary groundwork for moralizations regarding Western moral superiority (except in America where slavery had not yet been abolished) *and* for a scopophilia concocted of an unstable mix of sexual desire, cultural domination, and misogyny.

> Gérôme offered up pictures of Near Eastern sexuality for tired businessmen in the guise of high art, but it was a sensibility he shared with his audience. He associated the Orient with escapist sexual fantasies and deployed all the clichés like harems, slaves, baths, veils, dancing girls and boys.
>
> [He] is obsessed with . . . scenes of human beings subject to involuntary servitude and overwhelming power. He himself was waited upon hand and foot during his safaris or at home, and he obviously identified with the dominant classes in society.[44]

All this notwithstanding, art history remains divided on the subject of the nude, especially those of the orientalist variety, and the case of Gérôme provides an opportunity to describe a little of the situation. As recently as 1986 the principal Gérôme scholar felt it necessary to mount a moral defense of this painting, condemning the "dreadful practice" of the slave market and arguing that this image, and others like it, "could only be seen as abolitionist"! As he put it, "the cruel act of inspecting the teeth . . . is meant to communicate the utter humiliation of slavery; the chaste nudity accentuates the woman's helplessness."[45] To make such a statement depends upon a momentary forgetting of how paintings of female nudes *as a whole* functioned in Europe and America in the second half of the nineteenth century; of the widespread practice of prostitution in Europe involving girls and women of the poor classes and among nonwhites; of the absence of any suggestion whatsoever that abolitionists made use of such imagery; and finally of the look of the painting itself. That is, the painting's compositional center involves an examination of teeth and a barely metaphoric sexual penetration. We are *not* invited by Gérôme to gaze at this image in order to critique slavery; we are invited to look and to salivate, all the while saying out loud to anyone within earshot, "Tsk, tsk." Gérôme's considerable popularity with the French colonialist government and with wealthy art buyers was not the product of his social criticism, for he produced none on any subject. And to single out the slave-market nudes as social commentaries is to separate them from his other works, without any more reason than *wishing* to do so, for large numbers of Gérôme nudes—harem scenes, baths, and the like—enjoy no such cover of putative political correctness.

It is no less amazing to displace regressive politics by calling it progressive, in order to "save" an artist for a supposedly liberal audience of twentieth-century viewers, than it is to cash in politics altogether and call it comedy, as in this 1972 reading by still another art historian of Gérôme's *The Slave Market:*

> It is just possible that this painting betrays a touch of humor, macabre though it may be—a personal reaction which is otherwise suppressed in the deadly serious and imperturbedly realistic manner of Gérôme's paintings—because here the young female slave has been disrobed to present her beautiful body, but the critical examination is devoted to . . . [elision in the original, presumably to signal the punch line:] her teeth.[46]

Such commentary at the least chooses to forget that the woman's external surfaces are already available to the gaze by nature of her nudity. But that humiliation, made more striking by the degree of overdress of the picture's principal males, is not sufficient. Her interiority must also be subject to the look. Gérôme's painting is an explicit forecast of the latter-day girlie magazine imagery, wherein it no longer suffices to photograph a woman's naked skin; she must display to the camera her vagina via spread-leg crotch shots as well and, in many instances, use her fingers to open her body's interior to the probing lens. There is a difficulty in all this, however, one that threatens to undercut the fantasies such imagery functions to provoke. Already hinted at by the situation Gérôme paints, the sexual setting of late twentieth-century eroticism is commonly moved from the dimly lit, seductive pleasures of the bedroom to the fluorescent, unforgiving brightness more common to the clinical examining table. Under these conditions of spectatorship, the act of looking increasingly demands to be recognized as degrading to the self-dehumanizing viewer, and under this circumstance, the putative pleasure of domination turns out to have quite a bill attached.

To the extent that Gérôme paints violence, it is enacted by the Others he paints against their own people. Gérôme's own violent performance is self-effacing, displaced by the dark Others of his fertile imagination. Real history is conveniently erased. In particular, Gérôme eschews the violence of European colonialism in the Middle East, like the French Society of Missionaries, which in 1867 during widespread famine in Algeria offered starving children food—provided they converted to Christianity. Indeed, to look at his paintings one would never know that any European except him had been there. Westerners do not intrude into his orientalist space, which is made to appear undisturbed, like some perverse Eden of sexual possibilities, as Linda Nochlin has pointed out in an insightful critique of Gérôme and his current promoters.[47]

Inviting Revenge

It is nearly impossible today to take seriously William Adolphe Bouguereau's gigantic canvas *Nymphs and Satyr* (Figure 9.8). By all our "standards" the painting's erotic impact, upon which Bouguereau concentrates his entire rhetorical effort, does not so much fall flat as appear ridiculous. But to laugh is not the point. Instead, I want to think about the painting as a serious effort by a major and highly successful late nineteenth-century artist to respond to the demand for nude spectacle that came from his largely upper-bourgeois buyers on both sides of the Atlantic.[48] It is a commonplace that during the Victorian age painting provided a principal and socially sanctioned outlet for representing the otherwise unrepresentable in a society obsessed with the human sexuality it worked so hard to control. As regards the male spectators of Bouguereau's paintings, the question to ask is what might they have seen, that is, how might they have "read" the image?

Typical of a number of pictures by Bouguereau, the male remains singular and solitary as a common denominator, around which women, much pluralized, seem held in his sway like electrons around the atomic nucleus. The painting's rhetorical impact is driven by an apparent, but unreal, reversal of power, to the extent that the male remains virtually static, placed in a reactive position, while the women move assertively and thus determine his action. The male is a satyr, at once highly sexualized but not quite a man, so that the apparent power reversal does not appear to apply to "real" men. The potential excitement from the image, in other words, derives from what the women— too many of them—*do to* a male. The nymph upon whom Bouguereau con-

Figure 9.8
William Adolphe
Bouguereau
(1825–1905), NYMPHS
AND SATYR (1873),
canvas, 260 × 180 cm.
Williamstown, Mass.,
Sterling and Francine
Clark Art Institute, acc.
no. 658.

centrates our attention at the right, and her companion facing us, both pull at the satyr's arms, in essence to make him rise, the erotic import of which is made the more apparent by his stiffened arms and outstretched fingers. In essence, they metaphorically coax his sexual excitement; they take control of his sexuality. But, contrarily, the nymph furthest to the left does exactly the opposite. She pushes her full weight against his head, forcing him down, while a fourth nymph grasps in her tight-fisted hand his goat's horn, the tip of which remains visible and vulgarly phallic.

The nymphs attempt to pull him into a pool—the clichéd reference to women's sexuality and, of course, to sea-born Venus—and he resists with all his might, if we pay attention solely to his feet. His upper torso is somewhat at odds with this resistance. The nymphs' facial expressions are unambiguously of the "come hither" variety, and they look more nineteenth-century French than mythological, as was noted in Bouguereau's own time. As one critic wrote in 1879 about this picture: "The trouble . . . is that the people are ladies, not Maenads or Bacchants. Their undressing is accidental or prurient, not ignorant. Look at any of their faces, and you feel that they need not insult your reason by pretending not to write modern French and read the fashion-newspaper."[49] "All the allusions to Greek mythology cannot conceal the fact that these women are no goddesses but high-class courtesans. Bouguereaus were hung in the drawing-rooms of bankers, industrialists and politicians, to be discussed 'scientifically' by the host and his male guests after the ladies had withdrawn for a conversation of their own."[50]

The painting's energy is dialectical. The male, heroic of body, attracts women by the swarm. Yet their very surplus seems to overwhelm him. Their sexual demands, in essence, threaten drowning. Bouguereau thus plays off a theme common to the late nineteenth century concerning female sexuality: Once awakened, it was (oddly) unnatural, unquenchable, and socially, morally, and physically destructive—notably of men.[51] Bouguereau attempts to make his appeal by simultaneously stimulating two enormously powerful, universally acknowledged male prerogatives: sexual desire (in the Victorian age officially denied to "good" women), and the will to dominate. The pleasure of looking at the women's bodies is clear enough. Their breasts and lower torsos are exaggerated, and Bouguereau takes fullest advantage of the particular Victorian fixation on women's backsides as a representational substitute for their genitals.[52] The will to dominate is stimulated by the apparent power reversal, in itself a call to action. That is, these women need to be firmly put in their place within the fantasy of the male spectator as he acts out revenge on yet another manifestation of Medusa. The mythological Medusa was repeatedly painted and sculpted during the nineteenth century. At once the object of hate and desire, she offered pleasure via her purportedly limitless and aggressive sexuality. Entwined snakes, supplanting her hair, visually overdetermined her aggressive phallic powers in an in-your-face manner. And for her rampant transgression of gender hierarchy, she *must* be punished. Her beheading by Perseus is her own castration and also the restoration of male sexual normalcy, the return of the phallus.[53]

Once again, however, there is a difficulty for the male spectator. To entertain the fantasy, to sense the need to reassert dominance, is to acknowledge that men's hierarchical superiority over women is not natural, but imposed, and that domination can never relax its grip, lest it be challenged. That men must force the issue admits to both the self-interest and the historical contingency of unequal gender relations. Finally, Bouguereau's decision to set his scene in a mythic past accomplishes two related feats: It provides a "cover" for painting the otherwise startlingly modern female flesh; and it accounts for women in nature *as nature,* undeveloped and primitive, driven by out-of-control physical appetites. The convenience of the satyr, as the male force, thereby is explained: Real men in essence have evolved (they do not look like satyrs); women have remained the same. Men are *not* satyrs, so Bouguereau informs us, solely driven by their goatlike sexual urges. The better to illustrate the claim, Bouguereau represents the satyr as already caught up in the evolutionary process. Bouguereau provides him with an upper torso that would be the envy of Apollo, a torso surmounted by a *thinking* head that already knows enough to control his lower, goat half by resisting the women.

Eve—Again

The nude child in Bouguereau's *Temptation*[54] (Figure 9.9), resolutely innocent, produces no libidinal response. Instead, she evokes the motherhood role of her adult companion—but with an edge. The painting's setting is allegorical, not natural; it serves to equate the female with nature. The mother wears a generic peasant costume that is essentially impossible to place in any very specific chronology or geography; the hairstyles of both females are clearly contemporaneous to the painting's date of execution. On balance, the picture evokes a warm and giving love between the infant and her mother. Yet Bouguereau is not content to leave it there. He introduces two "natural" but ancillary props (a little pond and an apple) and a textual label (the painting's name) and by these means attempts to immerse the picture's rhetoric fully in the discourse of Victorian sexual politics. In short, motherhood and childhood are connected to the sins, specifically female and sexual, that brought about the fall of the first Man and all men who succeeded him.

Figure 9.9
William Adolphe Bouguereau (1825–1905), TEMPTATION (1880), canvas,
97 × 130 cm. Minneapolis, The Minneapolis Institute of Arts, The Putnam Dana
McMillan and the M. Knoedler Fund, acc. no. 74.74.

Both females are situated at the edge of an improbable pond, its reflective
undisturbed surface the agent of narcissism. The pond functions analogously
to the mirror conventionally placed in the hands of women throughout art's
history as a sign and guarantee of their vanity, hence their moral weakness.
Ironically, male narcissism (the source for the sin is, after all, the young male
Narcissus) functionally remains little more than myth; for women, it is made
into a fact of their nature, a defining principle of their identity. The young
and beautiful mother takes her little girl to the pond, the place for looking at
the self, for self-absorption (read: selfishness). And just for good measure, she

takes along a single apple, ripe for eating. The apple provides the young woman with her putative name: Eve, she who cannot help herself, she who will consume the forbidden fruit, presumably while her child watches. Temptation, Bouguereau warns, stalks the female. The apple is magnificently painted, a nearly shocking patch of red and yellow in a painting otherwise devoid of those bright colors; it looks so delicious that we know it will be eaten—and shared. Temptation will win out. The story of Eve never ends; hence men's troubles have no conclusion.

From our own moment in history, we might argue that the apple is gratuitous, even cruel, like the painting's implicitly condemning label. But that would be to ignore the social truth revealed in Bouguereau's visual "remark" as regards women's situation, which, to be sure, he neither critiques nor condemns. Instead, his quasi-photo-realist style of painting lends the picture an air of (false) objectivity, hence truth. Provided we can "see through" what is going on, we can better understand how the rhetoric of inequality works. The position Bouguereau maintains on the matter presents itself to us as rhetoric, an effort to persuade and to make us believe. In the end, at least from the advantage of historical distance, we can see through his setup. Everything depends on the apple—without which the painting's condemnatory label loses its effectiveness. But the apple, its colors virtually jumping off the canvas, demanding our attention, protests just a bit too much. This most natural of substances, the fruit of health, the fruit of knowledge from the Tree of Knowledge, presents itself as Symbol, writ upper case. And the moment we can "see" Symbol in it (and not "just" the apple), we have come some distance toward realizing that we have been handed a plea, not a statement of fact. The painting's function unmasks itself and thereby unwittingly provides us with choice.

Chapter 10

The Male Nude: Identity and Denial

For Western painting over the past several centuries, the nude male body has presented a host of problems that intersect with but are distinct from those attached to the nude female body. These problems have confronted not only artists and the original audiences for their work but also the academic discipline of art history, responsible for organizing the more or less "official" discourse on the subject.

A Perplexing Sight

In the West, nakedness is culturally associated with the shame that extends historically to the first precepts of the Judeo-Christian religion. Adam and Eve, having lost their innocence, covered themselves to hide their nakedness, about which they became self-conscious for the first time; and Noah's sons covered their father's nakedness, the result of drunken excess. Indeed, even the ancient Romans were at least officially critical of the nakedness associated with Greek practice in sport, despite the Romans' inherited taste for Greek statuary representing nudes. For the most part, nakedness is culturally marked as demanding privacy. When made publicly visible, nakedness functions as a magnet of attraction by violating a taboo whose strength varies in time and by geography.

Whereas the state of nakedness requires a specific, culturally learned etiquette of looking, or better yet, an etiquette of *not* looking, the *painted* nude represents nakedness as a state specifically *made for concentrated looking*.

Unlike, say, catching an accidental glimpse of someone without clothes, when there may be no intention either to display nakedness to others or for others to see it, the nude in art exists *only* to be seen naked. It invites not the averted eye, but the stare. Whatever the apparent rationale for the painted body to be without clothes, for example, taking a bath, the visible fact of nudity itself takes precedence. Nudity as such, in other words, overwhelms the image. Of course, nudity as an art subject is not nudity itself but nudity's representation. But whatever subject is represented providing justification, explanation, or logic for the state of nudity, the nude in art challenges the cultural proscription not of nudity itself but of voyeurism. To be effective as a painting of a nude, the image must make us *want* to look at the body in the manner represented. A principal means by which this is accomplished is for the image to focus its rhetorical energies to trigger the viewer's fantasies (the imaginary)—and desire.

What we commonly take the state of nudity to mean centers on the making visible of the body's sexuality. Nudity involves genitals. Thus in the parlance of movies, references to "full frontal nudity" roughly equates with "real" nudity; seeing someone's backside on the screen falls short of authenticity. Sexuality functions as a principal locus for our sense of *embodied* identity; it *is* us at the core of our sense of being. It is also the site of psychic and physical desire and erotic pleasure, as well as the source of anxiety and a host of other emotions. Regarding the painted nude generally, and the male nude especially, the viewer's interest is overdetermined to the extent that what the nude makes visible is the usually invisible site of deepest social and personal concern. Why so, especially in the male nude? The answer hinges in large part on the presumed audience, which, in most instances concerning painted nudes of *both* sexes before our own century, was explicitly, if not quite exclusively, male. To be sure, women saw such images, though their access was sometimes more limited by comparison to that of men, but nudes were not usually painted either by or for women. Men painted them and other men paid for them and also organized and largely controlled the sites where such images could be viewed. There were needs addressed by representing nude men *for men*—but always with a price to pay.[1]

For the male viewer, access to the sight of the nude female ordinarily serves as confirmation of male power, if only imagined. Access to the sight of the male nude is more complicated. If nudity is associated with shame, it is likewise associated with sexuality. Yet to be *looked at sexually* is to be consumed or taken *by sight*. Not for nothing is the gaze—the stare—said to be penetrating. The look per se is constituted wholly within the history of gender relations. Until recently if a man stared at a woman, she was expected to avert her eyes, thereby marking her awareness of his look and quickly deferring to its putative power, allowing herself to be taken in by him. But if one man stares at another, and the two are strangers, a confrontation is likely: "What are you looking at?" might be the query, uttered as a challenge, unless there is an unspoken sexual interest that they share. The stare, in other words, functions—and is by men *expected* to function—as a challenge, and the historical constancy of this fact is evident in Western literature dating back to the ancients.

Let me begin with a nude so well known and so often reproduced that there is no need to illustrate it here, the sculpture *David* (1501–1504) by Michelangelo, in marble and eighteen feet high. In the presence of this sculpture in situ in the Academy Gallery, Florence, it is nearly as interesting to watch the people looking as it is to gaze at the sculpture itself. What I have noticed is that women tend to take it in easily and comfortably and that men often do not. Viewers of both sexes seem to find the piece riveting, but men exhibit signs of being disconcerted. There is, of course, the simple fact that the sculpture is so profoundly different from what most men see in their bathroom mirrors. But there is more to the problem of looking than the male failure to measure up. Michelangelo virtually demands that viewers take pleasure in confronting David's body. Enormous, heroic, physically perfect, a technical tour de force to be sure, and—most of all—powerfully sexual. It is David's sexuality that Michelangelo demands that we acknowledge, though not specifically as a sign of David's male agency but as a pleasurable sight in itself. Set on a pedestal, viewers must literally *look up* to take in the figure. The space of its current setting is somewhat confined in light of the sculpture's size; the viewer cannot take it in without active eye movement. The eyes must sweep from the figure's feet to its head, and since it is freestanding, viewers may move entirely around it, taking it in from every possible angle. The polished white body is there to be cruised; it is a spectacle, and the sculpture's confronting power is radically increased by the setting—a separate gallery in the museum, in which there is nothing else to look at.

If the male viewer looks away from the sculpted David, he is forced to acknowledge and confront his own discomfort; yet to look is to take in what in normal circumstances cannot be looked at. In the locker room, males learn early where *not* to focus their eyes and therefore go to self-conscious lengths to avoid such looking (or at least to avoid being caught at it). In short, in the presence of *David* many men do not know what to do with their eyes. Michelangelo is powerfully adept at making us want to look, but in looking we are forced to acknowledge, and at least partly to violate, a taboo. In essence, men are culturally forbidden to take pleasure in the look of the body of their own sex, though they are culturally required, at least in the present moment, to make their own specific bodies pleasurable sights to themselves and, presumably, to women.

The long-standing, still-current model for the most desirable and perfect body specimen is not from life but from art, not really from *David* but from its antecedents in the ancient world, in Greece and Rome. Yet from these beginnings the male body as an object of simultaneous emulation and desirability is also one of a contradiction that manifests itself in explicitly physical terms. As a sight, the ideal male body in art—and hence, so it would seem, in life—conflates with some sense of the physically and spiritually heroic, an embodied state and spiritual virtue seldom made available to women. Yet throughout the history of art the sort of male body that has been designated as "ideal" is consistently and paradoxically infused with female characteristics.

Thus ancient representations of Hercules commonly provided him with extremely exaggerated musculature distinctly, if oddly, feminizing—not unlike that of modern bodybuilders who attempt to emulate Hellenistic sculpture not only by isolating and hyperdeveloping separate muscles that can be pumped up for posing, but also by shaving all (presumably) but genital body hair and oiling their skin to replicate the surface texture of polished marble. Accordingly, their bodies become object-sights *as such.* The "strength" that they possess is literally for show only. Pumping iron is in part an activity preparatory to one's *being looked at by other men,* who populate the audience in posing competitions (so it seems, if to confuse things further, mostly for "straight" men). In contrast, exhibiting the same effect by different means, many nineteenth-century paintings represent a distinctly soft, even slight, and explicitly feminized male as the ideal form, as we shall see.

The affecting power of the male nude in art lies in its ability to produce tension *in the male viewer,* who, when looking, is forced to acknowledge the power exerted on him by the ideal body of another male. Conversely, the nonideal male nude in art is incapable of producing this tension, thereby transferring agency entirely to the viewer, who may look in contempt, not desire, on the body of the lesser male. Yet to exert this power, the idealized body must become an object of desire, a transformation that culturally feminizes both the figure represented *and* the male viewer, given the culturally established rules of gendered looking.

Until recently the academic discipline of art history has maintained a general silence on the male nude, except to treat it as a subject of formal or compositional interest. That is, the literature on the male nude has largely avoided (and seemingly claimed no investment in) the sociocultural and sexual issues that so powerfully inform the general subject. This is unquestionably a reflection of male art historians—like other men—being uncomfortable discussing the male body in a public forum, despite the centrality of the subject in the history of art. This situation began to change only with the development of feminist studies in the human sciences, and most recently, with the appearance of gay and lesbian studies. For example, well into our own century, the homosexuality of Michelangelo—let alone that of numerous other canonic artists of highest caliber—was barely acknowledged, as though it was an "unfortunate" and embarrassing fact best kept quiet, *especially* concerning its real or potential impact on his art. For example, when I studied art history as an undergraduate and graduate student in the 1960s, sexuality was seldom discussed even when it was the very subject of an artwork. And the sexuality of artists themselves was presumed, it seemed, to be irrelevant, or perhaps, as students, none of our business. The homoeroticism evident in much of Michelangelo's work was a topic still more taboo than the sexuality of the artist himself. Yet Michelangelo's work enjoyed lavish praise and considerable attention in our slide lectures. The discipline, in other words, mirrored perfectly in its repressed discourse what the art itself so effectively referenced. The refusal to "say" acknowledged what Michelangelo achieved. He made us see, and *want* to see, what we were not supposed to. And I suspect we will continue to stare at *David*—Florence's principal tourist attraction—as long as the male body in reality is situated dead center in its own impossible mix of contradictions.

Saintly Looks

In ecclesiastical painting, the representation of Saint Sebastian exemplifies how the male nude defines the paradoxes I have delineated. Sebastian was a Roman martyr, said to be a member of the Praetorian guard in the third century, secretly a Christian, and was executed for his beliefs by Emperor Diocletian. First shot through with arrows, he survived only to be beaten to death (Figure 10.1).[2] In this devotional picture, Sebastian is paired with the sainted Pope Fabian, because they share the same feast day in the Roman Catholic Church (at the bottom are also two small figures representing Brothers of the Misericordia). Sebastian is represented as a handsome and well-developed youth, his body repeatedly and rather decoratively pierced with arrows—which produce very little blood flow. Sebastian's refined face and elegant gestures acknowledge no suffering from his ordeal.

The sexuality of Sebastian's body is emphasized in numerous ways. In addition to his youth and general good looks, particular attention is given to highlighting his curly hair. His eyes are feminized by arching the eyebrows

Figure 10.1
Giovanni di Paolo (active 1420s; died 1482), SAINTS FABIAN AND SEBASTIAN, panel, 84.5 × 54.5 cm. London, National Gallery, inv. no. 3402. Reproduced by courtesy of the Trustees, The National Gallery, London.

and exaggerating their almond shape—no such sexualization is awarded to Fabian's features. The mouth is small and delicate. Typical of many early representations of this subject, the saint's loincloth, slung very low, is diaphanous, a type of fabric usually associated with women's costume. It allows the skin of his thighs to show through, though the genitals are discreetly, if barely, hidden. Sebastian's torso is heroic, almost surprisingly so in comparison with Fabian, virtually smothered in robes whose volume denies all sense of his corporeal being. Giovanni di Paolo carefully models Sebastian's chest and groin, delineating the anatomy—however inaccurately—and thereby making a visual issue of it. The sharply converging lines outlining the groin lead our eyes to what will *not quite* be shown and which, by being denied, is made all the more the focus of visual desire. In classical sculpture, male genitals are "stated"; they form part of a larger idealized whole, and relative to overall body proportions, they are often somewhat undersize, so that attention is taken from them. In much later art (by no means all), male genitals are, like those of women, hidden from view. But the hiding, characteristic of ecclesiastical art, often renders them a real issue, as an acknowledged taboo. The viewer is visually teased—and thereby made to want to look; officially speaking, the tease is a device for getting us to invest in the saint, and ideally, to desire to emulate him as we are drawn to his image. (Needless to say this is dangerous terrain; the desire produced can easily lead to its most secular of forms or to idolatry, or to both.)

The association of arrows to sexual love—Cupid's dart—is ancient, as is their association with male sexuality (later, the arrow became associated with plague, and it is ironic that Saint Sebastian came to serve as a protector against that disease). The penetration of Sebastian's body by arrows draws attention to his body and to his would-be martyrdom. But the lack of disfigurement, blood, and apparent suffering produce other effects. The arrows' explicitly decorative character, the attractive patterning they produce on his body, serve as adornment: The pierced body is made still more beautiful and desirable, an effect not out of keeping with religious veneration.

Visually speaking, Saint Fabian competes rather poorly. He is shoved off to the side, to such an extent that not all of his body can be accommodated within the frame (although the painting may have been cut down a bit at some point), and he is positioned in profile. He *is* merely his face and hands. Fabian is essentially reduced to his lavish vestments, the sign of his authority as pope. By contrast, Sebastian is, simply, body—"what a body"—and that is just the point. Every investment in looking is directed away from the distraction of Fabian's outfit and toward *flesh,* and only flesh, for there is nothing else to be looked at, due to the painting's empty background.

The altarpiece of Saint Sebastian's martyrdom ascribed to Antonio and Piero del Pollaiuolo (Figure 10.2) presents a particularly theatrical spectacle, richly colored and infinitely detailed. The viewer's eyes are tempted by a visual feast but supplied with one main course, Sebastian's body, at once entrée and dessert. The painting's religious sentiment is driven by secular pleasure, by *embodied* desire mapped onto the panel and transposed onto the viewer. The practically naked Sebastian is set on a pedestal of sorts that forms the apex of a compositional triangle whose base is outlined by the other men shooting arrows at him. The viewer's eyes are almost forcibly drawn upward to Sebastian's white body, bound *loosely* to the tree, weight shifted to one leg to affect a nearly relaxed stance, *almost* as though he were there voluntarily. The picture's climax is reached in Sebastian's face and head, inclining slightly backward and to the side, which thereby creates a visual tension by throwing the pyramid slightly off balance at its peak. The tilted head and the facial expression together replicate the look of ecstasy (one that the Roman Baroque sculptor Bernini later put to good use in his famous marble religious ecstasies of Saint Theresa and Blessed Lodovica Albertoni, whose visions of Christ Bernini represented as literally orgasmic).[3]

The painting's eroticism depends upon, and is partly driven by, the drapery covering the saint's body: "In the figurative arts, eroticism appears as a relationship between clothing and nudity."[4] Indeed, as Anne Hollander has shown, the nude in art is usually rendered in relation to the clothed figure of the same historical moment. The nude depends on its clothed "other," or counterpart, for its effect on the viewer, for its meanings, and indeed, for its very form. "The more significant clothing is, the more meaning attaches to its absence, and the more awareness is generated about any relation between the two states."[5] Sebastian's drapery produces the satisfaction in looking that comes from the frustrated realization that one can never be satisfied by looking. The painting freezes an action, an undressing that will only go *this* far. Sebastian is made the more sexual by his loincloth's not only being wrapped too low on his hips but also fastened by an obviously phallic knot that substitutes for and reminds the viewer of what is hidden. These sexual effects are increased by a subtle bit of color change at the groin that hints of pubic hair on his otherwise entirely smooth body.

Male homoerotic sexual desire is repeatedly inscribed in the bodies of his torturers, not least in the man in the lower left center who bends down to load his crossbow and, in the process, extends his well-shaped backside for our viewing pleasure. More important, there is an explicit pleasurable tension between the passive, even languid, Sebastian and the archers whose bodies, muscles bulging, are tensed to their aggressive task. Sebastian waits to be pen-

Figure 10.2
Attributed to Antonio del Pollaiuolo (1432–1498) and Piero del Pollaiuolo
(c.1441–before 1496), ALTARPIECE: THE MARTYRDOM OF SAINT SEBASTIAN
(c.1475), panel, 291.5 × 202.6 cm. London, National Gallery, inv. no. 292.
Reproduced by courtesy of the Trustees, The National Gallery, London.

etrated—deeply: The arrows in the bows are far longer than the visible parts of those already piercing him. The active-passive binary driving the relationship is virtually one of violent courtship. In short, it is neither accidental nor surprising that the Saint Sebastian story provided a narrative through which homoerotic desire could be sanctioned as a sight.[6] Anne Hollander, writing about a different Saint Sebastian painting, provides an apt summary:

> Saint Sebastian is the outstanding example of the emphatically sexy saint, shown over and over in the Renaissance as a sort of sacrificial Adonis. . . . In this forest scene some of the tender youth's garments are shown delicately unfastened and pushed downward, as if by a lover's caressing hand. He gazes languishingly at the beholder; and his torso wears the elegant lozenge shape dictated by the prevailing mode, so that he seems a more deliberately desirable figure. His torturers are very near him, like prospective rapists pretending to be archers.[7]

Phallic Disappointment

Antonio del Pollaiuolo's famous engraving from the late fifteenth century of a combat of nude men (Figure 10.3) erases the quasi-passive, feminized discourse typical to Saint Sebastian imagery in favor of an aggressive, highly physical masculinity, yet one at least as improbable as the sort imagined for the saint. Pollaiuolo exaggerates musculature: He shows each body in tension, even that of the man at the lower right at the moment of his impaling. The black and white of the print, subtly modeled, adds to the starkness of the overall effect. The male bodies are inexplicably nude, since nudity in battle renders them more vulnerable to attack. The illogic of their nudity serves to focus more attention on the state of nudity itself. It makes an issue of the nude body as a metaphor, perhaps, as some scholarly work suggests, providing a critique of the "despicable body" as the prison of the soul.[8]

The engraving strips men of their clothes, provides them with heroic bodies, and *duplicates* them. Masculinity is portrayed as a *physical* trait, entirely divorced from the abstractions of character, notably *virtus* (manly excellence). Masculinity *is* aggression. The actors' grimacing faces are not the locus of attraction. Arguably, we look quickly away from their faces, spending our time on the male flesh that is conventionally hidden from view. However coarse their features, without exception each man "behaves" heroically to the extent that he does battle with enemies who are his physical equal. Indeed, the men's physicality nearly guarantees the event represented: What else do such bodies do; for what other reason might they exist? "Women, as objects of desire, may remove their clothes at any time (in art anyway), but men need an excuse."[9] The battleground serves as a principal site on which to display the "reality"

Figure 10.3
Antonio del Pollaiuolo (1432–1498), A COMBAT OF NUDE MEN (1460–1480),
engraving, 39.4 × 60.3 cm. London, British Museum, Department of Prints and
Drawings, inv. no. VI 33.

and impact of masculinity envisioned in hyperbolic physical form: Entire
Body as Phallus. But herein lies a problem for the very masculine identity the
image attempts so forcefully to imagine.

It is worth noting that the majority of male nudes in the history of Western
painting have their genitals shielded from view, a representational decision
that is about more than modesty. Shielding gives to the male body an effect
similar to that of the female whose sexual parts are by nature anatomically
"invisible," hence never quite to be visually "had." The crucial myth consti-
tuting masculinity remains intact by not being subjected to visual testing.
That is, to make visible the male sexual parts in art causes considerable risk to
the fragile state of male identity that hinges, culturally speaking, on genital
accounts of masculinity (men constructing themselves by the common de-

nominator of their sexual parts, to which are assigned putatively heroic tasks and physical proportions).

But as Pollaiuolo's image broadly hints, the male genitals when made visible prove to be the *least* heroic parts of their otherwise heroic bodies. Every muscle in Pollaiuolo's nude combatants is tensed save the "muscle" of their sexual erectal tissue. That hangs limply and with extreme vulnerability, given the circumstances of the narrative. To "tense" that organ, after all, would only render it more vulnerable and also admit to a different kind of excitement in the presence of other men, thereby violating one of the strongest cultural proscriptions. Pollaiuolo's engraving, in other words, at the beginning of a long period during which the male nude dominated art practice, maps out a terrain of endless loss in the face of purported gain. Not the least difficulty of "showing" the phallus, as it were *documenting* its presence, is, in the end, its considerably disappointing sight. As that part of male body geography marked as the locus for masculinity, hence agency, the phallus does not add up to all that much, visually speaking. Volumetrically it is far less "impressive" than the female breasts that painters so obsessively painted as the acceptable locus for an otherwise nonvisible female sexuality. The penis, in other words, works its cultural "charm" more effectively as an *imaginary* object. Rather small, and entirely defenseless, all the more so in painting, when it is framed by the heroic male body, it measures up poorly against its myriad visual substitutes: clubs, spears, arrows, swords, rifles, pistols, and even the occasional cigar.

> Even the most beautiful male body, then, contains an inherent and perplexing contradiction. The penis, symbol of masculine virility, a source of sexual pleasure and focus of male pride, is also the most vulnerable piece of human flesh. Those few inches that should epitomize male strength and potency need more protection than any other part of the male or female anatomy. The sight of the limp penis sparks off the anxiety and ambivalence that men feel about their own sexuality.[10]

And, in a related insight: "Whenever the penis is directly drawn, it is realized for what it actually is, a rather small, fleshy piece of skin, which validates Lacan's notion that the phallus only works as the 'privileged signifier' when it is veiled. When the organ it depends upon is revealed, then its privileged centrality is challenged."[11]

There is a related issue concerning the male genitals and the act of looking, namely, *who* is looking and what they make of what they see. Most art was acquired by men, and it therefore functioned principally in their interests and as a barometer of their concerns. But for art to function to its full potential as a sociocultural agent, it must be seen by others and not just by its "owner." With very few exceptions, art was displayed with the presumption that both men *and women* would see it. In regard to the male nude, exposure of the penis to the sight of women presented a psychological and political problem for men, to the extent that men's own identity and agency visibly hung by such a visually disappointing thread: "Women may feel cheated, as if the terrorist who has held them hostage and threatened with the pistol in his pocket, turns out to be armed only with a finger!"[12] During the Renaissance, the reawakened fascination with the male body was by no means confined to visual art. It was, for example, powerfully articulated as well in upper-class male fashion. In their costuming, men sought to accentuate their sexual bulges. They inserted codpieces to amplify their genitals to a degree that now appears almost comical and wore brightly colored, attention-getting, form-fitting tights that accentuated their buttocks—not least because they were seamed in the back. All was kept fully visible by wearing only very short doublets that barely extended below the waist.[13]

Body Reversal?

Sandro Botticelli's *Venus and Mars* (Figure 10.4) invests heavily in the nude male. The painting's unusual dimensions—its extreme and unconventional horizontal length—at once makes possible the supine repose of the principal protagonist and attracts viewers' attention by its strange shape. In essence a bedroom scene,[14] the painting's subject is denoted, if problematically, by the phallic lance pointing paradoxically *toward* Mars, as though it were an instrument of Venus, and not Mars's own weapon. Venus's eyes, and ours, are on his body, whose head assumes roughly the same pose and "look" of Pollaiuolo's Saint Sebastian. In this instance, by nature of the identified subject, involving two of mythology's most famous lovers, the erotic intent is underscored.

Anne Hollander argues that the painting's erotic content is precipitated by the fashion of a completely dressed Venus wearing a modern costume, in contrast to Mars, whose drapery is merely standard issue for a mythological deity, having nothing to do with Renaissance modernity. "It is her complete, unruffled clothing that provides the sexual voltage for his nakedness, to a much greater degree than if she, too, were wearing loose drapery. Her modern clothes show her sexual dominance as much as her wakefulness does, and they make his bareness more erotic, despite his mythological trappings."[15] The

Figure 10.4
Allesandro (Sandro) Botticelli (c. 1445–1510), VENUS AND MARS (c. 1485–1486), panel, 69.2 × 173.4 cm. London, National Gallery, inv. no. 915. Reproduced by courtesy of the Trustees, The National Gallery, London.

eroticism of Botticelli's painting depends upon a stark reversal in which the nude male is made subject to a woman and to the gaze, both hers and ours.

The articulation of Mars's body employs rhetorical devices conventionally reserved in Western painting for the female body. The warrior god is transformed into a piece of well-shaped, smooth and highly refined (vaguely delicate), and oddly *soft,* sculpture. His lower torso is virtually feminine, his color is notably light, and his body is hairless in those locales where painters would commonly hint of hair, at the groin and armpits. On balance, Mars is very much something to look at, and he is made a sight by means of a quite obvious fiction. He assumes—quite theatrically—a *pose* of sleep, for the position he assumes does not replicate any body position in which true sleep is possible. He actually props himself up slightly—there is nothing behind him to support the upper part of his back. His left arm, though limp, implies its use as a support for his position. His right leg, prominently bent, would fall to the side, were he asleep. Yet his right hand and his facial expression resonate with loss of consciousness. The myth, told by Homer and Ovid,[16] makes clear a sexual adventure, and his own nudity essentially insists on that as a pretext to the picture—valorous Mars, god of war, does not let down his guard for no purpose.

Mars sleeps, but only sort of; postcoital bliss is hinted at, though the lovers do not lie side by side but face one another. Venus's facial beauty is striking, and her full breasts and left leg are emphasized and well defined under the thin drapery, all of it making her distinctly sexual. Yet she is *not* in a postorgasmic state. Instead, she is pensive, reserved, and indeed, she very much commands the scene by her own act of looking. She holds Mars in *her* gaze and by this means leads our eyes to him, where we find our own point of concentration.

Mars's very name carries the cachet of masculinity. This allows Botticelli the opportunity to preserve the prerogative of masculinity's conventional associations simply by naming him Mars—rather like calling him John Wayne today. At the same time, he takes off Mars's armor to show what is underneath: his sensual body, whose powers are more subtle but no less real. Mars captivates Venus and the viewer, who must be presumed to be male. Venus's staring at Mars tacitly acknowledges that she cannot take her eyes off him. Even in a state of unconsciousness, in other words, Mars's agency remains intact. Nonetheless, what those riveted eyes see is Mars having lost himself to a woman, having *become* a sight instead of using his own gaze as a sign and source of his power.

The Mars mythology, virtually a cliché to Botticelli's audience, defines one side of his power; his physical beauty defines another. Put in our own parlance: "Mars, he's the man!" And yet Botticelli makes that masculinity depend on Mars's looking androgynous—a characteristic in the Italian Renaissance that more than once defined the ideal *imaginary* male. As one sixteenth-century art theorist put it with regard to Titian's 1554 painting of Venus and Adonis, a man having "a touch of the beautiful woman [was] a difficult and pleasing mixture."[17] On balance, the painting plays brilliantly with a visually destabilizing blend of excitement, attraction, response, and—not least important—with reversal of culturally assigned sexual identities and sexual roles, as well as with an alternative to sanctioned discourses of seeing. Seeing *Venus and Mars,* in other words, invites us to imagine physical and psychic delights that might result from seeing things differently.

Youth, Death, and Sanctioned Desire

The Genesis story of Cain's murder of his brother Abel (4:1–15) provided artists with an opportunity for display of the male body in a state of collapse, specifically the young and athletically beautiful body, whose nudity was sanctioned by scriptural account, paralleling the sanction available by resorting to the mythologies of pagan deities and heroes. Abel was a shepherd, an "early" version of the human, hence "naturally" close to nature. His parents' expulsion from the Garden of Eden had been told only two Bible verses prior to the introduction of Abel's character (Genesis 3:24, the final verse of the chapter, and Genesis 4:2, respectively). In God's eyes, Abel is the good brother, whose sacrifice of the first of his flock to God's honor serves to prefigure Christ as the Good Shepherd, whose self-sacrifice brings the promise of salvation to all children of Adam. The moral good spiritually embodied in Abel is made visible in representation by the usual means, by assigning him great physical beauty and showing him in the tragic state of his recent demise, cut down in his early prime.

In a culture long since given to marking the body as, at best, the prison of the nobler soul and, at worst, as that which drives our sinful, notably lustful natures, the sight of Abel's body lends itself to a paradoxical reading. Abel's story prefigures Christ's self-sacrifice, hence it carries enormous theological significance. But François-Xavier Fabre's *Death of Abel* (Figure 10.5) treats its subject more like a fallen god, as much at home in a Homeric myth as a scriptural narrative. Anything that might pass for specifically religious convictions attending the representation is extinguished by the powerful impact of Abel's beautiful dead body, essentially made a *sexual* spectacle—with no sign of disfigurement from his being murdered. The painting's devotional content, overwhelmed by its sensualism, is not terribly surprising in that the painting was produced during the French Revolution, a period in French history not noted for its ecclesiastical fervor. It is fair to say that this painting, like many other erotic images produced during the eighteenth and nineteenth centuries, fundamentally made use of both religious and mythological stories as convenient "covers" for representing what otherwise might not be represented.

Our eyes are brought into the picture at the lower left, where light is concentrated. Abel's refined and handsome face, surrounded by dark curly hair, is strongly modeled by light and shadow and framed by the left arm. Made pure spectacle, his body is twisted to accentuate the musculature of his arms and legs. Abel's body is defined compositionally as a strong diagonal cutting across a picture surface otherwise marked mostly by forms that are fundamentally upright, thus accentuating the effect of his collapse. And he is shown close up, so that his body dominates the image. The chest muscles are exaggerated near the neck, made to form a deeply cut V, whose edges are highlighted and recesses darkened. That V leads to the breastbone centerline defining the two sides of the rib cage. This line, once again exaggerated by Fabre, leads the eye toward the genital region, discreetly covered and framed from below by the legs that form another, though this time inverted, V. At this crucial juncture, looking is compositionally focused *and* frustrated, but not before the "promise" of what remains hidden is explicitly evoked. Fabre takes up his brush and with a few strokes paints a triangular dark patch, half shade, half pubic hair. In other words, everything about Abel's body is sexualized: The arms, legs, and torso are elongated, the musculature highly modeled, and the pose organized so that the eye is encouraged to rationalize his body around

Figure 10.5
François-Xavier Fabre (1766–1837), DEATH OF ABEL (1791), canvas. Montpellier, Musée Fabre, inv. no. 825.1.60. Photo: Frédéric Jaulmes.

his barely covered sexuality. The body radiates toward a "center" that is the phallus, formally located just above the intersection of diagonals connecting the painting's corners.

Fabre's Abel is painted as an ephebe, in ancient Greece an athletic youth of eighteen to twenty years—part boy, but mostly man. And entirely typical of ephebe representations from the late eighteenth century and throughout the nineteenth, he is masculine but also feminine. The ephebe is not hard and heroic in the Herculean sense, as is evident, for example, in the exaggerated male musculature seen on Roman breastplates. Instead, he is marked with boyish softness. The ephebe resonates with sexuality precisely to the extent that his sexuality is ambiguous or, perhaps better, unstable. His body and its beauty is unfixed, momentary, and evolving. It is represented at an *imagined* moment, frozen in art, suspended between states, as omnisexual: boy-man, feminine-masculine.

Indeed, in nineteenth-century painting, representation of the dead Abel finds him posed analogously, though not identically, as a type of reclining female nude popular then, called by Bram Dijkstra the "nymph with the broken back" (Figure 10.6).[18] The feminization of Abel's pose in both paintings, organized around physical passivity and the availability to the gaze that such passivity both invites and even compels, drives the erotic charge. In fact, Bouguereau's painting, even more than Fabre's, blatantly references Abel's sexuality by elevating, hence emphasizing, the body's pelvic region. Nor are these isolated examples: "French history painting provides numerous examples of ephebic passivity, debility, helplessness and impotence, charged with an eroticism that is rarely matched in contemporary images of femininity."[19]

The audience for this art was principally male and, it must be presumed, not on balance homosexual, despite the obvious homoerotic appeal.[20] It is this seeming paradox that lays challenge to any neat boundaries we prefer to establish between either-or sexualities. All people learn by looking: Establishing identity depends on looking at one's own gender, at others like oneself.

Figure 10.6 William Adolphe Bouguereau (1825–1905), FIRST MOURNING (THE DEATH OF ABEL) (1888), canvas, 203 × 252 cm. Buenos Aires, Museo Nacional de Bellas Artes, inv. no. 2770, gift of the Estate of Francisco Uriburu, 1939.

That is, "the stability of masculinity depends upon the visibility of the male body; to be learnt or consolidated, masculinity requires a visual exchange between men."[21] Furthermore, looking engenders not only "education" but also desires, which by their very nature inevitably involve the body and commonly—though not always—the erotic, narrowly conceived. Yet because of powerful proscriptions against homoeroticism, the male looking at the self through the same-sex Other is at best problematic. In no small part this explains why men organize their looking at other men in specifically sanctioned venues, those of professional sports especially, which, after all, exist to be viewed.[22]

Nor is it an accidental by-product that in sport we have located a terrain where a kind of physical contact between men is acceptable that would elsewhere be regarded as intolerable: the embracing and butt-slapping that occur when points are scored. Likewise, cable-television ads for bodybuilding equipment devise their appeal to men by negotiating a very thin line that separates the purportedly straight from the gay. To appeal to men, the ads mark themselves as straight; but to sell the product the beautiful male body must be made an object of desire to men who, since childhood, have been cautioned against looking at men. Moreover, the body that is the object of the gaze is itself objectified in ways very similar to the objectification of female nudes—with the crucial exception that the male body is made active, always on the move. Nonetheless, the body is principally made an object for display, hence looking. Its pumped-up muscles are not presented as necessary to any sort of physical labor (apart from body "sculpting"), save for the identity of masculinity that they presumably produce. Muscle-machine muscles are in essence designer muscles: They operate as pure and simple aesthetics, and aesthetics is a geography in our culture principally labeled as feminine. Moreover, the male body of the ads is not only deeply tanned but oiled. It is made into a reflective surface, the more eye-catching on that account, though functionally the oiled body is utterly illogical—except as spectacle (it makes a mess on the bodybuilding machine itself, stains gym shorts, etc.). The male bodies in the ads are *cosmetically* adjusted by the oiling—and makeup has long been culturally designated feminine. But like Fabre's painting of the dead Abel, the negotiation between accepted and forbidden male sexuality defines the effectiveness of the advertisements. They operate by highlighting as desirable a body that few men possess, *and* by carefully and indirectly acknowledging culturally suppressed desires and practices.

It is not going too far to suggest that these video ads—which incidentally prospective buyers can obtain free from the manufacturer for private home-viewing—are part and parcel of the same discourse defined nearly two centuries ago by the appearance of ephebe paintings. Both delineate the outlines of a long-standing crisis in male identity.[23] Representation played a crucial role as part of the discursive apparatus through which identities were constructed and projected. As such, representation is entirely caught up in the process both as mirror and agent: "A confusion at the level of sexuality brings with it a disturbance of the visual field."[24] Ephebe imagery provided men, whether hetero- or homosexual, with a visual source by which to re-view themselves not as they were but as they might be (or might have been): young and literally physically free to be what culturally was disallowed—beautiful, ambiguous, and *desirable*. Bodybuilding equipment advertising smartly plays off identical ambiguities regarding desire. It avoids both the dangerous choice of same-sex desire and the cliché of opposite-sex attraction such as 1950s comic book back-cover ads for Charles Atlas bodybuilding (how to get the girl of your dreams with a dream body). Nowadays, such advertising centers around narcissism—whose referent, Narcissus, was long a popular theme in painting—the desirous looking at the male self, a self-directed, but still homoerotic, falling in love *with a look,* one that conveniently excludes women by making them entirely irrelevant. This narcissism, however, does not ignore the feminine but, in effect, "colonizes" it, takes it in as part and parcel of the masculine. In one sense we might argue for a progressive masculinity that both acknowledges and valorizes the feminine, but this is an insufficient accounting, to the extent that a masculinity defined in these terms simultaneously seems to excise the female (as opposed to the feminine) entirely from the visual field.[25]

Phallus as Hidden Delight

The visual pleasure taken by adults in the representation of children was, by the second half of the eighteenth century, commonly mapped onto the body of the racially alien Other. Whereas the earliest manifestations of this tendency were undeniably discreet, even subtle, by the late nineteenth century full-blown eroticism was commonplace—but with a cautionary diversion. For its time, Jean-Léon Gérôme's orientalist *The Snake Charmer* (Figure 10.7), an extraordinarily phallocentric image, references an especially problematic sexualization of children, namely, the homoerotic. A boy stands erect—even shaftlike, with his legs tightly together—and holds out to view an enormous snake, among the most clichéd psychic fantasies of male sexual potency; this, in a painting whose composition is overdetermined by columnar forms, straight lines, and angularity. Virtually every figure in the picture, all of them male, holds a stick, plays a wind instrument, or has a saber. And at the center of the back wall Gérôme places a rather-too-obvious shield and spear replicating the outline of the male genitalia, serving almost like a non-verbal label for the painting's subject. All of the males but one—the standing boy—are very dark skinned. The exception, strikingly light by comparison, hence catching our eyes, is the only one among them who is sexualized as such. He *is* sex; and he is also feminized, despite the phallicism of his pose and his snake prop. The painting makes a visual fetish of his buttocks. Nothing else in the painting so effectively catches the light entering from the right, modeling their shape to the point of lavishing attention and riveting the gaze.

Gazing as such is directly referenced. The image is *about* looking. The audience within the image is provided with a set of visual interests different from those of the painting's audience outside the frame. To the extent that those within pay direct heed to the boy, they appear to be interested in the reptile he holds aloft, the gigantic phallus substitute. Their looking, hidden

Figure 10.7
Jean-Léon Gérôme (1824–1904), THE SNAKE CHARMER (1880), canvas, 83.8 × 122.1 cm. Williamstown, Mass., Sterling and Francine Clark Art Institute, acc. no. 51.

from our sight, is privileged, since of course they can also see the "real" thing should they so choose. The viewer outside the picture is made to want to see what is hidden because of the "promise" provided by the child's backside. Desire is mapped out as the pleasure taken from imagining, not from having. That is, the boy's highlighted posterior becomes the imagined substitute for the view that Gérôme refuses us, and by that means he makes us look the more—his own power as a painter is caught up in the scene. And yet the gaze that is invited is one forbidden by the demands of Victorian morality as well as by the already highly elaborated homophobic panic emerging in Western Europe, quite aside from what the image might suggest about adult sexual desire for children, homo- or heterosexual. The sight, in other words, is tacitly taboo. The viewer's fixated look gains moral sanction from the subject represented being that of the racial Other, the Not Us. Hence, the viewer can take pleasure *and* utter whatever cultural critique and moral condemnation may be felt necessary.

The typical orientalist nude claims the prerogative of a sexuality that is feminine not only because of the sex of its favored subject, the harem girl, but also because of the mystery—mysteriousness being culturally marked as a feminine trait—attending the putative geographical setting, as Linda Nochlin has pointed out.[26] The site did not compute with anything that most Europeans or Americans had experienced; the Middle East was a land of the imaginary, a place of fantasy. And the native people were made no less mysterious. They were represented as living without history, in a timeless, exotic, and old-fashioned present. As I discussed in a previous chapter, racial Others, *especially* people of the Middle East, were consistently feminized in Western consciousness and representation, not least as a means to assert and reassure the Western "self" of Western cultural mastery and masculinized political dominance. Gérôme's hiding the boy's genitals from sight feminizes him by rendering him less dangerous. Hence he becomes desirable not for his prowess, not as a model of, say, heroic male agency, but because he can be—in part—*taken,* here visually, not physically. To invest male Middle Eastern sexuality in a feminized child rather than an adult helps render the sight *safe* to be seen.

The nineteenth century's increasingly frenzied obsession to account for the scope of children's sexuality (to a degree not evident in any earlier period of Western history),[27] found common release in the desire to see naked children, whether in paintings or photographs (*many* photographs). This is not to suggest that every image, whether painting or photograph, of a nude child is either immoral or pornographic. But it is said to acknowledge that the enormous fascination for the representation of children's unclothed bodies has a complicated history that to this day remains as poorly understood as its importance to many adults is certain.

Anti-Narcissism
and Zones of (Dis)Pleasure

I want to end the discussion with two drawings by Egon Schiele produced around 1910–1911 (Figures 10.8, 10.9), when the artist was twenty years old. (Schiele died in 1919, aged twenty-eight, during the great influenza epidemic that followed World War I.) Both are self-portraits, thus they involve a particularly high degree of intimacy in regard to the artist's own gaze—he draws himself by looking into a mirror, focusing his entire attention on the representation of the self. This is a matter of special note when the self-portrait involves the nude, for the entire visible body surface is at issue, by definition, as the sum of a self-directed and deeply psychological discourse. Schiele eliminates a setting; in both drawings his body simply *is* what there is. Context is absent, except for that provided in the second by his open jacket. Accordingly, the identity Schiele provides for himself via representation—via making his body visible as a sight to himself (and others)—is radically confined to his flesh and the pose and facial expression he provides for it. Pose and gesture, however, are not culturally vacant signs but are richly and powerfully discursive. In order to produce either drawing Schiele had to set down his pencil and brush, strike a pose, remember it, and take up his drawing tools once again, in a process that would be repeated many times. In other words, Schiele *posed,* and he did so because pose and gesture were the sole means by which he could make his body—otherwise entirely like countless other bodies—singular, the bearer of particular identity. In essence, he observed so as to compose himself.

Both drawings at first glance exhibit hasty execution due to the broad brush strokes used to fill in the body outline—"fast" parallel lines—and the small variation in color. And yet parts of the body, often small parts, are carefully modeled, almost lavished over, like the lips, hands, and not least important, the genitals. Schiele began with a sheet of white paper, upon which he fashioned the body, after which, using very pale beige watercolor, he filled in entirely around the figure, leaving a narrow band of white (Figure 10.8), thereby framing the body, the better to catch the gaze.

Schiele articulates his body against pictorial tradition. His self-image is at strong odds with either the heroic or the beautiful male body; in neither image is the body in any sense feminized. In the first drawing he makes himself extremely skinny and considerably elongates the right arm and both hands. The mouth is open in a kind of grimace or snarl that seems to articulate something like pain or anger. Schiele goes to considerable trouble to "put back" what is nearly always removed in images of men (and women)—body hair. Apart from a pubic tuft, Western imagery defoliates the male body, making smooth its surfaces, not allowing visual divergence from male muscula-

Figure 10.8
Egon Schiele
(1890–1919), SELF-
PORTRAIT NUDE (c.
1910), gouache, pencil,
watercolor, and white
heightening, 55.8 × 36.9
cm. Vienna, Graphische
Sammlung Albertina,
inv. no. 30.766.

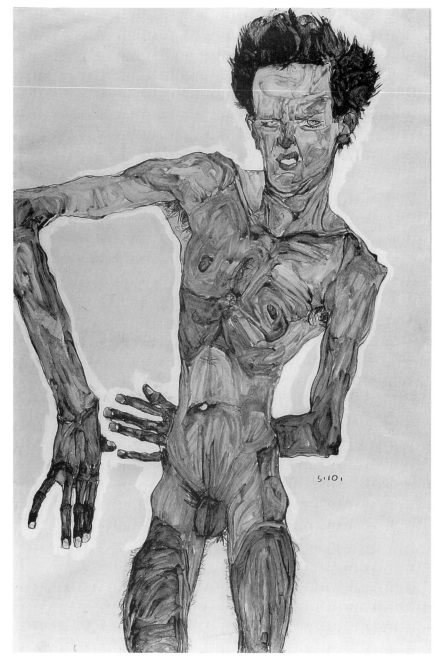

Figure 10.9
Egon Schiele
(1890–1919), SELF-
PORTRAIT NUDE MAS-
TURBATING (1911),
gouache, pencil, and wa-
tercolor, 48 × 32.1 cm.
Vienna, Graphische
Sammlung Albertina,
inv. no. 31.159.

ture. Body hair detracts from, even covers musculature, which must in the end substitute for the phallus that remains hidden. Regarding the nude, body hair becomes a second set of clothing: It hides too much of what the removal of clothing is intended to expose. Schiele, however, pencils in underarm hair and leg hair as well as genital hair and does so in a way that specifically seems to render its presence the least visually attractive: present sparsely, not luxuriantly, all the more drawing attention to its every strand.

The long-standing relation of hair to masculinity and male virility is inevitably problematic. In art its discreet visual presence in the genital region serves the expected purpose—and also marks a means by which to establish a transitional zone between the torso and the genitals, whose color is notably different among whites from the rest of the body.[28] To paint "too much" hair runs counter to the pictorial conventions relative to idealizing the male body, taken over from smooth marble sculpture; in short, the hirsute body risks visual association with brutishness. And this issue remains very much in modern consciousness. In the recent cable-television commercial for bodybuilding equipment described earlier, the "before" sequence exposes a hirsute male chest, and the "after" shows the same chest now duly pumped up, tanned, oiled, and entirely shaved! This is a risky business; the defoliation promotes the glistening of the oil that resonates with hardening and all that that implies. But the defoliation simultaneously is culturally marked as effeminizing. The risk is, of course, part of the appeal, for the newly remade man seemingly has the agency to transgress even the established boundaries of gender taboo.

The male self-portrait is an open invitation to narcissistic observation, especially evident in the work of young painters—one can compare those by Rembrandt produced throughout his career; the differences between the first and last are as profound as one would expect. And the self-portrait is a convenient way that young artists, often in poor economic straits, can avoid having to employ a model.[29] Schiele's self-portraits as a young man, contrary to expectations, are antinarcissistic, none more than the second drawing (Figure 10.9), in fact representing the artist masturbating. In this instance, clothing is putatively shed not for looking but for self-pleasure. The man's eyes are enlarged, so as to delineate sexual excitement, yet they are set in a face that expresses little pleasure—more sadness perhaps, but clearly reserve. Desire in this instance takes on a distinctly philosophical quality, ironically so in an image whose literal sexual "event" is almost never represented in the history of art. Indeed, the representation of masturbation, whether by males or females, was principally confined to the realm of pornography and bedroom erotica. It was not a subject for painting, but for drawing and engraving. Drawings, in usual function, were collected as a kind of private imagery, whatever the subject. Highly vulnerable to damage by light, they were kept in cartons or put into scrapbooks, where they could be viewed at will. But viewing in this instance tends to be highly privatized, both by nature of drawings' typically small size, by their fragility (they cannot be passed from person to person without causing them harm), by the need to keep them near a light source for viewing, and the like.

Schiele's drawing makes use of the open, dark coat as a frame around the naked torso, as a dark patch that sets off the hands fondling his genitals. The V-shape that narrows toward the face of the coat's opening and the light-colored area of his torso and chest together pull our eyes upward to note his expression. At the same time, the distinctly transgressive representation of his hands in action pulls our gaze downward. In essence, our eyes establish the linkage between genitals and face, as it were, the corporeal markers of body and soul by which our culture has chosen to define human identity. It is noteworthy that in regard to masturbation Schiele "shows" us virtually nothing. Almost "everything" is hidden, yet the impact of this hiding seems not to produce the desire to see what cannot be seen. In fact, it is quite possible that we may desire to see even less, due to the violation of representational taboo that defines the image—a sort of self-manifested demasculinization. Scholars have pointed out that Schiele arranges the fingers of his right hand in such a way to effect the appearance of female sexual parts—specifically, he parts his second and third fingers and colors pink the flesh thereby made visible.[30]

If our culture defines masculinity around the phallus as an agent for the domination of all that is outside the self—whether other men, women, or nature—the phallus as an instrument of self-pleasure becomes extremely problematic *as representation.* This is so because the pleasure is one that since the late eighteenth century has been read as "self-abuse" (the specific terms have changed historically, but this word, still in semicurrent usage, provides a convenient summary). As such, masturbation is culturally defined as an act against the self, whereby presumably the phallus turns self-parasitic. Pleasure for men has often been read as weakness, and sexual pleasure *with the self only* is by these terms made notably effeminizing—ironically so, in light of the virtual universality of the practice. "Self-control" is the usual name for masturbatory abstinence, a synonym for self-domination.

Schiele's drawing, nonetheless, does not precisely attempt to take issue with the dominant ideology—and in his lifetime the cultural strictures against masturbation were extreme, far more so than today.[31] Critique as such remains ambivalent. Instead, Schiele acknowledges the body and its drives. But what sexual drive produces is uncertain. The sexual drive itself leads to self-stimulation, yet self-satisfaction as an end point does not seem achievable, judging from his facial expression. Mostly, I think, Schiele reminds himself of the *a*sociality of his situation: He undressed for himself, to scrutinize his own body, to stimulate a desire that seems as much driven by clinical curiosity as sensual longing. Ultimately, the matter hinges on loneliness, a fact that becomes evident by looking at the calm, warmly embracing nudes he later painted of himself and his wife.

> His own appearance obsessed him. . . . He used wild, unnaturalistic colours to indicate states of mind, to make himself ugly, to draw attention to his genitals, nipples, to make them appear as wounds. He drew or painted himself . . . always in bondage to the facts of the body, and, as again and again emphasized, its (for Schiele) pathetic sexual needs.[32]

  Schiele's drawings, as a place to stop, iterate with unusual directness the central role that visual representation plays in the psychic, social, and cultural formation of consciousness and identity. His drawings demonstrate the underlying earnestness with which identity (inordinately abstract) is mapped onto and through the (inordinately concrete) body. In the history of Western representation, the body passes continuously and uneasily between its spiritual values as the seat of being and its objective manifestation as (just) an object—a form of un-stilled life—to be colonized by meaning.

Notes

Introduction

1. The monumental study by Martin Jay, *Downcast Eyes: The Denigration of Vision in Twentieth-Century French Thought* (Berkeley and Los Angeles: University of California Press, 1993), opens with a brief paragraph in which he self-consciously incorporates no fewer than twenty-one visual metaphors as a demonstration of the degree to which seeing and language are mutually dependent. See further Norman Bryson, *Word and Image: French Painting of the Ancien Régime* (Cambridge: Cambridge University Press, 1981), pp. 1–28. For a useful summary of the history and theory of representation see Richard Bernheimer, *The Nature of Representation: A Phenomenological Inquiry,* ed. H. W. Janson (New York: New York University Press, 1961).

2. Donald Preziosi, *Rethinking Art History: Meditations on a Coy Science* (New Haven: Yale University Press, 1989), p. 45; see further pp. 44–53. See also John Tagg, "Postmodernism and the Born-Again Avant-Garde," in *Grounds of Dispute: Art History, Cultural Politics and the Discursive Field* (Minneapolis: University of Minnesota Press, 1992), pp. 157–169.

3. Quoted from Ernst H. Gombrich, *Art and Illusion: A Study in the Psychology of Pictorial Representation,* 2d ed., rev. (Princeton: Princeton University Press, 1961), p. 15; compare Gombrich, p. 394: "We have come to realize more and more . . . that we can never neatly separate what we see from what we know. . . . With some self-discipline and self-observation we can all find out for ourselves that what we call seeing is invariably coloured and shaped by our knowledge (or belief) of what we see."

4. Gombrich, *Art and Illusion,* p. 298.

5. John Berger, *Ways of Seeing* (London: British Broadcasting Corporation, and Harmondsworth: Penguin Books, 1972), p. 10.

6. Quoted in Gombrich, *Art and Illusion,* p. 64.

7. Preziosi, *Rethinking Art History,* p. 153. See further to p. 155.

8. Ibid., p. 11.

9. See Keith Moxey, *The Practice of Theory: Poststructuralism, Cultural Politics, and Art History* (Ithaca: Cornell University Press, 1994); David Carrier, *Artwriting* (Amherst: University of Massachusetts Press, 1987); and Craig Owens, "Representation, Appropriation and Power," *Art in America* 70 (May 1982), pp. 9–21.

10. The major formulation of the difference between seeing and perceiving is in Gombrich's *Art and Illusion.* Gombrich's principal interest is to trace the history of representation as response to a mimetic impulse, a supposed inborn urge to strive for the Essential Copy, dependent upon the notion that art is essentially a record of per-

ception. This formulation has been much critiqued, but in particular see the sustained engagement by Norman Bryson, *Vision and Painting: The Logic of the Gaze* (New Haven: Yale University Press, 1983). Bryson argues that Gombrich suppresses the social character of representation and the historicity of the maker and viewer alike.

A great deal has recently been written concerning the historicity and contingency of seeing. For an introduction to this important work see Jay, *Downcast Eyes,* which includes an excellent historical account from the ancient Greeks to the present; Donald M. Lowe, *History of Bourgeois Perception* (Chicago: University of Chicago Press, 1982); Jonathan Crary, *Techniques of the Observer: On Vision and Modernity in the Nineteenth Century* (Cambridge, Mass.: MIT Press, 1990); and Hal Foster, ed., *Discussions in Contemporary Culture (Dia Art Foundation) Number Two: Vision and Visuality* (Seattle: Bay Press, 1988).

11. See John Rajchman, "Foucault's Art of Seeing," *October* 44 (Spring 1988), pp. 89–117.

12. For a succinct critique of this issue see Preziosi, *Rethinking Art History,* pp. 27–33.

13. Barbara Maria Stafford, *Body Criticism: Imaging the Unseen in Enlightenment Art and Medicine* (Cambridge, Mass.: MIT Press, 1991), p. 477.

14. On this issue see Joseph Leo Koerner, *The Moment of Self-Portraiture in German Renaissance Art* (Chicago: University of Chicago Press, 1993), p. 52, discussing Walter Benjamin's 1931 essay on the future of literary history, "Literaturgeschichte und Literaturwissenschaft."

15. Literature concerning the institution of the public museum, art and otherwise, both in the West and throughout the rest of the world, has burgeoned in the past decade. Limiting myself to a few of the more important works, the following are recommended merely as places to start. Ivan Karp and Steven D. Lavine, eds., *Exhibiting Cultures: The Poetics and Politics of Museum Display* (Washington, D.C.: Smithsonian Institution Press, 1991); Ivan Karp, Christine Mullen Kreamer, and Steven D. Lavine, eds., *Museums and Communities: The Politics of Public Culture* (Washington, D.C.: Smithsonian Institution Press, 1992); Kenneth Hudson, *Museums of Influence* (Cambridge: Cambridge University Press, 1987); Robert Hewison, *The Heritage Industry: Britain in a Climate of Decline* (London: Metheun, 1987); Martin Feldstein, ed., *The Economics of Art Museums* (Chicago: University of Chicago Press, 1991); Jeanette Greenfield, *The Return of Cultural Treasures* (New York: Cambridge University Press, 1989); Donald Horne, *The Great Museum: The Re-Presentation of History* (London: Pluto Press, 1984); Gaynor Kavanagh, ed., *Museum Languages: Objects and Texts* (Leicester: Leicester University Press, 1991); Peter Vergo, ed., *The New Museology* (London: Reaktion Books, 1989); Edward P. Alexander, *Museum Masters: Their Museums and Their Influence* (Nashville, Tenn.: American Association for State and Local History, 1983); Douglas Crimp, "On the Museum's Ruins," in *The Anti-Aesthetic: Essays on Postmodern Culture,* ed. Hal Foster (Port Townsend, Wash.: Bay Press, 1983), pp. 43–56; Tony Bennett, "The Exhibitionary Complex,"

New Formations 4 (Spring 1988), pp. 73–102; Carol Duncan and Alan Wallach, "The Universal Survey Museum," *Art History* 3 (1980), pp. 448–469; Andrew L. McClellan, "The Politics and Aesthetics of Display: Museums in Paris 1750–1800," *Art History* 7 (1984), pp. 438–464; Marie-Claude Chaudonneret, "Historicism and 'Heritage' in the Louvre, 1820–40: From the Musée Charles X to the Galerie d'Apollon," *Art History* 14 (1991), pp. 488–520; and William S. Hendon, Frank Costa, and Robert A. Rosenberg, "The General Public and the Art Museum: Case Studies of Visitors to Several Institutions Identify Characteristics of Their Publics," *American Journal of Economics and Sociology* 48, no. 2 (1989), pp. 231–243. Thanks to my colleague John Archer for drawing my attention to a number of these texts.

16. Compare Pierre Bourdieu, *Distinction: A Social Critique of the Judgement of Taste,* trans. Richard Nice (Cambridge, Mass.: Harvard University Press, 1984), p. 30. "Nothing more totally manifests and achieves the autonomizing of aesthetic activity vis-à-vis extra-aesthetic interests or functions than the art museum's juxtaposition of works. Though originally subordinated to quite different or even incompatible functions (crucifix and fetish, Pietà and still life), these juxtaposed works tacitly demand attention to form rather than function, technique rather than theme, and, being constructed in styles that are mutually exclusive but all equally necessary, they are a practical challenge to the expectation of realistic representation as defined by the arbitrary canons of an everyday aesthetic, and so lead naturally from stylistic relativism to the neutralization of the very function of representation."

17. Constance Perin, "The Communicative Circle: Museums as Communities," in *Museums and Communities,* ed. Karp, Kreamer, and Lavine, p. 185.

18. Jean Baudrillard, *For a Critique of the Political Economy of the Sign,* trans. Charles Levin (St. Louis, Mo.: Telos Press, 1981), pp. 112–122. The quotations are from p. 113. On a related note, see Craig Owens, "The Birth and Death of the Viewer: On the Public Functions of Art," in *Discussions in Contemporary Culture (Dia Art Foundation) Number One,* ed. Hal Foster (Seattle: Bay Press, 1987), pp. 16–23, which opens with an excellent discussion of the 1987 auction purchase by a Japanese insurance company of one of Vincent van Gogh's sunflower still lifes for $38.9 million.

Chapter 1

1. Quoted from the exhibition catalog by Eddy de Jongh, *Still-Life in the Age of Rembrandt* (Auckland: Auckland City Art Gallery, 1982), p. 145. See also on this artist Svetlana Alpers, *The Art of Describing: Dutch Art in the Seventeenth Century* (Chicago: University of Chicago Press, 1983), pp. 58–64, 76–79.

2. For a brief summary of this frequently told early history, see Cis Amaral, "'Be What You Would Seem to Be,'" *Art and Artists* 11 (August 1976), pp. 26–28; and Gillian Saunders, "Trompe l'Oeil: Visual Deception in European Art," *Victoria and Albert [Museum] Album* 5 (1986), pp. 58–67. For thorough treatment of this history see Norman Bryson, *Looking at the Overlooked: Four Essays on Still Life Painting*

(Cambridge, Mass.: Harvard University Press, 1990), pp. 17–59, regarding the famous accounts of ancient trompe l'oeil still life by Philostratus and Pliny (the latter describing the contest between Parrhasios and Zeuxis to fashion the most convincingly mimetic representation), with briefer comments on Plato and Vitruvius. Other worthwhile studies, fundamentally surveys of the genre's entire history, include M. L. d'Otrange Mastai, *Illusion in Art: Trompe l'Oeil, A History of Pictorial Illusionism* (New York: Abaris Books, 1975); Célestine Dars, *Images of Deception: The Art of Trompe-l'Oeil* (Oxford: Phaidon, 1979); Miriam Milman, *Trompe-l'Oeil Painting: The Illusions of Reality* (New York: Skira/Rizzoli, 1982); and Martin Battersby, *Trompe l'Oeil: The Eye Deceived* (New York: St. Martin's Press, 1974).

3. For more concerning technique, see Battersby, *Trompe l'Oeil: The Eye Deceived,* pp. 19–22.

4. Arthur C. Danto, "Trompe l'oeil," *Nation* 254 (4 May 1992), p. 604.

5. Saunders, "Trompe l'Oeil: Visual Deception in European Art," p. 63.

6. Jennifer Mundy, "Surrealism and Painting: Describing the Imaginary," *Art History* 10 (1987), p. 504. On Magritte and the problematics of representation, see Bernard Noël, *Magritte,* trans. Jeffrey Arsham (New York: Crown Publishers, 1977); and Michel Foucault, *This Is Not a Pipe,* trans. and ed. James Harkness (Berkeley and Los Angeles: University of California Press, 1983), especially for Foucault's insightful discussion about visual representation's problematic relationship to words. Concerning *La condition humaine* see the exhibition catalog by Sarah Whitfield, *Magritte* (London: The South Bank Centre, 1992), cat. no. 62.

7. Bryson, *Looking at the Overlooked,* p. 143; see further pp. 140–145.

8. Susan L. Siegfried, "Boilly and the Frame-up of *Trompe l'oeil,*" *Oxford Art Journal* 15, 2 (1992), p. 31.

9. See further on this image Alfred Frankenstein, "Fooling the Eye," *Art Forum* 12, 9 (May 1974), pp. 32–33.

10. Albert Pomme de Mirimonde, "Les peintres flamands de trompe l'oeil et des natures mortes au XVIIe siècle, et les sujets de musique," *Jaarboek, Koninklijk Museum voor Schone Kunsten* [Antwerp] (1971), p. 229; and Norbert Schneider, *The Art of the Still Life: Still Life Painting in the Early Modern Period,* trans. Hugh Beyer (Cologne: Benedikt Taschen Verlag, 1990), p. 23. Gijsbrechts's paintings were executed in great numbers for the Danish kings Frederick III and Christian V, whom he served as court painter; such pictures as this one were likely amusements for the kings and their guests. From Jongh, *Still-Life in the Age of Rembrandt,* p. 146. See further Georges Marlier, "C. N. Gijsbrechts, l'illusionniste," *Connaissance des Arts* 145 (March 1964), pp. 96–105. See also Gertrude Grace Sill, "The Reversed Canvas," *Portfolio* 3, 1 (January-February 1981), pp. 48–51, reproducing as well twentieth-century examples by Roy Lichtenstein and Jasper Johns, among others.

11. Other artists produced trompe l'oeil painting of easels, including Cornelis-Norbertus Gijsbrechts (now in Copenhagen, National Museum of Art); for a reproduction see Dars, *Images of Deception,* p. 37, fig. 26, about which see Celeste Brusati, "Stilled Lives: Self-Portraiture and Self-Reflection in Seventeenth-Century Nether-

landish Still-Life Painting," *Simiolus* 20 (1990/1991), p. 180; and Poul Gammelbo, *Dutch Still-Life Painting from the 16th to the 18th Centuries in Danish Collections* (Copenhagen: Munksgaard, 1960), pp. 166–167.

12. The prints are after Perelle and Le Clerc, that is, they are copied from actual prints. See further Milman, *Trompe-l'oeil Painting,* p. 92.

13. Quoted from Mastai, *Illusion in Art,* pp. 207–208; and Milman, *Trompe-l'oeil Painting,* pp. 112–113 n. 15.

14. Georges de Loye, "Le Trompe-l'oeil d'Antoine Fort-Bras," *Revue des Arts* 10 (1960), p. 19.

15. See further the discussion by Siegfried, "Boilly and the Frame-up of *Trompe l'oeil,*" pp. 27–28.

16. Danto, "Trompe l'oeil," pp. 605–606. Perhaps the best account of the genre's limitations is by Jean Baudrillard, "The Trompe-l'Oeil," in *Calligram: Essays in New Art History from France,* ed. Norman Bryson (Cambridge: Cambridge University Press, 1988), pp. 53–62.

17. David Summers, "Real Metaphor: Towards a Redefinition of the 'Conceptual' Image," in *Visual Theory: Painting and Interpretation,* ed. Norman Bryson, Michael Ann Holly, and Keith Moxey (New York: HarperCollins, 1991), p. 241.

18. See the excellent essay by Dorinda Evans, "Raphaelle Peale's *Venus Rising from the Sea*: Further Support for a Change in Interpretation," *American Art Journal* 14 (Summer 1982), pp. 63–72; my information on the X ray is from p. 63 n. 1. Evans clarifies that the figure behind the curtain is based on a 1772 engraving after a painting by James Barry, *Birth of Venus* or *Venus Rising from the Sea;* the engraving is reproduced on p. 64. Peale's painting's title, *After the Bath,* has no historical basis. Nonetheless, the pose of the arm holding aloft a woman's long hair, together with the bare foot, duly inscribe contemporaneous conventions for representing a nude; whether a bath is involved is fundamentally irrelevant.

19. See Roger B. Stein, "Charles Willson Peale's Expressive Design: The Artist in His Museum," *Prospects: The Annual of American Cultural Studies,* ed. Jack Salzman, 6 (1981), pp. 174–175, who suggests that this painting is a "mordantly witty covert parody of *The Artist in His Museum,*" the famous painting by Charles Willson Peale, Raphaelle Peale's father.

20. This matter is brilliantly articulated with regard to trompe l'oeil paintings in general by Siegfried, "Boilly and the Frame-up of *Trompe l'oeil,*" see in particular pp. 34–36. She describes the Parrhasios versus Zeuxis contest as characteristic of male rivalries, pointing to the traditional contents of trompe l'oeil paintings as taken from male pastimes (hunting, smoking, gaming, etc.) and finally to the cool, ironic stance typical of these pictures in their relation to the beholder.

21. The major work on American still lifes of this sort is by Alfred Frankenstein, *After the Hunt: William Harnett and Other American Still Life Painters, 1870–1900,* rev. ed. (Berkeley and Los Angeles: University of California Press, 1969); and by the same author, the exhibition catalog *The Reality of Appearance: The Trompe l'Oeil Tradition in American Painting* (Greenwich, Conn.: New York Graphic Society,

1970). See further on the general topic the more recent studies by Roxana Barry, "Plane Truths: 19th-Century American Trompe l'Oeil Painting," *Arts & Antiques* 4 (September-October 1981), pp. 100–106; Robert F. Chirico, "Language and Imagery in Late Nineteenth-Century Trompe l'Oeil," *Arts Magazine* 59 (March 1985), pp. 110–114; Johanna Drucker, "Harnett, Haberle, and Peto: Visuality and Artifice among the Proto-Modern Americans," *Art Bulletin* 74 (1992), pp. 37–50. On Haberle, see Robert F. Chirico, "John Haberle and *Trompe-l'Oeil,*" *Marsyas: Studies in the History of Art* 19 (1977–1978), pp. 37–43. The leading American trompe l'oeil painter was William Harnett, concerning whom see the recent and excellent exhibition catalog edited by Doreen Bolger, Marc Simpson, and John Wilmerding, *William M. Harnett* (New York: Harry N. Abrams, 1992). Of particular relevance to this discussion see the essays in this volume by Nicolai Cikovsky, Jr., "'Sordid Mechanics' and 'Monkey-Talents': The Illusionistic Tradition," pp. 19–29; and Doreen Bolger, "The Patrons of the Artist: Emblems of Commerce and Culture," pp. 73–86.

22. Edward J. Nygren, "The Almighty Dollar: Money as a Theme in American Painting," *Winterthur Portfolio: A Journal of American Material Culture* 23 (1988), p. 130.

23. Reproduced in Nygren, "The Almighty Dollar," p. 143, discussed on pp. 142–143.

24. Ibid., pp. 142–143. For other images of this sort, see pp. 144–150.

25. Paul J. Staiti, "Illusionism, Trompe l'Oeil, and the Perils of Viewership," in the exhibition catalog edited by Bolger, Simpson, and Wilmerding, *William M. Harnett,* pp. 42–43.

26. See Miles Orvell, *The Real Thing: Imitation and Authenticity in American Culture, 1880–1940* (Chapel Hill: University of North Carolina Press, 1989), pp. 120–121.

27. See Lynn Glaser, *Counterfeiting in America* (New York: Clarkson N. Potter, 1968).

28. Drucker, "Harnett, Haberle, and Peto," p. 41. See Staiti, "Illusionism, Trompe l'Oeil, and the Perils of Viewership," pp. 31–35, re the perceived relation in the late nineteenth century of trompe l'oeil paintings to con games.

29. From the fascinating account by Lawrence Weschler, "Onward and Upward with the Arts (Boggs)," *New Yorker,* 63 (18 January 1988), p. 43. The entire profile is on pp. 33–56; with continuation (25 January 1988), pp. 88–98; and a follow-up, "Money Changes Everything," 68 (18 January 1993), pp. 38–41. See also J.S.G. Boggs, "Art Under Arrest," *Art and Antiques* (October 1987), pp. 99–104, 126–127.

30. Weschler, "Onward and Upward," p. 49.

31. Ibid., p. 44, and (25 January 1988) p. 90.

32. On the relation of trompe l'oeil money paintings to twentieth-century Modernism, see Drucker, "Harnett, Haberle, and Peto," p. 50; and Walter Benn Michaels, *The Gold Standard and the Logic of Naturalism: American Literature at the Turn of the Century* (Berkeley and Los Angeles: University of California Press, 1987), pp. 162–165.

Chapter 2

1. See Pierre Skira, *Still Life: A History,* trans. Jean-Marie Clarke (New York: Skira/Rizzoli, 1989), pp. 21–22; Charles Sterling, *Still Life Painting: From Antiquity to the Present Time,* trans. James Emmons, rev. ed. (New York: Universe Books, 1959), p. 11; and Norman Bryson, *Looking at the Overlooked: Four Essays on Still Life Painting* (Cambridge, Mass.: Harvard University Press, 1990), pp. 8–9, 17–32.

2. Norbert Schneider, *The Art of the Still Life: Still Life Painting in the Early Modern Period,* trans. Hugh Beyer (Cologne: Benedikt Taschen Verlag, 1990), p. 7. See pp. 7–16 for a solid introduction to the early theory, place, and practice of still life painting in Western Europe. Some of my subsequent general remarks about still life are indebted to this study. See also Sterling, *Still Life Painting,* pp. 43–44, for more on the history of the genre's terminology.

3. See further Andrea Gasten, "Dutch Still-Life Painting: Judgements and Appreciation," in the exhibition catalog by Eddy de Jongh, *Still-Life in the Age of Rembrandt* (Auckland: Auckland City Art Gallery, 1982), pp. 13–16. On reassessment of still life since the nineteenth century, see pp. 17–22.

4. Arthur K. Wheelock, Jr., "Still Life: Its Visual Appeal and Theoretical Status in the Seventeenth Century," in the exhibition catalog *Still Lifes of the Golden Age: Northern European Paintings from the Heinz Family Collection,* catalog entries by Ingvar Bergström, ed. Arthur K. Wheelock, Jr. (Washington, D.C.: National Gallery of Art, 1989), p. 12.

5. See on this point and on still life in a general theory of "the gaze," Norman Bryson, "In Medusa's Gaze," in the exhibition catalog by Bernard Barryte, *In Medusa's Gaze: Still Life Paintings from Upstate New York Museums* (Rochester, N.Y.: Memorial Art Gallery of the University of Rochester, 1991), p. 6, and thereafter to p. 30, for his important essay as a whole. Much of this is developed at greater length in Bryson, *Looking at the Overlooked,* especially following p. 60.

6. See John Michael Montias, "Art Dealers in the Seventeenth-Century Netherlands," *Simiolus* 18 (1988), pp. 244–253.

7. See on this point Lawrence O. Goedde, "A Little World Made Cunningly: Dutch Still Life and Ekphrasis," in Bergström, *Still Lifes of the Golden Age,* p. 36; and Schneider, *Art of the Still Life,* p. 10, who retells the account of a flower still life by Ambrosius Bosschaert fetching 1,000 Dutch guilders at a time when a standard portrait required payment of only 60.

8. Not that these claims invariably went unchallenged; thus Denis Diderot championed the still lifes of Jean-Baptiste Chardin, insisting that they could more than hold their own against history pictures. See Schneider, *Art of the Still Life,* p. 9.

9. Roland Barthes, "The World as Object," trans. Richard Howard, in *A Barthes Reader,* ed. Susan Sontag (New York: Hill and Wang, 1982), pp. 65 and 67.

10. Schneider, *Art of the Still Life,* p. 16.

11. Wheelock, "Still Life: Its Visual Appeal," p. 11.

12. Bryson, "In Medusa's Gaze," pp. 6–7.

13. Compare Michel Foucault, *The History of Sexuality,* vol. 1, *An Introduction,* trans. Robert Hurley (New York: Pantheon Books, 1978).

14. Ernst H. Gombrich, "Tradition and Expression in Western Still Life," in *Meditations on a Hobby Horse and Other Essays on the Theory of Art* (Chicago: University of Chicago Press, 1963), p. 104.

15. Bryson, *Looking at the Overlooked,* p. 108: "The construction of such gardens was an undertaking so colossal that only a prince or the state could find the resources to fund it, and what such patronage brought with it was a symbolic association between horticulture and political power that conferred on Dutch flower painting a high value of social prestige (and the supporters of the earliest flower painters were decidedly more courtly than bourgeois)."

16. Marie-Louise Hairs, *The Flemish Flower Painters in the XVIIth Century,* trans. Eva Grzelak (Brussels: Lefebvre et Gillet, 1985), p. 5.

17. Simon Schama, *The Embarrassment of Riches: An Interpretation of Dutch Culture in the Golden Age* (Berkeley and Los Angeles: University of California Press, 1988), p. 353. See pp. 350–371 for a general account of the tulip mania and its social impact.

18. N. W. Posthumus, "The Tulip Mania in Holland in the Years 1636 and 1637," *Journal of Economic and Business History* 1 (1928), pp. 438–440, 443, 448.

19. Schama, *Embarrassment of Riches,* p. 354.

20. Hairs, *Flemish Flower Painters,* p. 6; and Schama, *Embarrassment of Riches,* p. 617. Tulip mania produced a sociocultural backlash led by Calvinist preachers as vain folly, not least because of the dynamics of speculation and the desire it produced for fast and excessive profit. Concerning Dutch guilt over wealth in general, see further Schama, pp. 289–371.

21. Hairs, *Flemish Flower Painters,* p. 5. Regarding the costs and numbers of paintings (not only those of flowers) produced in Holland, see Ad van der Woude, "The Volume and Value of Paintings in Holland at the Time of the Dutch Republic," in *Art in History, History in Art: Studies in Seventeenth-Century Dutch Culture,* ed. David Freedberg and Jan de Vries (Santa Monica, Calif.: The Getty Center for the History of Art and the Humanities, 1991), pp. 285–329. Van der Woude estimates that between 1580 and 1800 the staggering number of nearly 9 million paintings was produced (p. 315). He suggests that the cheapest of paintings were affordable by the lowest social orders, though the most expensive works were only had by the wealthiest.

22. On this painter see Klaus Ertz, *Jan Brueghel der Ältere (1568–1625): Die Gemälde mit kritischem Oeuvrekatalog* (Cologne: DuMont Buchverlag, 1979), the standard monograph; concerning the flower paintings, see pp. 252–327. See also Klaus Ertz, "Introduction: Some Thoughts on the Paintings of Jan Brueghel the Elder (1568–1625)," *Jan Brueghel the Elder: A Loan Exhibition of Paintings* (London: Brod Gallery, 1979), pp. 8–21. See further Fritz Baumgart, *Blumen Brueghel (Jan Brueghel d. Ä.) Leben und Werk* (Cologne: DuMont Buchverlag, 1978); concerning the flower paintings, see pp. 139–154.

23. Hairs, *Flemish Flower Painters,* pp. 33–37; the discussion of Brueghel continues to p. 115.

24. For a discussion of this painting's formal composition see Ertz, *Brueghel,* pp. 264, 267.

25. Elisabeth Blair MacDougall, "Flower Importation and Dutch Flower Paintings, 1600–1750," in Bergström, *Still Lifes of the Golden Age,* p. 31. The exhibition catalog by Sam Segal, *A Flowery Past: A Survey of Dutch and Flemish Flower Painting from 1600 until the Present,* trans. P. M. van Tongeren-Woodland (Amsterdam: Gallery P. de Boer, 1982), p. 27, provides a list of twenty-five stylistic characteristics of early flower still lifes like Brueghel's. He points out that the apparent accuracy of the painted flowers is deceiving to the extent that proportions between flowers are commonly altered, larger ones being painted smaller, smaller ones larger, the better to fit the compositional scheme. Moreover, flowers at the top of a pyramidal bouquet could not have stems sufficiently long to reach the vase.

26. See Ertz, *Jan Brueghel der Ältere,* pp. 528–529.

27. Ertz, "Introduction: Some Thoughts on the Paintings of Jan Brueghel the Elder," pp. 8, 19. Bryson, *Looking at the Overlooked,* p. 108: "Flower painting is labour-intensive to a degree that exceeds other still life genres: short-cuts are technically impossible. As a result, it can flourish only when the demand for painting is sufficiently buoyant to permit the necessary and considerable outlay for a painter's labour."

28. B. Brenninkmeyer-de Rooij, "Zeldzame bloemen, 'Fatta tutti del natturel' door Jan Brueghel I," *Oud Holland* 104 (1990), p. 248. Regarding the various flowers typically depicted in northern still life paintings, see further MacDougall, "Flower Importation and Dutch Flower Paintings," pp. 27–33.

29. Wheelock, "Still Life: Its Visual Appeal," p. 15.

30. Ibid., p. 18. Wheelock suggests that Cardinal Borromeo likely saw Brueghel's still life as a celebration of God's natural creation in all its diversity and visual splendor, a reading characteristic of the Catholic Counter-Reformation and directly opposing Calvinist interpretation.

31. Hairs, *Flemish Flower Painters,* pp. 58–59, 62.

32. See further MacDougall, "Flower Importation and Dutch Flower Paintings," pp. 27–33; on time, and the breaking of the bonds between man and the cycles of nature, see Bryson, *Looking at the Overlooked,* p. 105.

33. Wheelock, "Still Life: Its Visual Appeal," pp. 16–17; see also George Ferguson, *Signs and Symbols in Christian Art* (New York: Oxford University Press, 1961).

34. See further Sam Segal, *The Sumptuous Still Life in the Netherlands, 1600–1700,* ed. William B. Jordan (The Hague: SDU Publishers, 1988), p. 100. A principal difficulty with symbolic readings is the radical moral ambiguity of the signs involved— thus presenting a challenge that compliments the viewer's intelligence (but is quite apart from the issue of whether to "read" the signs as symbols at all). In *Flowery Past,* pp. 28–29, Segal observes: "The fly, for example, is a transitorial symbol but can also be one of sin and corruption. When one strikes it, it returns, just like temptation and sin. It can also be a symbol of tenacity (to Truth). We see a pair of lizards, a lizard is man's friend, '*vitae defensor,*' it gives a warning against snakes, Evil. It is also a symbol of tenacity as once it has grasped its prey he does not easily release it, by which it triumphs over its difficulties. But again, the lizard can be interpreted as a symbol for hypocrisy and deceit when seen in the context of a witches representation." See further pp. 12–35.

Further, aside from the fact that few viewers of still lifes—or of any other paintings—in our own age have cultural access to the history and use of symbols, we have little way of knowing the extent to which the painting's "original" viewers could carry out such interpretations or whether they were interested in so doing. The question of symbolic, especially emblem-based, readings of Dutch painting—from still lifes to genre scenes and even landscapes—has recently been subject to an intensive debate, a good introduction to which is the volume edited by David Freedberg and Jan de Vries, *Art in History, History in Art: Studies in Seventeenth-Century Dutch Culture* (Santa Monica, Calif.: The Getty Center for the History of Art and the Humanities, 1991). In particular see the essays by Gary Schwarz, "Art in History," pp. 7–16; Eddy de Jongh, "Some Notes on Interpretation," pp. 119–136; and David Freedberg, "Science, Commerce, and Art: Neglected Topics at the Junction of History and Art History," pp. 377–428.

35. Brenninkmeyer-de Rooij, "Zeldzame bloemen," p. 248.

36. Wheelock, "Still Life: Its Visual Appeal," p. 14.

37. Hairs, *Flemish Flower Painters,* p. 7.

38. Bryson, *Looking at the Overlooked,* p. 106.

39. Ruysch was born into a wealthy family; her father was the famous anatomist and botanist Fredrik Ruysch, discussed later on in Chapter 6. She was sent by her father to study art with Willem van Aelst. She later married the portrait painter Juriaen Pool, by whom she had ten children. Her paintings were well known and sought after during her own lifetime throughout Europe; her work commanded high prices— 750 to 1,000 Dutch florins. In 1708 she was appointed Court Painter to Johann Wilhelm, the prince elector of the Palatinate of the Rhine, at Düsseldorf, though she continued to live and work in The Hague. She continued painting until she was at least eighty-three. She painted this still life when she was twenty-two. See further Bergström, *Still Lifes of the Golden Age,* p. 123; Barryte, *In Medusa's Gaze,* pp. 58–59; and Marianne Berardi, "The Nature Pieces of Rachel Ruysch," *Porticus,* vols. 10 and 11 (1987–1988), pp. 3–15, whence my information.

40. The extreme attention to detail, whether of plants or insects, reflects not only the fact that she worked from natural specimens but also the likelihood that she took advantage of her father's collections—of which he had engravings made, published in installments after 1700 as *Thesaurus animalium* and *Thesaurus anatomicus.* From Jongh, *Still-Life in the Age of Rembrandt,* p. 177. For an excellent general account of the fascination with the unusual, the rare, the well-made, and so on see the exhibition catalog edited by Joy Kenseth, *The Age of the Marvelous* (Hanover, N.H.: Hood Museum of Art, Dartmouth College, 1991).

41. Barryte, *In Medusa's Gaze,* p. 58. The created effect of a spatial gap may be similar to that of the dioramas she helped design for her father's famous *Wunderkammer* of natural history.

42. For more on the symbolic potential of these creatures, see Schneider, *Art of the Still Life,* pp. 195–201.

43. See Introduction, n. 18, this volume.

44. Sterling, *Still Life Painting,* p. 114.

Chapter 3

1. The exhibition catalog by Alberto Veca, *Vanitas: Il simbolismo des tempo* (Bergamo: Galleria Lorenzelli, 1981), with abbreviated English text, pp. 163–221, provides information on the history of death as a literary and visual subject and includes numerous Italian sources. See also Norbert Schneider, *The Art of the Still Life: Still Life Painting in the Early Modern Period,* trans. Hugh Beyer (Cologne: Benedickt Taschen Verlag, 1990), pp. 76–87.

2. For other relevant scriptural sources, as well as relevant secular literature and emblems relative to the Vanitas topos, see Ingvar Bergström, *Dutch Still-Life Painting in the Seventeenth Century,* trans. Christina Hedström and Gerald Taylor (London: Faber and Faber, 1956), pp. 155–156. For a general introduction to the Vanitas theme, see pp. 154–190, whence much of my basic information. Bergström is the best source in English for traditional interpretations of this genre. For an important revisionist view see Svetlana Alpers, *The Art of Describing: Dutch Art in the Seventeenth Century* (Chicago: University of Chicago Press, 1983), especially pp. 90–91, 103–109, 114–115. On musical subject matter in these paintings see Richard Leppert, *The Theme of Music in Flemish Paintings of the Seventeenth Century,* 2 vols. (Munich and Salzburg: Musikverlag Emil Katzbichler, 1977), vol. 1, pp. 75–84.

3. For an excellent account of the tension between the visible and the invisible, the image and the unseen text in Vanitas painting, see Norman Bryson, "In Medusa's Gaze," in the exhibition catalog by Bernard Barryte, *In Medusa's Gaze: Still Life Paintings from Upstate New York Museums* (Rochester, N.Y.: Memorial Art Gallery of the University of Rochester, 1991), pp. 9–14.

4. See further on Pereda the exhibition catalog by William B. Jordan, *Spanish Still Life in the Golden Age, 1600–1650* (Fort Worth, Tex.: Kimball Art Museum, 1985), pp. 206–219.

5. Albert Pomme de Mirimonde, "Les sujets de musique chez les Caravagistes Flamands," *Jaarboek, Koninklijk Museum for Schone Kunsten* [Antwerp] (1965), pp. 165–167.

6. The sexual meaning of *zingen* in the proverb is clarified by its use in another Dutch proverb: "*Voor het zingen de kerk uit*" ("Before singing leave the church"), a reference to coitus interruptus. On the lute and prostitution, see Albert Pomme de Mirimonde, "Musique et symbolisme chez Jan-Davidszoon de Heem, Cornelis-Janszoon et Jan II Janzoon de Heem," *Jaarboek, Koninklijk Museum voor Schone Kunsten* [Antwerp] (1970), p. 287; and Leppert, *Theme of Music in Flemish Paintings,* vol. 1, p. 185.

7. Albert Pomme de Mirimonde, "Les natures mortes à instruments de musique de Peter Boel," *Jaarboek, Koninklijk Museum voor Schone Kunsten* [Antwerp] (1964), pp. 114–117.

8. On the matter of making a moral choice as a function of these images, see Anne Walter Lowenthal, "Response to Peter Hecht," *Simiolus* 16 (1986), pp. 188–190; and by the same author, *Joachim Wtewael and Dutch Mannerism* (Doornspijk: Davaco, 1986), pp. 57–60; and Bryson, "In Medusa's Gaze," pp. 10–12.

9. See Norman Bryson, *Looking at the Overlooked: Four Essays on Still Life Painting* (Cambridge, Mass.: Harvard University Press, 1990), pp. 115–121. The quotation is from p. 116.

10. Bryson, "In Medusa's Gaze," p. 11.

11. The factual information contained in my discussion of this painting is from Barryte, *In Medusa's Gaze,* pp. 112–113.

12. See also the discussion of this print in Barryte, *In Medusa's Gaze,* pp. 114–125.

Chapter 4

1. Carolyn Chute, *The Beans of Egypt, Maine* (New York: Warner Books, 1985), pp. 117–118.

2. The foregoing summarizes research by Scott A. Sullivan, *The Dutch Gamepiece* (Totowa, N.J.: Allanheld and Schram, 1984), especially the chapter "Hunting and Dutch Society," pp. 33–45; see also by the same author, "Rembrandt's *Self-Portrait with a Dead Bittern,*" *Art Bulletin* 62 (1980), pp. 236–243; Norbert Schneider, *The Art of the Still Life: Still Life Painting in the Early Modern Period,* trans. Hugh Beyer (Cologne: Benedickt Taschen Verlag, 1990), pp. 50–63; and Ingvar Bergström, *Dutch Still-Life Painting in the Seventeenth Century,* trans. Christina Hedström and Gerald Taylor (London: Faber and Faber, 1956), pp. 247–259.

3. Sullivan, *Dutch Gamepiece,* p. 64.

4. See Richard Leppert, *Music and Image: Domesticity, Ideology and Socio-Cultural Formation in Eighteenth-Century England* (Cambridge: Cambridge University Press, 1988), the chapter "Music and the Body: Dance, Power, Submission," pp. 71–106.

5. Sullivan, *Dutch Gamepiece,* p. 62, indicates knowledge of approximately 130 gamepieces by Weenix.

6. See the exhibition catalog Fred G. Meijer, *Still Life Paintings from the Golden Age* (Rotterdam: Museum Boymans-van Beuningen, 1989), p. 116, concerning this very painting.

7. Covering a slightly later period, the classic account is that by Michel Foucault, *Discipline and Punish: The Birth of the Prison,* trans. Alan Sheridan (New York: Vintage Books, 1979).

8. The hunt-as-slaughter was represented in seventeenth-century images of Diana the Huntress, among which versions by Jan Brueghel the Elder, in collaboration with Rubens, are especially noteworthy. In these pictures, and adding to the equation I have otherwise been constructing, Diana and her female companions were conventionally painted in the nude. See Klaus Ertz, *Jan Brueghel der Ältere (1568–1625): Die Gemälde mit kritischem Oeuvrekatalog* (Cologne: DuMont Buchverlag, 1979), pp. 391–406.

The English painter Arthur Devis (1712–1787) in a portrait of the Cross family made use of dead game in an equally powerful and direct way. He posed husband, wife, and small child on the grounds of their estate at Shudy Camps Park, Cambridgeshire, with the family home in the background separated from the sitters by an expansive lawn. Mr. Cross, just back from the hunt, hands his wife a small dead bird. Seated on a bench, book in hand, she looks up and quite literally shrinks back from the little carcass being presented to her. On her other side, her husband's hound looks on with interest at the trophy. To choose this gesture for the husband and this response for the wife was a blatant, raw expression of hierarchical difference. The painting is reproduced in Sydney H. Pavière, *The Devis Family of Painters* (Leigh-on-the-Sea, England: F. Lewis, 1950), plate 29.

9. Sullivan, *Dutch Gamepiece,* pp. 19–20.

10. See further Neil Maclaren, *National Gallery Catalogues: The Spanish School,* 2d ed., rev. by Allan Braham (London: The National Gallery, 1970), pp. 101–108, from which my information concerning this picture is taken.

11. Ibid., pp. 102–103: "Areas in which boars had been located were enclosed by a continuous wall of canvas supported on stakes (the *tela*), sometimes as much as a league in circumference. The stakes were transported on wagons like the one visible behind the tree in the lower right-hand corner of the present composition. The nearest level piece of ground was then cleared of bushes and undergrowth and enclosed with canvas; this second enclosure, known as the *contratela,* was about 100 yards in diameter, and is the arena represented [in the painting]. A passage was then made from the *tela* to the *contratela,* in which the King and his companions awaited the boar. . . . The Queen and her ladies watched from coaches within the enclosure, and were guarded by huntsmen on foot with lances."

12. Olivar Millar, *The Queen's Pictures* (New York: Macmillan, 1977), p. 172.

13. Derek Jarrett, *England in the Age of Hogarth* (New Haven: Yale University Press, 1986), p. 132: "The social unit was not the individual but the family or the household, a fact which gave great importance to the actual houses in which these units were contained. The possession of a hearth, traditionally the centre and focus not only of the house but also of the people who lived in it, was the thing that defined a man's position and gave him a place in society."

14. See further Schneider, *Art of the Still Life,* pp. 26–29, tracing the relation between changing economic conditions and the production of market scene paintings.

15. On Aertsen's painting see the fine essay by Kenneth M. Craig, "Pieter Aertsen and *The Meat Stall,*" *Oud Holland* 96 (1982), pp. 1–15. My own reading of this painting moves in a somewhat different direction from Craig's. For more on Aertsen, see Bergström, *Dutch Still-Life Painting,* pp. 16–24; and R. L. Falkenburg, "Iconographical Connections Between Antwerp Landscapes, Market Scenes and Kitchen Pieces, 1500–1580," *Oud Holland* 102 (1988), pp. 114–126. Following Aertsen's death, and that of Joachim Beuckelaer who, contemporaneously, painted similar subjects, no other such pictures were produced in the Netherlands for two decades. See Sullivan, *Dutch Gamepiece,* p. 9.

16. Craig, "Pieter Aertsen and *The Meat Stall,*" p. 3.

17. Regarding iconographical issues, see further Jan A. Emmens, "'Eins aber ist nötig': Zu Inhalt und Bedeutung von Markt- und Küchenstücken des 16. Jahrhunderts," in *Album Amicorum J. G. van Gelder,* ed. Josua Bruyn (The Hague:

Nijhoff, 1973), pp. 93–101. See also Norman Bryson, *Looking at the Overlooked: Four Essays on Still Life Painting* (Cambridge, Mass.: Harvard University Press, 1990), pp. 146–150.

18. Compare a discussion of Goya's *Sheep's Head* (Louvre) by Charles Sterling, *Still Life Painting: From Antiquity to the Present Time,* trans. James Emmons (New York: Universe Books, 1959), p. 97.

19. Schneider, *Art of the Still Life,* pp. 40–41: "Also, there is the associative connection between fresh meat and eroticism (*voluptas carnis* or, as Luther puts it, the 'wilful wickedness of the flesh'). Ancient notions of magic probably played a part, too, whereby a person's libido could be influenced by the consumption of meat." Schneider's discussion concerns a painting similar to Aertsen's by Pieter Cornelisz van Ryck, *Kitchen Scene* (1604) (Brunswick, Herzog-Anton-Ulrich Museum), reproduced in color, pp. 42–43.

20. Craig, "Pieter Aertsen and *The Meat Stall,*" pp. 10–12, suggests that the painting was likely commissioned by the Antwerp Butcher's Guild and was to be hung in the Butchers' Hall. The reading I have suggested seems entirely congruent with this possibility, not least because the image thus awards guild members prominent *literal* place in defining the future. The guild had both status and wealth—in 1551, the year of the painting, guild members were celebrating the fiftieth anniversary of their guild-hall's construction, at that moment the largest secular building in the city, as Craig points out.

21. See Kenneth M. Craig, "Rembrandt and *The Slaughtered Ox,*" *Journal of the Warburg and Courtauld Institutes* 46 (1983), pp. 235–239; and Avigdor W.G. Posèq, "The Hanging Carcass Motif and Jewish Artists," *Jewish Art,* vols. 16 and 17 (1990/1991), pp. 139–156. On the first Netherlandish representations of this subject see also Craig, "Pieter Aertsen and *The Meat Stall,*" p. 14 n. 29.

22. Posèq, "Hanging Carcass Motif," p. 144; and Craig, "Rembrandt and *The Slaughtered Ox,*" pp. 235–236, re linkages between the ox and Christ.

23. The painting's embedded subjectivity surely bears some relation to Rembrandt's own recent and repeated experiences with death—of several of his infant children, his wife, and his mother—just as his 1655 Louvre painting came at a time of "financial collapse and professional near-ruin." See Craig, "Rembrandt and *The Slaughtered Ox,*" p. 239. See also Mieke Bal, "Dead Flesh, or the Smell of Painting," in *Visual Culture: Images and Interpretations,* ed. Norman Bryson, Michael Ann Holly, and Keith Moxey (Hanover, N.H.: Wesleyan University Press, 1994), pp. 371–378.

24. See further Esti Dunow, "Soutine's Still Lifes," in the exhibition catalog edited by Ernst-Gerhard Güse, *C. Soutine (1893–1943)* (London: Arts Council of Great Britain, 1981), pp. 73–97; and Avigdor W.G. Posèq, "Soutine's Paraphrase of Rembrandt's *Slaughtered Ox,*" *Konsthistorisk tidskrift* 60 (1991), pp. 210–222, the latter for a psychoanalytical-biographical read of this group of paintings.

25. Dunow, "Soutine's Still Lifes," p. 74.

26. Ibid.

27. See on this painting José López-Rey, *Velázquez: A Catalogue Raisonné of His Oeuvre, with an Introductory Study* (London: Faber and Faber, 1963), p. 272; Jonathan Brown, *Velázquez: Painter and Courtier* (New Haven: Yale University Press, 1986), pp. 197–200; Enriqueta Harris, *Velázquez* (Ithaca: Cornell University Press, 1982), pp. 147–151; Joseph-Émile Muller, *Velázquez,* trans. Jane Brenton (London: Thames and Hudson, 1976), pp. 191–198.

28. Posèq, "Hanging Carcass Motif," p. 152.

29. Donald Kuspit, "Francis Bacon: The Authority of Flesh," *Artforum* 13 (Summer 1975), p. 51.

30. For more on Bacon's many paintings on this general topos, see Dawn Ades and Andrew Forge, *Francis Bacon* (New York: Harry N. Abrams, 1985), especially pp. 12–15; and [Francis Bacon and David Sylvester] *Francis Bacon: Interviewed by David Sylvester* (New York: Pantheon Books, 1975), pp. 24–29, 37–38, 48–50, 71–73.

31. Kuspit, "Francis Bacon: The Authority of Flesh," pp. 53–55; the quotation is from p. 55.

32. Gilles Deleuze, "Interpretations of the Body: A New Power of Laughter for the Living," *Art International* 8 (Autumn 1989), p. 38.

33. Kuspit, "Francis Bacon: The Authority of Flesh," p. 56.

34. For a related discussion, see the excellent study by Ernst van Alphen, *Francis Bacon and the Loss of Self* (Cambridge, Mass.: Harvard University Press, 1993), especially pp. 111–113, focused on the relationship between representability and subjectivity. Valuable insights are also offered by John Russell, *Francis Bacon,* rev. ed. (London: Thames and Hudson, 1993), pp. 41–42.

Chapter 5

1. Norbert Schneider, *The Art of the Still Life: Still Life Painting in the Early Modern Period,* trans. Hugh Beyer (Cologne: Benedikt Taschen Verlag, 1990) p. 65; see further to p. 75.

2. Pierre Skira, *Still Life: A History,* trans. Jean-Marie Clarke (New York: Skira/Rizzoli, 1989), p. 100; see further his discussion of the sacred associations, pp. 100–101.

3. For a detailed discussion of this image see Richard Leppert, "Music, Representation, and Social Order in Early-Modern Europe," *Cultural Critique* 12 (Spring 1989), pp. 41–55. See also Albert Pomme de Mirimonde, "Les 'Cabinets de musique,'" *Jaarboek, Koninklijk Museum voor Schone Kunsten* [Antwerp] (1966), pp. 141–178; Richard Leppert, *The Theme of Music in Flemish Paintings of the Seventeenth Century,* 2 vols. (Munich and Salzburg: Musikverlag Emil Katzbichler, 1977), vol. 1, pp. 109–114; vol. 2, pp. 24–29, and 242–243 for plates 24–25. See cat. no. 100, reproduced as plate 24, for a virtually exact replica of the Prado original; Simone Speth-Holteroff, *Les peintres flamands de cabinets d'amateurs au XVIIe siècle* (Paris: Elsevier, 1957); Klaus Ertz, *Jan Brueghel der Ältere (1568–1625): Die Gemälde, mit kritischem Oeuvrekatalog* (Cologne: DuMont Buchverlag, 1979), pp. 328–362,

concerning Brueghel's entire series of allegories of the senses paintings; see pp. 329, 350–352, in regard to the paintings on hearing; Fritz Baumgart, *Blumen Brueghel (Jan Brueghel d. Ä.): Leben und Werk* (Cologne, DuMont Buchverlag, 1978), pp. 121–131; and Hans Kauffmann, "Die Fünfsinne in der niederländischen Malerei des 17. Jahrhunderts," in *Kunstgeschichtliche Studien: Festschrift für Dagobert Frey,* ed. Hans Tintelnot (Breslau: Gauverlag, 1943), pp. 133–157. On the general subject, see Chu-tsing Li, "The Five Senses in Art: An Analysis of Its Development in Northern Europe" (Ph.D. diss., State University of Iowa, 1955).

4. Schneider, *Art of the Still Life,* p. 65.

5. Roland Barthes, "The Plates of the *Encyclopaedia,*" in *New Critical Essays,* trans. Richard Howard (New York: Hill and Wang, 1980), p. 27.

6. See Roland Barthes, "Dare to Be Lazy," in *The Grain of the Voice: Interviews, 1962–1980,* trans. Linda Coverdale (New York: Hill and Wang, 1985), pp. 38–45.

7. See further Ertz, *Jan Brueghel,* pp. 355–356.

8. See Alain Corbin, *The Foul and the Fragrant: Odor and the French Social Imagination* (New York: Berg Publishers, 1986), "The New Calculus of Olfactory Pleasure," pp. 71–85, concerning this matter in the eighteenth and the early nineteenth centuries.

9. Gertraude Winckelmann-Rhein, *The Paintings and Drawings of Jan "Flower" Bruegel,* trans. Leonard Mins (New York: Harry N. Abrams, 1968), p. 28.

10. See further Richard Leppert, "David Teniers the Younger and the Image of Music," *Jaarboek, Koninklijk Museum voor Schone Kunsten* [Antwerp] (1978), pp. 63–155. For a different reading of the owls, see pp. 77–78.

Chapter 6

1. Michel Foucault's *Discipline and Punish: The Birth of the Prison,* trans. Alan Sheridan (New York: Vintage Books, 1979) remains the most influential recent theoretical-historical account of the subject. For a useful and heavily illustrated introduction to this subject see Lionello Puppi, *Torment in Art: Pain, Violence and Martyrdom,* trans. Jeremy Scott (New York: Rizzoli, 1991), treating the subject from the twelfth to nineteenth centuries; and Edward Peters, *Torture* (Oxford: Basil Blackwell, 1985).

2. Puppi, *Torment in Art,* p. 15. See further Pieter Spierenburg, *The Spectacle of Suffering: Executions and the Evolution of Repression; from a Preindustrial Metropolis to the European Experience* (Cambridge: Cambridge University Press, 1984), especially pp. 43–80, dealing with the staging and dramatization of executions.

3. Puppi, *Torment in Art,* pp. 124–125. On the painting's date and condition, see Donald Posner, *Annibale Carracci: A Study in the Reform of Italian Painting Around 1590,* 2 vols. (London: Phaidon, 1971), vol. 2, p. 3.

4. Julia Kristeva, "Holbein's Dead Christ," trans. Leon S. Roudiez, in *Fragments for a History of the Human Body,* ed. Michel Feher, with Ramona Naddaff and Nadia Tazi, 3 vols. (New York: Zone, 1989), vol. 1, pp. 238–269. For a useful gloss of and reponse to Kristeva, see John Lechte, "Kristeva and Holbein, Artist of Melancholy,"

British Journal of Aesthetics 30 (1990), pp. 342–350. See also John Rowlands, *Holbein: The Paintings of Hans Holbein the Younger. Complete Edition* (Oxford: Phaidon, 1985), pp. 52–53, 127–128; and Heinrich Klötz, *Hans Holbein d. J.: Christus im Grabe* (Stuttgart: Philipp Reclam Jun., 1968).

5. Puppi, *Torment in Art*, p. 89, explains that as a patron saint of sailors Erasmus was portrayed holding a windlass handle with a cable around it. This attribute in turn gave rise to accounts that his death came via evisceration. For another version of the St. Erasmus martyrdom, painted by Nicolas Poussin, see p. 152. Poussin himself may have witnessed a disemboweling in Rome early in the seventeenth century. See also the exhibition catalog *Dieric Bouts* (Brussels: Éditions de la Connaissance, 1957), pp. 33–37.

6. Puppi, *Torment in Art*, p. 29. For a good introduction to the general subject of anatomy and its representation in art see Albert S. Lyons and R. Joseph Petrucelli, Jr., *Medicine: An Illustrated History* (New York: Harry N. Abrams, 1978). On the general subject see Charles Singer, *A Short History of Anatomy from the Greeks to Harvey*, 2d ed. (New York, Dover, 1957); and the excellent study by Barbara Maria Stafford, *Body Criticism: Imagining the Unseen in Enlightenment Art and Medicine* (Cambridge, Mass.: MIT Press, 1991).

7. William S. Heckscher, *Rembrandt's Anatomy of Dr. Nicholaas Tulp: An Iconographical Study* (New York: New York University Press, 1958), p. 105: "But in a deeper sense public anatomies were magic precautions taken in order to protect society against the criminal's power to do evil, which the execution alone had by no means managed to annihilate. In primitive societies the evildoer must be vivisected or dissected so that the king, or the medicine man who does the dissecting, may discover the diseased organ, seat of the demoniacal power—the *evu* or *likundu*—which can then be properly destroyed."

8. See further Ronald Paulson, *Hogarth's Graphic Works*, 3d ed., rev. (London: The Print Room, 1989), pp. 151–152; and by the same author, *The Art of Hogarth* (London: Phaidon, 1975), pp. 61–62.

9. Heckscher, *Rembrandt's Anatomy*, p. 32.

10. I am quoting from Thomas R. Forbes, "'To Be Dissected and Anatomized,'" *Journal of the History of Medicine and Allied Sciences* 36 (1981), pp. 490–491. See also K. B. Roberts and J.D.W. Tomlinson, *The Fabric of the Body: European Traditions of Anatomical Illustration* (Oxford: Clarendon Press, 1992), pp. 475–484, including information of the practice of robbing graves for anatomical dissection.

11. See further John Bertrand deC. M. Saunders and Charles D. O'Malley, *The Anatomical Drawings of Andreas Vesalius: With Annotations and Translations, a Discussion of the Plates and Their Background, Authorship and Influence, and a Biographical Sketch of Vesalius* (1950; reprint, New York: Bonanza Books, 1982); Marion H. Spielmann, *The Iconography of Andreas Vesalius* (London: J. Bale, Sons, and Danielsson, 1925); and the excellent discussion in Roberts and Tomlinson, *Fabric of the Body*, pp. 126–165. I have reproduced images from the second edition, recut from the first edition's woodblocks and often considered superior.

For a general description of the anatomical book illustrations by Vesalius, and the others to be considered in due course in this chapter (by Ruysch, Albinus, Bidloo, and Gautier D'Agoty), see Roberts and Tomlinson, *Fabric of the Body;* and Ludwig Choulant, *History and Bibliography of Anatomic Illustration,* trans. and annotated by Mortimer Frank (New York: Hafner Publishing, 1962). The book was first published in 1852.

12. The grave digger's spade is also literally functional; it serves as a device for stabilizing a standing skeleton, as Vesalius himself advises. See Saunders and O'Malley, *Anatomical Drawings of Andreas Vesalius,* p. 84.

13. Ibid., p. 104.

14. Vesalius's illustrations of the viscera encased within the human torso are based on torsos of fragmented antique sculptures—upon idealized bodies, not real ones. See Glen Harcourt, "Andreas Vesalius and the Anatomy of Antique Sculpture," *Representations* 17 (Winter 1987), pp. 28–61. Harcourt further suggests that the contextualizing illustrations of skeletons in Vesalius provided the opportunity to show how the skeleton functions while gesturing, walking, bending, and so on. See also Jonathan Sawday, "The Fate of Marsyas: Dissecting the Renaissance Body," in *Renaissance Bodies: The Human Figure in English Culture, c. 1540–1660,* ed. Lucy Gent and Nigel Llewellyn (London: Reaktion Books, 1990), p. 126.

15. See James Elkins, "Michelangelo and the Human Form: His Knowledge and Use of Anatomy," *Art History* 7 (1984), pp. 176–186. Regarding the connection of artist's brush to anatomist's scalpel, see the psychoanalytic readings of the nineteenth-century paintings by Thomas Eakins of surgery (not anatomy) by Michael Fried, "Realism, Writing, and Disfiguration in Thomas Eakins' *Gross Clinic,*" *Representations* 9 (Winter 1985), pp. 33–104; and a critical response by Marcia Pointon, "Psychoanalysis and Art History: Freud, Fried and Eakins," in *Naked Authority: The Body in Western Painting, 1830–1908* (Cambridge: Cambridge University Press, 1990), pp. 35–58.

16. France Borel, *The Seduction of Venus: Artists and Models,* trans. Jean-Marie Clarke (New York: Skira/Rizzoli, 1990), p. 163.

17. Ibid., pp. 162–163.

18. Heckscher, *Rembrandt's Anatomy,* p. 88.

19. Roberts and Tomlinson, *Fabric of the Body,* p. 291.

20. Robert James, *Medicinal Dictionary . . .* (London, 1743); quoted from Roberts and Tomlinson, *Fabric of the Body,* p. 293.

21. Antoine M. Luyendijk-Elshout, "Death Enlightened: A Study of Frederik Ruysch," *Journal of the American Medical Association* 212 (1970), p. 122. This source provides a useful biography of Ruysch, a quite detailed description of his collections, and an account of its preservation in St. Petersburg and elsewhere in Russia up to 1970. Part of my general account of Ruysch's display pieces is endebted to this essay. See also Rosamond Wolff Purcell and Stephen Jay Gould, "Dutch Treat: Peter the Great and Frederik Ruysch," in *Finders, Keepers: Treasures and Oddities of Natural History; Collectors from Peter the Great to Louis Agassiz* (New York: W. W. Norton, 1992), pp. 13–32, which includes superb color plates by Purcell, among which are six of preserved whole infants or body parts. In 1995 *Eighteenth Century Studies* will

publish an excellent essay on Ruysch's collection by Meg Spilleth with color photographs by Rosamond Wolff Purcell.

22. Luyendijk-Elshout, "Death Enlightened," p. 122. Following the sale of his collection to Peter the Great, Ruysch proceeded to start another; that one was sold to the king of Poland after Ruysch's death. (Parts of Peter's collection still exist in St. Petersburg.) See Roberts and Tomlinson, *Fabric of the Body,* p. 294. The number of specimens I cited (2,000) comes from Purcell and Gould, "Dutch Treat: Peter the Great and Frederik Ruysch," p. 20; Roberts and Tomlinson, p. 294, put the total at 1,300. For a brief account on the state of the collection in 1960, see Gunter Mann, "Museums: The Anatomical Collections of Frederik Ruysch at Leningrad," *Bulletin of the Cleveland Medical Library* 11 (1964), pp. 10–13.

23. Fredrik Ruysch, *Thesaurus anatomicus primus. Het eerste anatomisch cabinet* (Amsterdam, 1739), pp. 10–11.

24. Quoted from Roberts and Tomlinson, *Fabric of the Body,* p. 293. The several first pages of each section of the catalog are devoted to detailed descriptions of the display pieces, whereas descriptions of the scientific specimens tend to be very brief.

25. Luyendijk-Elshout, "Death Enlightened," p. 125.

26. The various passages quoted are from Fredrik Ruysch, *Thesaurus anatomicus tertius. Het derde anatomisch cabinet,* in *Alle de ontleed- Genees- en Heelkundige Werken,* 3 vols. (Amsterdam, 1744), vol. 2, pp. 565–569.

27. Roberts and Tomlinson, *Fabric of the Body,* p. 294.

28. See the excellent discussion by Stafford, *Body Criticism,* pp. 29–33, 254–279; however, on the Enlightenment's distrust of the visual, see pp. 392–396. See also Stafford's account of the "cabinet of cutaneous horrors" in the museum of the Hôpital Saint-Louis in Paris, pp. 282–305: "This medical panorama, unfurling the universal garb of rot, instantaneously clarifies the premium placed during the Enlightenment on an aesthetics of immaculateness" (p. 283). Stafford traces the cultural impact of diseases of the skin and a fascination with perfect body surfaces, in fact attainable only via the idealizing brush of artists.

29. Stafford, *Body Criticism,* has much to say on this subject; for a flavor of it, see pp. 12–18, 148–150.

30. For a detailed description of Albinus's methods, see Roberts and Tomlinson, *Fabric of the Body,* pp. 323–324.

31. For a fascinating account of the connection between anatomical study and gender politics, see Londa Schiebinger, "Skeletons in the Closet: The First Illustrations of the Female Skeleton in Eighteenth-Century Anatomy," *Representations* 14 (Spring 1986), pp. 42–82.

32. For an example of an artist's borrowing from an anatomist, in this instance Albinus, see the picture by Joseph Wright of Derby, *Old Man and Death,* painted in two versions, reproduced, along with the Albinus anatomical print, in Benedict Nicolson, *Joseph Wright of Derby: Painter of Light,* 2 vols. (London: Routledge and Kegan Paul, 1968), vol. 1, pp. 55–56, and vol. 2, plate 123; also in the exhibition catalog by Judy Egerton, *Wright of Derby* (New York: Metropolitan Museum of Art, 1990), pp. 83–84.

For more on the confrontation between anatomy and art over the body as a terrain of meaning, see the studies of Rembrandt's *The Anatomy Lesson of Dr. Tulp* (The Hague, Mauritshuis Museum) by Francis Barker, *The Tremulous Private Body: Essays on Subjection* (London: Methuen, 1984), pp. 71–84; Heckscher, *Rembrandt's Anatomy* (Heckscher provides a great deal of valuable information concerning the theatricality and staging of anatomy lessons in the seventeenth century); and William Schupbach, *The Paradox of Rembrandt's "Anatomy of Dr. Tulp"*, Medical History, supplement no. 2 (London: Wellcome Institute for the History of Medicine, 1982).

33. Choulant, *History and Bibliography of Anatomic Illustration,* p. 252. See also Mario Perniola, "Between Clothing and Nudity," trans. Roger Freidman, in *Fragments for a History of the Human Body,* ed. Michel Feher, with Ramona Naddaff and Nadia Tazi, 3 vols. (New York: Zone, 1989), vol. 2, pp. 258–259.

34. See also the illustrations thereof in his *Exposition anatomique des maux vénériens, sur les parties de l'homme & de la femme . . .* (Paris 1773). Choulant, *History and Bibliography of Anatomic Illustration,* p. 270: "His anatomic illustrations . . . impress the critical observer with their arrogance and charlatanry and do not recommend themselves to the student of anatomy either for their faithfulness and reliability or for their technique."

35. The figure is feminized, though it is difficult to ascertain gender with certainty.

36. Borel, *Seduction of Venus,* p. 176.

37. My information on these paintings is from two sources: (1) the excellent essay by Nina Athanassoglou-Kallmyer, "Géricault's Severed Heads and Limbs: The Politics and Aesthetics of the Scaffold," *Art Bulletin* 74 (1992), pp. 599–618. Arguing against traditional wisdom that these images were mere studies for *The Raft of the Medusa* (1819), she suggests that they were finished images that should properly be understood in relation to Géricault's leftist politics, notably including his opposition to capital punishment. She further relates the images' history to early Romantic fascination with the grotesque and morbid and to Romanticism's attack on classical notions of beauty and idealization; (2) Lorenz E.A. Eitner, *Géricault: His Life and Work* (London: Orbis Publishing, 1983), pp. 180–185, and p. 345 n. 133, which provides a list of the eight paintings and drawings of this sort by the artist.

38. Eitner, *Géricault,* p. 183.

39. Athanassoglou-Kallmyer, "Géricault's Severed Heads and Limbs," develops this line of argument throughout her essay.

40. Compare Athanassoglou-Kallmyer, "Géricault's Severed Heads and Limbs," p. 610.

41. Ibid., p. 614, in turn quoting Charles Clément, *Géricault: Étude biographique et critique* (1879), new ed., ed. Lorenz E.A. Eitner (Paris: L. Laget, 1973), p. 304 n. 107.

Chapter 7

1. John Evans, *Juvenile Pieces: Designed for the Youth of Both Sexes,* 3d ed. (London, [1797]), from chapter "On the Utility of Paintings," p. 71.

2. Regarding the very large sums of money made by the most successful English portrait painters in the last half of the eighteenth century, see Gerald Reitlinger, *The Economics of Taste: The Rise and Fall of Picture Prices, 1760–1960,* 3 vols. (London: Barrie and Rockliff, 1961–1970), vol. 1, pp. 57–65, and, especially, Marcia Pointon, "Portrait-Painting as a Business Enterprise in London in the 1780s," *Art History* 7 (1984), pp. 187–205. Reynolds, the richest of the lot, died the equivalent of a millionaire in modern terms. Important recent work has explored the relation of portraiture to the public sphere. See especially John Barrell, ed., *Painting and the Politics of Culture: New Essays on British Art, 1700–1850* (Oxford: Oxford University Press, 1992); and, focusing on art, the economy, and cultural production, a fascinating study by David H. Solkin, *Painting for Money: The Visual Arts and the Public Sphere in Eighteenth-Century England* (New Haven: Yale University Press, 1993).

3. Norman Bryson, "In Medusa's Gaze," in *In Medusa's Gaze: Still Life Paintings from Upstate New York Museums,* ed. Bernard Barryte (Rochester, N.Y.: Memorial Art Gallery of the University of Rochester, 1991), p. 7.

4. James Thomson Shotwell, "Richelieu, Cardinal," *The Encyclopaedia Britannica,* 11th ed. (1911), vol. 23, p. 303.

5. Ibid., p. 304.

6. Ibid., p. 305.

7. See Cecil Weatherly, "Knighthood," *The Encyclopaedia Britannica,* 11th ed. (1911), vol. 15, p. 863.

8. My principal sources on the paintings are Bernard Dorival, *Philippe de Champaigne (1602–1674): La vie, l'oeuvre, et le catalogue raisonné de l'oeuvre,* 2 vols. (Paris: Léonce Laget Libraire, 1976); concerning the two Richelieu portraits, among more than a dozen of this sitter that Champaigne painted, see vol. 2, cat. no. 207, pp. 115–116, and cat. no. 213, pp. 120–121; and Martin Davies, *National Gallery Catalogues: French School,* 2d ed., rev. (London: National Gallery of Art, 1957), pp. 25–27. On the triple portrait, see also Claude Keisch, "Portraits in mehrfacher Ansicht: Überlieferung und Sinnwandel einer Bildidee," *Staatliche Museen zu Berlin, Forschungen und Berichte,* Kunsthistorische und Volkskundliche Beiträge, no. 17 (Berlin: Akamedie-Verlag, 1976), especially pp. 215–216. Regarding the issue of retouching, see Dorival, *Philippe de Champaigne,* vol. 2, p. 119.

9. Dorival, *Philippe de Champaigne,* vol. 1, p. 42.

10. Be that as it may, it is simply not the case that facial expression in painting is semantically constant, nor is it ever to be presumed naturalistic. On the dangers of reading Renaissance facial expressions, see John Oliver Hand and Martha Wolff, *The Collections of the National Gallery of Art Systematic Catalogue: Early Netherlandish Painting* (Washington, D.C.: National Gallery of Art; and New York: Cambridge University Press, 1986), p. 106 n. 13. See further on merchant paintings Thomas S. Holman, "Holbein's Portraits of the Steelyard Merchants: An Investigation," *Metropolitan Museum Journal* 14 (1979), pp. 139–158.

11. Sadja J. Herzog, "Jan Gossaert, Called Mabuse (ca. 1478–1532), a Study of His Chronology with a Catalogue of His Works," 3 vols. (Ph.D. diss., Bryn Mawr College, 1968), vol. 1, pp. 142–143.

12. Jakob Rosenberg, "A Portrait of a Banker (Jerome Sandelin?) by Jan Gossaert, Called Mabuse," *National Gallery of Art: Report and Studies in the History of Art 1967* (Washington, D.C.: National Gallery of Art, 1967), p. 41.

13. Quoted from John F. Moffitt, "Observations on the Origins and Meanings of Goya with the Devils in the 1820 *Self-Portrait with Dr. Arrieta*," *Minneapolis Institute of Arts Bulletin* 65 (1981–1982), p. 37.

14. Fred S. Licht, *Goya: The Origins of the Modern Temper in Art* (New York: Universe Books, 1979), p. 162.

15. Regarding the background figures and various interpretations of their significance see in particular Moffitt, "Observations on the Origins and Meanings of Goya," which addresses this matter at length; for an opposing view see Robert W. Baldwin, "Healing and Hope in Goya's *Self-Portrait with Dr. Arrieta*," *Source: Notes in Art History* 4, 4 (Summer 1985), pp. 31–36. The literature on this picture is considerable; Moffitt provides an accounting, p. 47 n. 1.

16. Richard Brilliant, *Portraiture* (Cambridge, Mass.: Harvard University Press, 1991), pp. 110, 112–113.

17. Brilliant, *Portraiture,* p. 151. Compare a parallel remark by Oscar Wilde cited on p. 82.

18. The most thorough account of the life, work, and later impact of this painter is the volume edited by Pontus Hulten, developed around an exhibition at the Palazzo Grassi, Venice: *The Arcimboldo Effect: Transformations of the Face from the 16th to the 20th Century* (New York: Abbeville Press, 1987). The few facts known about Arcimboldo's life are repeated in this volume.

19. Roland Barthes, "Arcimboldo, or Magician and Rhétoriqueur," in *The Responsibility of Forms: Critical Essays on Music, Art, and Representation,* trans. Richard Howard (Berkeley and Los Angeles: University of California Press, 1991), p. 138. Barthes's essay is famous for its reading of Arcimboldo's work as rhetoric, calling forth the precise techniques of literary practice.

20. James Hall, *Dictionary of Subjects and Symbols in Art* (New York: Harper and Row, 1974), p. 321; and Catherine B. Avery, ed., *The New Century Classical Handbook* (New York: Appleton-Century-Crofts, 1962), pp. 1138–1139. For further information concerning this painting see Thomas DaCosta Kaufmann, *The School of Prague: Painting at the Court of Rudolf II* (Chicago: The University of Chicago Press, 1988), pp. 171–172; and by the same author "Arcimboldo's Imperial Allegories: G. B. Fonteo and the Interpretation of Arcimboldo's Painting," *Zeitschrift für Kunstgeschichte* 39 (1976), pp. 275–296, and concerning this painting, pp. 295–296 in particular; and "The Allegories and Their Meaning," in Hulten, ed., *Arcimboldo Effect,* pp. 89–108. My commentary is considerably indebted to Kaufmann's research and insights.

21. Kaufmann, *School of Prague,* p. 171.

22. The original source for this reading is a 310-line Latin poem by Giovanni Baptista Fonteo dedicated to Maximilian II, a gloss on Arcimboldo's seasons and elements paintings; see Kaufmann, "Arcimboldo's Imperial Allegories," p. 276. Hulten, ed., *Arcimboldo Effect,* pp. 147–164, provides the full translated text of the poem.

Gregorio Comanini, in a 1591 treatise on painting, discusses the Rudolf II image and identifies Vertumnus as the painting's subject; on this point see Kaufmann, "The Allegories and Their Meaning," pp. 99, 103–104; the text in question is quoted in Hulten, ed., *Arcimboldo Effect*, pp. 182–194.

23. Three other versions of this painting, of uncertain attribution, exist. They are reproduced in Sven Alfons, "The Museum as Image of the World," in Hulten, ed., *Arcimboldo Effect*, p. 86, and are discussed on pp. 79–81. See further Kaufmann, *School of Prague*, p. 169; and Giancarlo Maiorino, *The Portrait of Eccentricity: Arcimboldo and the Mannerist Grotesque* (University Park: Pennsylvania State University Press, 1991), pp. 46–49.

24. Barthes, "Arcimboldo, or Magician and Rhétoriqueur," p. 142.

Chapter 8

1. The painting was first studied in detail by P.J.J. van Thiel, "Marriage Symbolism in a Musical Party by Jan Miense Molenaer," *Simiolus* 2 (1967), pp. 90–99; and I have discussed it at length in Richard Leppert, *The Sight of Sound: Music, Representation, and the History of the Body* (Berkeley and Los Angeles: University of California Press, 1993), pp. 1–12. Much of what appears here is taken from these two sources, especially the latter. See further David R. Smith, *Masks of Wedlock: Seventeenth-Century Dutch Marriage Portraiture* (Ann Arbor, Mich.: UMI Research Press, 1982). Most of Smith's study, however, concerns the pair portrait (separate pendant pictures for husband and wife), by far the more common type of marriage picture produced by Dutch artists. See also the exhibition catalog by Eddy de Jongh, *Portretten van echt en trouw: Huwelijk en gezin in de Nederlandse kunst van de zeventiende eeuw* (Zwolle: Uitgeverij Waanders; and Haarlem: Frans Halsmuseum, 1986); on Molenaer's picture see Thomas Kren, "Chi non vuol Baccho: Roeland van Laer's Burlesque Painting About Dutch Artists in Rome," *Simiolus* 11 (1980), pp. 75–78; and David R. Smith, "Courtesy and Its Discontents: Frans Hals's *Portrait of Isaac Massa and Beatrix van der Laen*," *Oud Holland* 100 (1986), pp. 21–22.

2. Van Thiel, "Marriage Symbolism," p. 99. The visual antithesis to the temperance emblem is the servant at the left peering into the jug. He is a *kannekijker*, that is, a tippler; in emblematic literature such a figure commonly signifies gluttony (p. 93). On the uniqueness of the monkey-cat representation see pp. 95–96. The "domestic" enclosure at the right, not likely the representation of a real dwelling, is a symbolic fortress of the marriage vows; it is metaphorically mirrored on the painting's left by the ivy-covered wall topped by two pots of carnations. Van Thiel describes the emblematic associations; the wall alludes to the husband, the ivy to the wife, and the flowers to fidelity; see pp. 98–99. For more on the broad range of symbols conventionally employed in Dutch marriage portraiture, see Smith, *Masks of Wedlock*, pp. 57–89.

3. Emblems, commonly published in large collections, consist of an image accompanied by a verbal gloss. Emblem illustrations, sans text, found their way into the cultural vocabulary of other discursive practices like painting (and, indeed, music).

See further John Landwehr, *Emblem and Fable Books Printed in the Low Countries, 1542–1813: A Bibliography* (Utrecht: HES Publishers, 1988); Eddy de Jongh, *Zinne-en minnebeelden in de schilderkunst van de zeventiende eeuw* (Antwerp: Openbare Kunstbezit in Vlaanderen, 1967); and Mario Praz, *Studies in Seventeenth-Century Imagery* 2d ed. (Rome: Storia, 1964).

4. See Simon Schama, *The Embarrassment of Riches: An Interpretation of Dutch Culture in the Golden Age* (Berkeley and Los Angeles: University of California Press, 1987), especially the detailed discussion on pp. 388–480 in the chapter titled "Housewives and Hussies: Homeliness and Worldliness." As mentioned earlier (see Chapter 3, n. 6, this volume), Dutch prostitutes even carried lutes with them into taverns as a sonoric-visual device advertising their profession. Numerous Dutch paintings visually connect the lute to prostitution in particular via the visual subject of the procuress. These representations conflict with emblematic associations of the lute with the virtue of temperance (on which see Van Thiel, "Marriage Symbolism," p. 91).

5. See Petrus Johannes Blok, *History of the People of the Netherlands,* vol. 3, *The War with Spain,* trans. Ruth Putnam (New York: Putnam, 1900); Pieter Geyl, *The Revolt of the Netherlands (1555–1609),* 2d ed. (London: Ernest Benn, 1958); Pieter Geyl, *The Netherlands Divided (1609–1648),* trans. S. T. Bindoff, in collaboration with Pieter Geyl (London: Williams and Norgate, 1936); and Geoffrey Parker, *The Dutch Revolt* (Ithaca: Cornell University Press, 1977).

6. See Schama, *Embarrassment of Riches.* The book contains an up-to-date bibliographic guide to the study of Dutch culture, pp. 655–670.

7. See Richard Leppert, *Music and Image: Domesticity, Ideology, and Socio-Cultural Formation in Eighteenth-Century England* (Cambridge: Cambridge University Press, 1988), for the situation in England, and Richard Leppert, "*Concert in a House:* Musical Iconography and Musical Thought," *Early Music* 7 (1979), pp. 3–17, for the Low Countries. Although the concern was continentwide, the severity of the complaint varied over time and place, across religious and other divides.

8. On the musical opposition between noise and order see Jacques Attali, *Noise: The Political Economy of Music,* trans. Brian Massumi (Minneapolis: University of Minnesota Press, 1985).

9. Despite notable stylistic differences, there is little ideological divergence between Teniers's representations of the lower classes and those of many other Dutch and Flemish painters, such as Cornelis Bega, Pieter de Bloot, Andries Both, Joos van Craesbeek, Egbert van Heemskerck, Frans van Mieris the Elder, Bartholomeus Molenaer, Adriaen van Ostade, Isaac van Ostade, David Ryckaert the Younger, Pieter Verelst, and even Jan Miense Molenaer. Examples of relevant work by these painters are reproduced in Walter Bernt, *The Netherlandish Painters of the Seventeenth Century,* trans. P. S. Falla, 3 vols., 3d ed. (London: Phaidon, 1970).

10. In musical practice the instrument's nasal, reedy sound locates it as Dionysian. See Richard Leppert, "David Teniers the Younger and the Image of Music," *Jaarboek, Koninklijk Museum voor Schone Kunsten* [Antwerp] (1978), p. 141 n. 140.

11. See Chapter 3, n. 6.

12. Roland Barthes, "The World as Object," trans. Richard Howard, in *A Barthes Reader,* ed. Susan Sontag (New York: Hill and Wang, 1982), pp. 67–68.

13. Albert S. Lyons and R. Joseph Petrucelli, Jr., *Medicine: An Illustrated History* (New York: Harry N. Abrams, 1978), p. 445.

14. Gerard Knuttel, *Adriaen Brouwer: The Master and His Work,* trans J. G. Talma-Schilthuis and Robert Wheaton (The Hague: L.J.C. Boucher, 1962), p. 150. Brouwer's career lasted for only about fifteen years. See pp. 9 and 30.

15. See n. 8, above.

16. See Richard Leppert, *The Theme of Music in Flemish Paintings of the Seventeenth Century,* 2 vols. (Munich: Musikverlag Emil Katzbichler, 1977), vol. 1, pp. 199–200; and Mary Frances Durantini, *The Child in Seventeenth-Century Dutch Painting* (Ann Arbor, Mich.: UMI Research Press, 1983), especially pp. 288–289, 292–296.

17. See also Susan Koslow, "Frans Hals's *Fisherboys:* Exemplars of Idleness," *Art Bulletin* 57 (1975), pp. 418–432, re other broadly grinning children. On the representation of begging, see Richard Leppert, *Arcadia at Versailles: Noble Amateur Musicians and Their Musettes and Hurdy-Gurdies at the French Court (c. 1660–1789)* (Amsterdam: Swets and Zeitlinger, 1978), pp. 11–23.

18. *Annals of Agriculture,* 17 (1792), p. 156. Quoted from Dorothy Marshall, *English People in the Eighteenth Century* (London: Longmans, 1956), p. 237. Arthur Young was himself fond of music. For additional remarks by Arthur Young and others on this matter, see Gordon E. Mingay, *English Landed Society in the Eighteenth Century* (London: Routledge and Kegan Paul, 1963), pp. 254–256. These views were common as the eighteenth century drew to a close, but similar, if not identical, expressions of concern occasionally occurred much earlier. See, for example, an anonymous pamphlet, *The Grand Concern of England Explained . . .* (London, 1673), reprinted in *The Harleian Miscellany; or, A Collection of Scarce, Curious, and Entertaining Pamphlets and Tracts . . . ,* 12 vols. (London, 1808–1811), vol. 8, pp. 51–53.

19. Allatson M. Burgh, *Anecdotes of Music, Historical and Biographical in a Series of Letters from a Gentleman to His Daughter,* 3 vols. (London, 1814), vol. 1, pp. v–vi.

20. *Gentleman's Magazine,* 71 (1801), p. 587. Quoted from Marshall, *English People in the Eighteenth Century,* p. 238.

21. See Mary Dorothy George, *Catalogue of Political and Personal Satires Preserved in the Department of Prints and Drawings in the British Museum,* vol. 8, *1801–1810* (London: The British Museum, 1947), no. 11444, pp. 885–886.

22. By contrast, for a fascinating account of the sexuality of nineteenth-century English working-class women as perceived by middle-class men, see Griselda Pollock, "The Dangers of Proximity: The Spaces of Sexuality and Surveillance in Word and Image," *Discourse* 16 (Winter 1993–1994), pp. 3–50.

23. James Hall, *Dictionary of Subjects and Symbols in Art* (New York: Harper and Row, 1974), pp. 62–63. Some of my information on this painting is from William R. Crelly, *The Paintings of Simon Vouet* (New Haven: Yale University Press, 1962), pp. 170–172. Crelly points out that the picture is rather carelessly executed and that it might have been produced as the cartoon for a tapestry.

24. See John A. Walker, "Art and the Peasantry," *Art & Artists* 13, 9 (January 1979), pp. 26–27; and on Brueghel paintings in particular, pp. 28–29, 31, to which I am indebted; and Walter S. Gibson, *Bruegel* (New York: Oxford University Press, 1977), pp. 146–149, 156–159.

25. Compare the famous painting by Jean-François Millet in the Boston Museum of Fine Arts, *Harvesters Resting* (1850–1853), reproduced and discussed in the exhibition catalogue by Alexandra R. Murphy, *Jean-François Millet* (Boston: Museum of Fine Arts, 1984), pp. 60–64.

26. Anne Hollander, *Moving Pictures* (New York: Alfred A. Knopf, 1989), pp. 96–97.

27. Iain Buchanan, "The Collection of Niclaes Jongelinck: II, The 'Months' by Pieter Bruegel the Elder," *Burlington Magazine* 132 (1990), p. 541. See also R. H. Marijnissen and M. Seidel, *Bruegel* (New York: Harrison House, 1984), pp. 47–48. For a summary of discussions relative to the months of the year represented— whether, for example, July-August or August-September—see Hans J. van Miegroet, "*The Twelve Months* Reconsidered: How a Drawing by Pieter Stevens Clarifies a Bruegel Enigma," *Simiolus* 16 (1986), pp. 29–35, and Buchanan, "Collection of Niclaes Jongelinck," *passim.*

28. Walter S. Gibson, "In Detail: Pieter Bruegel's *The Harvesters*," *Portfolio: The Magazine of the Visual Arts* 3 (May/June 1981), p. 41.

29. Norman Bryson, *Looking at the Overlooked: Four Essays on Still Life Painting* (Cambridge, Mass.: Harvard University Press, 1990), p. 101, comments on this issue, in reference to Brueghel's *The Battle Between Carnival and Lent,* a picture with a much more pronounced bird's-eye view than *The Harvesters:* "Brueghel's painting is an exact record of class division: the superior viewing-class peers down through the painting at the diminutive insect life of the peasantry far below. They are ridiculous, but happy; there is even a sense of bucolic charm in their gross communal life. . . . Brueghel's image does everything that might flatter a governing class into conviction of its own superiority and right to oversee a population which . . . presents no threat to its own existence." See also Margaret Sullivan, *Bruegel's Peasants: Art and Audience in the Northern Renaissance* (Cambridge: Cambridge University Press, 1994).

30. John Barrell, *The Dark Side of the Landscape: The Rural Poor in English Painting, 1730–1840* (Cambridge: Cambridge University Press, 1980), p. 149.

31. See the exhibition catalog by Judy Egerton, *George Stubbs, 1724–1806* (London: Tate Gallery, 1984), pp. 166–168. Stubbs's *Reapers,* and a companion image, *Haymakers,* were engraved and sold by subscription for the considerable sum of £2 10s. See Christopher Lennox-Boyd, Rob Dixon, and Tim Clayton, *George Stubbs: The Complete Engraved Works* (London: Stipple Publishing, 1989), cat. nos. 89–90; on costs and techniques see pp. 38–39. (The subscription advertisement for the two engravings is reproduced in Egerton, *George Stubbs, 1724–1806,* cat. no. 171.) See also the exhibition catalog by Christiana Payne, *Toil and Plenty: Images of the Agricultural Landscape in England, 1780–1890* (New Haven: Yale Center for British Art and Yale University Press, 1994), pp. 81–84. This volume contains useful back-

ground information concerning rural unrest and the economic conditions of agricultural workers; see especially pp. 5–22; and concerning the audience for agricultural paintings, see pp. 47–49. Both *Reapers* and *Haymakers* are discussed by Barrell, *Dark Side of the Landscape,* pp. 25–31. See also on this topic the excellent study by Ann Bermingham, *Landscape and Ideology: The English Rustic Tradition, 1740–1860* (Berkeley and Los Angeles: University of California Press, 1986).

32. Monica Juneja, "The Peasant in French Painting: Millet to Van Gogh," *Museum* 36 (1984), pp. 168–172. The literature concerning the nineteenth century, on Millet in particular, is extensive, but among recent studies the following should be consulted: T. J. Clark, *The Absolute Bourgeois: Artists and Politics in France, 1848–1851* (Princeton: Princeton University Press, 1982), pp. 72–98; Raymond Crew, "Picturing the People: Images of the Lower Orders in Nineteenth-Century French Art," and Elizabeth Johns, "The Farmer in the Works of William Sidney Mount," both in *Art and History: Images and Their Meaning,* ed. Robert I. Rotberg and Theodore K. Rabb (Cambridge: Cambridge University Press, 1988), pp. 203–231, 257–281, respectively; Laura L. Meixner, "Popular Criticism of Jean-François Millet in Nineteenth-Century America," *Art Bulletin* 65 (1983), pp. 94–105; the exhibition review by Bernard Denvir, "Jean Francois Millet: The Sour Taste of Success," *Art & Artists* 10, 10 (January 1976), pp. 20–23; the exhibition catalog by Robert L. Herbert, *Jean-François Millet* (London: Hayward Gallery, 1976); André Fermigier, *Jean-François Millet,* trans. Dinah Harrison (New York: Skira/Rizzoli, 1977); and the aforementioned (n. 25, this chapter) exhibition catalog by Murphy, *Jean-François Millet.* See also Richard R. Brettell and Caroline B. Brettell, *Painters and Peasants in the Nineteenth Century* (New York: Skira/Rizzoli, 1983); and Griselda Pollock, "Van Gogh and the Poor Slaves: Images of Rural Labour as Modern Art," *Art History* 11 (1988), pp. 408–432, for an excellent account of the historical inadequacy of seeing artists like van Gogh as belonging, simply, to one side or another of the political spectrum.

33. See, for example, his two paintings, "Reaper with Sickle," and "The Sheaf-Binder," reproduced in Louis van Tilborgh, ed., *Van Gogh and Millet* (Amsterdam: Rijksmuseum Vincent van Gogh, 1989), pp. 130, 134.

34. The bibliography pertaining to the representation of racial difference is staggering in proportion. Two areas of principal focus are the imagery of blacks and of orientalism. Regarding the former, the best starting place is the massive, well-illustrated set, *The Image of the Black in Western Art,* Ladislas Bugner, ed., 4 vols. in 6 (Houston: Menil Foundation, 1976–1989). The series begins with ancient Egypt and ends with America at the start of World War I. Other major studies include: Albert Boime, *The Art of Exclusion: Representing Blacks in the Nineteenth Century* (Washington, D.C.: Smithsonian Institution Press, 1990); the exhibition catalog by Guy C. McElroy, *Facing History: The Black Image in American Art, 1710–1940* (Washington, D.C.: Bedford Arts, in association with The Corcoran Gallery of Art, 1990); Jan Nederveen Pieterse, *White on Black: Images of Africa and Blacks in Western Popular Culture* (New Haven: Yale University Press, 1992); the exhibition catalog by Peter H. Wood and Karen C.C. Dalton, *Winslow Homer's Images of Blacks: The Civil*

War and Reconstruction Years (Austin: University of Texas Press, 1988); David Dabydeen, *Hogarth's Blacks: Images of Blacks in Eighteenth Century English Art* (Athens: University of Georgia Press, 1987); and Alain Locke, ed., *The Negro in Art: A Pictorial Record of the Negro Artist and of the Negro Theme in Art* (Chicago: Afro-Am Press, 1969). Most of these texts include extensive bibliographies.

35. My information on this painting is from the exhibition catalog *Jean-Léon Gérôme (1824–1904)* (Dayton, Ohio: The Dayton Art Institute, 1972), p. 91; and MaryAnne Stevens, ed., *The Orientalists: Delacroix to Matisse: The Allure of North Africa and the Near East* (London: Thames and Hudson, and the National Gallery of Art, 1984), p. 148.

36. Edward Said, *Orientalism* (New York: Vintage Books, 1978).

37. Stevens, *The Orientalists*, p. 148.

38. Hugh Honour, *The Image of the Black in Western Art*, vol. 4, *From the American Revolution to World War I, Part 2: Black Models and White Myths* (Houston: Menil Foundation, 1989), pp. 12–13.

39. Sander L. Gilman, "Black Bodies, White Bodies: Toward an Iconography of Female Sexuality in Late Nineteenth-Century Art, Medicine, and Literature," *Critical Inquiry* 12 (1985), pp. 204–242; Leonard Bell, *Colonial Constructs: European Images of the Maori, 1840–1914* (Melbourne: Melbourne University Press, 1992); and by the same author, "Artists and Empire: Victorian Representations of Subject People," *Art History* 5 (1982), pp. 73–86.

40. For a good account of the racism embedded in this color binary, see Boime, *Art of Exclusion,* pp. 1–13. On the merging of imperialism with moral crusade, with the pseudoscientific backing of evolutionary doctrines, see Patrick Brantlinger, "Victorians and Africans: The Genealogy of the Myth of the Dark Continent," *Critical Inquiry* 12 (1985), pp. 166–203.

41. Bell, "Artists and Empire," p. 74.

42. Hugh Honour, *The Image of the Black in Western Art,* vol. 4, *From the American Revolution to World War I, Part 1: Slaves and Liberators* (Houston: Menil Foundation, 1989), p. 282.

43. Harriet Guest, "Curiously Marked: Tattooing, Masculinity, and Nationality in Eighteenth-Century British Perceptions of the South Pacific," *Painting and the Politics of Culture,* ed. John Barrell (Oxford: Oxford University Press, 1992), p. 102. This is a brilliant essay on the gendering of the Other in Western representation.

44. Honour, *Image of the Black in Western Art,* vol. 4, part 2, pp. 38–40; the quotations appear on p. 38. See also Marc Sandoz, *Théodore Chassériau (1819–1856): Catalogue raisonné des peintures et estampes* (Paris: Arts et Métiers Graphiques, 1974), p. 40.

45. Barbara Maria Stafford, *Body Criticism: Imaging the Unseen in Enlightenment Art and Medicine* (Cambridge, Mass.: MIT Press, 1991), p. 84; see further to p. 104.

46. See Patrizia Magli, "The Face and the Soul," trans. Ughetta Lubin, in *Fragments for a History of the Human Body,* ed. Michel Feher, with Ramona Naddaff and Nadia Tazi, 3 vols. (New York: Zone, 1989), vol. 2, p. 88.

47. See the excellent study by Mary Cowling, *The Artist as Anthropologist: The Representation of Type and Character in Victorian Art* (Cambridge: Cambridge University Press, 1989).

48. Stafford, *Body Criticism,* p. 91. On Lavater see pp. 91–102.

49. Ibid., p. 102. See also Pieterse, *White on Black,* on the "science of race," pp. 45–51.

50. Samuel R. Wells, *New Physiognomy, or, Signs of Character . . .* (New York: Fowler and Wells, 1866), p. 61.

51. Ibid., p. 189.

52. Ibid., p. 193.

53. Ibid., p. 239.

54. Ibid., p. 266.

55. Ibid., pp. 382–383.

56. Ibid., pp. 398–399.

57. Ibid., p. 391.

58. McElroy, *Facing History,* p. xi. Regarding fruit and the representation of blacks, especially in the modern media, see Pieterse, *White on Black,* pp. 199–203.

In 1933 Sterling A. Brown assessed the treatment of blacks in American literature, suggesting that seven types of character emerge. Among these, Hovenden's young boy falls all too neatly into what Brown named "Local Color Negro." See Sterling A. Brown, "Negro Character as Seen by White Authors," *Journal of Negro Education* 2 (1933), pp. 179–203. The others are: The Contented Slave, The Wretched Freeman, The Comic Negro, The Brute Negro, The Tragic Mulatto, and The Exotic Primitive (p. 180). For more on this general subject see Henry Louis Gates, Jr., "The Face and Voice of Blackness," in the exhibition catalog by Guy C. McElroy, *Facing History: The Black Image in American Art, 1710–1940* (Washington, D.C.: Bedford Arts, in association with the Corcoran Gallery of Art, 1990), pp. xxix–xlviii, which provides a valuable summary of blacks' own efforts to reclaim their subjecthood in practice and representation alike. See also Henry Louis Gates, Jr., "The Trope of a New Negro and the Reconstruction of the Image of the Black," *Representations* 24 (Fall 1988), pp. 129–155; and Elizabeth Johns, *American Genre Painting: The Politics of Everyday Life* (New Haven: Yale University Press, 1991), pp. 100–136.

Chapter 9

1. Kenneth Clark, *The Nude: A Study in Ideal Form* (Garden City, N.Y.: Doubleday, 1959), p. 23.

2. Ibid., p. 29.

3. John Berger, *Ways of Seeing* (London: British Broadcasting Corporation, and Harmondsworth: Penguin Books, 1972), pp. 45–64.

4. Ibid., pp. 46–47.

5. Ibid., pp. 52, 54.

6. Laura Mulvey, "Visual Pleasure and Narrative Cinema," in *Visual and Other Pleasures* (Bloomington: Indiana University Press, 1989), pp. 14–26. See also

"Afterthoughts on 'Visual Pleasure and Narrative Cinema' Inspired by King Vidor's *Duel in the Sun* (1946)" in the same volume, pp. 29–38.

7. This topic is the subject of Berger's final chapter in *Ways of Seeing,* pp. 129–154.

8. Mulvey, "Visual Pleasure and Narrative Cinema," p. 19.

9. See Gill Saunders, *The Nude: A New Perspective* (London: Herbert Press, 1989), pp. 21–29.

10. Feminist scholarship on the "female gaze"—in effect, on women "looking back"—has for the most part to date come from work on popular culture, contemporary painting, and photography by women, often of male nudes. See, for example, Lorraine Gamman and Margaret Marshment, eds., *The Female Gaze: Women as Viewers of Popular Culture* (Seattle: Real Comet Press, 1989); and Sarah Kent and Jacqueline Morreau, *Women's Images of Men* (London: Writers and Readers Publishing, 1985). Other noteworthy texts are cited in notes that follow.

11. The bibliography of feminist art history, both by women and more recently by men, is already enormous. See Cassandra L. Langer, *Feminist Art Criticism: An Annotated Bibliography* (New York: G. K. Hall, 1993). Much of this work has been conducted as a recovery project designed to acknowledge the presence of women artists throughout Western history and to delineate the ideological issues surrounding their exclusion from art history, as in Rozsika Parker and Griselda Pollock, *Old Mistresses: Women, Art and Ideology* (London: Routledge and Kegan Paul, 1986); Deborah Cherry, *Painting Women: Victorian Women Artists* (London: Routledge, 1993). More recent work has sought to define the nature of feminist art discourse, as in Arlene Raven, Cassandra L. Langer, and Joanna Frueh, eds., *Feminist Art Criticism: An Anthology* (Ann Arbor, Mich.: UMI Research Press, 1988); other recent feminist art history has in essence claimed by its very practice an agency of female spectatorship; and some of this scholarship also addresses the work of women artists; see, for example, Rozsika Parker and Griselda Pollock, eds., *Framing Feminism: Art and the Women's Movement, 1970–85* (London: Pandora, 1987); Rosemary Betterton, ed., *Looking On: Images of Femininity in the Visual Arts and Media* (London: Pandora, 1987); Norma Broude and Mary D. Garrard, eds., *Feminism and Art History: Questioning the Litany* (New York: Harper and Row, 1982); and by the same editors, *The Expanding Discourse: Feminism and Art History* (New York: HarperCollins, 1992); Linda Nochlin, *Women, Art, and Power and Other Essays* (New York: Harper and Row, 1988); Susan R. Suleiman, ed., *The Female Body in Western Culture: Contemporary Perspectives* (Cambridge, Mass.: Harvard University Press, 1986); Griselda Pollock, *Vision and Difference: Femininity, Feminism and the Histories of Art* (London: Routledge, 1988); Hilary Robinson, ed., *Visibly Female: Feminism and Art: An Anthology* (New York: Universe Books, 1988); and Marina Warner, *Monuments and Maidens: The Allegory of the Female Form* (New York: Atheneum, 1985). Other important studies appear in notes that follow.

12. Luce Irigaray, quoted by Amelia G. Jones, "The Ambivalence of Male Masquerade: Duchamp as Rrose Sélavy," in *The Body Imaged: The Human Form and Visual Culture Since the Renaissance,* ed. Kathleen Adler and Marcia Pointon (Cambridge: Cambridge University Press, 1993), p. 30.

13. Marcia Pointon, *Naked Authority: The Body in Western Painting, 1830–1908* (Cambridge: Cambridge University Press, 1990). Pointon provides a good critique of both Clark and Berger, pp. 11–23. The best, most sustained critique of Clark in particular is by Lynda Nead, *The Female Nude: Art, Obscenity and Sexuality* (London: Routledge, 1992); see especially pp. 17–22.

14. Rosemary Betterton, "How Do Women Look? The Female Nude in the Work of Suzanne Valadon," in *Visibly Female. Feminism and Art: An Anthology,* ed. Hilary Robinson (New York: Universe Books, 1988), p. 255.

15. Pointon, *Naked Authority,* pp. 17–23.

16. See also Edward Snow, "Theorizing the Male Gaze: Some Problems," *Representations* 25 (Winter 1989), pp. 30–41: "Under the aegis of demystifying and excoriating male vision, the critic systematically deprives images of women of their subjective or undecidable aspects—to say nothing of their power—and at the same time eliminates from the onlooking 'male' ego whatever elements of identification with, sympathy for, or vulnerability to the feminine such images bespeak" (p. 31).

17. See Anne Hollander, *Seeing Through Clothes* (New York: Penguin Books, 1978), pp. 84–89.

18. Joseph Leo Koerner, *The Moment of Self-Portraiture in German Renaissance Art* (Chicago: University of Chicago Press, 1993), p. 295. This is a brilliant study on all accounts, and as regards the discussion at hand, the chapter "Death as Hermeneutic" is particularly apropos; see pp. 292–316; this painting is discussed on pp. 309–310. For a briefer, earlier account by the same author see "The Mortification of the Image: Death as a Hermeneutic in Hans Baldung Grien," *Representations* 10 (Spring 1985), pp. 52–101. Two other essays on this painting are noteworthy: A. Kent Hieatt, "Eve as Reason in a Tradition of Allegorical Interpretation of the Fall," *Journal of the Warburg and Courtauld Institutes* 43 (1980), pp. 221–226; and by the same author, "Hans Baldung Grien's Ottawa *Eve* and Its Context," *Art Bulletin* 65 (1983), pp. 290–304.

19. On the textual sources for the association of the serpent with the phallus, see Hieatt, "Eve as Reason," p. 223; and Hieatt, "Hans Baldung Grien's Ottawa *Eve,*" pp. 298–299.

20. Hieatt, "Eve as Reason," p. 223; Hieatt, "Hans Baldung Grien's Ottawa *Eve,*" pp. 292–298, describes the bite as vicious, which to me seems questionable. The bite causes no depression on Adam as Death's arm, nor do the serpent's jaws show the slightest sign of being tensed.

21. Koerner, *Moment of Self-Portraiture,* p. 298, and p. 503 n. 18.

22. Ibid., p. 303.

23. Cecil Gould, *The Sixteenth-Century Italian Schools: National Gallery Catalogues* (London: The National Gallery, 1975), p. 42. See also Allan Braham, *Italian Paintings of the Sixteenth Century: The National Gallery Schools of Painting* (London: The National Gallery, in association with William Collins, 1985), p. 64.

24. See Emmanuel Cooper, *The Sexual Perspective: Homosexuality and Art in the Last 100 Years in the West* (London: Routledge and Kegan Paul, 1986), p. 17, re this and other Bronzino paintings evoking incest.

25. On the issue of the painting's commission, see *National Gallery: Illustrated General Catalogue,* 2d ed., rev. (London: The National Gallery, 1986), p. 73; Braham, *Italian Paintings of the Sixteenth Century,* p. 64; and Gould, *Sixteenth-Century Italian Schools,* p. 43.

26. J. F. Conway, "Syphilis and Bronzino's London Allegory," *Journal of the Warburg and Courtauld Institutes* 49 (1986), pp. 250–255, maintains that the allegorical figure cited by scholars as representing Jealousy in fact makes allusion to syphilis, a common and then devastating venereal disease. He argues that the painting critiques illicit sexuality—prostitution via the incestuous kiss of Venus and her son; sodomy via Cupid's pose. Cosimo sought to control both (sodomy by burning at the stake for a third conviction, on which see p. 255). Bronzino's allegory has received a great deal of scholarly attention; for a fairly complete bibliography see Thomas Frangenberg, "Der Kampf und den Schlerer: Zur Allegorie Agnolo Bronzinos in der National Gallery London," *Wallraf-Richartz-Jahrbuch: Westdeutsches Jahrbuch für Kunstgeschichte* 46/47 (1985–1986), p. 383 n. 1. Among the major interpretations of the painting's complex allegory see Erwin Panofsky, *Studies in Iconology: Humanistic Themes in the Art of the Renaissance* (1939; reprint, New York: Harper and Row, 1972), pp. 86–91 (focused on the figure of Time); Graham Smith, "Jealousy, Pleasure and Pain in Agnolo Bronzino's 'Allegory of Venus and Cupid,'" *Pantheon: International Art Journal* 39 (1981), pp. 250–258; Charles Hope, "Bronzino's *Allegory* in The National Gallery," *Journal of the Warburg and Courtauld Institutes* 45 (1982), pp. 239–243 (discussing identities of the various figures represented). Finally, Michael Levey, "Sacred and Profane Significance in Two Paintings by Bronzino," in *Studies in Renaissance and Baroque Art, Presented to Anthony Blunt on His 60th Birthday* (London: Phaidon, 1967), pp. 32–33, discusses the painting as an allegory of the erotic power of Venus, hence providing a substitute title ("Venus Disarming Cupid").

27. Ovid, *Metamorphoses,* trans. Rolfe Humphries (Bloomington: Indiana University Press, 1955), pp. 24–25 (1:690–712).

28. See further N.G.L. Hammond and H. H. Scullard, eds., *The Oxford Classical Dictionary,* 2d ed. (Oxford: Clarendon Press, 1970), p. 773; and Catherine B. Avery, ed., *The New Century Classical Handbook* (New York: Appleton-Century-Crofts, 1962), pp. 808–809.

29. See Richard Leppert, *Arcadia at Versailles: Noble Amateur Musicians and Their Musettes and Hurdy-Gurdies at the French Court (c. 1660–1789)* (Amsterdam and Lisse: Swets and Zeitlinger, 1978).

30. See Eunice Lipton, "Woman, Pleasure, and Painting (e.g., Boucher)," *Genders* 7 (March 1990), pp. 69–86, an insightful feminist—and distinctly sympathetic—reading of Boucher's female nudes, together with a capsule account of women's place in court society; and Joan B. Landes, *Women and the Public Sphere in the Age of the French Revolution* (Ithaca: Cornell University Press, 1988), especially pp. 17–38, tracing the influence of elite women on political events and public language of the Old Regime via the urban salon, as distinct from the absolutist court. See Donald Posner, "Mme. de Pompadour as a Patron of the Visual Arts," *Art Bulletin* 72

(1990), pp. 74–105, for a recent revisionist account of Mme de Pompadour's impact on French art.

31. The exhibition catalog *François Boucher, 1703–1770,* catalog entries by Alastair Laing (New York: The Metropolitan Museum of Art, 1986), p. 252.

32. Concerning engravings, drawings, similar images, and copies related to this painting, see Alexandre Ananoff and Daniel Wilderstein, *François Boucher,* 2 vols. (Paris: La Bibliothèque des Arts, 1976), vol. 2, p. 190.

33. Leopold D. Ettlinger, "Taste and Patronage: The Role of the Artist in Society," in *The Eighteenth Century: Europe in the Age of Enlightenment,* ed. Alfred Cobban (New York: McGraw Hill, 1969), p. 218.

34. See on this point Norman Bryson, *Tradition and Desire: From David to Delacroix* (Cambridge: Cambridge University Press, 1984), p. 130. See also Robert Rosenblum, *Jean-Auguste-Dominique Ingres* (New York: Harry N. Abrams, 1985), p. 78; and Eldon N. Van Liere, "Solutions and Dissolutions: The Bather in Nineteenth-Century French Painting," *Arts Magazine* 54 (May 1980), pp. 104–105.

35. See the exhibition catalog by Donald A. Rosenthal, *Orientalism: The Near East in French Painting, 1800–1880* (Rochester, N.Y.: Memorial Art Gallery of the University of Rochester, 1982), pp. 119–125.

36. Rosenblum, *Jean-Auguste-Dominique Ingres,* p. 170. This painting has been much studied. In particular see Hélène Toussaint, *Le Bain turc d'Ingres* (Paris: Musée du Louvre, 1971), and a brilliant essay by Marilyn R. Brown, "The Harem Dehistoricized: Ingres' *Turkish Bath,*" *Arts Magazine* 61 (June 1987), pp. 58–68. For more concerning Lady Mary Wortley Montagu's letter memoir, see Marcia Pointon, *Hanging the Head: Portraiture and Social Formation in Eighteenth-Century England* (New Haven: Yale University Press, 1993), pp. 147, 152–153.

37. See Bryson, *Tradition and Desire,* pp. 156–157.

38. See Brown, "The Harem Dehistoricized," pp. 62–66.

39. A close, slightly later, variant is in the Walters Art Gallery, Baltimore, concerning which see the exhibition catalog *The Orientalists: Delacroix to Matisse: The Allure of North Africa and the Near East,* ed. MaryAnne Stevens (London: Thames and Hudson, and the National Gallery of Art, 1984), pp. 171–172. On the version under discussion, at Harvard University, see also Rosenblum, *Jean-Auguste-Dominique Ingres,* pp. 142–145.

40. Bryson, *Tradition and Desire,* pp. 141–142.

41. Richard Ettinghausen, "Jean-Léon Gérôme as a Painter of Near Eastern Subjects," in the exhibition catalog *Jean-Léon Gérôme (1824–1904)* (Dayton, Ohio: The Dayton Art Institute, 1972), pp. 16–17.

42. Gerald M. Ackerman, "Gérôme's Oriental Paintings and the Western Genre Tradition," *Arts Magazine* 60 (March 1986), p. 75; and by the same author, *The Life and Work of Jean-Léon Gérôme, with a Catalogue Raisonné* (London: Sotheby's Publications, 1986), p. 46.

43. See MaryAnne Stevens, "Western Art and Its Encounter with the Islamic World, 1798–1914," in the exhibition catalog Stevens, ed., *The Orientalists: Delacroix to Matisse,* p. 21.

44. Albert Boime, "Gérôme and the Bourgeois Artist's Burden," *Arts Magazine* 57 (January 1983), pp. 67, 68. This essay contains good background on Gérôme's political connections to the court of Napoléon III.

45. Ackerman, "Gérôme's Oriental Paintings and the Western Genre Tradition," p. 79.

46. Ettinghausen, "Jean-Léon Gérôme as a Painter of Near Eastern Subjects," pp. 21–22.

47. Linda Nochlin, "The Imaginary Orient," *Art in America* 71 (1983), pp. 118–131, 186–191. Nochlin is my source for the story of the French missionaries, p. 126.

48. Louise d'Arnencourt, "Bouguereau and the Art Market in France," in *William Bouguereau, 1825–1905* (exhibition catalog) (Montreal: The Montreal Museum of Fine Arts, 1984), p. 95: His works were collected by a wealthy international clientele "most vividly personified by the millionaires of the New World, who were as eager to decorate the newly plastered walls of their luxurious mansions as they were to construct the pedestals of their infant culture."

49. Quoted from Bram Dijkstra, *Idols of Perversity: Fantasies of Feminine Evil in Fin-de-Siècle Culture* (New York: Oxford University Press, 1986), p. 276.

50. Alfred Werner, "The Return of Monsieur Bouguereau," *Art & Artists* 9, 12 (March 1975), p. 28.

From the early 1880s to 1901 the painting was hung in the bar of the Hoffman House Hotel in New York, following a sale by its original American owner. There it was seen "by the wealthy and influential, since the Hoffman House was the social center for the rich and famous of business, politics, and show business—from Buffalo Bill to Ulysses S. Grant." From William H. Gerdts, *The Great American Nude: A History in Art* (New York: Praeger Publishers, 1974), p. 103.

There is a considerable bibliography for this painting, for which, together with much additional information about its history, see the exhibition catalog *William Bouguereau (1825–1905)*, pp. 182–186. This volume contains useful essays on French *pompier* art in general, a biography and assessment of Bouguereau's work, and information on the marketing and collecting of his paintings. See also Hollis Clayson, *Painted Love: Prostitution in French Art of the Impressionist Era* (New Haven: Yale University Press, 1991), an excellent account of related subject matter (the discussion of a once-famous painting by Henri Gervex, *Rolla* [1878], pp. 79–90, is particularly good). Probably the most famous painting of a nude prostitute is Manet's *Olympia,* on which see T. J. Clark, *The Painting of Modern Life: Paris in the Art of Manet and His Followers* (Princeton: Princeton University Press, 1984), pp. 79–146; and Peter Brooks, "Storied Bodies, or Nana at Last Unveil'd," *Critical Inquiry* 16 (1989), pp. 1–32.

51. Michel Foucault, *The History of Sexuality,* vol. 1, *An Introduction,* trans. Robert Hurley (New York: Pantheon Books, 1978).

52. See Sander Gilman, "Black Bodies, White Bodies: Towards an Iconography of Female Sexuality in Late Nineteenth-Century Art, Medicine, and Literature," *Critical Inquiry* 12 (1985), pp. 204–242.

53. See, for example, Neil Hertz, "Medusa's Head: Male Hysteria Under Political Pressure," and a series of exchanges ("More About 'Medusa's Head'") by Catherine Gallagher, Joel Fineman, and Neil Hertz, in *Representations* 4 (Fall 1983), pp. 27–72.

54. See further *William Bouguereau, 1825–1905,* pp. 217–219; and Robert Isaacson, "The Evolution of Bouguereau's Grand Manner," *Bulletin of the Minneapolis Institute of Arts* 62 (1975), pp. 74–83.

Chapter 10

1. See remarks by Norman Bryson, "Géricault and 'Masculinity,'" in *Visual Culture: Images and Interpretations,* ed. Norman Bryson, Michael Ann Holly, and Keith Moxey (Hanover, N.H.: Wesleyan University Press, 1994), pp. 228–259, whose approach here is principally psychoanalytic but is read within a specific historical and cultural context.

2. James Hall, *Dictionary of Subjects and Symbols in Art* (New York: Harper and Row, 1974), pp. 276–277; and Louis Réau, *Iconographie de l'art chrétien,* 3 vols. in 6 (Paris: Presses Universitaires de France, 1955–1959), vol. 3, part 2, pp. 1190–1199.

3. See Rudolf Wittkower, *Gian Lorenzo Bernini: The Sculptor of the Roman Baroque,* 2d ed. (London: Phaidon, 1966), pp. 216–219 and 257–259.

4. Mario Perniola, "Between Clothing and Nudity," trans. Roger Freidman, in *Fragments for a History of the Human Body,* ed. Michel Feher, with Ramona Naddaff and Nadia Tazi, 3 vols. (New York: Zone, 1989), vol. 2, p. 237.

5. Anne Hollander, *Seeing Through Clothes* (Harmondsworth: Penguin Books, 1988), p. 83; see also p. xiii.

6. For more on this painting see Leopold D. Ettlinger, *Antonio and Piero Pollaiuolo: Complete Edition with a Critical Catalogue* (Oxford: Phaidon, 1978), pp. 48–51, 139–140.

7. Hollander, *Seeing Through Clothes,* pp. 182–183. In Renaissance literary tradition "Sebastian" was a code name for a homosexual. See Janet Cox-Rearick, "A 'St Sebastian' by Bronzino," *Burlington Magazine* 129 (March 1987), p. 161 n. 29.

8. See further Patricia Emison, "The Word Made Naked in Pollaiuolo's *Battle of the Nudes,*" *Art History* 13 (1990), p. 265. Also on this engraving see Ettlinger, *Antonio and Piero Pollaiuolo,* pp. 146–147; and L. Richards, "Antonio Pollaiuolo, *Battle of Naked Men,*" *Bulletin of the Cleveland Museum of Art* 55 (1968), pp. 62–70.

9. The exhibition catalog by David Martocci, *The Male Nude* (Williamstown, Mass.: Sterling and Francine Clark Art Institute, 1980), [unpaginated, p. 2].

10. Sarah Kent, "Looking Back," in *Women's Images of Men,* ed. Sarah Kent and Jacqueline Morreau (London: Writers and Readers Publishing, 1985), pp. 72–73. See also by Sarah Kent, in the same volume, "The Erotic Male Nude," pp. 75–105, addressing the question of women's pleasure in looking at male nudes intended for male audiences; she also discusses male nudes (photographs and paintings) by twentieth-century women artists. See also Margaret Walters, *The Nude Male: A New Perspective* (New York: Paddington Press, 1978).

11. Richard Easton, "Canonical Criminalizations: Homosexuality, Art History, Surrealism, and Abjection," *differences: A Journal of Feminist Cultural Studies* 4, 3 (1992), p. 164.

12. Kent, "Looking Back," p. 72.

13. Hollander, *Seeing Through Clothes,* p. 234.

14. See Herbert P. Horne, *Botticelli: Painter of Florence* (Princeton: Princeton University Press, 1980), p. 140, according to whom it was "probably executed for the panel of a bed, or couch, or some such piece of furniture."

15. Hollander, *Seeing Through Clothes,* p. 179.

16. See Hall, *Dictionary of Subjects and Symbols in Art* (New York: Harper and Row, 1974), p. 320.

17. Quoted in Sharon Fermor, "Movement and Gender in Sixteenth-Century Italian Painting," in *The Body Imaged: The Human Form and Visual Culture Since the Renaissance,* ed. Kathleen Adler and Marcia Pointon (Cambridge: Cambridge University Press, 1993), p. 129. For information concerning homoerotic themes in the Renaissance, see Leonard Barkan, *Ganymede and the Erotics of Humanism* (Stanford: Stanford University Press, 1991); James M. Saslow, *Ganymede in the Renaissance: Homosexuality in Art and Society* (New Haven: Yale University Press, 1986); and Emmanuel Cooper, *The Sexual Perspective: Homosexuality and Art in the Last 100 Years in the West* (New York: Routledge and Kegan Paul, 1986), pp. 1–23. For more on Botticelli's *Venus and Mars,* including detailed accounts of the allegory it unfolds, see Ronald Lightbown, *Sandro Botticelli: Life and Work* (Berkeley and Los Angeles: University of California Press, 1978), pp. 90–93; Liana Cheney, *Quattrocento Neoplatonism and Medici Humanism in Botticelli's Mythological Paintings* (Lanham, Md.: University Press of America, 1985), pp. 35–37, 60–61, 66–70; and Homan Potterton, *The National Gallery, London* (London: Thames and Hudson, 1977), p. 36.

18. Bram Dijkstra, *Idols of Perversity: Fantasies of Feminine Evil in Fin-de-Siècle Culture* (New York: Oxford University Press, 1986), pp. 104–109. Thomas Crow, however, has convincingly demonstrated the role played by French revolutionary politics in the *The Sleep of Endymion* (1791), the painting by Anne-Louis Girodet of a similar androgynous ephebe. See "Revolutionary Activism and the Cult of Male Beauty in the Studio of David," in *Fictions of the French Revolution,* ed. Bernadette Ford (Chicago: Northwestern University Press, 1991), especially pp. 72–79. This essay was revised and expanded as "Observations on Style and History in French Painting of the Male Nude, 1785–1794," in *Visual Culture: Images and Interpretations,* ed. Bryson, Holly, and Moxey, pp. 141–167. In the same volume, Whitney Davis, "The Renunciation of Reaction in Girodet's *Sleep of Endymion,*" pp. 168–201, formulates an extremely interesting response to Crow via a well-historicized discussion of the homoerotic appeal of this painting.

19. Abigail Solomon-Godeau, "Male Trouble: A Crisis in Representation," *Art History* 16 (1993), p. 298. On Fabre's painting see also pp. 295–296. This is an extraordinary essay, highly recommended for a detailed historical account of the visual

history I am addressing. See also George Levitine, *Girodet-Troison: An Iconographical Study* (New York: Garland Publishing, 1978), pp. 117–135, 205–211.

20. See Solomon-Godeau, "Male Trouble," pp. 311–312 n. 37.

21. Michael Hatt, "Muscles, Morals, Mind: The Male Body in Thomas Eakins' *Salutat*," in *The Body Imaged: The Human Form and Visual Culture Since the Renaissance,* ed. Kathleen Adler and Marcia Pointon (Cambridge: Cambridge University Press, 1993), p. 63.

22. See the valuable study by Whitney Davis, "Erotic Revision in Thomas Eakins's Narratives of Male Nudity," *Art History* 17 (1994), pp. 301–341.

23. The best-known account of this phenomenon is by Michel Foucault, *The History of Sexuality,* vol. 1, *An Introduction,* trans. Robert Hurley (New York: Pantheon Books, 1978).

24. Jacqueline Rose, *Sexuality in the Field of Vision* (London: Verso, 1986), p. 228.

25. I am taking the notion of colonization from Solomon-Godeau, "Male Trouble," p. 295.

26. Linda Nochlin, "The Imaginary Orient," *Art in America* 71 (1983), pp. 118, 122.

27. See Foucault, *History of Sexuality,* vol. 1: *An Introduction.*

28. Hollander, *Seeing Through Clothes,* p. 136.

29. See France Borel, *The Seduction of Venus: Artists and Models,* trans. Jean-Marie Clarke (New York: Skira/Rizzoli, 1990), pp. 40–51, which includes a discussion of Schiele.

30. Simon Wilson, *Egon Schiele* (Ithaca: Cornell University Press, 1980), pp. 30, 57. See also Jane Kallir, *Egon Schiele: The Complete Works* (New York: Harry N. Abrams, 1990), pp. 69–70; and Alessandra Comini, *Egon Schiele's Portraits* (Berkeley and Los Angeles: University of California Press, 1974), pp. 88–89.

31. See Foucault, *History of Sexuality,* vol. 1, *An Introduction.*

32. Janet Hobhouse, *The Bride Stripped Bare: The Artist and the Nude in the Twentieth Century* (London: Jonathan Cape, 1988), p. 58; regarding the later nudes, see pp. 68–69, and on p. 72, the couple, again nude, with their child. Between 1912 and 1917 he painted no nude self-portraits.

Works Cited

Ackerman, Gerald M. "Gérôme's Oriental Paintings and the Western Genre Tradition." *Arts Magazine* 60 (March 1986), pp. 75–80.

————. *The Life and Work of Jean-Léon Gérôme, with a Catalogue Raisonne.* London: Sotheby's Publications, 1986.

Ades, Dawn, and Andrew Forge. *Francis Bacon.* New York: Harry N. Abrams, 1985.

Albinus, Bernhard Siegfried. *Tabulae sceleti et musculorum corporis humani.* Leiden, 1747.

Alexander, Edward P. *Museum Masters: Their Museums and Their Influence.* Nashville, Tenn.: American Association for State and Local History, 1983.

Alfons, Sven. "The Museum as Image of the World." In *The Arcimboldo Effect: Transformations of the Face from the 16th to the 20th Century,* edited by Pontus Hulten, pp. 67–88. New York: Abbeville Press, 1987.

Alpers, Svetlana. *The Art of Describing: Dutch Art in the Seventeenth Century.* Chicago: University of Chicago Press, 1983.

Alphen, Ernst van. *Francis Bacon and the Loss of Self.* Cambridge, Mass.: Harvard University Press, 1993.

Amaral, Cis. "'Be What You Would Seem to Be.'" *Art and Artists* 11 (August 1976), pp. 26–29.

Ananoff, Alexandre, and Daniel Wilderstein. *François Boucher.* 2 vols. Paris: La Bibliothèque des Arts, 1976.

Arnencourt, Louise d'. "Bouguereau and the Art Market in France." In *William Bouguereau, 1825–1905* [exhibition catalog], pp. 95–103. Montreal: Montreal Museum of Fine Arts, 1984.

Athanassoglou-Kallmyer, Nina. "Géricault's Severed Heads and Limbs: The Politics and Aesthetics of the Scaffold." *Art Bulletin* 74 (1992), pp. 599–618.

Attali, Jacques. *Noise: The Political Economy of Music.* Translated by Brian Massumi. Minneapolis: University of Minnesota Press, 1985.

Avery, Catherine B., ed. *The New Century Classical Handbook.* New York: Appleton-Century-Crofts, 1962.

[Bacon, Francis, and David Sylvester.] *Francis Bacon: Interviewed by David Sylvester.* New York: Pantheon Books, 1975.

Bal, Mieke. "Dead Flesh, or the Smell of Painting." In *Visual Culture: Images and Interpretations,* edited by Norman Bryson, Michael Ann Holly, and Keith Moxey, pp. 365–383. Hanover, N.H.: Wesleyan University Press, 1994.

Baldwin, Robert W. "Healing and Hope in Goya's *Self-Portrait with Dr. Arrieta.*" *Source: Notes in Art History* 4, 4 (Summer 1985), pp. 31–36.

Barkan, Leonard. *Ganymede and the Erotics of Humanism.* Stanford: Stanford University Press, 1991.

Barker, Francis. *The Tremulous Private Body: Essays on Subjection.* London: Methuen, 1984.

Barrell, John. *The Dark Side of the Landscape: The Rural Poor in English Painting, 1730–1840.* Cambridge: Cambridge University Press, 1980.

Barrell, John, ed. *Painting and the Politics of Culture: New Essays on British Art, 1700–1850.* Oxford: Oxford University Press, 1992.

Barry, Roxana. "Plane Truths: 19th-Century American Trompe l'Oeil Painting." *Arts & Antiques* 4 (September-October 1981), pp. 100–106.

Barthes, Roland. "Arcimboldo, or Magician and Rhétoriqueur." In *The Responsibility of Forms: Critical Essays on Music, Art, and Representation,* translated by Richard Howard, pp. 129–148. Berkeley and Los Angeles: University of California Press, 1991.

————. "Dare to Be Lazy." In *The Grain of the Voice: Interviews, 1962–1980,* translated by Linda Coverdale, pp. 38–45. New York: Hill and Wang, 1985.

————. "The Plates of the *Encyclopaedia.*" In *New Critical Essays,* translated by Richard Howard, pp. 23–39. New York: Hill and Wang, 1980.

————. "The World as Object." Translated by Richard Howard. In *A Barthes Reader,* edited by Susan Sontag, pp. 62–73. New York: Hill and Wang, 1982.

Battersby, Martin. *Trompe l'Oeil: The Eye Deceived.* New York: St. Martin's Press, 1974.

Baudrillard, Jean. *For a Critique of the Political Economy of the Sign.* Translated by Charles Levin, pp. 112–122. St. Louis: Telos Press, 1981.

————. "The Trompe-l'Oeil." In *Calligram: Essays in New Art History from France,* edited by Norman Bryson, pp. 53–62. Cambridge: Cambridge University Press, 1988.

Baumgart, Fritz. *Blumen Brueghel (Jan Brueghel d. Ä.) Leben und Werk.* Cologne: DuMont Buchverlag, 1978.

Bell, Leonard. "Artists and Empire: Victorian Representations of Subject People." *Art History* 5 (1982), pp. 73–86.

————. *Colonial Constructs: European Images of the Maori, 1840–1914.* Melbourne: Melbourne University Press, 1992.

Bennett, Tony. "The Exhibitionary Complex." *New Formations* 4 (Spring 1988), pp. 73–102.

Berardi, Marianne. "The Nature Pieces of Rachel Ruysch." *Porticus,* vols. 10 and 11 (1987–1988), pp. 3–15.

Berger, John. *Ways of Seeing.* London: British Broadcasting Corporation, and Harmondsworth: Penguin Books, 1972.

Bermingham, Ann. *Landscape and Ideology: The English Rustic Tradition, 1740–1860.* Berkeley and Los Angeles: University of California Press, 1986.

Bernheimer, Richard. *The Nature of Representation: A Phenomenological Inquiry.* Edited by H. W. Janson. New York: New York University Press, 1961.

Bernt, Walter. *The Netherlandish Painters of the Seventeenth Century.* Translated by P. S. Falla. 3d ed. 3 vols. London: Phaidon, 1970.

Betterton, Rosemary. "How Do Women Look? The Female Nude in the Work of Suzanne Valadon." In *Visibly Female: Feminism and Art: An Anthology,* edited by Hilary Robinson, pp. 250–271. New York: Universe Books, 1988.

———, ed. *Looking On: Images of Femininity in the Visual Arts and Media.* London: Pandora, 1987.

Bidloo, Govard. *Anatomia humani corporis . . .* Amsterdam, 1685.

Blok, Petrus Johannes. *History of the People of the Netherlands.* Vol. 3, *The War with Spain.* Translated by Ruth Putnam. New York: Putnam, 1900.

Boggs, J.S.G. "Art Under Arrest." *Art and Antiques* (October 1987), pp. 99–104, 126–127.

Boime, Albert. *The Art of Exclusion: Representing Blacks in the Nineteenth Century.* Washington, D.C.: Smithsonian Institution Press, 1990.

———. "Gérôme and the Bourgeois Artist's Burden." *Arts Magazine* 57 (January 1983), pp. 64–73.

Bolger, Doreen. "The Patrons of the Artist: Emblems of Commerce and Culture." In *William M. Harnett* [exhibition catalog], edited by Doreen Bolger, Marc Simpson, and John Wilmerding, pp. 73–86. New York: Harry N. Abrams, 1992.

Bolger, Doreen, Marc Simpson, and John Wilmerding, eds. *William M. Harnett* [exhibition catalog]. New York: Harry N. Abrams, 1992.

Borel, France. *The Seduction of Venus: Artists and Models.* Translated by Jean-Marie Clarke. New York: Skira/Rizzoli, 1990.

Bourdieu, Pierre. *Distinction: A Social Critique of the Judgement of Taste.* Translated by Richard Nice. Cambridge, Mass.: Harvard University Press, 1984.

Braham, Allan. *Italian Paintings of the Sixteenth Century: The National Gallery Schools of Painting.* London: The National Gallery, in association with William Collins, 1985.

Brantlinger, Patrick. "Victorians and Africans: The Genealogy of the Myth of the Dark Continent." *Critical Inquiry* 12 (1985), pp. 166–203.

Brenninkmeyer-de Rooij, B. "Zeldzame bloemen, 'Fatta tutti del natturel' door Jan Brueghel I." *Oud Holland* 104 (1990), pp. 218–248.

Brettell, Richard R., and Caroline B. Brettell. *Painters and Peasants in the Nineteenth Century.* New York: Skira/Rizzoli, 1983.

Brilliant, Richard. *Portraiture.* Cambridge, Mass.: Harvard University Press, 1991.

Brooks, Peter. "Storied Bodies, or Nana at Last Unveil'd." *Critical Inquiry* 16 (1989), pp. 1–32.

Broude, Norma, and Mary D. Garrard, eds. *The Expanding Discourse: Feminism and Art History.* New York: HarperCollins, 1992.

———. *Feminism and Art History: Questioning the Litany.* New York: Harper and Row, 1982.

Brown, Jonathan. *Velázquez: Painter and Courtier.* New Haven: Yale University Press, 1986.

Brown, Marilyn R. "The Harem Dehistoricized: Ingres' *Turkish Bath.*" *Arts Magazine* 61 (June 1987), pp. 58–68.

Brown, Sterling A. "Negro Character as Seen by White Authors." *Journal of Negro Education* 2 (1933), pp. 179–203.

Brusati, Celeste. "Stilled Lives: Self-Portraiture and Self-Reflection in Seventeenth-Century Netherlandish Still-Life Painting." *Simiolus* 20 (1990/1991), pp. 168–182.

Bryson, Norman. "Géricault and 'Masculinity.'" In *Visual Culture: Images and Interpretations,* edited by Norman Bryson, Michael Ann Holly, and Keith Moxey, pp. 228–259. Hanover, N.H.: Wesleyan University Press, 1994.

———. "In Medusa's Gaze." In *In Medusa's Gaze: Still Life Paintings from Upstate New York Museums* [exhibition catalog], edited by Bernard Barryte, pp. 6–30. Rochester, N.Y.: Memorial Art Gallery of the University of Rochester, 1991.

———. *Looking at the Overlooked: Four Essays on Still Life Painting.* Cambridge, Mass.: Harvard University Press, 1990.

———. *Tradition and Desire: From David to Delacroix.* Cambridge: Cambridge University Press, 1984.

———. *Vision and Painting: The Logic of the Gaze.* New Haven: Yale University Press, 1983.

———. *Word and Image: French Painting of the Ancien Régime.* Cambridge: Cambridge University Press, 1981.

Buchanan, Iain. "The Collection of Niclaes Jongelinck: II, The 'Months' by Pieter Bruegel the Elder." *Burlington Magazine* 132 (1990), pp. 541–550.

Bugner, Ladislas, ed. *The Image of the Black in Western Art.* 4 vols. in 6. Houston: Menil Foundation, 1976–1989.

Burgh, Allatson M. *Anecdotes of Music, Historical and Biographical in a Series of Letters from a Gentleman to His Daughter.* 3 vols. London, 1814.

Carrier, David. *Artwriting.* Amherst: University of Massachusetts Press, 1987.

Chaudonneret, Marie-Claude. "Historicism and 'Heritage' in the Louvre, 1820–40: From the Musée Charles X to the Galerie d'Apollon." *Art History* 14 (1991), pp. 488–520.

Cheney, Liana. *Quattrocento Neoplatonism and Medici Humanism in Botticelli's Mythological Paintings.* Lanham, Md.: University Press of America, 1985.

Cherry, Deborah. *Painting Women: Victorian Women Artists.* London: Routledge, 1993.

Chirico, Robert F. "John Haberle and *Trompe-l'Oeil.*" *Marsyas: Studies in the History of Art* 19 (1977–1978), pp. 37–43.

———. "Language and Imagery in Late Nineteenth-Century Trompe l'Oeil." *Arts Magazine* 59 (March 1985), pp. 110–114.

Choulant, Ludwig. *History and Bibliography of Anatomic Illustration.* Translated and annotated by Mortimer Frank. 1852. Reprint, New York: Hafner Publishing, 1962.

Chute, Carolyn. *The Beans of Egypt, Maine.* New York: Warner Books, 1985.

Cikovsky, Nicolai, Jr. "'Sordid Mechanics' and 'Monkey-Talents': The Illusionistic Tradition." In *William M. Harnett* [exhibition catalog], edited by Doreen Bolger, Marc Simpson, and John Wilmerding, pp. 19–29. New York: Harry N. Abrams, 1992.

Clark, Kenneth. *The Nude: A Study in Ideal Form.* Garden City, N.Y.: Doubleday, 1959.

Clark, T. J. *The Absolute Bourgeois: Artists and Politics in France, 1848–1851.* Princeton: Princeton University Press, 1982.

———. *The Painting of Modern Life: Paris in the Art of Manet and His Followers.* Princeton: Princeton University Press, 1984.

Clayson, Hollis. *Painted Love: Prostitution in French Art of the Impressionist Era.* New Haven: Yale University Press, 1991.

Clément, Charles. *Géricault: Étude biographique et critique.* 1879. New ed., edited by Lorenz E.A. Eitner, Paris: L. Laget, 1973.

Comini, Alessandra. *Egon Schiele's Portraits.* Berkeley and Los Angeles: University of California Press, 1974.

Conway, J. F. "Syphilis and Bronzino's London Allegory." *Journal of the Warburg and Courtauld Institutes* 49 (1986), pp. 250–255.

Cooper, Emmanuel. *The Sexual Perspective: Homosexuality and Art in the Last 100 Years in the West.* London: Routledge and Kegan Paul, 1986.

Corbin, Alain. *The Foul and the Fragrant: Odor and the French Social Imagination.* New York: Berg Publishers, 1986.

Cowling, Mary. *The Artist as Anthropologist: The Representation of Type and Character in Victorian Art.* Cambridge: Cambridge University Press, 1989.

Cox-Rearick, Janet. "A 'St Sebastian' by Bronzino." *Burlington Magazine* 129 (March 1987), pp. 155–162.

Craig, Kenneth M. "Pieter Aertsen and *The Meat Stall.*" *Oud Holland* 96 (1982), pp. 1–15.

———. "Rembrandt and *The Slaughtered Ox.*" *Journal of the Warburg and Courtauld Institutes* 46 (1983), pp. 235–239.

Crary, Jonathan. *Techniques of the Observer: On Vision and Modernity in the Nineteenth Century.* Cambridge, Mass.: MIT Press, 1990.

Crelly, William R. *The Paintings of Simon Vouet.* New Haven: Yale University Press, 1962.

Crew, Raymond. "Picturing the People: Images of the Lower Orders in Nineteenth-Century French Art." In *Art and History: Images and Their Meaning,* edited by Robert I. Rotberg and Theodore K. Rabb, pp. 203–231. Cambridge: Cambridge University Press, 1988.

Crimp, Douglas. "On the Museum's Ruins." In *The Anti-Aesthetic: Essays on Postmodern Culture,* edited by Hal Foster, pp. 43–56. Port Townsend, Wash.: Bay Press, 1983.

Crow, Thomas. "Observations on Style and History in French Painting of the Male Nude, 1785–1794." In *Visual Culture: Images and Interpretations,* edited by

Norman Bryson, Michael Ann Holly, and Keith Moxey, pp. 141–167. Hanover, N.H.: Wesleyan University Press, 1994.

———. "Revolutionary Activism and the Cult of Male Beauty in the Studio of David." In *Fictions of the French Revolution,* edited by Bernadette Ford, pp. 55–83. Chicago: Northwestern University Press, 1991.

Dabydeen, David. *Hogarth's Blacks: Images of Blacks in Eighteenth Century English Art.* Athens: University of Georgia Press, 1987.

d'Agoty, Jacques Fabien Gautier. *Anatomie de la tête . . .* Paris, 1748.

———. *Exposition anatomique des maux vénériens, sur les parties de l'homme & de la femme . . .* Paris, 1773.

———. *Myologie complètte en couleur et grandeur naturelle . . .* Paris, 1745.

Danto, Arthur C. "Trompe l'oeil." *Nation* 254 (4 May 1992), p. 604.

Dars, Célestine. *Images of Deception: The Art of Trompe-l'Oeil.* Oxford: Phaidon, 1979.

Davies, Martin. *National Gallery Catalogues: French School.* 2d ed., rev. London: National Gallery of Art, 1957.

Davis, Whitney. "Erotic Revision in Thomas Eakins's Narratives of Male Nudity." *Art History* 17 (1994), pp. 301–341.

———. "The Renunciation of Reaction in Girodet's *Sleep of Endymion.*" In *Visual Culture: Images and Interpretations,* edited by Norman Bryson, Michael Ann Holly, and Keith Moxey, pp. 168–201. Hanover, N.H.: Wesleyan University Press, 1994.

Deleuze, Gilles. "Interpretations of the Body: A New Power of Laughter for the Living." *Art International* 8 (Autumn 1989), pp. 34–40.

Denvir, Bernard. "Jean François Millet: The Sour Taste of Success." *Art & Artists* 10, 10 (January 1976), pp. 20–23.

Dijkstra, Bram. *Idols of Perversity: Fantasies of Feminine Evil in Fin-de-Siècle Culture.* New York: Oxford University Press, 1986.

Dorival, Bernard. *Philippe de Champaigne (1602–1674): La vie, l'oeuvre, et le catalogue raisonné de l'oeuvre.* 2 vols. Paris: Léonce Laget Libraire, 1976.

Drucker, Johanna. "Harnett, Haberle, and Peto: Visuality and Artifice Among the Proto-Modern Americans." *Art Bulletin* 74 (1992), pp. 37–50.

Duncan, Carol, and Alan Wallach. "The Universal Survey Museum." *Art History* 3 (1980), pp. 448–469.

Dunow, Esti. "Soutine's Still Lifes." *C. Soutine (1893–1943)* [exhibition catalog], edited by Ernst-Gerhard Güse, pp. 73–97. London: Arts Council of Great Britain, 1981.

Durantini, Mary Frances. *The Child in Seventeenth-Century Dutch Painting.* Ann Arbor, Mich.: UMI Research Press, 1983.

Easton, Richard. "Canonical Criminalizations: Homosexuality, Art History, Surrealism, and Abjection." *differences: A Journal of Feminist Cultural Studies* 4, 3 (1992), pp. 133–175.

Egerton, Judy. *George Stubbs, 1724–1806* [exhibition catalog]. London: Tate Gallery, 1984.

————. *Wright of Derby* [exhibition catalog]. New York: The Metropolitan Museum of Art, 1990.

Eitner, Lorenz E.A. *Géricault: His Life and Work.* London: Orbis Publishing, 1983.

Elkins, James. "Michelangelo and the Human Form: His Knowledge and Use of Anatomy." *Art History* 7 (1984), pp. 176–186.

Emison, Patricia. "The Word Made Naked in Pollaiuolo's *Battle of the Nudes.*" *Art History* 13 (1990), pp. 261–275.

Emmens, Jan A. "'Eins aber ist nötig': Zu Inhalt und Bedeutung von Markt- und Küchenstücken des 16. Jahrhunderts." In *Album Amicorum J. G. van Gelder,* edited by Josua Bruyn, pp. 93–101. The Hague: Nijhoff, 1973.

Ertz, Klaus. "Introduction: Some Thoughts on the Paintings of Jan Brueghel the Elder (1568–1625)." In *Jan Brueghel the Elder: A Loan Exhibition of Paintings* [exhibition catalog], pp. 8–21. London: Brod Gallery, 1979.

————. *Jan Brueghel der Ältere (1568–1625): Die Gemälde mit kritischem Oeuvrekatalog.* Cologne: DuMont Buchverlag, 1979.

Ettinghausen, Richard. "Jean-Léon Gérôme as a Painter of Near Eastern Subjects." In *Jean-Léon Gérôme (1824–1904)* [exhibition catalog], pp. 16–26. Dayton, Ohio: The Dayton Art Institute, 1972.

Ettlinger, Leopold D. *Antonio and Piero Pollaiuolo: Complete Edition with a Critical Catalogue.* Oxford: Phaidon, 1978.

————. "Taste and Patronage: The Role of the Artist in Society." In *The Eighteenth Century: Europe in the Age of Enlightenment,* edited by Alfred Cobban, pp. 217–258. New York: McGraw Hill, 1969.

Evans, Dorinda. "Raphaelle Peale's *Venus Rising from the Sea:* Further Support for a Change in Interpretation." *American Art Journal* 14 (Summer, 1982), pp. 63–72.

Evans, John. *Juvenile Pieces: Designed for the Youth of Both Sexes.* 3d ed. London, [1797].

Falkenburg, R. L. "Iconographical Connections Between Antwerp Landscapes, Market Scenes and Kitchen Pieces, 1500–1580." *Oud Holland* 102 (1988), pp. 114–126.

Feldstein, Martin, ed. *The Economics of Art Museums.* Chicago: University of Chicago Press, 1991.

Ferguson, George. *Signs and Symbols in Christian Art.* New York: Oxford University Press, 1961.

Fermigier, André. *Jean-François Millet.* Translated by Dinah Harrison. New York: Skira/Rizzoli, 1977.

Fermor, Sharon. "Movement and Gender in Sixteenth-Century Italian Painting." In *The Body Imaged: The Human Form and Visual Culture Since the Renaissance,* edited by Kathleen Adler and Marcia Pointon, pp. 129–145. Cambridge: Cambridge University Press, 1993.

Forbes, Thomas R. "'To Be Dissected and Anatomized.'" *Journal of the History of Medicine and Allied Sciences* 36 (1981), pp. 490–492.

Foster, Hal, ed. *Discussions in Contemporary Culture (Dia Art Foundation) Number Two: Vision and Visuality.* Seattle: Bay Press, 1988.

Foucault, Michel. *The Archaeology of Knowledge and the Discourse on Language*. Translated by A. M. Sheridan Smith. New York: Pantheon Books, 1972.

————. *Discipline and Punish: The Birth of the Prison*. Translated by Alan Sheridan. New York: Vintage Books, 1979.

————. *The History of Sexuality*. Vol. 1, *An Introduction*. Translated by Robert Hurley. New York: Pantheon Books, 1978.

————. *This Is Not a Pipe*. Translated and edited by James Harkness. Berkeley and Los Angeles: University of California Press, 1983.

François Boucher, 1703–1770 [exhibition catalog]. Catalog entries by Alastair Laing. New York: The Metropolitan Museum of Art, 1986.

Frangenberg, Thomas. "Der Kampf und den Schlerer: Zur Allegorie Agnolo Bronzinos in der National Gallery London." *Wallraf-Richartz-Jahrbuch: West-deutsches Jahrbuch für Kunstgeschichte*, vols. 46 and 47 (1985–1986), pp. 377–386.

Frankenstein, Alfred. *After the Hunt: William Harnett and Other American Still Life Painters, 1870–1900*. Rev. ed. Berkeley and Los Angeles: University of California Press, 1969.

————. "Fooling the Eye." *Art Forum* 12, 9 (May 1974), pp. 32–35.

————. *The Reality of Appearance: The Trompe l'Oeil Tradition in American Painting* [exhibition catalog]. [Greenwich, Conn.:] New York Graphic Society, 1970.

Freedberg, David. "Science, Commerce, and Art: Neglected Topics at the Junction of History and Art History." In *Art in History, History in Art: Studies in Seventeenth-Century Dutch Culture*, edited by David Freedberg and Jan de Vries, pp. 376–428. Santa Monica, Calif.: The Getty Center for the History of Art and the Humanities, 1991.

Fried, Michael. "Realism, Writing, and Disfiguration in Thomas Eakins's *Gross Clinic*." *Representations* 9 (Winter 1985), pp. 33–104.

Gallagher, Catherine, Joel Fineman, and Neil Hertz. "More About 'Medusa's Head.'" *Representations* 4 (Fall 1983), pp. 55–72.

Gamman, Lorraine, and Margaret Marshment, eds. *The Female Gaze: Women as Viewers of Popular Culture*. Seattle: Real Comet Press, 1989.

Gammelbo, Poul. *Dutch Still-Life Painting from the 16th to the 18th Centuries in Danish Collections*. Copenhagen: Munksgaard, 1960.

Gasten, Andrea. "Dutch Still-Life Painting: Judgements and Appreciation." In *Still-Life in the Age of Rembrandt* [exhibition catalog], edited by Eddy de Jongh, pp. 13–25. Auckland: Auckland City Art Gallery, 1982.

Gates, Henry Louis, Jr. "The Face and Voice of Blackness." In *Facing History: The Black Image in American Art, 1710–1940* [exhibition catalog], edited by Guy C. McElroy, pp. xxix–xlviii. Washington, D.C.: Bedford Arts, in association with the Corcoran Gallery of Art, 1990.

————. "The Trope of a New Negro and the Reconstruction of the Image of the Black." *Representations* 24 (Fall 1988), pp. 129–155.

Geertz, Clifford. "Art as a Cultural System." *Modern Language Notes* 91 (1976), pp. 1473–1499.

George, Mary Dorothy. *Catalogue of Political and Personal Satires Preserved in the Department of Prints and Drawings in the British Museum.* Vol. 8, *1801–1810.* London: The British Museum, 1947.

Gerdts, William H. *The Great American Nude: A History in Art.* New York: Praeger Publishers, 1974.

Geyl, Pieter. *The Netherlands Divided (1609–1648).* Translated by S. T. Bindoff, in collaboration with Pieter Geyl. London: Williams and Norgate, 1936.

———. *The Revolt of the Netherlands (1555–1609).* 2d ed. London: Ernest Benn, 1958.

Gibson, Walter S. *Bruegel.* New York: Oxford University Press, 1977.

———. "In Detail: Pieter Bruegel's *The Harvesters.*" *Portfolio: The Magazine of the Visual Arts* 3 (May/June 1981), pp. 40–45.

Gilman, Sander L. "Black Bodies, White Bodies: Toward an Iconography of Female Sexuality in Late Nineteenth-Century Art, Medicine, and Literature." *Critical Inquiry* 12 (1985), pp. 204–242.

Glaser, Lynn. *Counterfeiting in America.* New York: Clarkson N. Potter, 1968.

Goedde, Lawrence O. "A Little World Made Cunningly: Dutch Still Life and Ekphrasis." In *Still Lifes of the Golden Age: Northern European Paintings from the Heinz Family Collection* [exhibition catalog], edited by Arthur K. Wheelock, Jr., pp. 35–44. Washington, D.C.: National Gallery of Art, 1989.

Gombrich, Ernst H. *Art and Illusion: A Study in the Psychology of Pictorial Representation.* 2d ed., rev. Princeton: Princeton University Press, 1961.

———. "Tradition and Expression in Western Still Life." In *Meditations on a Hobby Horse and Other Essays on the Theory of Art,* pp. 95–105. Chicago: University of Chicago Press, 1963.

Gould, Cecil. *The Sixteenth-Century Italian Schools: National Gallery Catalogues.* London: The National Gallery, 1975.

Greenfield, Jeanette. *The Return of Cultural Treasures.* New York: Cambridge University Press, 1989.

Guest, Harriet. "Curiously Marked: Tattooing, Masculinity, and Nationality in Eighteenth-Century British Perceptions of the South Pacific." In *Painting and the Politics of Culture,* edited by John Barrell, pp. 101–134. Oxford: Oxford University Press, 1992.

Hairs, Marie-Louise. *The Flemish Flower Painters in the XVIIth Century.* Translated by Eva Grzelak. Brussels: Lefebvre et Gillet, 1985.

Hall, James. *Dictionary of Subjects and Symbols in Art.* New York: Harper and Row, 1974.

Hammond, N.G.L., and H. H. Scullard, eds. *The Oxford Classical Dictionary.* 2d ed. Oxford: Clarendon Press, 1970.

Hand, John Oliver, and Martha Wolff. *The Collections of the National Gallery of Art Systematic Catalogue: Early Netherlandish Painting.* Washington, D.C.: National Gallery of Art; and New York: Cambridge University Press, 1986.

Harcourt, Glen. "Andreas Vesalius and the Anatomy of Antique Sculpture." *Representations* 17 (Winter 1987), pp. 28–61.

The Harleian Miscellany; or, A Collection of Scarce, Curious, and Entertaining Pamphlets and Tracts . . . 12 vols. London, 1808–1811.

Harris, Enriqueta. *Velézquez.* Ithaca: Cornell University Press, 1982.

Hatt, Michael. "Muscles, Morals, Mind: The Male Body in Thomas Eakins' *Salutat.*" In *The Body Imaged: The Human Form and Visual Culture Since the Renaissance,* edited by Kathleen Adler and Marcia Pointon, pp. 57–69. Cambridge: Cambridge University Press, 1993.

Heckscher, William S. *Rembrandt's Anatomy of Dr. Nicholaas Tulp: An Iconographical Study.* New York: New York University Press, 1958.

Hendon, William S., Frank Costa, and Robert A. Rosenberg. "The General Public and the Art Museum: Case Studies of Visitors to Several Institutions Identify Characteristics of Their Publics." *American Journal of Economics and Sociology* 48, 2 (1989), pp. 231–243.

Herbert, Robert L. *Jean-François Millet* [exhibition catalog]. London: Hayward Gallery, 1976.

Hertz, Neil. "Medusa's Head: Male Hysteria Under Political Pressure." *Representations* 4 (Fall 1983), pp. 27–54.

Herzog, Sadja J. "Jan Gossaert, Called Mabuse (ca. 1478–1532), A Study of His Chronology with a Catalogue of His Works," 3 vols. Ph.D. diss., Bryn Mawr College, 1968.

Hewison, Robert. *The Heritage Industry: Britain in a Climate of Decline.* London: Metheun, 1987.

Hieatt, A. Kent. "Eve as Reason in a Tradition of Allegorical Interpretation of the Fall." *Journal of the Warburg and Courtauld Institutes* 43 (1980), pp. 221–226.

———. "Hans Baldung Grien's Ottawa *Eve* and Its Context." *Art Bulletin* 65 (1983), pp. 290–304.

Hobhouse, Janet. *The Bride Stripped Bare: The Artist and the Nude in the Twentieth Century.* London: Jonathan Cape, 1988.

Hollander, Anne. *Moving Pictures.* New York: Alfred A. Knopf, 1989.

———. *Seeing Through Clothes.* New York: Penguin Books, 1978.

Holman, Thomas S. "Holbein's Portraits of the Steelyard Merchants: An Investigation." *Metropolitan Museum Journal* 14 (1979), pp. 139–158.

Honour, Hugh. *The Image of the Black in Western Art.* Vol. 4, *From the American Revolution to World War I, Part 1: Slaves and Liberators.* Houston: Menil Foundation, 1989.

———. *The Image of the Black in Western Art.* Vol. 4, *From the American Revolution to World War I, Part 2: Black Models and White Myths.* Houston: Menil Foundation, 1989.

Hope, Charles. "Bronzino's *Allegory* in The National Gallery." *Journal of the Warburg and Courtauld Institutes* 45 (1982), pp. 239–243.

Horne, Donald. *The Great Museum: The Re-Presentation of History.* London: Pluto Press, 1984.

Horne, Herbert P. *Botticelli: Painter of Florence.* Princeton: Princeton University Press, 1980.

Hudson, Kenneth. *Museums of Influence.* Cambridge: Cambridge University Press, 1987.

Hulten, Pontus, ed. *The Arcimboldo Effect: Transformations of the Face from the 16th to the 20th Century.* New York: Abbeville Press, 1987.

Isaacson, Robert. "The Evolution of Bouguereau's Grand Manner." *Bulletin of the Minneapolis Institute of Arts* 62 (1975), pp. 74–83.

Jarrett, Derek. *England in the Age of Hogarth.* New Haven: Yale University Press, 1986.

Jay, Martin. *Downcast Eyes: The Denigration of Vision in Twentieth-Century French Thought.* Berkeley and Los Angeles: University of California Press, 1993.

Jean-Léon Gérôme (1824–1904) [exhibition catalog]. Dayton, Ohio: The Dayton Art Institute, 1972.

Johns, Elizabeth. *American Genre Painting: The Politics of Everyday Life.* New Haven: Yale University Press, 1991.

———. "The Farmer in the Works of William Sidney Mount." In *Art and History: Images and Their Meaning,* edited by Robert I. Rotberg and Theodore K. Rabb, pp. 257–281. Cambridge: Cambridge University Press, 1988.

Jones, Amelia G. "The Ambivalence of Male Masquerade: Duchamp as Rrose Sélavy." In *The Body Imaged: The Human Form and Visual Culture Since the Renaissance,* edited by Kathleen Adler and Marcia Pointon, pp. 21–31. Cambridge: Cambridge University Press, 1993.

Jongh, Eddy de. *Portretten van echt en trouw: Huwelijk en gezin in de Nederlandse kunst van de zeventiende eeuw* [exhibition catalog]. Zwolle: Uitgeverij Waanders; and Haarlem: Frans Halsmuseum, 1986.

———. "Some Notes on Interpretation." In *Art in History, History in Art: Studies in Seventeenth-Century Dutch Culture,* edited by David Freedberg and Jan de Vries, pp. 118–136. Santa Monica, Calif.: The Getty Center for the History of Art and the Humanities, 1991.

———. *Still-Life in the Age of Rembrandt* [exhibition catalog]. Auckland: Auckland City Art Gallery, 1982.

———. *Zinne- en minnebeelden in de schilderkunst van de zeventiende eeuw.* Antwerp: Openbare Kunstbezit in Vlaanderen, 1967.

Jordan, William B. *Spanish Still Life in the Golden Age, 1600–1650* [exhibition catalog]. Fort Worth, Tex.: Kimball Art Museum, 1985.

Juneja, Monica. "The Peasant in French Painting: Millet to Van Gogh." *Museum* 36 (1984), pp. 168–172.

Kallir, Jane. *Egon Schiele: The Complete Works.* New York: Harry N. Abrams, 1990.

Karp, Ivan, Christine Mullen Kreamer, and Steven D. Lavine, eds. *Museums and Communities: The Politics of Public Culture.* Washington, D.C.: Smithsonian Institution Press, 1992.

Karp, Ivan, and Steven D. Lavine, eds. *Exhibiting Cultures: The Poetics and Politics of Museum Display.* Washington, D.C.: Smithsonian Institution Press, 1991.

Kauffmann, Hans. "Die Fünfsinne in der neiderländischen Malerei des 17.

Jahrhunderts." In *Kunstgeschichtliche Studien: Festschrift für Dagobert Frey*, edited by Hans Tintelnot, pp. 133–157. Breslau: Gauverlag, 1943.

Kaufmann, Thomas DaCosta. "The Allegories and Their Meaning." In *The Arcimboldo Effect: Transformations of the Face from the 16th to the 20th Century*, edited by Pontus Hulten, pp. 89–108. New York: Abbeville Press, 1987.

———. "Arcimboldo's Imperial Allegories: G. B. Fonteo and the Interpretation of Arcimboldo's Painting." *Zeitschrift für Kunstgeschichte* 39 (1976), pp. 275–296.

———. *The School of Prague: Painting at the Court of Rudolf II.* Chicago: University of Chicago Press, 1988.

Kavanagh, Gaynor, ed. *Museum Languages: Objects and Texts.* Leicester: Leicester University Press, 1991.

Keisch, Claude. "Portraits in mehrfacher Ansicht: Überlieferung und Sinnwandel einer Bildidee." In *Staatliche Museen zu Berlin, Forschungen und Berichte*, pp. 205–239. Kunsthistorische und Volkskundliche Beiträge, no. 17. Berlin: Akamedie-Verlag, 1976.

Kenseth, Joy, ed. *The Age of the Marvelous* [exhibition catalog]. Hanover, N.H.: Hood Museum of Art, Dartmouth College, 1991.

Kent, Sarah. "The Erotic Male Nude." In *Women's Images of Men*, edited by Sarah Kent and Jacqueline Morreau, pp. 75–105. London: Writers and Readers Publishing, 1985.

———. "Looking Back." In *Women's Images of Men*, edited by Sarah Kent and Jacqueline Morreau, pp. 55–74. London: Writers and Readers Publishing, 1985.

Kent, Sarah, and Jacqueline Morreau. *Women's Images of Men.* London: Writers and Readers Publishing, 1985.

Klötz, Heinrich. *Hans Holbein d. J.: Christus im Grabe.* Stuttgart: Philipp Reclam Jun., 1968.

Knuttel, Gerard. *Adriaen Brouwer: The Master and His Work.* Translated by J. G. Talma-Schilthuis and Robert Wheaton. The Hague: L.J.C. Boucher, 1962.

Koerner, Joseph Leo. *The Moment of Self-Portraiture in German Renaissance Art.* Chicago: University of Chicago Press, 1993.

———. "The Mortification of the Image: Death as a Hermeneutic in Hans Baldung Grien." *Representations* 10 (Spring 1985), pp. 52–101.

Koslow, Susan. "Frans Hals's *Fisherboys*: Exemplars of Idleness." *Art Bulletin* 57 (1975), pp. 418–432.

Kren, Thomas. "Chi non vuol Baccho: Roeland van Laer's Burlesque Painting About Dutch Artists in Rome." *Simiolus* 11 (1980), pp. 63–80.

Kristeva, Julia. "Holbein's Dead Christ." Translated by Leon S. Roudiez. In *Fragments for a History of the Human Body*, edited by Michel Feher, with Ramona Naddaff and Nadia Tazi, vol. 1, pp. 238–269. 3 vols. New York: Zone, 1989.

Kuspit, Donald. "Francis Bacon: The Authority of Flesh." *Artforum* 13 (Summer 1975), pp. 50–59.

Landes, Joan B. *Women and the Public Sphere in the Age of the French Revolution.* Ithaca: Cornell University Press, 1988.

Landwehr, John. *Emblem and Fable Books Printed in the Low Countries, 1542–1813: A Bibliography.* Utrecht: HES Publishers, 1988.

Langer, Cassandra L. *Feminist Art Criticism: An Annotated Bibliography.* New York: G. K. Hall, 1993.

Lechte, John. "Kristeva and Holbein, Artist of Melancholy." *British Journal of Aesthetics* 30 (1990), pp. 342–350.

Lennox-Boyd, Christopher, Rob Dixon, and Tim Clayton. *George Stubbs: The Complete Engraved Works.* London: Stipple Publishing, 1989.

Leppert, Richard. *Arcadia at Versailles: Noble Amateur Musicians and Their Musettes and Hurdy-Gurdies at the French Court (c. 1660–1789).* Amsterdam: Swets and Zeitlinger, 1978.

————. "*Concert in a House:* Musical Iconography and Musical Thought." *Early Music* 7 (1979), pp. 3–17.

————. "David Teniers the Younger and the Image of Music." *Jaarboek, Koninklijk Museum voor Schone Kunsten* [Antwerp] (1978), pp. 63–155.

————. *Music and Image: Domesticity, Ideology and Socio-Cultural Formation in Eighteenth-Century England.* Cambridge: Cambridge University Press, 1988.

————. "Music, Representation, and Social Order in Early-Modern Europe." *Cultural Critique* 12 (Spring 1989), pp. 25–55.

————. *The Sight of Sound: Music, Representation, and the History of the Body.* Berkeley and Los Angeles: University of California Press, 1993.

————. *The Theme of Music in Flemish Paintings of the Seventeenth Century.* 2 vols. Munich and Salzburg: Musikverlag Emil Katzbichler, 1977.

Levey, Michael. "Sacred and Profane Significance in Two Paintings by Bronzino." In *Studies in Renaissance and Baroque Art, Presented to Anthony Blunt on His 60th Birthday* (London: Phaidon, 1967), pp. 30–33.

Levitine, George. *Girodet-Troison: An Iconographical Study.* New York: Garland Publishing, 1978.

Li, Chu-tsing. "The Five Senses in Art: An Analysis of Its Development in Northern Europe." Ph.D. diss., State University of Iowa, 1955.

Licht, Fred S. *Goya: The Origns of the Modern Temper in Art.* New York: Universe Books, 1979.

Lightbown, Ronald. *Sandro Botticelli: Life and Work.* Berkeley and Los Angeles: University of California Press, 1978.

Lipton, Eunice. "Woman, Pleasure, and Painting (e.g., Boucher)." *Genders* 7 (March 1990), pp. 69–86.

Locke, Alain, ed. *The Negro in Art: A Pictorial Record of the Negro Artist and of the Negro Theme in Art.* Chicago: Afro-Am Press, 1969.

López-Rey, José. *Velázquez: A Catalogue Raisonné of His Oeuvre, with an Introductory Study.* London: Faber and Faber, 1963.

Lowe, Donald M. *History of Bourgeois Perception.* Chicago: University of Chicago Press, 1982.

Lowenthal, Anne Walter. *Joachim Wtewael and Dutch Mannerism.* Doornspijk: Davaco, 1986.

————. "Response to Peter Hecht." *Simiolus* 16 (1986), pp. 188–190.

Loye, Georges de. "Le Trompe-l'oeil d'Antoine Fort-Bras." *Revue des Arts* 10 (1960), pp. 19–24.

Luyendijk-Elshout, Antoine M. "Death Enlightened: A Study of Frederik Ruysch." *Journal of the American Medical Association* 212 (1970), pp. 121–126.

Lyons, Albert S., and R. Joseph Petrucelli, Jr. *Medicine: An Illustrated History.* New York: Harry N. Abrams, 1978.

McClellan, Andrew L. "The Politics and Aesthetics of Display: Museums in Paris 1750–1800." *Art History* 7 (1984), pp. 438–464.

MacDougall, Elisabeth Blair. "Flower Importation and Dutch Flower Paintings, 1600–1750." In *Still Lifes of the Golden Age: Northern European Paintings from the Heinz Family Collection* [exhibition catalog], edited by Arthur K. Wheelock, Jr., pp. 27–31. Washington, D.C.: National Gallery of Art, 1989.

McElroy, Guy C. *Facing History: The Black Image in American Art, 1710–1940* [exhibition catalog]. Washington, D.C.: Bedford Arts, in association with the Corcoran Gallery of Art, 1990.

Maclaren, Neil. *National Gallery Catalogues: The Spanish School,* 2d ed., rev. by Allan Braham. London: The National Gallery, 1970.

Magli, Patrizia. "The Face and the Soul." Translated by Ughetta Lubin. In *Fragments for a History of the Human Body,* edited by Michel Feher, with Ramona Naddaff and Nadia Tazi, vol. 2, pp. 86–127. 3 vols. New York: Zone, 1989.

Maiorino, Giancarlo. *The Portrait of Eccentricity: Arcimboldo and the Mannerist Grotesque.* University Park: Pennsylvania State University Press, 1991.

Mann, Gunter. "Museums: The Anatomical Collections of Frederik Ruysch at Leningrad." *Bulletin of the Cleveland Medical Library* 11 (1964), pp. 10–13.

Marijnissen, R. H., and M. Seidel. *Bruegel.* New York: Harrison House, 1984.

Marlier, Georges. "C. N. Gijsbrechts, l'illusionniste." *Connaissance des Arts* 145 (March 1964), pp. 96–105.

Marshall, Dorothy. *English People in the Eighteenth Century.* London: Longmans, 1956.

Martocci, David. *The Male Nude* [exhibition catalog]. Williamstown, Mass.: Sterling and Francine Clark Art Institute, 1980.

Mastai, M. L. d'Otrange. *Illusion in Art: Trompe l'Oeil, A History of Pictorial Illusionism.* New York: Abaris Books, 1975.

Meijer, Fred G. *Still Life Paintings from the Golden Age* [exhibition catalog]. Rotterdam: Museum Boymans-van Beuningen, 1989.

Meixner, Laura L. "Popular Criticism of Jean-François Millet in Nineteenth-Century America." *Art Bulletin* 65 (1983), pp. 94–105.

Michaels, Walter Benn. *The Gold Standard and the Logic of Naturalism: American Literature at the Turn of the Century.* Berkeley and Los Angeles: University of California Press, 1987.

Miegroet, Hans J. van. "*The Twelve Months* Reconsidered: How a Drawing by Pieter Stevens Clarifies a Bruegel Enigma." *Simiolus* 16 (1986), pp. 29–35.

Millar, Olivar. *The Queen's Pictures.* New York: Macmillan, 1977.

Milman, Miriam. *Trompe-l'Oeil Painting: The Illusions of Reality.* New York: Skira/Rizzoli, 1982.

Mingay, Gordon E. *English Landed Society in the Eighteenth Century.* London: Routledge and Kegan Paul, 1963.

Mirimonde, Albert Pomme de. "Les 'Cabinets de musique.'" *Jaarboek, Koninklijk Museum voor Schone Kunsten* [Antwerp] (1966), pp. 141–178.

———. "Musique et symbolisme chez Jan-Davidszoon de Heem, Cornelis-Janszoon et Jan II Janzoon de Heem." *Jaarboek, Koninklijk Museum voor Schone Kunsten* [Antwerp] (1970), pp. 241–295.

———. "Les natures mortes à instruments de musique de Peter Boel." *Jaarboek, Koninklijk Museum voor Schone Kunsten* [Antwerp] (1964), pp. 107–141.

———. "Les peintres flamands de trompe l'oeil et des natures mortes au XVIIe siècle, et les sujets de musique." *Jaarboek, Koninklijk Museum voor Schone Kunsten* [Antwerp] (1971), pp. 223–272.

———. "Les sujets de musique chez les Caravagistes Flamands." *Jaarboek, Koninklijk Museum voor Schone Kunsten* [Antwerp] (1965), pp. 113–170.

Moffitt, John F. "Observations on the Origins and Meanings of Goya with the Devils in the 1920 *Self-Portrait with Dr. Arrieta.*" *Minneapolis Institute of Arts Bulletin* 65 (1981–1982), pp. 36–49.

Montias, John Michael. "Art Dealers in the Seventeenth-Century Netherlands." *Simiolus* 18 (1988), pp. 244–253.

Moxey, Keith. *The Practice of Theory: Poststructuralism, Cultural Politics, and Art History.* Ithaca: Cornell University Press, 1994.

Muller, Joseph-Émile. *Velázquez.* Translated by Jane Brenton. London: Thames and Hudson, 1976.

Mulvey, Laura. "Afterthoughts on 'Visual Pleasure and Narrative Cinema' Inspired by King Vidor's *Duel in the Sun* (1946)." In *Visual and Other Pleasures,* pp. 29–38. Bloomington: Indiana University Press, 1989.

———. "Visual Pleasure and Narrative Cinema." In *Visual and Other Pleasures,* pp. 14–26. Bloomington: Indiana University Press, 1989.

Mundy, Jennifer. "Surrealism and Painting: Describing the Imaginary." *Art History* 10 (1987), pp. 492–508.

Murphy, Alexandra R. *Jean-François Millet* [exhibition catalog]. Boston: Museum of Fine Arts, 1984.

National Gallery: Illustrated General Catalogue. 2d ed., rev. London: The National Gallery, 1986.

Nead, Lynda. *The Female Nude: Art, Obscenity and Sexuality.* London: Routledge, 1992.

Nicolson, Benedict. *Joseph Wright of Derby: Painter of Light.* 2 vols. London: Routledge and Kegan Paul, 1968.

Nietzsche, Friedrich. *The Birth of Tragedy and the Genealogy of Morals.* Translated by Francis Golffing. New York: Doubleday Anchor Books, 1956.

Nochlin, Linda. "The Imaginary Orient." *Art in America* 71 (1983), pp. 118–131, 186–191.

————. *Women, Art, and Power and Other Essays.* New York: Harper and Row, 1988.

Noël, Bernard. *Magritte.* Translated by Jeffrey Arsham. New York: Crown Publishers, 1977.

Nygren, Edward J. "The Almighty Dollar: Money as a Theme in American Painting." *Winterthur Portfolio: A Journal of American Material Culture* 23 (1988), pp. 129–150.

Orvell, Miles. *The Real Thing: Imitation and Authenticity in American Culture, 1880–1940.* Chapel Hill: University of North Carolina Press, 1989.

Ovid. *Metamorphoses.* Translated by Rolfe Humphries. Bloomington: Indiana University Press, 1955.

Owens, Craig. "The Birth and Death of the Viewer: On the Public Functions of Art." In *Discussions in Contemporary Culture (Dia Art Foundation) Number One,* edited by Hal Foster, pp. 16–23. Seattle: Bay Press, 1987.

————. "Representation, Appropriation and Power." *Art in America* 70 (May 1982), pp. 9–21.

Panofsky, Erwin. *Studies in Iconology: Humanistic Themes in the Art of the Renaissance.* 1939. Reprint, New York: Harper and Row, 1972.

Parker, Geoffrey. *The Dutch Revolt.* Ithaca: Cornell University Press, 1977.

Parker, Rozsika, and Griselda Pollock. *Old Mistresses: Women, Art and Ideology.* London: Routledge and Kegan Paul, 1986.

————, eds. *Framing Feminism: Art and the Women's Movement, 1970–85.* London: Pandora, 1987.

Paulson, Ronald. *The Art of Hogarth.* London: Phaidon, 1975.

————. *Hogarth's Graphic Works.* 3d ed., rev. London: Print Room, 1989.

Pavière, Sydney H. *The Devis Family of Painters.* Leigh-on-the-Sea, England: F. Lewis, 1950.

Payne, Christiana. *Toil and Plenty: Images of the Agricultural Landscape in England, 1780–1890* [exhibition catalog]. New Haven: Yale Center for British Art and Yale University Press, 1994.

Perin, Constance. "The Communicative Circle: Museums as Communities." In *Museums and Communities: The Politics of Public Culture,* edited by Ivan Karp, Christine Mullen Kreamer, and Steven D. Lavine, pp. 182–220. Washington, D.C.: Smithsonian Institution Press, 1992.

Perniola, Mario. "Between Clothing and Nudity. " Translated by Roger Freidman. In *Fragments for a History of the Human Body,* edited by Michel Feher, with Ramona Naddaff and Nadia Tazi, vol. 2, pp. 236–265. 3 vols. New York: Zone, 1989.

Peters, Edward. *Torture.* Oxford: Basil Blackwell, 1985.

Pieterse, Jan Nederveen. *White on Black: Images of Africa and Blacks in Western Popular Culture.* New Haven: Yale University Press, 1992.

Pointon, Marcia. *Hanging the Head: Portraiture and Social Formation in Eighteenth-Century England.* New Haven: Yale University Press, 1993.

————. *Naked Authority: The Body in Western Painting, 1830–1908.* Cambridge: Cambridge University Press, 1990.

———. "Portrait-Painting as a Business Enterprise in London in the 1780s." *Art History* 7 (1984), pp. 187–205.

———. "Psychoanalysis and Art History: Freud, Fried and Eakins." In *Naked Authority: The Body in Western Painting, 1830–1908,* pp. 35–58. Cambridge: Cambridge University Press, 1990.

Pollock, Griselda. "The Dangers of Proximity: The Spaces of Sexuality and Surveillance in Word and Image." *Discourse* 16 (Winter 1993–1994), pp. 3–50.

———. "Van Gogh and the Poor Slaves: Images of Rural Labour as Modern Art." *Art History* 11 (1988), pp. 408–432.

———. *Vision and Difference: Femininity, Feminism and the Histories of Art.* London: Routledge, 1988.

Posèq, Avigdor W.G. "The Hanging Carcass Motif and Jewish Artists." *Jewish Art,* vols. 16 and 17 (1990/1991), pp. 139–156.

———. "Soutine's Paraphrase of Rembrandt's *Slaughtered Ox.*" *Konsthistorisk tidskrift* 60 (1991), pp. 210–222.

Posner, Donald. *Annibale Carracci: A Study in the Reform of Italian Painting Around 1590.* 2 vols. London: Phaidon, 1971.

———. "Mme. de Pompadour as a Patron of the Visual Arts." *Art Bulletin* 72 (1990), pp. 74–105.

Posthumus, N. W. "The Tulip Mania in Holland in the Years 1636 and 1637." *Journal of Economic and Business History* 1 (1928), pp. 434–449.

Potterton, Homan. *The National Gallery, London.* London: Thames and Hudson, 1977.

Praz, Mario. *Studies in Seventeenth-Century Imagery.* 2d ed. Rome: Storia, 1964.

Preziosi, Donald. *Rethinking Art History: Meditations on a Coy Science.* New Haven: Yale University Press, 1989.

Puppi, Lionello. *Torment in Art: Pain, Violence and Martyrdom.* Translated by Jeremy Scott. New York: Rizzoli, 1991.

Purcell, Rosamond Wolff, and Stephen Jay Gould. "Dutch Treat: Peter the Great and Frederik Ruysch." In *Finders, Keepers: Treasures and Oddities of Natural History; Collectors from Peter the Great to Louis Agassiz,* pp. 13–32. New York: W. W. Norton, 1992.

Rajchman, John. "Foucault's Art of Seeing." *October* 44 (Spring 1988), pp. 89–117.

Raven, Arlene, Cassandra L. Langer, and Joanna Frueh, eds. *Feminist Art Criticism: An Anthology.* Ann Arbor, Mich.: UMI Research Press, 1988.

Réau, Louis. *Iconographie de l'art chrétien.* 3 vols. in 6. Paris: Presses Universitaires de France, 1955–1959.

Reitlinger, Gerald. *The Economics of Taste: The Rise and Fall of Picture Prices, 1760–1960.* 3 vols. London: Barrie and Rockliff, 1961–1970.

Richards, L. "Antonio Pollaiuolo, *Battle of Naked Men.*" *Bulletin of the Cleveland Museum of Art* 55 (1968), pp. 62–70.

Roberts, K. B., and J.D.W. Tomlinson. *The Fabric of the Body: European Traditions of Anatomical Illustration.* Oxford: Clarendon Press, 1992.

Robinson, Hilary, ed. *Visibly Female: Feminism and Art: An Anthology.* New York: Universe Books, 1988.

Rose, Jacqueline. *Sexuality in the Field of Vision.* London: Verso, 1986.

Rosenberg, Jakob. "A Portrait of a Banker (Jerome Sandelin?) by Jan Gossaert, Called Mabuse." In *National Gallery of Art: Report and Studies in the History of Art 1967,* pp. 39–43. Washington, D.C.: National Gallery of Art, 1967.

Rosenblum, Robert. *Jean-Auguste-Dominique Ingres.* New York: Harry N. Abrams, 1985.

Rosenthal, Donald A. *Orientalism: The Near East in French Painting, 1800–1880* [exhibition catalog]. Rochester, N.Y.: Memorial Art Gallery of the University of Rochester, 1982.

Rowlands, John. *Holbein: The Paintings of Hans Holbein the Younger. Complete Edition.* Oxford: Phaidon, 1985.

Russell, John. *Francis Bacon.* Rev. ed. London: Thames and Hudson, 1993.

Ruysch, Fredrik. *Epistola anatomica, problematica, quarta & decima . . .* Amsterdam, 1732.

———. *Thesaurus anatomicus primus. Het eerste anatomisch cabinet.* Amsterdam, 1739.

———. *Thesaurus anatomicus tertius. Het derde anatomisch cabinet.* In *Alle de ontleed- Genees- en Heelkundige Werken.* 3 vols. Amsterdam, 1744.

Said, Edward. *Orientalism.* New York: Vintage Books, 1978.

Sandoz, Marc. *Théodore Chassériau (1819–1856): Catalogue raisonné des peintures et estampes.* Paris: Arts et Métiers Graphiques, 1974.

Saslow, James M. *Ganymede in the Renaissance: Homosexuality in Art and Society.* New Haven: Yale University Press, 1986.

Saunders, John Bertrand deC. M., and Charles D. O'Malley. *The Anatomical Drawings of Andreas Vesalius: With Annotations and Translations, a Discussion of the Plates and Their Background, Authorship and Influence, and a Biographical Sketch of Vesalius.* 1950. Reprint, New York: Bonanza Books, 1982.

Saunders, Gill. *The Nude: A New Perspective.* London: Herbert Press, 1989.

Saunders, Gillian. "Trompe l'Oeil: Visual Deception in European Art." *Victoria and Albert [Museum] Album* 5 (1986), pp. 58–67.

Sawday, Jonathan. "The Fate of Marsyas: Dissecting the Renaissance Body." In *Renaissance Bodies: The Human Figure in English Culture, c. 1540–1660,* edited by Lucy Gent and Nigel Llewellyn, pp. 112–135. London: Reaktion Books, 1990.

Schama, Simon. *The Embarrassment of Riches: An Interpretation of Dutch Culture in the Golden Age.* Berkeley and Los Angeles: University of California Press, 1988.

Schiebinger, Londa. "Skeletons in the Closet: The First Illustrations of the Female Skeleton in Eighteenth-Century Anatomy." *Representations* 14 (Spring 1986), pp. 42–82.

Schneider, Georges. "C. N. Gijsbrechts, l'illusionniste." *Connaissance des Arts* 145 (March 1964), pp. 96–105.

Schneider, Norbert. *The Art of the Still Life: Still Life Painting in the Early Modern Period.* Translated by Hugh Beyer. Cologne: Benedikt Taschen Verlag, 1990.

Schupbach, William. *The Paradox of Rembrandt's "Anatomy of Dr. Tulp."* Medical History, supplement no. 2. London: Wellcome Institute for the History of Medicine, 1982.

Schwarz, David. "Art in History." In *Art in History, History in Art: Studies in Seventeenth-Century Dutch Culture,* edited by David Freedberg and Jan de Vries, pp. 7–25. Santa Monica, Calif.: The Getty Center for the History of Art and the Humanities, 1991.

Segal, Sam. *A Flowery Past: A Survey of Dutch and Flemish Flower Painting from 1600 Until the Present* [exhibition catalog]. Translated by P. M. van Tongeren-Woodland. Amsterdam: Gallery P. de Boer, 1982.

———. *The Sumptuous Still Life in the Netherlands, 1600–1700.* Edited by William B. Jordan. The Hague: SDU Publishers, 1988.

Shotwell, James Thomson. "Richelieu, Cardinal." *The Encyclopaedia Britannica.* 11th ed. (1911), vol. 23, pp. 303–305.

Siegfried, Susan L. "Boilly and the Frame-up of *Trompe l'oeil." Oxford Art Journal* 15, 2 (1992), pp. 27–37.

Sill, Gertrude Grace. "The Reversed Canvas." *Portfolio* 3, 1 (January-February 1981), pp. 48–51.

Singer, Charles. *A Short History of Anatomy from the Greeks to Harvey.* 2d ed. New York: Dover, 1957.

Skira, Pierre. *Still Life: A History.* Translated by Jean-Marie Clarke. New York: Skira/Rizzoli, 1989.

Smith, David R. "Courtesy and Its Discontents: Frans Hals's *Portrait of Isaac Massa and Beatrix van der Laen." Oud Holland* 100 (1986), pp. 2–34.

———. *Masks of Wedlock: Seventeenth-Century Dutch Marriage Portraiture.* Ann Arbor, Mich.: UMI Research Press, 1982.

Smith, Graham. "Jealousy, Pleasure and Pain in Agnolo Bronzino's 'Allegory of Venus and Cupid.'" *Pantheon: International Art Journal* 39 (1981), pp. 250–258.

Snow, Edward. "Theorizing the Male Gaze: Some Problems." *Representations* 25 (Winter 1989), pp. 30–41.

Solkin, David H. *Painting for Money: The Visual Arts and the Public Sphere in Eighteenth-Century England.* New Haven: Yale University Press, 1993.

Solomon-Godeau, Abigail. "Male Trouble: A Crisis in Representation." *Art History* 16 (1993), pp. 286–312.

Speth-Holteroff, Simone. *Les peintres flamands de cabinets d'amateurs au XVIIe siècle.* Paris: Elsevier, 1957.

Spielmann, Marion H. *The Iconography of Andreas Vesalius.* London: J. Bale, Sons, and Danielsson, 1925.

Spierenburg, Pieter. *The Spectacle of Suffering: Executions and the Evolution of Repression; from a Preindustrial Metropolis to the European Experience.* Cambridge: Cambridge University Press, 1984.

Stafford, Barbara Maria. *Body Criticism: Imagining the Unseen in Enlightenment Art and Medicine.* Cambridge, Mass.: The MIT Press, 1991.

Staiti, Paul J. "Illusionism, Trompe l'Oeil, and the Perils of Viewership." In *William M. Harnett* [exhibition catalog], edited by Doreen Bolger, Marc Simpson, and John Wilmerding, pp. 31–48. New York: Harry N. Abrams, 1992.

Starobinski, Jean. *The Living Eye.* Translated by Arthur Goldhammer. Cambridge, Mass.: Harvard University Press, 1989.

Stein, Roger B. "Charles Willson Peale's Expressive Design: The Artist in His Museum." In *Prospects: The Annual of American Cultural Studies* 6 (1981), edited by Jack Salzman, pp. 139–185.

Sterling, Charles. *Still Life Painting: From Antiquity to the Present Time.* Translated by James Emmons. Rev. ed. New York: Universe Books, 1959.

Stevens, MaryAnne. "Western Art and Its Encounter with the Islamic World, 1798–1914." In *The Orientalists: Delacroix to Matisse: The Allure of North Africa and the Near East* [exhibition catalog], edited by MaryAnne Stevens, pp. 15–23. London: Thames and Hudson, and the National Gallery of Art, 1984.

————, ed. *The Orientalists: Delacroix to Matisse: The Allure of North Africa and the Near East* [exhibition catalog]. London: Thames and Hudson, and the National Gallery of Art, 1984.

Suleiman, Susan R., ed. *The Female Body in Western Culture: Contemporary Perspectives.* Cambridge, Mass.: Harvard University Press, 1986.

Sullivan, Margaret. *Bruegel's Peasants: Art and Audience in the Northern Renaissance.* Cambridge: Cambridge University Press, 1994.

Sullivan, Scott A. *The Dutch Gamepiece.* Totowa, N.J.: Allanheld and Schram, 1984.

————. "Rembrandt's *Self-Portrait with a Dead Bittern*." *Art Bulletin* 62 (1980), pp. 236–243.

Summers, David. "Real Metaphor: Towards a Redefinition of the 'Conceptual' Image." In *Visual Theory: Painting and Interpretation,* edited by Norman Bryson, Michael Ann Holly, and Keith Moxey, pp. 231–259. New York: HarperCollins, 1991.

Tagg, John. "Postmodernism and the Born-Again Avant-Garde." In *Grounds of Dispute: Art History, Cultural Politics and the Discursive Field,* pp. 157–169. Minneapolis: University of Minnesota Press, 1992.

Thiel, P.J.J. van. "Marriage Symbolism in a Musical Party by Jan Miense Molenaer." *Simiolus* 2 (1967), pp. 90–99.

Tilborgh, Louis van, ed. *Van Gogh and Millet.* Amsterdam: Rijksmuseum Vincent van Gogh, 1989.

Toussaint, Hélène. *Le Bain turc d'Ingres.* Paris: Musée du Louvre, 1971.

Van Liere, Eldon N. "Solutions and Dissolutions: The Bather in Nineteenth-Century French Painting." *Arts Magazine* 54 (May 1980), pp. 104–114.

Veca, Alberto. *Vanitas: Il simbolismo des tempo* [exhibition catalog]. Bergamo: Galleria Lorenzelli, 1981.

Vergo, Peter, ed. *The New Museology.* London: Reaktion Books, 1989.

Vesalius, Andreas. *De humani corporis fabrica.* 2d ed., rev. Basel, 1555.

Walker, John A. "Art and the Peasantry." *Art & Artists* 13, 9 (January 1979), pp. 26–35.

Walters, Margaret. *The Nude Male: A New Perspective.* New York: Paddington Press, 1978.

Warner, Marina. *Monuments and Maidens: The Allegory of the Female Form.* New York: Atheneum, 1985.

Weatherly, Cecil. "Knighthood." *The Encyclopaedia Britannica.* 11th ed. (1911), vol. 15, pp. 851–867.

Wells, Samuel R. *New Physiognomy, or, Signs of Character . . .* New York: Fowler and Wells, 1866.

Werner, Alfred. "The Return of Monsieur Bouguereau." *Art & Artists* 9, 12 (March 1975), pp. 25–31.

Weschler, Lawrence. "Money Changes Everything." *New Yorker,* 68 (18 January 1993), pp. 38–41.

———. "Onward and Upward with the Arts (Boggs)." *New Yorker,* 63 (18 January 1988), pp. 33–56; (25 January 1988), pp. 88–98.

Wheelock, Arthur K., Jr. "Still Life: Its Visual Appeal and Theoretical Status in the Seventeenth Century." In *Still Lifes of the Golden Age: Northern European Paintings from the Heinz Family Collection* [exhibition catalog], edited by Arthur K. Wheelock, Jr., pp. 11–25. Washington, D.C.: National Gallery of Art, 1989.

Whitfield, Sarah. *Magritte* [exhibition catalog]. London: The South Bank Centre, 1992.

Wilson, Simon. *Egon Schiele.* Ithaca: Cornell University Press, 1980.

Winckelmann-Rhein, Gertraude. *The Paintings and Drawings of Jan "Flower" Bruegel.* Translated by Leonard Mins. New York: Harry N. Abrams, 1968.

Wittkower, Rudolf. *Gian Lorenzo Bernini: The Sculptor of the Roman Baroque.* 2d ed. London: Phaidon, 1966.

Wood, Peter H., and Karen C.C. Dalton. *Winslow Homer's Images of Blacks: The Civil War and Reconstruction Years* [exhibition catalog]. Austin: University of Texas Press, 1988.

Woude, Ad van der. "The Volume and Value of Paintings in Holland at the Time of the Dutch Republic." In *Art in History, History in Art: Studies in Seventeenth-Century Dutch Culture,* edited by David Freedberg and Jan de Vries, pp. 285–329. Santa Monica, Calif.: The Getty Center for the History of Art and the Humanities, 1991.

About the Book and Author

In *Art and the Committed Eye* Richard Leppert examines Western European and American art from the fifteenth to the twentieth century. He studies the complex relation between the "look" of images and the variety of social and cultural uses to which they are put and demonstrates that the meaning of any image is significantly determined by its function, which changes over time. In particular, he emphasizes the ways in which visual culture is called on to mediate social differences defined by gender, class, and race.

In Part 1, Leppert addresses the nature and task of representation, discussing how meaning accrues to images and what role vision and visuality play in the history of modernity. Here he explains imagery's power to attract our gaze by triggering desire and focuses on the long history of the use of representation to enact a deception, whether in painting or advertising.

Part 2 explores art's relation to the material world, to the ways in which images mark our various physical and psychic ties to objects. The author analyzes still life paintings whose subject matter is both extraordinarily diverse and deeply paradoxical—from flower bouquets to grotesque formal arrangements of human body parts. Leppert demonstrates that even in "innocent" still lifes, formal design and technical execution are imbued with cultural conflict and social power.

Part 3 is devoted to the representation of the human body—as subject to obsessive gazing and as an object of display, spectacle, and transgression. The variety of body representation is enormous: pleased or tortured, gorgeous or monstrous, modest or lascivious, powerful or weak, in the bloom of life or under the anatomist's knife, clothed or naked. But it is the sexual body, Leppert shows, that has provided the West with its richest, most complex, contradictory, conflicted, and paradoxical accounts of human identity in relation to social ideals.

Richard Leppert is professor and chair of the Department of Cultural Studies and Comparative Literature at the University of Minnesota. His most recent books include *The Sight of Sound: Music, Representation, and the History of the Body* (1993) and *Music and Image* (1988).

Index

References to illustrations are printed in **bold** type. Book titles are not indexed except for those few receiving detailed discussion; authors are indexed. Only significant references to persons and places are indexed.